ED BULLINS

Twelve Plays & Selected Writings

ED BULLINS   *Edited by Mike Sell*

THE UNIVERSITY OF MICHIGAN PRESS
ANN ARBOR

Published in the United States of America by
The University of Michigan Press
Manufactured in the United States of America
⊛ Printed on acid-free paper

2009   2008   2007   2006   4   3   2   1

A CIP catalog record for this book is available from the British Library.

Library of Congress Cataloging-in-Publication Data

Bullins, Ed.
    [Selections. 2006]
    Ed Bullins : twelve plays and selected writings / Ed Bullins ;
  edited by Mike Sell.
        p.   cm.
    ISBN-13: 978-0-472-11407-8 (cloth : acid-free paper)
    ISBN-10: 0-472-11407-7 (cloth : acid-free paper)
    ISBN-13: 978-0-472-03182-5 (pbk. : acid-free paper)
    ISBN-10: 0-472-03182-1 (pbk. : acid-free paper)
      1. Sell, Mike, 1967–   II. Title.
    PS3552.U45A6   2006
    812'.54—dc22   2006015260

Acknowledgment: "A Short Statement on Street Theater" originally appeared in TDR/The
Drama Review 12, no 4 (1968).

Contents

ESSAYS & LETTERS

     BY MIKE SELL AND GABRIEL A. SMITH

Introduction

A Literary Gangster from Those Primitive Times of the Twentieth Century

by Mike Sell

ED BULLINS IS, by his own admission, one of the most important and controversial playwrights of the Cold War era (1945–91). It's hard not to agree with him. Since the production in 1965 of the edgy and still eminently performable trio *How Do You Do*, *Dialect Determinism (or the Rally)*, and *Clara's Ole Man*, he has persistently shattered critical and theatrical orthodoxy (including the paradoxical orthodoxy of the so-called avant-garde), recast the basic terms of dramatic criticism, engaged with some of the most pressing issues surrounding race and racial representation, and written provocative, fascinating, and quite often beautiful drama. Though critical of experiment for its own sake and better known as a realist, Bullins has challenged the mainstream as a hard-core avant-gardist, experimenting widely, audaciously, even dangerously with dramatic form and theatrical event. He has composed happenings, rituals, historical pageants, Grand Guignol, *opéra bouffe*, and dramatic shaggy dogs. He helped develop (with Amiri Baraka and Ben Caldwell) one new genre, the revolutionary commercial, and invented another all by himself, what I would call the "agitprop closet drama," a form of political theater that deconstructs the lines between theatrical representation and insurrectionary action, art as utilitarian means and art as end in itself.

He's been a first-rate scandal, too, regularly and mercurially antagonizing those around him for both the most high-minded and the lowest-down and meanest purposes. Bullins has never been shy about starting a fight, that's certain, and has done so for both personal, situational reasons and as a participant in two of the most important and controversial philosophical and political movements of our times: black nationalism and feminism. This combination of critical acumen, craft work, experimental urge, pugnacious contrariness, and a serious concern for ideas and politics is a rare find in theater history but is typical of those whose reputation lasts and whose plays persist in the world repertoire. This is certainly why he's received the kind of broad recognition evidenced by his many awards. He is the recipient of three Obies, a New York Drama Critics Circle Award, a Drama Desk–Vernon Rice Award, two Guggenheim fellowships, four Rockefeller Foundation grants, Two National Endowment for the Arts fellowships, an Otto Award for innovative political theater, a National Black Theatre Festival Living Legend Award, and scores of other honors.

Yet, when I asked him in 2005 what he thought he'd be best known for, he responded, "I'll probably be known for obscurity." Punctuated with low, warm chuckles, he expanded on the notion:

> That's the way that it's spelled out in the last twenty years, but I shouldn't be pessimistic. I was once asked to make an epitaph and I chose to write, "Hope is like a dry bone." Something like that. I guess that I was in one of my negative nihilistic periods. I don't know . . . I write plays I hope will last. I try to do them that way. Hundreds of years. Probably won't, seeing how the world is going. They will all be, probably, all my plays and literary works, gathered and piled in a huge bonfire and set ablaze . . . but then I remember that this is the electronic era, so it will be on somebody's disc or chip or whatever. Maybe I will be remembered as a literary gangster from those primitive times of the twentieth century.

Obscurity, celebrity, negative nihilism, and gangsterism aren't especially bad terms to keep in mind as we read the works, though they're certainly not the whole story. The man's capacity for self-obfuscation, literary tricksterism, spells of wild-swinging cynicism, and fits of deep distrust has always played in unpredictable ways with his commitment to making a difference in the lives of others in both the broadest and the most personal ways.

As is the rule with the plays, we need to think of the person himself without falling into rigid categories and orthodox approaches. Bullins is, bottom line, a *militant*, though a militant not always committed to the specific people, institutions, or ideologies of the political or social causes in which he participates. A militant without a cause? No. A "revolutionary gadfly" might be the best way to capture it. The singular commitment of his life is *probity*, though what he probes and how he goes about that probing have often proven troubling and distasteful to others, not least due to the fact that his probing sometimes lacks an obvious moral or political purpose. When I asked him whether or not his most provocative works—especially those that deal with rape, a common theme in his first decade's work—had been treated fairly, he responded, "Fair? Well, there's no fairness in war, is there?" Again, the low chuckle. "I mean. I don't take quarter and I don't give it in certain aesthetic arenas." His "enemies" might respond that the problem is that one is never entirely sure when, where, and why the shots fly.

Although he was hardly an overnight sensation—he was thirty when his first plays were written and produced—Bullins enjoyed during the middle 1960s a rapid rise in the public eye after getting a lot of buzz for the wickedly funny *Clara's Ole Man*, earning a reputation as a "Black Radical" for his association with headline-catching organizations on the West Coast, and getting hired as playwright in residence at Robert Macbeth's New Lafayette Theatre in 1967. To properly understand his early works, we need to keep in mind this conjunction of celebrity, politics, and institution building. *Malcolm: '71, or Publishing Blackness; We Righteous Bombers; The Play of the Play; A Short Play for a Small Theater; It Bees Dat Way;* and the short film scenario "The Box Office" can all be read as metadramas that investigate the social, economic, political, ethical, and material questions surrounding so-called Black theater. Not just assertions of Blackness, they are also probing explorations of the grounds for the assertion itself.

"The Box Office," for example, situates the preparations of a new theater, highly reminiscent of the Lafayette, in a tangle of sidewalk sight lines (of two cops, a drunken passerby, a man with a movie camera, the writer himself) and ethical issues (the exploitation of two women—"I sho don't like this stoop labor, honey. I ain't no sharecropper"—and lack of concern for the drunk, who disappears into the crowd). *We Righteous Bombers* punctures the certitudes of Black radicals and existentialist nihilists alike by placing its characters (and Albert Camus's *Les Justes*, from which it liberally borrows) in a dizzying whirlwind of theatrical frames, obliterating distinctions between revolutionary "truth" and ideological blindness. The agit-prop closet drama *Malcolm: '71* is, on one level, a call to action to Black scholars to circle their wagons. Although its action is simple—"Blackman" hangs up on a white editor of a proposed anthology of radical literature after learning her dog is named after Malcolm X—its framing of the action is not. Leading its reader to consider not just the dramatic action but the text in her hands (a copy of the journal *Black Scholar*, in which the play was first published, or this anthology, for that matter), it asks us to consider drama not just a thing for the *stage* but a critical problem for the *page*. Bullins is a playwright acutely conscious of the politics of representation and a savvy negotiator of those politics. His most dedicated critic, Samuel Hay, has gone so far as to characterize his oeuvre as a virtual recapitulation of the history of African-American theater that dexterously confronts not only the contradictions within that tradition but the contradictions in that tradition's relations with the broader arena of U.S. and world drama and theater.[1] In this respect, his work fully embodies the Black Arts Movement's commitment to Blackness—not Blackness, as Kimberly Benston puts it, as "a self-deceived discourse declaring itself unambiguously to be a mode of authentic being unprecedented in African-American history" but Blackness as a "critical appraisal . . . account[ing] for its animating tensions in terms which reduce neither their contradictory nor productive character."[2]

His broad popularity—was there another living playwright whose work was produced more often in the 1960s and 1970s?—was due at least in part to his personal efforts to promote the growth of new audiences, theaters, and playwrights. Indeed, he is rightfully considered a central figure not just in American drama but in three of the most significant trends in post–World War II theater: the Black Arts Movement, identity theater, and the move "beyond Broadway" (to recall C. W. E. Bigsby's phrase).[3] This centrality is assured not just by the plays. As I've mentioned, Bullins played an active role in key theater-critical institutions of the day, shaping the ways in which people understand, perceive, and discuss theater and drama, especially (though not exclusively) in terms of race. The late August Wilson was not the first to insist on the validity of race-based casting and staffing. Nor was Wilson the first to draw attention to the deep hypocrisy of those who would dare to accuse the self-proclaimed "Black" playwright of "self-segregation." Bullins's open letters to the *New York Times* and other papers during the 1970s sparked public debate and put the heat on white critics, especially, to achieve greater fluency in the assumptions and history of African-American theater and to take responsibility for racist comments (conscious or otherwise). That particular issue was so heated for Bullins that he, Macbeth, and the cast and crew of the New Lafayette banned white reviewers from their productions, a decision that stood until funding difficulties demanded a rethink.

Bullins didn't just react to the criticisms of others. His achievements as editor and essayist are also considerable. The 1968 Black theater issue of *The Drama Review*, which Bullins edited, is often and appropriately called "the Bible of the Black Arts Movement." Although it gives a highly selective perspective on that movement, it enabled the wide diffusion of self-consciously "Black" dramatic texts, theater documents, and theory. Read with an eye to that selective perspective, the special issue also provides some interesting insights into the highly reticulated politics of the U.S. theater scene at the time. One could go so far as to claim that the issue is a kind of "textualized performance" of those politics.[4] Bullins also edited two anthologies of plays featuring new work by African-American playwrights, many of them associated with the New Lafayette, and without doubt required reading for anyone interested in U.S. drama. He was the chief editor of the New Lafayette's *Black Theatre* magazine, whose six issues have yet to be fully mined for their historical and critical riches. Last, his essays, particularly "Black Theater: The 70s—Evolutionary Changes," "Black Theater, Bourgeois Critics," and the preface to *The New Lafayette Theatre Presents*, stand as signal moments in the development of contemporary African-American theater and dramatic criticism. He stands with such luminaries as Larry Neal and Addison Gayle for his efforts to ask and answer what Errol Hill and James Hatch (luminaries themselves) have characterized as the "key questions": "What is Black theatre? Does it have a separate aesthetic? Who is its audience? Who should write its criticism? What is theatre's fundamental purpose?"[5]

Looking back beyond 1965, though, it's hard to imagine him ever becoming a playwright, let alone an editor, critic, and theater developer. When he wrote his first plays, Bullins carried with him a rather colorful resume: North Philadelphia "rude boy," former navy pugilist, recent recipient of a General Education Diploma (GED), struggling real-estate developer, increasingly militant Black Nationalist. Like so many young African Americans of his generation, he suffered from profound despair about himself and his world. He was nonplussed by Old Left attitudes toward antiracist activism, was reading a lot of existentialist literature (Camus would prove an enduring interest) and educating himself on the history and issues affecting the African diaspora (his roommate at Los Angeles City College was Ron Everett, later to change his name to Maulana Karenga and found the US organization and create Kwanzaa). However, the opportunities to create and motivate weren't coming—his white writing teacher apparently took special pleasure in reminding him of his unworthiness as a writer. He was, as he put it in a 1969 interview, a "frustrated and evil cat."[6]

The shape of that frustration is mapped in his mutinous 1973 novel

The Reluctant Rapist, a semiautobiographical work (with emphasis on the *semi*) written over the course of the 1960s. As with many of the plays, attention to the form is as vital as attention to content. That form describes a deep and obscure coherence of experience, an experience shattered across three decades and a continent. As if trying to pin down a moving target on a shifting, shadowy landscape, the novel shuttles from the main character's childhood to adolescence to adulthood, throwing the reader from urban Philadelphia to a state adoption farm near Chester, Pennsylvania, to Los Angeles and in so doing juxtaposing the sexual and economic manipulation of youth by hypocritical religious leaders to the rhetorical and emotional manipulation of disaffected youths by self-proclaimed "Black leaders" to the casual, brutal exploitation of women by men, the narrator included. The thematic unity of these apparently disparate moments and places suggests that whatever meaning and coherence its narrator can find will be found not in ideology or theology or any kind of "commitment" but in an aggressive, nihilistic rebellion against the sexual, economic, emotional, and rhetorical exploitation that surrounds him.

It's a bleak, fascinating read. Bullins has characterized it as a lampoon of Eldridge Cleaver's claim, in *Soul on Ice* (1968), that rape is an insurrectionary act whose methods are best developed by practicing them on the black women in one's neighborhood prior to moving on to white women elsewhere. The satirical edge can be tough to find, though. Perhaps the very failure of its narrator and protagonist, Steve Benson, to take his sexual aggression into some larger sociopolitical arena is part of the point. Bullins has also described it as coming out of long familiarity with the work of Henry Miller and Chester Himes.[7] In that respect, one can appreciate it as an effort to find and define the most basic dimensions of existence without relying on politics and ideology—a work, in other words, advertising a kind of brutarian humanism, if you will.

In the end, it's a book that roughhouses with some very difficult issues yet requires a very sensitive reading to make sense of its approach. Many readers haven't bothered, and even those who do will find it a hard trick to pull off. The novel's constant, brutal disparagement of politics and politicos and its apparently casual treatment of sexual violence earned him the scathing contempt of *Village Voice* editor Erika Munk, for one, who had to that point been his champion. Two of Munk's complaints—with the third, the absurd idea that he is "pro-rape," not worth addressing—have become critical commonplaces among his detractors. Spending a few moments considering them can help us understand some of the characteristics of the work more generally, especially the plays. Frustration and evilness, it turns out, are a creative and critical wellspring for Bullins.

First, Munk condemns the fact that "there's no distancing, no disapproval, of his rather autobiographical narrator's ideas and actions."[8] Regarding the first accusation, Munk's right on target. Indeed, Bullins was regularly called out for not adequately guiding audience perceptions through the thorny issues raised in the work, most notably at a 1968 forum called by Robert Macbeth to debate the New Lafayette's production of *We Righteous Bombers*. At that forum, the influential activist and political theorist Askia Touré criticized the play for failing to make its intentions clear (is it a satire or a "serious portrayal of the lives of certain Black activists"?), for failing to mark a distinction between the "fool" and the "true revolutionary," and for creating characters (especially the female character Bonnie Brown) who come across as "vacillating" and "schizophrenic."[9] But the refusal to moralize is neither necessary nor unprecedented. Indeed, one could link Bullins's full-frontal approach to the sordid realities of this world to the nineteenth-century naturalists, who are often accused of dragging humanity into the muck without a straw to grasp; to the dadas and surrealists, who were perfectly willing to expose the most perturbing, difficult dimensions of life without affording a consistent out (Isidore Ducasse's *Maldoror* is perhaps the most unshakably disconcerting example); to the so-called gangstas of hip-hop, with their incisive descriptions of the day-to-day pleasures and pains of the angry underclass; or to the Camus of *The Stranger*. Brett Easton Ellis's *American Psycho* comes to mind, too.

But I'd argue that the most rewarding and relevant lineage to trace is that of the great blues singers and composers: Robert Johnson, Joe Williams, Bessie Smith, Gertrude "Ma" Rainey, Muddy Waters. Munk ultimately doesn't account for the twist that Bullins applies in the epigraph and at the conclusion of *The Reluctant Rapist*, as well as the deeper cultural grounds for the novel's apparently nihilistic perspective. The final lines reveal that the novel has been addressed not to a general readership but to a "luscious black shape" lying beside the narrator. "You really tell some good dirty stories, baby," she tells him. "But they ain't nasty enough . . . and they so weird." The novel ends by quoting one of the more delicious double entendres in the blues tradition: "Mah poppa's a jockey an he teach me how ta ride . . . oh, yah, mah poppa's a jockey an he teach me how ta ride . . . he said, git in da middle, son, an ya move from side to side . . ."[10] If there's frustration and "negative nihilism" to be found in the novel—and in the life it portrays—that frustration needs to be understood in terms of an expressive tradition that has always understood sex and violence to be the most fundamental realities of existence; has always understood the act of public contrariness to be a most positive expression of commitment to life, liberty, and community; and has always understood expression as inseparable from seduction and the inevitability of betrayal.

Describing the "blues ethos," Bullins's friend and compatriot Larry Neal notes that "the essential motive behind the best blues song is the acquisition of insight, wisdom" but adds that such insight is not to be had within the frameworks of traditional morality or ideology. In fact, it's often found in overt rejection of those frameworks: "for the blues singer, the world is his text."[11] And that world—and the reading strategies required of it—cannot be comprehended in the comforting terms of theological and ideological orthodoxy. This is not to excuse or explain away the brutality to be found in Bullins's creative work—in fact, quite the opposite. Sexual violence is central to the history of African America, a weapon used against African Americans both in reality (in slave quarters, in maximum security prisons) and rhetoric (as justification for the lynch mob). Even if we dismiss the idea that rape is insurrection, there is no denying that rape is a political act.

I'd suggest that sexual violence in the work should be considered as one aspect of Bullins's effort to tell what might be called a *blues history* of African America, a history understood as determined in part (though only in part) by racialized sex and violence. Following Angela Davis's incisive delineation of the "politics" of the great blues singers Ma Rainey and Bessie Smith, we might characterize it as an effort to name a social condition in the absence of any acceptable or amenable political avenues or language for addressing that condition. Thus it can be read as "encourage[ing] a critical attitude and urg[ing] its audience to challenge social conditions, but it cannot establish the terrain of protest by itself."[12] The history told in *The Reluctant Rapist* can be told neither in the language of traditional ideology nor in the form of a traditional realistic novel (which it often resembles). The "critical attitude" here—and this is where the comparison to Rainey and Smith finds its limits—is voiced by someone who is simultaneously victim and victimizer.

Understood not just as a formal influence but as a worldview shared by many within the Black Arts Movement, the blues help us comprehend in the plays and fiction a deeper level of community sensibility at work. Bullins is a writer acutely aware not only of his audience—no good playwright can be otherwise—but of the cultural legacies that both empower and hinder the relationship between artist and audience. In this respect, Bullins's work can be considered as part of what Kimberly Benston has characterized as the "methectic" tendency in African-American culture, a tendency emblematized by the call-and-response structure of the African-American field holler, sermon, and blues.[13] His writings—dramatic, fictional, critical—systematically engage the function of audience in art, at once celebrating the many traditions of call-and-response and challenging those traditions and their assumptions. Just as surely as the theater and the printed page are the objects of critical inquiry for Bullins, so is the relationship between artist and audience. *The Theme Is Blackness*, for one, plunges the spectators into darkness, challenging the long-standing theatrical tradition of constructing the theater event around the visual. The fortunately unproduced *A Short Play for a Small Theater* asks its solo performer to ritually apply face paint—an allusion to blackface minstrelsy—load a gun, then systematically murder the white spectators.

By contrast, in *The Reluctant Rapist*, the audience, the implied community in the act of public remembrance, is palpably absent. The woman at the conclusion is a sudden, even somewhat clumsy device. Regardless of who the story is addressed to, this is a story of an alienated man whose medium (the novel) is, in some respects, the apotheosis of alienation. Novel reading, in our times, is most often a solitary act. Theater, on the other hand, categorically demands an audience—and the African-American audience has often been characterized as an active, even unruly presence in the theater event. From all accounts, those at the New Lafayette Theatre were especially so. Thus, if there's a lack of moral or ideological guidance in the work, that lack needs to be understood as the reflection of a deep respect for the audience, a most precise assessment of the audience's role, and a firm refusal to assume shared belief in the face of economic, social, and political factors that impact—often fatally—any act of communication.

Munk's second criticism is that the work reflects a "profound cynicism . . . a conman's nihilism." This criticism is harder to shake—after all, Bullins characterizes himself in exactly those terms. Even if we do tune into the blues sensibility, it's hard not to read works such as *The Reluctant Rapist*, *The Fabulous Miss Marie*, *Jo Anne!!!*, or "The Hungered One" as ultimately providing no sense of hope, no dramatic or conceptual "out" for the characters and their situations. That said, Bullins's cynicism and nihilism are not just affectations; they're hard earned, the result of paying his dues in many political and artistic organizations. Hard earned, too, from a long, unflinching look at the history of race, class, and sex in this country. However, understanding and justifying the personal attitude isn't entirely relevant to the claim that the *creative work* expresses a similar viewpoint. For that, we must follow Hill and Hatch once again and attend strictly to what they have characterized as Bullins's portrayal of a "delicate balance of humanity."[14] Without such attention, the deep commitment and genuine love many of his characters have for each other will be misperceived (if not entirely ignored) and understood as simply the moment-to-moment rationalizations of characters living in bad faith. Lacking such attention, we will simply miss the point and lose the drama.

The cynicism and satire of *The Fabulous Miss Marie*, for example, come across as simply a rehash of the old avant-gardist *épater le bourgeois* gesture unless they are placed in careful relationship to the deep, perennial love of Marie and Bill. There is no doubt that Bullins is attacking the frivolity of African-American working-class people with pretensions of "upward mobility"—not to mention the hand-to-mouth "love" offered by Marco or the "revolutionary" Gafney—but he is also mapping with real affection the contours of its tenuous existence and the impact of that frivolity, fragility, and survivalist mentality on love and friendship. The protagonist's commitment to the little monster in "The Hungered One" is, at first glance, a freak every bit as much as the monster itself, but it's also evidence of a sense of compassion and pity that overcomes so-called common sense. This is an affection that surpasses all social convention.

Likewise, we find in many of Bullins's plays relations between men and women that are troubling in large part due to the way they intertwine love, violence, and rebelliousness. The gang rape that concludes *The Corner*; the demented, demi-pornographic, fun-house whirl of *Jo Anne!!!*; the wicked ironies of *It Has No Choice* (in which an act of sexual aggression between a black man and a white woman turns out to be a regular thing); and the Obie-winning *The Taking of Miss Janie* are all troubling in exactly this way. In each of these works, we see Bullins delving deeply into a dimension of sexual violence that has only recently attracted the attention it deserves. Rape, after all, is most often committed against women by the men closest to them. This suggests that rape and love—and I use the term *love* neither ironically nor as mitigative of the violence of rape—are not mutually exclusive; moreover, comprehending their connections is vital to any effort not just to define *true love* but to make sense of sexual violence. A director approaching these plays will fail utterly if she or he fails to manifest the profoundly paradoxical nature of the relationships between the men who rape and the women who are raped. Cliff Dawson's decision to abandon Stella to his drunken friends must be at once agonized, utterly and cruelly "cool," and comprehended as a kind of "founding violence" leading to the tragic love affair of Cliff and Lou in *In the Wine Time*.

Taking this all into account—and returning to the moment in 1965 when Bullins fully committed to playwriting, Black Power, and Black Art—it would appear that at the very moment he felt himself more and more drawn to that most political, most community-oriented art form, theater, he felt less and less confidence in the strength, unity, and intelligence of any community to honestly assess its origins and assumptions or to face up to its pervasive, inevitable, hypocrisy. But then he heard that somebody—a *Black* somebody—was shaking up the New York scene and doing so in a way that wasn't caught in the representational cul-de-sacs of the absurdists, that plumbed deeply the ancient sensibility of Blackness, and engaged seriously—despite the underlying cynicism—the possibility of social change and justice. Familiar with Amiri Baraka's poetry from underground magazines such as *Wild Dog*, he caught the plays *Dutchman* and *The Slave* when they toured San Francisco in 1965. Inspired by the wicked knotting of deep irony and complete emotional commitment in those works, Bullins got drunk one night, wrote *How Do You Do* (epigraph courtesy of Baraka's "The Revolutionary Theatre"), followed it up two weeks later with *Dialect Determinism (or The Rally)*, then followed that up with *Clara's Ole Man*. These first plays evince the characteristic traits of much of his work to this day: ill-tempered irony; the dramatic potential of class differences within African America; a masterful grasp of the variety, rhythm, music, and ironies of African American vernacular; a keen sense of audience perspective and presence; fluency in many dramatic styles and a willingness to mix them up; and a solid sense of what works on stage.

The ice broke in other ways, too, enabling his "frustration" and "evilness" to be put to good use. As he put it to me, he discovered at the time a way to align his passion for theater and drama with his social concerns—at least for a moment or two. In 1965, he would not only start his career as a playwright but also help organize Black House, working closely with former actor Bobby Seale and the up-and-coming playwright and poet Marvin X. Eldridge Cleaver's role in the organization was also engineered by Bullins, who invited him to Oakland after they were put in touch by X. Although he was later expelled from Black House over disagreements concerning the participation of white radicals, Bullins remained a friend and ally of the Black Panthers, especially after getting big-time notice with his triple bill at the American Place Theatre in Manhattan. As fund-raiser for the Panthers and agitator for their cause, Bullins would write quite a few agitprop theater pieces characterized by a disarming self-reflexivity (e.g., *A Short Play for a Small Theater*, *It Bees Dat Way*, *Death List*).

Supposedly, Bullins wasn't satisfied with this kind of dramatic work. As the story is typically told, he felt a real lack of fit between his so-called revolutionary work and the more naturalistic, nondidactic plays, which portrayed, without any distancing or disapproval, the day-to-day lives of African-American lumpen-, working-, and middle-class people. This version of the story leads one to assume that Bullins abandoned politics for art. That's the way Nathan L. Grant spins it in his excellent entry on Bullins in *The Oxford Companion to African-American Literature*: "Bullins's commitment to art over ideology was in early evidence when the Black House experienced a schism between members who wanted to use theatre for revolutionary propaganda and those who saw theatre's potential for cultural change."[15] The thing is, marking a strong distinction between the revolutionary and the cultural in his work isn't an especially smart way to slice the pie. First of all, such a claim does a disservice to the Black Arts Movement's "animating tensions" (to recall Benston again). What gets left out, too, is *probity*, a function of art that Bullins was able and willing to apply regardless of genre and purpose. Finally, the distinction between politics and art doesn't match the facts, since, after arriving in New York City, Bullins continued to write the kind of overtly political and didactic works of which he had supposedly grown weary.

Indeed, the kind of "naturalism" Bullins developed with the New Lafayette and for which he is best known is hardly lacking in self-reflexivity and attention to social, political, and economic issues; just as surely, it compels the audience into forms of self-recognition and self-critique that are the proprietary trademark of so-called revolutionary drama. We should recall that, as he told Clayton Riley, Baraka's impact on him was not just due to the fact that he was "concerned with the same realities" as Bullins but also because he was concerned with the same "contradictions."[16] Bullins called what he was doing "natural" playwriting, neatly trimming the "-ism" and, by extension, the dogmatism and positivism typical of naturalism. Like the synonymous hairstyle, the natural play maneuvers soulfully and stylistically across the wilds of performativity and essentialism, appearing utterly natural in the midst of the most outrageous fictions and misperceptions.

The Pig Pen, for one example, presents an apparently shapeless, undramatic picture of a group of 1960s Afro- and Anglo-bohemians. Naturalism to the hilt, it would seem, very much in the spirit of the unaltered reportage tradition of naturalist playwriting. However, remembering another key musical influence on the man's work, we can delineate a distinctly jazzy shape to this social gathering, a coalescence of language, gesture, and theme. In addition, we find in the play the "intellectual/artistic/pseudo-bohemian type," Len Stover, whose call to action and consciousness are cast in the starkest of lights by the entrance of a policeman, unheard and unseen by the other characters, who traipses through the party, blowing his whistle. Completely unexpected and absolutely surreal, the dancing cop terminally ruptures any putative "fourth wall" and calls our attention to our own surveillance of and judgment on the scene. Though not as aggressively as, say, *It Bees Dat Way*—which takes the documentarian claims of naturalism to an absurd and frightening conclusion—*The Pig Pen* is a perfect example of how Bullins could at once represent

African-America "realistically" and yet make his audience uncomfortably aware of the power relations involved in all theater experience.

The issue for Bullins as far as the West Coast was concerned was, ultimately, money and time. Not seeing any chance of developing as a professional playwright on the West Coast, he pondered leaving the country altogether. Fortunately, an invitation came at the last minute that kept him closer to home, an invitation from Macbeth, who offered him the post of playwright in residence at a new theater, the New Lafayette, named after an old Harlem institution. With Macbeth, Bullins would develop one of the most significant institutions in U.S. theater history, an institution that would premiere some of his most important plays, including *In the Wine Time, Goin' a Buffalo, We Righteous Bombers, The Duplex,* and *The Fabulous Miss Marie.* As head of the theater's playwriting workshop, Bullins mentored a generation of writers, including J. E. "Sonny Jim" Gaines (also his most trusted lead actor), Martie Charles, OyamO, and Richard Wesley. In fact, there is a veritable New Lafayette School of playwriting, which focuses on the everyday lives of the African American urban underclass, uses a range of vernaculars, favors sudden shifts between dramatic modes, and favors irony over dramatic resolution.

Beyond the work itself, any consideration of the "politics" of Bullins's work after he left the West Coast needs to account for the causes to which he contributed. Not only was his activism constant during this period; it crossed national boundaries. In 1969, two years into his work with the Lafayette, he attended, with Cleaver and others, the first Pan-African Cultural Festival, held in Algiers, Algeria. There he would state, "We have to revolutionize our culture, the Black culture in America, and hook up with the third world and our Black African brothers"—and then have it published in *Black Theatre.* This is hardly the statement of a cynical con man. Quite the contrary; it stands as evidence of Bullins's efforts to internationalize Blackness and promote collaboration between the Black Arts Movement and international decolonization tendencies.

There's another way to look at Bullins's dissatisfaction with "political" drama, a perspective that demands we read the plays with an eye to larger tendencies in the Black Arts Movement. We ought to recall, for starters, that the New Lafayette Theatre burned down shortly after Bullins arrived in Manhattan following a violent dispute at a party for Harold Cruse's *The Crisis of the Negro Intellectual.* The impact of Cruse's book on the Black Arts Movement generally and the Lafayette specifically can hardly be overstated. Of particular importance was his assertion that unless African-America produced institutions that simultaneously served political, economic, and cultural ends it would surely fail in its greater aspirations for justice and equality. This "triple-front" approach to Black Power suggested to the more critically sophisticated members of the movement—Bullins and Macbeth among them—that any artistic representation must draw attention to its institutional bases, community connections, and means of production. This approach to drama is clearly visible in a short piece, like *Malcolm: '71* a drama about literary anthologies and the politics of editorial control, published in a journal dedicated to radical scholarship. But it's also apparent in more subtle ways in "natural" works such as *The Fabulous Miss Marie*, which peppers its moving, funny, and absurd representation of African-American working-class life with moments of insidious self-consciousness about the mediation of "Blackness"; specifically, televised coverage of police attacks on civil rights activists, pornographic films, and the soft-shoe shuffling of the minstrel show tradition. I'd argue that, rather than reflecting cynicism and a desire to manipulate his subjects, Bullins's acute sensitivity to the cultural, political, economic, and media contexts of his work pressed him to ask questions that many of those around him were simply not ready to hear.

However we judge the work's hard edges, Bullins is committed to mentoring, collaboration, and institution building. As part of the New York Shakespeare Festival Writers' Unit and the Cherry Lane Theatre Mentor Project, he's helped shape the careers of Amhir Bahati, Doug Fallon, Fatisha, J.e. Franklin, Kermit Frazier, Abbie Gehman, Neil Harris, Herb Liebman, Winston Lovett, Sonia Sanchez, Barbara Schneider, and Shirley Timmreck. As an editor of anthologies and journals, Bullins has guaranteed wider attention to the work of Sanchez, Adrienne Kennedy, Ben Caldwell, James Garrett, Marvin X, Baraka, and others. As editor of the Black theater issue of *The Drama Review*, he catapulted the movement into the national and international spotlight. And, though *Black Theatre* magazine was peppered with the kind of language that has earned the Black Arts Movement a reputation as misogynist, homophobic, and anti-Semitic, it also put forward to its eight thousand subscribers the work of black women and emphasized the accomplishments of African American theater workers across the United States and the Caribbean. Last, he founded the New Lafayette Theatre Play Service, which promoted production and reading not only of his works but those of Sanchez, Macbeth, Charles, Gaines, Marvin X, Ben Caldwell, Sharon Stockard, Richard Wesley, Salimu, and OyamO.

The pace that Bullins kept during his first decade is remarkable. The 1970s saw him producing some great plays, including *The Duplex, The Taking of Miss Janie, Street Sounds,* and *The Fabulous Miss Marie* (an Obie winner and, for my money, his best play). His works were produced twice at Manhattan's Lincoln Center, and awards came in at a rapid pace from fringe and mainstream alike. But a series of historical and personal events in the mid-1970s turned the firebrand of the countercultural theater scene into something of an outcast. The work itself played a role, as I've mentioned. The sex, violence, vulgar language, and lower-depths focus had always offended (and continue to offend) delicate sensibilities, but the reaction took on a particularly ad hominem cast. Bullins was perceived by many to be a misogynist, particularly after the publication of *The Reluctant Rapist*, whose title pretty much said it all to his detractors. Munk's incisive, cruel, and highly personal attack on Bullins was published in a 1976 *Village Voice* review of the Theatre of the Riverside Church's production of *Jo Anne!!!* Shortly thereafter, a row over the Lincoln Center production of *The Duplex* captured theater headlines. Once again, naturalism was the issue, with Bullins arguing that director Gilbert Moses (who he characterized as a "mercenary")[17] and Lincoln Center artistic director Jules Irving had lost a sense of the play's aesthetic bases and its characters' thoroughly ritualized lives. Lacking a cultural ground, the play came across to the audience as a dramatically shapeless minstrel show. He told Clayton Riley, "They turned the whole thing into a burlesque show, complete with a 'Darktown Strutters Ball' kind of musical score and an overall mood that's straight out of *Amos 'n' Andy*. It's not the play I wrote, and doesn't say anything about any Black people I know."[18] Although he received solid support for his cause from the off- and off-off-Broadway community (including significant support from the Queer Theater scene), he earned a bad reputation among the bigwigs that dovetailed nicely with the feminist backlash. Outside the theater world, trouble was brewing, too. As an activist, he received his fair share of abuse from government representatives and freelance reactionaries alike. And the economic crisis of 1973 dried up money for all art, the New Lafayette Theatre included. A place that had truly become a home for the nomadic Bullins shut down in 1973, taking *Black Theatre* and the New Lafayette Theatre Play Service with it, and serving a blow to the wider Black Arts Movement. What also went was an artistic community that had inspired Bullins to produce some of his best work. Most painful of all, his son, Edward Jr., died in 1978.

Many are under the mistaken assumption that this was the year that marked the end of his career. This is hardly the case. Certainly, the 1980s was a quiet, introspective, scholarly time for Bullins. He taught at Amherst, Columbia, Hofstra, Dartmouth, and other colleges and universities and earned a degree from Antioch University–San Francisco in 1989, continuing with an master of fine arts at San Francisco State University in 1994.

The quiet wasn't uncreative; he continued to write, producing plays that probed the boundaries between musical and dramatic form and also writing a number of works devoted to historical subjects (Phyllis Wheatley, Louis Armstrong, Lucy Terry, and Adam Clayton Powell Jr.). He revisited his epic *Twentieth Century Cycle* with *Boy x Man*, which premiered in 1995 at the Second Annual National Symposium on African American Theatre.

A playwright who quite literally thinks in dramatic terms—who truly believes Aristotle's old maxim that drama is a thinking poised between history and philosophy—it would be hard to imagine him ever stopping. Thus, it's important that the reader of this anthology not mistake the table of contents for a covert pronouncement on the quality of the work Bullins has done in the 1980s and 1990s. I believe that the entire range of his work should be put back in arm's reach of the general public, including recent works such as *Boy x Man* and *Harlem Diva* (and, indeed, it is, thanks to the Alexander Street Press's online database). However, the decision in this anthology has been to focus primarily on his first decade's work and include only one recent play—2005's *Harlem Diva*. This decision is based on the notion that any reconsideration of Bullins's work has to begin at the beginning and be based in a fair appraisal of both his most celebrated and most nettlesome works.

Another challenge of anthologizing Bullins is contending with the sheer volume of his work—a challenge that isn't abated even if we work only with the best and most familiar. So, it's incumbent that the choices made here be explained. The bulk of the pages that follow are devoted to the most remarkable and often noted years of his career, 1965–76. Within that period, we find plays that are generally recognized as part of the "Bullins canon" and as tried-and-true members of the modern dramatic tradition. But we also find in that period plays that mark Bullins as a member of the vanguard. And it is in that period, too, that he wrote most of the public statements and open letters that established the key theatrical-political concerns of our day. In sum, there's good reason to focus on the earlier works. Early on, the decision was made to include not just the significant and best-known texts but the most provocative and troubling works, too. In this sense, the anthology learns the lesson of *Malcolm: '71* and doesn't try to domesticate the radical. Thus, in addition to the classic Bullins plays *How Do You Do, The Electronic Nigger, Clara's Ole Man*, and *In the Wine Time*, passages from *The Reluctant Rapist* and the theater pieces *It Bees Dat Way* and *A Short Play for a Small Theater* are included.

Even following these criteria, there are far too many plays to include in a single volume, particularly given the desire here to include fiction, essays, and correspondence—a decision intended to promote a more nuanced reading of the theatrical work and of the time period in which Bullins began his career. As a consequence, plays that duplicate themes, forms, and/or characters were deemed "expendable" despite their excellence. This is why, for example, *Goin' a Buffalo*, *In New England Winter*, *The Taking of Miss Janie*, and *The Duplex* aren't included—they duplicate themes, forms, and/or characters found in *The Fabulous Miss Marie*, *Jo Anne!!!* and *In the Wine Time*. I believe that, ultimately, the selections included herein will provide the reader with the most comprehensive, interesting, and challenging perspective on the work as a whole—and, hopefully, inspiration to seek out the rest.

Another challenge concerns providing assistance to readers not necessarily familiar with the historical and cultural references that pepper the plays and essays. For reasons of space, notes are provided for antiquated colloquialisms, names of historical figures, and obscure cultural references, but notes are not provided for the names of playwrights and plays. It is hoped that readers of this material will be at least superficially familiar with the dramatic tradition. Texts are ordered chronologically within each section.

Thanks are due to both individuals and institutions for their assistance and support. This reader received grants, gifts, and help from all over Indiana University of Pennsylvania's campus, including its Faculty Senate, former College of Humanities and Social Sciences Dean Brenda Carter, English Department, African American Cultural Center, and Stapleton Library Interlibrary Loan department. Tony Leon, Kevin Sanders, and Gabriel Smith put in long hours as copy editors and, in the case of Smith, the creation of the chronology. LeAnn Fields provided her typically acute editorial eye, as did Rebecca Mostov. The anonymous reader also provided extremely useful advice to ensure that this book would be as relevant and readable as possible. Marva Sparks was a gracious and lovely host during a visit to Boston. This reader is inconceivable without the path-blazing work of Samuel Hay, who both organized the Bullins archive and wrote a reference book that has never been out of reach, *Ed Bullins: A Literary Biography*. The ongoing critical conversations I've had with David Krasner, Harry Elam Jr., and Jim Smethurst have been both affirming and educational. I also thank Robert Macbeth, whose honesty and generosity have impacted my understandings of Bullins and his moments in fundamental ways. Of course, much gratitude and respect is due the author himself; though the process has had its characteristically testy moments, it has been a remarkable one for me, and I hope it will have a positive, persistent impact on Ed's work and life. Last, my gratitude and respect go to Kate Sell, my wife, for her dedication, support, and love and the three graceful and intelligent boys she is raising.

Notes

1. Samuel Hay, *Ed Bullins: A Literary Biography* (Detroit: Wayne State University Press, 1997).

2. Kimberly W. Benston, *Performing Blackness: Enactments of African-American Modernism* (New York and London: Routledge, 2000), 4.

3. C. W. E. Bigsby, *A Critical Introduction to Twentieth-Century American Drama*, vol. 3: *Beyond Broadway* (New York: Cambridge University Press, 1985).

4. On Bullins as editor, see Mike Sell, "Bullins as Editorial Performer: Textual Power and the Limits of Performance in the Black Arts Movement," *Theatre Journal* 53, no. 3 (October 2001): 411–28.

5. Erroll G. Hill and James V. Hatch, *A History of African American Theatre* (New York: Cambridge University Press, 2003), 428.

6. Marvin X, interview, in *New Plays from the Black Theatre*, ed. Ed Bullins (New York: Bantam, 1969).

7. Interview with the author, July 3, 2005.

8. Erika Munk, "Bullins: 'I Had My Way with Her,'" *Village Voice*. November 8, 1976, 87–88.

9. "Lafayette Theatre Reaction to *Bombers*, May 11, 1969," *Black Theatre* 4 (1969): 17.

10. Ed Bullins, *The Reluctant Rapist* (New York: Harper and Row, 1973), 165–66.

11. Larry Neal, "The Ethos of the Blues," in *Visions of a Liberated Future* (New York: Thunder's Mouth Press, 1989), 108.

12. Angela Davis, *Blues Legacies and Black Feminism: Gertrude "Ma" Rainey, Bessie Smith, and Billie Holiday* (New York: Pantheon, 1998), 113.

13. Kimberly W. Benston, "The Aesthetic of Modern Black Drama: From *Mimesis* to *Methexis*," in *The Theatre of Black Americans: A Collection of Critical Essays*, edited by Errol Hill (New York: Applause Theatre Book Publishers, 1987).

14. Hill and Hatch, *A History of African American Theatre*, 392.

15. Nathan L. Grant, "Ed Bullins," in *The Oxford Companion to African American Literature* (New York: Oxford University Press, 1997), 110.

16. Clayton Riley, "Bullins: 'It's Not the Play I Wrote.'" *New York Times*, March 19, 1972).

17. Ibid.

18. Ibid.

PLAYS

How Do You Do reflects a postabsurdist perspective in the attention it pays to the emptiness of language and culture in America in the Cold War Era. But it also reflects the politically engaged work of Amiri Baraka—a quote from his incendiary "The Revolutionary Theatre" serves as the epigraph. Thus, we see here an early example of Bullins's attempt to turn the absurdity of mass-mediated racism against itself, to move through nonsense to sense, through ugliness to beauty, through absurdity to significance. It was first produced at the Firehouse Repertory Theatre, San Francisco, in 1965 and first published by Illumination Press (San Francisco, 1967). It was reprinted in Black Fire, *edited by LeRoi Jones and Larry Neal (New York: Morrow, 1968).*

How Do You Do

A Nonsense Drama

(1965)

All their faces turned into the lights and you work on
them black nigger magic and cleanse them at having
seen the ugliness and, if the beautiful see themselves,
they will love themselves.

—LeRoi Jones

SETTING: *There must be music throughout, rhythmic music of a blues harmonica or guitar. A long, backless, rough bench is at front stage; a lone, blinking spot focuses upon the bench. As the play progresses, the white spot is alternated with red, orange, green, blue—any color to suggest changes of mood. The two male players are young, but nearly out of their youth; the matron is well-fleshed and attractive.* ROGER *is shabbily dressed;* PAUL's *clothes do not matter. The look and import of taste must be apparent in* DORA's *dress and mannerisms, except when she becomes excited. The players are black. When the curtain rises,* PAUL *sits on one end of the bench. A Georgia chain-gang song plays, and the light is steady.*

PAUL: I must make music today, poet music. I've sat here too long making nothing, and I know I've been born to make song. (*A figure appears from the wings. It dances in the shadows to a small plaintive melody, mingled with the blues, and* DORA *bumps and grinds into the light to the incongruous music. She stops behind the man and, when the music changes to barrel-house blues, she dances like a child around the bench.*) How shall I begin? Should I find the words first or the melody? Should I suggest a theme?

DORA, *strutting in front of* PAUL *like a streetwalker:* What are you doing? Are you talking to yourself, man? Why are you here alone?

PAUL: Who the hell are you?

DORA: I asked you first! If you're talking to yourself, that means you're crazy. I think I'd better report you. (*She starts off, twisting her hips to the quickly blinking light.*)

PAUL: GO TO HELL!

(DORA *reaches the shadows and slows, then hesitates, and stops as she meets* ROGER *striding briskly toward the light.*)

ROGER: Why hello! Fancy meeting you here.

DORA, *taking* ROGER's *arm and re-entering the light with him:* Fine, thank you. And you?

ROGER, *offers her a seat on the far end of the bench from* PAUL. *He sits next to her and puts his arm around her waist:* Did I ask you how do you do? Oh, I guess it doesn't matter, now does it, old top? As you can see, I'm in wonderful shape. In face (*grimaces*), I'm marvelous. (PAUL *sits silently, no longer outwardly brooding. He is ignored by the couple and looks lost in thought.*)

DORA: Do I know you? I has assumed as much. That suit fits you so well. How much did it cost?

ROGER: One hundred and fifty dollars. One of my cheaper numbers. I have sixty-two of them. All exactly like this one. I only wear them on Wednesdays. They were made especially for me. I look so beautiful in my clothes.

DORA: You sho' does.

ROGER: It's nice that you know. You have a fine . . . uhhh . . . intellect.

DORA: I'm president of three clubs!

ROGER: Really!

DORA: And I have color TV!

ROGER: How grand!

DORA: How much do you make?

ROGER: I have a very good job. I'm classified very highly. I'm a G-OOOO. And my credit rating is magnificent.

DORA: How magnificent!

ROGER: Are you married?

DORA, *clutching between his legs:* Would it matter?

ROGER: How do you do?

DORA: Fine, thank you.

ROGER: Fancy meeting you here.

DORA: Yes, one turns up in such exotic surroundings. Especially when one is so cultured and refined.

ROGER: How obvious.

DORA: I have fifty-seven pairs of drawers.

ROGER: Tremendous! Tremendous!

DORA: I don't have my shoes reheeled.

ROGER: Reheeled?

DORA: Yes!

ROGER: I buy my socks by the box.

DORA: How ecstatic!

ROGER: How do you do?

DORA: I'm fine.

ROGER: I know that . . . ha, ha, ha.

PAUL, *not turning from his contemplative position:* OH, FUCK!

ROGER, *to* DORA: Did you fart?

DORA: I'm a lady.

ROGER: Oh, how could I have forgotten? I'm so refined that I sometimes forget the larger issues, you know.

DORA: Is that a British accent?

ROGER: French.

DORA: Sorbonne?

ROGER: Berlitz.[1]

DORA: They're the most pretentious on the continent!

ROGER: How do you do?

DORA, *laying her head upon his shoulder, but only resting her hand on his leg:* I can positively hear the mandolins playing. It's as if we were floating down the Grand Canal in Venice.

(*The off-key blues gives a funky squeal.*)

ROGER, *shoves* DORA, *who takes a pratfall behind the bench:* Bitch! Get yo' greasy head off'a mah rags!

DORA, *looking up from the floor:* I have a run in my hose, but I got twenty-eight mo' boxes.

---

1. Berlitz: A popular language instruction company.

ROGER, *inspecting his manicure:* I say there, old girl, the membrane in the cochlea on which is located the Organ of Corti . . . etc., etc., etc.

DORA: How true.

PAUL, *stands and walks over to* ROGER: Shut up!

ROGER, *looking down at* DORA: Did you say something, Sweetcake?

DORA, *rising and edging toward the bench:* Yes, I said I liked your gold tooth.

ROGER, *flashing his gold tooth and showing her the large diamond on his finger:* You do? What's your name, Honeychile?

DORA: Dora. What's yours?

ROGER: Roger.

DORA: Dodger?

ROGER: No, Stereotype.

DORA: My, my, Sugarpie, so am I.

ROGER: What?

DORA: Of the same breed.

ROGER, *looking at* PAUL's *back, retreating to his seat:* Who's dat?

DORA: Just some ole nigger. Dirty, no-count Southern boogie, probably.

ROGER: He must be here for some reason. (*calling to* PAUL *in the voice of a white man*) Hey, boy! (PAUL *glowers back at him.*) Yeah, you, fellah. Come down here! (PAUL *stands and saunters back to* ROGER. *The lights change color when* PAUL *gets in position and continue to change throughout the play. The music also picks up in tempo and, in* PAUL's *longer speeches, a funeral dirge is played.*)

DORA: He's not a bad-looking chap when you get used to him, a bit coarse, but . . . hummph, probably couldn't pay my taxi fare to town.

ROGER: What's your name, boy?

PAUL: It's Paul.

ROGER: What are you hanging around here for? You're not of our class and quality.

PAUL: No, I'm not.

DORA: What do you do, Honey?

PAUL: I'm an image-maker.

DORA: How do you do?

ROGER: Fine, how are you?

DORA: Better, if the weather holds.

ROGER: How clever. Why didn't I think of that?

DORA: I'm in the society pages of *The Coloured Courier* every day. I'm a debutante.

ROGER: Your ole man did an excellent job shining my shoes dis' mornin'. Tipped the ole nigger a dollah. Some days when I feel good, I tip him two.

DORA: I'm the president of three clubs.

PAUL, *speaking as a lecturer:* Build into the black/white consciousnesses of the Western Judeo-Christian culture the reality of the diabolical black sociopath that it has created.

ROGER: I pay fifty-two fifty for my shoes. I don't support my bastards. I drink forty percent of the scotch imported in dis great country of my fantasies. I'll work for a white man, when I works. A black woman can't do anything fo' me 'cept lead me to a white one. I hate myself.

DORA: Mink and ermine . . . ohhh, chile . . . it's enough to give me an organism . . . besides poker. My husband ain't a man. He makes love to my brother.

PAUL: Know that man can philosophize himself into any and all positions to justify his greed for power and his cowardice.

ROGER: I can bullshit mah boss just like dat. "You're one out of a thousand niggers, Roger Stereotype," he says. "Y'all sho' knows wha yo' talkin' 'bout, bossman, suh," I tell him.

DORA: I haven't had an organism since I was beaten by my last white lover. He didn't know how to put a good nigger whuppin' on me like mah ole man usta, but I didn't have patience ta larn him.

PAUL: Tell your victim you are goin' to kill him but giggle, buck dance,[2] and break wind before you pull your razor.

DORA, *jumping slightly from her seat:* 'Scuse me.

ROGER: See bitch, I tole you you farted.

DORA: I'm a lady. You don't go 'round talkin' ta ya white bitch like dat.

ROGER: She's refined.

DORA: And me?

ROGER, *turning to* PAUL: Go on, man. Get on with your shit.

PAUL: Give the lady her say.

DORA, *brazen and free:* Yeah, you black mothafucker. How can you expect me to be a fictitious pile of shit when you ain't even man enough to be mah man? If you want to go for that mythical bullshit about the white goddess, then respect yourself by makin' your own dreams. Put a black goddess on her own pedestal beside that white one who's shittin' on your dumb black head as well as her white man's. Don't wait for a white cat to glorify me before you come sniffin' on round home, black sucker. (*Pauses*) And another thing, fool. Start takin' care of your nine bastards that you got from showin' me how much man you was and take me down to the Club on your arm. I've been a waitress enough

---

2. Buck dance: A pre-tap-dance routine performed in the middle nineteenth century by minstrel and vaudeville performers, though perhaps originally on slave ships. Thus the term *buck*, a derogatory term for the black male.

times to know what fork to stir mah soup with. Yeah, instead of takin' your latest white girl, take me to Sardi's[3] fo' cocktails, and see how you feel with a fine black woman on your arm.

ROGER, *singing girlishly:* I'm so fine. I have the finest rags on my behind.

PAUL, *resolutely, not getting through at all:* Know that evil is the inverse of good, that violence is the basis of power, that hate works to meet its own ends.

ROGER: That Jew boy I work fo' is no older den me. I could wheel 'n deal as good as him. I got mo' on the ball den dat square-ass paddy mothafucker. (*He feels* DORA's *thigh.*) Hey, baby, have ya seen mah new Cadillac?

DORA: Your boss drives a Volkswagen.

PAUL, *recollecting:* Should Jews . . . should Jews buy VW's?[4]

ROGER: I's a boss nigger. I'm so hip, I can't even talk. It ain't mah language anyway . . . dat's why I talk in an Oxfordian accent. Yawhl.

PAUL: Scratch your head, shuffle, pray to his gods until you decide what day you'll call Judgment.

DORA: I think it's just a shame that we Americans tolerate all those damned . . . pardon me . . . that isn't ladylike, is it? (ROGER *has his hand up her dress now.*) I think something should be done about Cuba and Red China and the black Congolese. At least that's what my white boyfriend tells me in bed.

PAUL: Imitate him. Become an alter-ego Superman, Lone Ranger, and Tarzan, in blackface, but really turn into the Shadow.

ROGER: Are you familiar with karate, chaps?

DORA: Mah white man can do seven pushups!

PAUL: Make him think that you don't know anything about language. That you can't logically think because you say, "I ain't never done no nothin' . . ." DESTROY HIS INSTITUTIONALIZED, STRUCTURED LOGIC THROUGH ILLOGIC . . . YAWHL!

(PAUL *is tiring. The couple on the bench are in hot embrace but still speak their lines as if they were having an elocution lesson.*)

ROGER: I live in a hundred-thousand-dollar house, drive a nine-thousand-dollar car, am in debt for sixty thousand. I do well on ten thousand a year.

PAUL: Never let him know you have any brains.

DORA: Chile, that was the grooviest thing I ever fell into. I really, but I mean really, baby, dig all that action . . .

---

3. Sardi's: A famous Times Square restaurant and bar, hangout of the stars.

4. Should Jews buy VWs?: The prototype of the popular Volkswagen Beetle was created by Hitler; the German Volkswagen Group utilized forced Jewish labor during the 1930s and 1940s.

ROGER: We drank twenty fifths of White Label at Blue's last Sadee.[5] Naw, I don't eat watermelon, fried chicken, and I don't know what chittlins, hog maws, and corn bread is, chile. I just don't think of it! . . . Oh Jesus! . . . It's all so unrefined. (ROGER *is becoming more effeminate.* DORA's *voice is turning husky.* PAUL's *speeches don't carry conviction.*)

DORA: You should try my beef stroganoff, darling.

ROGER: My tummy might tumble. (*They break their embrace.*)

DORA: No, it wouldn't, Sweetcake.

ROGER: I'm Ivy League, you know.

DORA: Yes, I was born in Georgia, but my parents left before I was born.

ROGER: You should just see my last golf score.

DORA: Why, of course I buy flesh-colored Maiden Forms.[6]

ROGER: I'm the first one in my firm.

DORA: I sit next to the window where everyone can see me.

ROGER: How do you do?

DORA: Fine, how are you?

ROGER: Fine day, if it doesn't cloud up and shit.

DORA: Really!

PAUL: Don't rape his women, seduce them—you don't have to rape anybody—everyone wants to screw your black ass. RIGHT! (PAUL's *voice is now a whisper, and* ROGER *feels his manhood returning.*)

ROGER: I wonder if that white bitch will say "yeah" if I put a one-hundred-dollah bill on the table.

DORA: I've been to every white motel in town.

PAUL: Don't blow up all dat good technology—cough, cough—and them there institutions at your disposal. Infiltrate his technology with Ph.D.'s.

(*The harmonica brays like a jackass and the lights flicker as never before.*)

DORA: Let's all turn white.

ROGER: I'm de best, 'cause I just know it. Don't need to go any further den dat. I can't git any better.

DORA: I got to percents in school and, shit, dat's all I could do to pass. Nex' year I was pregnant.

ROGER: Read a book? Sheet! Ain't gonna be wastin' mah time readin' some fuckin' book. I read one once in school. Just sat up dere and finished it to see what it was all about. Found out dat readin' ain't shit. Ain't gonna be wastin' mah time.

---

5. Sadee = Saturday.

6. Maiden Forms: A pun on Maidenform, a popular brand of women's underwear in the 1960s; the company's bras were touted for their ability to "lift and separate." The pun alludes to Plato's theory of ideal forms.

PAUL: Kill him in the mind—the age of the body is done. Imitate the State, it kills its questioners in the cerebrum. Become a guerrilla warrior of ideas.

ROGER, *speaking to* DORA: How bout lettin' me buy ya a drink, baby?

DORA: Where?

ROGER: Some little out-of-the-way place I know.

DORA: No!

ROGER: Why?

DORA: You got to take me some place where I can be seen.

PAUL: Sell illogic like he sells soap—his mind is tuned like yours to pick up any crap that comes along and sounds just as good as the other crap.

ROGER: Socratic irony without compassion is Fascism.

DORA: Sophist rhetoric without sympathy is Salesmanship.

PAUL: Right, children. (*Motioning them to leave*) Now go out and play, children. Go out and burn and turn and learn. Go spread the word.

ROGER: I can take you to the bar of the biggest white motel in the state.

DORA, *smoothing her dress and pulling up her stockings:* I'll be a knockout.

ROGER: All the white chicks will look at me.

DORA, *looking in a hand mirror:* I'm so fine.

ROGER, *standing, holding out his hand to* DORA: How do you do?

DORA: Fine, thank you.

ROGER: Qu'est que c'est?

DORA: Trés bien, merci.

ROGER: ARE YOU INDIAN?

DORA: My great grandfather told many tales . . .

ROGER: I have great empathy with the cause of human rights. But I'm so refined I can never get any farther than a white bar in spreading brotherhood.

DORA: You have great promise and proportions.

ROGER: How do you do? (*They leave the stage doing versions of the latest dances—the twist, swim, frug, etc.*)

PAUL: Fine day, thank you. (*He walks back to his end of the bench and sits.*) I must make music today, poet music. I know that I can make song. (*He seems inspired and begins singing.*) How do you do? Fine, thank you. And you? Trés bien, merci. Really! Fine day if it doesn't open up and swallow us. CAN'T SAY IF I SEE THE QUIET SUBTLETY IN NO HOPE . . . How do you do . . . I have a gold tooth . . . etc., etc., etc.

Curtain

A model one-act play, Clara's Ole Man *systematically ratchets up the dramatic tension until a climactic act of violence brings the curtain down. Although it is based on a very old-fashioned dramatic premise—an illicit rendezvous is interrupted by the return of one lover's "ole man"—it frames this premise in three innovative ways. First, much of the dramatic tension of the play occurs on the level of language. Second, the drama here is distinctly musical—rhythm 'n' blues plays in the background, making this a kind of "blues drama." Third, the sexual conflict is dislodged from the usual heterosexual framework; the "ole man" in this South Philadelphia apartment isn't who Jack (or, most likely, the viewer) expects. It was first produced at the Firehouse Repertory Theatre, San Francisco, in 1965 and first published in* Five Plays, *edited by Ed Bullins (New York: Bobbs-Merrill, 1969).*

Clara's Ole Man

A Play of Lost Innocence

(1965)

THE PEOPLE:

CLARA, *a light brown girl of eighteen, well built with long, dark hair. A blond streak runs down the middle of her head, and she affects a pony tail. She is pensive, slow in speech but feline. Her eyes are heavy-lidded and brown; she smiles— rather, blushes—often.*

BIG GIRL, *a stocky woman wearing jeans and tennis shoes and a tight-fitting blouse which accents her prominent breasts. She is of an indeterminable age, due partly to her lack of make-up and plain hair style. She is anywhere from 25 to 40 and is loud and jolly, frequently breaking out in laughter from her own jokes.*

JACK, *20 years old, wears a corduroy Ivy League suit and vest. At first,* JACK's *speech is modulated and too eloquent for the surroundings, but as he drinks his words become slurred and mumbled.*

BABY GIRL, BIG GIRL's *mentally retarded teenage sister. The girl has the exact same hairdo as* CLARA. *Her face is made up with mascara and eye shadow, and she has black arching eyebrows penciled darkly, the same as* CLARA.

MISS FAMIE, *a drunken neighbor.*

STOOGIE, *a local streetfighter and gang leader. His hair is processed.*[1]

BAMA, *one of* STOOGIE's *boys.*

HOSS, *another of* STOOGIE's *boys.*

C.C, *a young wino.*

TIME: *Early spring, the mid-1950s.*

SCENE: *A slum kitchen on a rainy afternoon in South Philadelphia. The room is very clean, wax glosses the linoleum and old wooden furniture; a cheap but clean red checkered oilcloth covers the table. If the room could speak it would say, "I'm cheap but clean."*

    A cheap AM radio plays rhythm 'n' blues music throughout the play. The furniture is made up of a wide kitchen table where a gallon jug of red wine sits. Also upon the table is an oatmeal box, cups, mugs, plates and spoons, ashtrays, and packs of cigarettes. Four chairs circle the table, and two sit against the wall at the back of the stage. An old-fashioned wood- and coal-burning stove takes up a corner of the room and a gas range of 1935 vintage is at the back next to the door to the yard. A large, smoking frying pan is on one of the burners.

    JACK *and* BIG GIRL *are seated at opposite ends of the table;* CLARA *stands at the stove fanning the fumes toward the door.* BABY GIRL *plays upon the floor with a homemade toy.*

CLARA, *fans fumes:* Uummm, uummm . . . well, there goes the lunch. I wonder how I was dumb enough to burn the bacon?

BIG GIRL: Just comes natural with you, honey, all looks and no brains . . . now with me and my looks, anybody in South Philly can tell I'm a person that naturally takes care of business . . . hee hee . . . ain't that right, Clara?

CLARA: Awww girl, go on. You's the worst messer'upper I knows. You didn't even go to work this mornin'. What kind of business is that?

---

    1. Processed: Chemically straightened, and consequently reddened, with a harrowing mix of lye and potato starch. Popular from the 1920s to 1950s and derided by many Black Nationalists of the 1960s as reactionary.

BIG GIRL: It's all part of my master plan, baby. Don't you worry none . . . Big Girl knows what she's doin'. You better believe that!

CLARA: Yeah, you may know what you're doin' but I'm the one who's got to call in for you and lie that you're sick.

BIG GIRL: Well, it ain't a lie. You know I got this cough and stopped-up feeling. (*Looking at* JACK) You believe that, don't you, youngblood?

JACK: Most certainly. You could very well have a respiratory condition and also have all the appearances of an extremely capable person.

BIG GIRL, *slapping table:* Hee hee . . . SEE, Clara? . . . SEE? Listen ta that, Clara. I told you anybody could tell it. Even ole hot lips here can tell.

CLARA, *pours out grease and wipes stove:* Awww . . . he just says that to be nice . . . he's always sayin' things like that.

BIG GIRL: Is that how he talked when he met you the other day out to your aunt's house?

CLARA, *hesitating:* Nawh . . . nawh he didn't talk like that.

BIG GIRL: Well, how did he talk, huh?

CLARA: Awww . . . Big Girl. I don't know.

BIG GIRL: Well, who else does? You know what kind of line a guy gives ya. You been pitched at enough times, haven't ya? By the looks of him I bet he gave ya the ole smooth college boy approach . . . (*To* JACK) C'mon, man, drink up. We got a whole lot mo' to kill. Don't you know this is my day off and I'm celebratin'?

JACK, *takes a drink:* Thanks . . . this is certainly nice of you to go to all this trouble for me. I never expected it.

BIG GIRL: What did you expect, youngblood?

JACK, *takes another sip:* Ohhh, well . . . I . . .

CLARA, *to* BABY GIRL: DON'T PUT THAT DIRTY THING IN YOUR MOUF, GAL! (*She walks around the table to* BABY GIRL *and tugs her arm*) Now, keep that out of your mouf!

BABY GIRL, *holds to toy sullenly:* No!

CLARA: You keep quiet, you hear, gal!

BABY GIRL: No ! ! !

CLARA: If you keep tellin' me no, I'm goin' ta take you upstairs ta Aunt Toohey.

BABY GIRL, *throws back head and drums feet on floor:* NO! NO! SHIT! DAMN! SHIT! NO!

CLARA, *disturbed:* Now stop that! We got company.

BIG GIRL, *laughs hard and leans elbows upon table:* HAW HAW HAW . . . I guess she told you, Clara. Hee hee . . . that little dirty mouf bitch (*pointing to* BABY GIRL *and becoming choked*) . . . that little . . . (*cough, cough*) . . . hooooee, boy!

CLARA: You shouldn't have taught her all them nasty words, Big Girl. Now we can't do anything with her. (*Turns to* JACK) What do you think of that?

JACK: Yes, it does seem a problem. But with proper guidance, she'll more than likely be conditioned out of it when she gets into a learning situation among her peer group.

BIG GIRL, *takes a drink and scowls:* BULLSHIT!

CLARA: Awww . . . B.G.

JACK: I beg your pardon, Miss?

BIG GIRL: I said bullshit! Whatta ya mean with proper guidance? . . . (*Points*) I taught that little bitch myself . . . the best cuss words I know before she ever climbed out of her crib . . . Whatta ya mean when she gets among her "peer group"?

JACK: I didn't exactly say that. I said when . . .

BIG GIRL, *cuts him off:* Don't tell me what you said, boy! I got ears. I know all them big horseshit doctor words . . . Tell him, Clara . . . Tell him what I do. Where do I work, Clara?

CLARA: Awww . . . B.G., please.

BIG GIRL: DO LIKE I SAY! DO LIKE BIG WANTS YOU TO!

CLARA, *surrenders:* She works out at the state nut farm.

BIG GIRL, *triumphant:* And tell mister smart and proper what I do.

CLARA, *automatically:* She's a technician.

JACK: Oh, that's nice. I didn't mean to suggest there was anything wrong with how you raised your sister.

BIG GIRL, *jolly again:* Haw haw haw . . . Nawh, ya didn't. I know you didn't know what you were sayin', youngblood. Do you know why I taught her to cuss?

JACK: Why no, I have no idea. Why did you?

BIG GIRL: Well, it was to give her freedom, ya know? (JACK *shakes his head.*) Ya see, workin' in the hospital with all the nuts and fruits and crazies and weirdos, I get ideas 'bout things. I saw how when they get these kids in who have cracked up and even with older people who come in out of their skulls, they all mostly cuss. Mostly all of them, all the time they out of their heads, they cuss all the time and do other wild things and boy do some of them really get into it and let out all of that filthy shit that's been stored up all them years. But when the docs start shockin' them and puttin' them on insulin, they quiets down. That's when the docs think they're gettin' better, but really they ain't. They're just learn'n like before to hold it in . . . just like before, that's one reason most of them come back or are always on the verge afterwards of goin' psycho again.

JACK, *enthusiastic:* Wow, I never thought of that! That ritual action of purging and catharsis can open up new avenues of therapy and in learning theory and conditioning subjects . . .

BIG GIRL: Saaay whaaa . . . ? What did you have for breakfast, man?

CLARA, *struck:* That sounds so wonderful . . .

JACK, *still excited:* But I agree with you. You have an intuitive grasp of very abstract concepts!

BIG GIRL, *beaming:* Yeah, yeah . . . I got a lot of it figured out . . . (*To* JACK) Here, fill up your glass again, man.

JACK, *to* CLARA: Aren't you drinking with us?

CLARA: Later. Big Girl doesn't allow me to start in drinking too early.

JACK, *confused:* She doesn't?

BIG GIRL, *cuts in:* Well, in Baby Girl's case, I said to myself that I'm teach'n her how in front and lettin' her use what she knows whenever it builds up inside. And it's really good for her, gives her spirit and everything.

CLARA: That's probably what warped her brain.

BIG GIRL: Hush up! You knows it was dat fuckin' disease. All the doctors said so.

CLARA: You don't believe no doctors 'bout nothin' else!

BIG GIRL, *glares at* CLARA: Are you showin' out, Clara? Are you showin' out to your little boyfriend?

CLARA: He ain't mah boyfriend.

JACK, *interrupts:* How do you know she might not have spirit if she wasn't allowed to curse?

BIG GIRL, *sullen:* I don't know anything, youngblood. But I can take a look at myself and see the two of us. Look at me! (*Stares at* JACK) LOOK AT ME!

JACK: Yes, yes, I'm looking.

BIG GIRL: Well, what do you see?

CLARA: B.G. . . . please!

BIG GIRL, *ignores:* Well, what do you see?

JACK, *worried:* Well, I don't really know . . . I . . .

BIG GIRL: Well, let me tell you what you see. You see a fat bitch who's twenty pounds overweight and looks ten years older than she is. You want to know how I got this way and been this way most of my life and would be worse off if I didn't let off steam some drinkin' this rotgut and speakin' my mind?

JACK, *to* BIG GIRL, *who doesn't listen but drinks:* Yes, I would like to hear.

(CLARA *finishes the stove and takes a seat between the two.* BABY GIRL *goes to the yard door but does not go out into the rain; she sits down and looks out through the door at an angle.*)

BIG GIRL: Ya see, when I was a little runt of a kid, my mother found out she couldn't keep me or Baby Girl any longer cause she had T.B.,[2] so I got shipped out somewheres and Baby Girl got shipped out somewheres else. People that Baby Girl went to exposed her to the disease. She was lucky. I ended up with some fuckin' Christians . . .

CLARA: Ohhh, B.G., you shouldn't say that!

BIG GIRL: Well, I sho as hell just did! . . . Damned kristers! I spent twelve years with those people, can you imagine? A dozen years in hell. Christians . . . haaa . . . always preachin' 'bout some heaven over yonder and building a bigger hell here den any devil have imagination for.

CLARA: You shouldn't go round sayin' things like dat.

BIG GIRL: I shouldn't! Well, what did your Christian mammy and pot-gutted pappy teach you? When I met you you didn't even know how to take a douche.

CLARA: YOU GOT NO RIGHT ! ! ! (*She momentarily rises as if she's going to launch herself on* BIG GIRL.)

BIG GIRL, *condescending:* Awww . . . forget it, sweetie . . . don't make no never mind, but you remember how you us'ta smell when you got ready fo bed . . . like a dead hoss or a baby skunk . . . (*To* JACK, *explaining*) That damned Christian mamma and pappa of hers didn't tell her a thing 'bout herself . . . ha ha ha . . . Thought if she ever found out her little things was used fo anything else 'cept squattin' she'd fall backwards right up in it . . . ZaaaBOOM . . . STRAIGHT TA HELL . . . ha ha . . . Didn't know that li'l Clara had already found her heaven, and on the same trail.

CLARA, *ashamed:* Sometimes . . . sometimes . . . I just want to die for bein' here.

BIG GIRL, *enjoying herself:* Ha ha ha . . . that wouldn't do no good. Would it? Just remember what shape you were in when I met you, kid. Ha ha ha. (*To* JACK) Hey, boy, can you imagine this pretty little trick here had her stomach seven months in the wind, waitin' on a dead baby who died from the same disease that Baby Girl had . . .

CLARA: He didn't have any nasty disease like Baby Girl!

BABY GIRL, *hears her name but looks out door:* NO! NO! SHIT! DAMN! SHIT! SHIT!

BIG GIRL: Haw haw haw . . . Now we got her started . . . (*She laughs for over a minute;* JACK *waits patiently, sipping.* CLARA *is grim.* BABY GIRL *has quieted.*) She . . . she . . . ha ha . . . was walkin' round with a dead baby in her and had no place to go.

---

2. T.B.: Tuberculosis.

CLARA, *fills a glass:* I just can't understand you, B.G. You know my baby died after he was born. Some days you just get besides yourself.

BIG GIRL: I'm only helpin' ya entertain your guest.

CLARA: Awww . . . B.G. It wasn't his fault. I invited him.

JACK, *dismayed:* Well, I asked, really. If there's anything wrong I can go.

BIG GIRL: Take it easy, youngblood. I'm just havin' a little fun. Now let's get back to the Clara Saga . . . ya hear that word, junior? . . . S-A-G-A, SUCKER! You college boys don't know it all. Yeah, her folks had kicked her out—and the little punk she was big for what had tried to put her out on the block—and when that didn't work out . . . (*Mocking and making pretended blushes*) because our sweet little thing here was soooo modest and sedate . . . the nigger split! . . . HAW HAW HAW . . . HE MADE IT TO NEW YORK! (*She goes into a laughing, choking, and crying fit.* BABY GIRL *rushes over to her and on tiptoe pats her back.*)

BABY GIRL: Big Girl! Big Girl! Big Girl!

(*A knocking sounds and* CLARA *exits to answer the door.*)

BIG GIRL, *catches her breath:* Whatcha want, little sister?

BABY GIRL: The cat! The cat! It's got some kittens! The cat got some kittens!

BIG GIRL, *still coughing and choking:* Awww, go on. You know there ain't no cats under there with no kittens. (*To* JACK) She's been makin' that story up for two months now about how some cat crawls up under the steps and has kittens. She can't fool me none. She just wants a cat but I ain't gonna get none.

JACK: Why not? Cats aren't so bad. My mother has one and he's quite a pleasure to her.

BIG GIRL: For your mammy maybe, but all they mean round here (*Singsong*) is fleas and mo' mouths to feed. With an invalid aunt upstairs, we don't need any mo' expenses.

JACK, *gestures toward* BABY GIRL: It shows that she has a very vivid imagination to make up that story about the kittens.

BIG GIRL: Yeah, her big sister ain't the biggest liar in the family.

(CLARA *returns with* MISS FAMIE *staggering behind her, a thin middle-aged woman in long seamen's raincoat, dripping wet and wearing house slippers that are soaked and squish water about the kitchen floor.*)

BIG GIRL: Hi, Miss Famie. I see you're dressed in your rainy glad rags today.

MISS FAMIE, *slurred speech of the drunk:* Hello, B.G. Yeah, I couldn't pass up seein' Aunt Toohey, so I put on my weather coat. You know that don't a day pass that I don't stop up to see her.

BIG GIRL: Yeah, I know, Miss Famie. Every day you go up there with that quart of gin under your dress and you two ole lushes put it away.

MISS FAMIE: Why, B.G. You should know better than that.

CLARA, *re-seated:* B.G., you shouldn't say that . . .

BIG GIRL: Why shouldn't I? I'm payin' for over half of that juice and I don't git to see none of it 'cept the empty bottles.

BABY GIRL: CAT! CAT! CAT!

MISS FAMIE: Oh, the baby still sees them there cats.

CLARA: You should be ashamed to talk to Miss Famie like that.

BIG GIRL, *to* JACK: Why you so quiet? Can't you speak to folks when they come in?

JACK: I'm sorry. (*To* MISS FAMIE) Hello, ma'am.

MISS FAMIE: Why howdie, son.

CLARA: Would you like a glass of wine, Miss Famie?

MISS FAMIE: Don't mind if I do, sister.

BIG GIRL: Better watch it, Miss Famie. Wine and gin will rust your gizzard.

CLARA: Ohhh . . . (*pours a glass of wine*) . . . Here, Miss Famie.

BABY GIRL: CAT! CAT!

BIG GIRL, *singsong, lifting her glass:* Mus' I tell' . . . muscatel . . . jitterbug champagne. (*Reminisces*) Remember, Clara, the first time I got you to take a drink? (*To* MISS FAMIE) You should of seen her. Some of this same cheap rotgut here. She'd never had a drink before but she wanted to show me how game she was. She was a bright little smart thing, just out of high school and didn't know her butt from a door knob.

MISS FAMIE: Yes, indeed, that was Clara all right.

BIG GIRL: She drank three waterglasses down and got so damned sick I had to put my finger down her throat and make her heave it up . . . HAW HAW . . . babbled her fool head off all night . . . Said she'd be my friend always . . . that we'd always be together . . .

MISS FAMIE, *gulps down her drink:* Wine will make you do that the first time you get good 'n high on it.

JACK, *takes a drink:* I don't know. You know . . . I've never really been wasted and I've been drinkin' for quite some time now.

BIG GIRL: Quite some time, huh? How long? Six months?

JACK: Nawh. My mother used to let me drink at home. I've been drinkin' since fifteen. And I drank all the time I was in the service.

BIG GIRL: Just because you been slippin' some drinks out of ya mammy's bottle and you slipped a few under ya belt with the punks in the barracks don't make ya a drinker, boy!

CLARA: B.G. , . . . do you have to?

MISS FAMIE, *finishes her second drink as* BIG GIRL *and* CLARA *stare at each other:*

Well, I guess I better get up and see Aunt Toohey. (*She leaves.*)

BIG GIRL, *before* MISS FAMIE *reaches top of stairs:* That ole ginhead tracked water all over your floor, Clara.

CLARA: Makes no never mind to me. This place stays so clean, I like when someone comes so it gets a little messy, so I have somethin' ta do.

BIG GIRL: Is that why Jackie boy is here? So he can do some messin' 'round?

CLARA: Nawh, B.G.

JACK, *stands:* Well, I'll be going. I see that . . .

BIG GIRL, *rises and tugs his sleeve:* Sit down an' drink up, youngblood. (*Pushes him back into his seat*) There's wine here . . . (*slow and suggestive*) . . . there's a pretty girl here . . . You go for that, don't you?

JACK: It's not that . . .

BIG GIRL: You go for fine little Clara, don't you?

JACK: Well, yes, I do . . .

BIG GIRL: HAW HAW HAW . . . (*slams the table and sloshes wine*) . . . HAW HAW HAW . . . (*slow and suggestive*) . . . What I tell ya, Clara? You're a winner. First time I laid eyes on you, I said to myself that you's a winner.

CLARA, *takes a drink:* Drink up, B.G.

BIG GIRL, *to* JACK: You sho you like what you see, youngblood?

JACK, *becomes bold:* Why, sure. Do you think I'd come out on a day like this for anybody?

BIG GIRL: HAW HAW HAW . . . (*peals of laughter and more coughs*)

JACK, *to* CLARA: I was going to ask you to go to the matinee 'round Pep's, but I guess it's too late now.

CLARA, *hesitates:* I never been.

BIG GIRL, *sobers:* That's right. You never been to Pep's and it's only 'round the corner. What you mean, it's too late, youngblood? It don't start gettin' good till 'round four.

JACK: I thought she might have ta start gettin' supper.

BIG GIRL: She'd only burn it the fuck up too if she did. (*To* CLARA) I'm goin' ta take you to Pep's this afternoon.

CLARA: You don't have ta, B.G.

BIG GIRL: It's my day off, ain't it?

CLARA: But it costs so much, don't it?

BIG GIRL: Nawh, not much . . . you'll like it. Soon as C.C comes over to watch Baby Girl, we can go.

CLARA, *brightens:* O.K.!

JACK: I don't know who's there now, but they always have a good show. Sometimes, Ahmad Jamal . . .

BABY GIRL, *cuts speech:* CAT! CAT! CAT!

BIG GIRL: Let's toast to that . . . (*Raising her glass*) . . . To Pep's on a rainy day!

JACK: HERE, HERE! (*He drains his glass.*)

(*A tumbling sound is heard from the backyard as they drink and* BABY GIRL *claps hands as* STOOGIE, BAMA, *and* HOSS *appear in the yard doorway. The three boys are no more than sixteen. They are soaked but wear only thin jackets, caps and pants. Under his cap,* STOOGIE *wears a bandanna to keep his processed hair dry.*)

BIG GIRL: What the hell is this?

STOOGIE, *goes to* BIG GIRL *and pats her shoulder:* The heat, B.G. The man was on our asses, so we had to come on in out of the rain, baby, dig?

BIG GIRL: Well, tell me somethin' I don't know, baby. Why you got to pick mah back door? I ain't never ready for any more heat than I gets already.

STOOGIE: It just happened that way, B.G. We didn't have any choice.

BAMA: That's right, Big Girl. You know we ain't lame 'nuf to be usin' yo pad fo no highway.

HOSS: Yeah, baby, you know how it is when the man is there.

BIG GIRL: Well, what makes a difference . . . (*Smiles*) . . . Hey, what'cha standin' there with your faces hangin' out for? Get yourselves a drink.

(HOSS *goes to the sink to get glasses for the trio.* STOOGIE *looks* JACK *over and nods to* BAMA, *then turns to* CLARA.)

STOOGIE: How ya doin', Clara? Ya lookin' fine as ever.

CLARA: I'm okay, Stoogie. I don't have to ask 'bout you none. Bad news sho' travels fast.

STOOGIE, *holds arms apart in innocence:* What'cha mean, baby? What'cha been hearin' bout poppa Stoogie?

CLARA: Just the regular. That your gang's fightin' the Peaceful Valley guys up in North Philly.

STOOGIE: Awww . . . dat's old stuff. Sheeet . . . you way behind, baby.

BAMA: Yeah, sweetcake, dat's over.

CLARA: Already?

HOSS: Yeah, we just finished sign'n' a peace treaty with Peaceful Valley.

BAMA: Yeah, we out ta cool the War Lords now from ov'va on Powelton Avenue.

HOSS: Ole Stoogie here is settin' up the war council now. We got a pact with Peaceful Valley and, man, when we come down on those punk War Lords . . . baby . . . it's just gonna be all ov'va.

BIG GIRL: Yeah, it's always one thing ta another with you punks.

STOOGIE: Hey, B.G., cool it! We can't help it if people always spreadin' rumors 'bout us. Things just happen an' people talk and don' understand and get it all wrong, dat's all.

BIG GIRL: Yeah, all of it just happens, huh? It's just natural . . . you's growin' boys.

STOOGIE: That's what's happen'n, baby. Now take for instance Peaceful Valley. Las' week, we went up there . . . ya know, only five of us in Crook's Buick.

CLARA: I guess ya was just lookin' at the scenery?

STOOGIE: Yeah, baby, dat's it. We was lookin' . . . lookin' fo' some jive half-ass niggers.

(*The boys laugh and giggle as* STOOGIE *enacts the story.*)

STOOGIE: Yeah, we spot Specs from offa Jefferson and Gratz walkin' with them bad foots down Master . . . ha ha ha . . .

BAMA: Tell them what happened to Specs, man.

HOSS: Awww, man, ya ain't gonna drag mah man Bama again?

(*They laugh more, slapping and punching each other, taking off their caps and cracking each other with them, gulping their wine and performing for the girls and* JACK. STOOGIE *has his hair exposed.*)

STOOGIE: Bama, here . . . ha ha ha . . . Bama burnt dat four-eyed mathafukker in the leg.

HOSS: Baby, you shoulda seen it!

CLARA: Yeah, that's what I heard.

STOOGIE: Yeah, but listen, baby. (*Points to BAMA*) He was holding the only heat we had . . . ha ho ho . . . and dis jive sucker was aimin' at Specs' bad foots . . . ha ha . . . while that blind mathafukker was blastin' from round the corner straight through the car window . . .

(*They become nearly hysterical with laughter and stagger and stumble around the table.*)

HOSS: Yeah . . . ha ha . . . mathafukkin' glass was flyin' all over us . . . ha ha . . . we almost got sliced ta death and dis stupid mathafukker was shootin' at the man's bad foots . . . ha ha . . .

BAMA, *scratching his head:* Well, man. Well, man . . . I didn't know what kind of rumble we was in.

(CLARA *and* BIG GIRL *laugh as they refill their glasses, nearly emptying the jug.* BIG GIRL *gets up and from out of the refrigerator pulls another gallon as laughter subsides.*)

BIG GIRL, *sits down:* What's the heat doin' after ya?

STOOGIE: Nothin'.

CLARA: I bet!

STOOGIE, *sneer:* That's right, baby. They just singled us out to make examples of.

(*This gets a laugh from his friends.*)

BIG GIRL: What did you get?

HOSS: Get?

BIG GIRL, *turns on him:* You tryin' ta get wise, punk?

STOOGIE, *patronizing:* Awww, B.G. You not goin' ta take us serious, are ya? (*Silence*) Well, ya see. We were walkin' down Broad Street by the State Store,[3] see? And we see this old rumdum come out and stagger down the street carryin' this heavy package . . .

CLARA: And? . . .

STOOGIE: And he's stumblin', see. Like he's gonna fall. So good ole Hoss here says, "Why don't we help that pore man out?" So Bama walks up and helps the man carry his package, and do you know what?

BIG GIRL: Yeah, the mathafukker "slips" down and screams and some cops think you some wrongdoin' studs . . . yeah, I know . . . of course you didn't have time to explain.

STOOGIE: That's right, B.G. So to get our breath so we could tell our side of it, we just stepped in here, dig?

BIG GIRL: Yeah, I dig. (*Menacing*) Where is it?

HOSS: Where's what?

(*Silence.*)

STOOGIE: If you had just give me another minute, B.G. (*Pulls out a quart of vodka*) Well, no use savin' it anyway. Who wants some hundred-proof tiger piss?

BAMA, *to* STOOGIE: Hey, man, how much was in dat mathafukker's wallet?

STOOGIE, *nods toward* JACK: Cool it, sucker.

HOSS, *to* STOOGIE: But, man, you holdin' the watch and ring, too!

STOOGIE, *advancing on them:* What's wrong with you jive-ass mathafukkers?

BIG GIRL: Okay, cool it! There's only one person gets out of hand 'round here, ya understand?

STOOGIE: Okay, B.G. Let it slide . . .

BABY GIRL: CAT! CAT! CAT!

STOOGIE, *to* JACK: Drink up, man. Not every day ya get dis stuff.

(BAMA *picks up the beat of the music and begins a shuffling dance.* BABY GIRL *begins bouncing in time to the music.*)

---

3. State Store: State-owned liquor store.

HOSS: C'mon, Baby Girl; let me see ya do the slide.

BABY GIRL: NO! NO! (*She claps and bounces.*)

HOSS, *demonstrates his steps, trying to outdance* BAMA: C'mon, Baby Girl, shake that thing!

CLARA: No, stop that, Hoss. She don't know what she's doin'.

BIG GIRL: That's okay, Clara. Go on, Baby Girl, do the thing.

(STOOGIE *grabs salt from the table and shakes it upon the floor, under the feet of the dancers.*)[4]

STOOGIE: DO THE SLIDE, MAN! SLIDE!

BABY GIRL, *lumbers up and begins a grotesque maneuver while grunting out strained sounds:* Uuuhhhhh . . . sheeeee . . . waaaa . . . uuhhhh . . .

BIG GIRL, *standing, toasting:* DO THE THING, BABY ! ! ! !

CLARA: Awww . . . B.G. Why don' you stop all dat?

STOOGIE, *to* JACK: C'mon, man, git with it.

(JACK *shakes his head and* STOOGIE *goes over to* CLARA *and holds out his hand.*)

STOOGIE: Let's go, baby.

CLARA: Nawh . . . I don't dance no mo'.

STOOGIE: C'mon, pretty mamma . . . watch this step . . . (*He cuts a fancy step.*)

BIG GIRL: Go on and dance, sister.

(STOOGIE *moves off and the three boys dance.*)

CLARA: Nawh . . . B.G., you know I don't go for that kind of stuff no mo'.

BIG GIRL: Go on, baby!

CLARA: No!

BIG GIRL: I want you to dance, Clara.

CLARA: Nawh . . . I just can't.

BIG GIRL: DO LIKE I SAY! DO LIKE BIG WANTS!

(*The dancers stop momentarily but begin again when* CLARA *joins them.* BABY GIRL *halts and resumes her place upon the floor, fondling her toy. The others dance until the record stops.*)

STOOGIE, *to* JACK: Where you from, man?

JACK: Oh, I live over in West Philly now, but I come from up around Master.

STOOGIE: Oh? Do you know Hector?

JACK, *trying to capture an old voice and mannerism:* Yeah, man. I know the cat.

STOOGIE: What's your name, man?

JACK: Jack, man. Maybe you know me by Tookie.

---

4. Grabs salt from the table and shakes it upon the floor: Done to improve sliding.

STOOGIE, *ritually:* Tookie . . . Tookie . . . yeah, man, I think I heard about you. You us'ta be in the ole Jet Cobras!

JACK: Well, I us'ta know some of the guys then. I been away for a while.

BAMA, *matter-of-factly:* Where you been, man? Jail?

JACK: I was in the marines for three years.

STOOGIE: Hey, man. That must'a been a gas.

JACK: It was okay. I seen a lot . . . went a lot of places.

BIG GIRL: Yeah, you must'a seen it all.

STOOGIE: Did you get to go anywhere overseas, man?

JACK: Yeah, I was aboard ship most of the time.

HOSS: Wow, man. That sounds cool.

BAMA: You really was overseas, man?

JACK: Yeah. I went to Europe and North Africa and the Caribbean.

STOOGIE: What kind of boat were you on, man?

JACK: A ship.

BIG GIRL: A boat!

JACK: No, a ship.

STOOGIE, *rising,* BAMA *and* HOSS *surrounding* JACK: Yeah, man, dat's what she said . . . a boat!

CLARA: STOP IT ! ! !

BABY GIRL: NO! NO! NO! SHIT! SHIT! SHIT! DAMN! SHIT!

MISS FAMIE's VOICE, *from upstairs:* Your aunt don't like all that noise.

BIG GIRL: You and my aunt better mind ya fukkin' ginhead business or I'll come up there and ram those empty bottles up where it counts!

BAMA, *sniggling:* Oh, baby. We forgot your aunt was up dere sick.

STOOGIE: Yeah, baby. Have another drink. (*He fills all glasses except* CLARA's; *she pulls hers away.*)

CLARA: Nawh, I don't want any more. Me and Big Girl are goin' out after a while.

BAMA: Can I go too?

BIG GIRL: There's always have ta be one wise mathafukker.

BAMA: I didn't mean nuttin', B.G., honest.

STOOGIE, *to* JACK: What did you do in the army, man?

JACK, *feigns a dialect:* Ohhh, man. I told you already I was in the marines!

HOSS, *to* CLARA: Where you goin'?

CLARA: B.G.'s takin' me to Pep's.

BAMA: Wow . . . dat's nice, baby.

BIG GIRL, *gesturing toward* JACK: Ole smoothie here suggested takin' Clara, but it seems he backed out, so I thought we might step around there anyway.

JACK, *annoyed:* I didn't back out!

STOOGIE, *to* JACK: Did you screw any of them foreign bitches when you were in Japan, man?

JACK: Yeah man. I couldn't help it. They were all over, ya know?

BIG GIRL: He couldn't beat them off.

STOOGIE: Yeah, man. I dig.

JACK: Especially in France and Italy. Course, the Spanish girls are the best, but the ones in France and Italy ain't so bad, either.

HOSS: You mean those French girls ain't as good as those Spanish girls?

JACK: Nawh, man, the Spanish girls are the best.

BAMA: I never did dig no Mexican nor Rican spic bitches too tough, man.

JACK: They ain't Mexican or Puerto Rican. They Spanish . . . from Spain . . . Spanish is different from Mexican. In Spain . . .

STOOGIE: Whatcha do now, man?

JACK: Ohhh . . . I'm goin' ta college prep on the G.I. Bill[5] now . . . and workin' a little.

STOOGIE: Is that why you sound like you got a load of shit in your mouth?

JACK: What do you mean!

STOOGIE: I thought you talked like you had shit in your mouth because you been ta college, man.

JACK: I don't understand what you're trying ta say, man.

STOOGIE: It's nothin', man. You just talk funny sometimes . . . ya know what I mean. Hey, man, where do you work?

JACK, *visibly feeling his drinks:* Nawh, man, I don't know what ya mean and I don't go to college, man, it's college prep.

STOOGIE: Thanks, man.

JACK: And I work at the P.O.

BAMA: Pee-who?

JACK: The Post Office, man.

STOOGIE: Thanks, George. I always like to know things I don't know anything about. (*He turns his back on* JACK.)

JACK, *to* BIG GIRL: Hey, what time ya goin' round to Pep's?

BIG GIRL: Soon . . . are you in a hurry, youngblood? You don't have to wait for us.

JACK, *now drunk:* That's okay . . . It's just gettin' late, ya know, man . . . and I was wonderin' what time Clara's ole man gets home . . .

---

5. G.I. Bill: The Servicemen's Readjustment Act of 1944, better known as the G.I. Bill of Rights, has provided billions of dollars to U.S. veterans for vocational training and higher education.

BIG GIRL: Clara's ole man? . . . What do you mean, man? . . .

(*The trio begins snickering, holding their laughter back;* JACK *is too drunk to notice.*)

JACK: Well, Clara said for me to come by today in the afternoon when her ole man would be at work . . . and I was wonderin' what time he got home . . .

BIG GIRL, *stands, tilting over her chair to crash backwards on the floor. Her bust juts out. She is controlled but furious:* Clara's ole man is home now . . .

(*A noise is heard outside as* C.C *comes in the front door. The trio is laughing louder but with restraint;* CLARA *looks stunned.*)

JACK, *starts up and feels drunk for the first time:* Wha . . . you mean he's been upstairs all this time?

BIG GIRL, *staring:* Nawh, man, I don't mean that!

JACK, *looks at* BIG GIRL, *then at the laughing boys and finally to* CLARA: Ohhh . . . jeezus! (*He staggers to the backyard door past* BABY GIRL *and becomes sick.*)

BIG GIRL: Didn't you tell him? Didn't you tell him a fukkin' thing?

(C.C *comes in. He is drunk and weaves and says nothing. He sees the wine, searches for a glass, bumps into one of the boys, is shoved into another, and gets booted in the rear before he reaches wine and seat.*)

BIG GIRL: Didn't you tell him?

CLARA: I only wanted to talk, B.G. I only wanted to talk to somebody. I don't have anybody to talk to . . . (*Crying*) . . . I don't have anyone . . .

BIG GIRL: It's time for the matinee. (*To* STOOGIE) Before you go, escort my friend out, will ya?

CLARA: Ohhh . . . B.G., I'll do anything, but please . . . Ohhh, Big . . . I won't forget my promise.

BIG GIRL: Let's go. We don't want to miss the show, do we?

CLARA: Please, B.G., please. Not that. It's not his fault! Please!

BIG GIRL: DO LIKE I SAY! DO LIKE I WANT YOU TO DO!

(CLARA *drops her head and rises and exits stage right followed by* BIG GIRL. STOOGIE *and his boys finish their drinks, stalk and swagger about.* BAMA *opens the refrigerator, and* HOSS *takes one long last guzzle.*)

BAMA: Hey, Stoogie babe, what about the split?

STOOGIE, *drunk:* Later, you square-ass, lame-ass mathafukker!

(HOSS *giggles.*)

BABY GIRL: CAT! CAT! CAT!

C.C, *seated, drinking:* Shut up, Baby Girl. Ain't no cats out dere.

MISS FAMIE, *staggers from upstairs, calling back:* GOOD NIGHT, TOOHEY. See ya tomorrow.

(*With a nod from* STOOGIE, BAMA *and* HOSS *take* JACK's *arms and wrestle him into the yard. The sound of* JACK's *beating is heard.* MISS FAMIE *wanders to the yard door, looks out, but staggers back from what she sees and continues sprawling toward the exit, stage right.*)

BABY GIRL: CAT! CAT! CAT!

C.C: SHUT UP! SHUT ON UP, BABY GIRL! I TOLE YA . . . DERE AIN'T NO CATS OUT DERE!!!

BABY GIRL: NO! DAMN! SHIT! SHIT! DAMN! NO! NO!

(STOOGIE *looks over the scene and downs his drink, then saunters outside. Lights dim out until there is a single soft spot on* BABY GIRL's *head, turned wistfully toward the yard; then blackness.*)

Curtain.

Like his compatriots in the Black Power and Black Arts Movements, Bullins was deeply concerned with education and educational reform. In this one-act play, Bullins extends the "drama of language" of How Do You Do *and* Clara's Ole Man *into the classroom of a Southern California junior college, pitting the well-meaning instructor Mr. Jones against the ridiculous but demonic student Carpentier. The play marks one of his first efforts at a decentered, nonlinear dramatic structure, as he counterpoints the conflict between the two major characters with the multiple, if minor, currents of the students witnessing their fight. It was firrst produced at the American Place Theatre in 1968 and first published in* Five Plays, *edited by Ed Bullins (New York: Bobbs-Merrill, 1969).*

The Electronic Nigger

(1968)

CHARACTERS:

MR. JONES, *A light-brown-skinned man. Thirty years old. Horn-rimmed glasses. Crewcut and small, smart mustache. He speaks in a clipped manner when in control of himself but is more than self-conscious, even from the beginning. Whatever, MR. JONES speaks as unlike the popular conception of how a negro speaks as is possible. Not even the fallacious accent acquired by many "cultured" or highly educated negroes should be sought, but that general cross-fertilized dialect found on various Ivy League campuses and those of the University of California. He sports an ascot.*

MR. CARPENTIER, *A large, dark man in his late thirties. He speaks in blustering orations, many times mispronouncing words. His tone is stentorian, and his voice has an absurdly ridiculous affected accent.*

BILL, *Twenty-two years old. Negro.*

SUE, *Twenty years old. White.*

LENARD, *Twenty-one. A fat white boy.*

MISS MOSKOWITZ, *Mid-thirties. An aging professional student.*

MARTHA, *An attractive negro woman.*

ANY NUMBER OF INTERRACIAL STUDENTS, *to supply background, short of the point of discouraging a producer.*

SCENE: *A classroom of a Southern California junior college. Modern decor. New facilities: Light green blackboards, bright fluorescent lighting, elongated rectangular tables, seating four to eight students facing each other, instead of the traditional rows of seats facing toward the instructor. The tables are staggered throughout the room and canted at angles impossible for the instructor to engage the eye of the student, unless the student turns toward him or the instructor leaves his small table and walks among the students.*

    It is seven o'clock by the wall-clock; twilight outside the windows indicates a fall evening. A "No Smoking" sign is beneath the clock, directly above the green blackboards, behind the instructor's table and rostrum. The bell rings.

    Half the STUDENTS *are already present.* MISS MOSKOWITZ *drinks coffee from a paper cup;* LENARD *munches an apple, noisily. More* STUDENTS *enter from the rear and front doors to the room and take seats. There is the general low buzz of activity and first-night anticipation of a new evening class.* BILL *comes in the back door to the room;* SUE *enters the other. They casually look about them for seats and indifferently sit next to each other.* JONES *enters puffing on his pipe and smoothing down his ascot. The bell rings.*

MR. JONES, *exhaling smoke:* Well . . . good evening . . . My name is Jones . . . ha ha . . . that won't be hard to remember, will it? I'll be your instructor this semester . . . ha ha . . . Now this is English 22E . . . Creative Writing.

LENARD: Did you say 22E?

MR. JONES: Yes, I did . . . Do all of you have that number on your cards? . . . Now look at your little IBM cards[1] and see if there is a little 22E in the upper left-hand corner. Do you see it? (CARPENTIER *enters and looks over the class.*)

MISS MOSKOWITZ, *confused:* Why . . . I don't see any numbers on my card.

MR. JONES, *extinguishing pipe:* Good . . . now that everyone seems to belong here who is here, we can get started with our creativity . . . ha ha . . . If I sort of . . .

---

1. Now look at your little IBM cards: When mass computerization of records began in the 1950s, information was stored on slips of cardboard through which a pattern of small holes was impressed representing letters and numbers. By the mid-1960s, these cards—and the ubiquitous warning not to "fold, crush, or mutilate"—had become a symbol of cultural alienation, especially for students.

MISS MOSKOWITZ, *protesting:* But I don't have a number!

LENARD, *ridicule:* Yes, you do!

MISS MOSKOWITZ: Give that back to me . . . give that card back to me right now!

LENARD, *pointing to card:* It's right here like he said . . . in the upper left-hand corner.

MISS MOSKOWITZ, *snatching card:* I know where it is!

MR. JONES: Now that we all know our . . .

A.T. CARPENTIER: Sir . . . I just arrived in these surroundings and I have not yet been oriented as to the primary sequence of events which have preceded my entrance.

MR. JONES: Well, nothing has . . .

A.T. CARPENTIER, *cutting:* If you will enlighten me, I'll be eternally grateful for any communicative aid that you may render in your capacity as professor *de la classe.*

MR. JONES: Well . . . well . . . I'm not a professor, I'm an instructor.

BILL: Just take a look at your card and see if . . .

A.T. CARPENTIER: Didn't your mother teach you any manners, young man?

BILL: What did you say, fellah?

A.T. CARPENTIER: Don't speak until you're asked to . . .

MR. JONES: Now you people back there . . . pay attention.

MISS MOSKOWITZ: Why, I never in all my life . . .

MR. JONES: Now to begin with . . .

SUE: You've got some nerve speaking to him like that. Where did you come from, mister?

MR. JONES: Class!

A.T. CARPENTIER: Where I came from . . . *mon bonne femme* . . . has no bearing on this situational conundrum . . . splendid word, "conundrum," heh, what? Jimmie Baldwin[2] uses it brilliantly on occasion . . .

MR. JONES: I'm not going to repeat . . .

A.T. CARPENTIER: But getting back to the matter at hand . . . I am here to become acquainted with the formal aspects of authorcraft . . . Of course I've been a successful writer for many years even though I haven't taken the time for the past ten years to practice the art forms of fiction, drama, or that very breath of the muse . . . poesy . . .

MR. JONES: Sir . . . please!

BILL: How do you turn it off?

---

2. Jimmie Baldwin: Pretentiously familiar reference to James Baldwin (1924–87), African-American writer, author of *Notes of a Native Son* (1955), *Blues for Mister Charlie* (1964), and many other highly regarded novels, essays, and plays.

LENARD: For Christ sake!

A.T. CARPENTIER: But you can find my name footnoted in numerous professional sociological, psychological, psychiatric, and psychedelic journals . . .

MR. JONES: If you'll please . . .

A.T. CARPENTIER: A.T. Carpentier is the name . . . notice the silent "T" . . . My profession gets in the way of art, in the strict aesthetic sense, you know . . . I'm a Sociological Data Research Analysis Technician Expert. Yes, penalology is my field, naturally, and I have been in over thirty-three penal institutions across the country . . . in a professional capacity, obviously . . . ha ho ho.

MR. JONES: Sir!

LENARD: Geez!

A.T. CARPENTIER: Here are some of my random findings, conclusions, etc. which I am re-creating into a new art form . . .

SUE: A new art form we have here already.

BILL: This is going to be one of those classes.

A.T. CARPENTIER: Yes, young lady . . . Socio-Drama . . .

MR. JONES: All right, Mr. Carpenter.

A.T. CARPENTIER, *corrects:* Carpentier! The "T" is silent.

MR. JONES: Okay. Complete what you were saying . . .

A.T. CARPENTIER: Thank you, sir.

MR. JONES: . . . and then . . .

A.T. CARPENTIER: By the way, my good friend J.J. Witherthorn is already dickering with my agent for options on my finished draft for a pilot he is planning to shoot of *Only Corpses Beat the Big House,* which, by the way, is the title of the first script, taken from an abortive *novella narratio* I had begun in my youth after a particularly torrid affair with one Eulah Mae Jackson . . .

MR. JONES: Good . . . now let's . . .

A.T. CARPENTIER: Of course, after I read it some of you will say it resembles in some ways *The Quare Fellow,* but I have documented evidence that I've had this plot outlined since . . .

BILL: Question!

SUE: Won't somebody do something?

BILL: Question!

MR. JONES, *to* BILL: Yes, what is it?

A.T. CARPENTIER, *over:* . . . Of course I'll finish it on time . . . the final draft, I mean . . . and have it to J. J. far ahead of the deadline but I thought that the rough edges could be chopped off here . . . and there . . .

MR. JONES, *approaching anger:* Mr. Carpentier . . . if you'll please?

A.T. CARPENTIER, *belligerent and glaring:* I beg your pardon, sir?

(MARTHA *enters.*)

MR. JONES: This class must get under way . . . immediately!

MARTHA, *to* MR. JONES: Is this English 22E?

A.T. CARPENTIER: Why, yes, you are in the correct locale, *mon jeune fil.*

MR. JONES: May I see your card, Miss?

A.T. CARPENTIER, *mutters:* Intrusion . . . non-equanimity . . .

MISS MOSKOWITZ: Are you speaking to me?

MR. JONES, *to* MARTHA: I believe you're in the right class, miss.

MARTHA: Thank you.

MR. JONES, *clears throat:* Hummp . . . huump . . . well, we can get started now.

A.T. CARPENTIER: I emphatically agree with you, sir. In fact . . .

MR. JONES, *cutting:* Like some of you, I imagine, this too is my first evening class . . . And I'd . . .

MISS MOSKOWITZ, *beaming:* How nice!

LENARD: Oh . . . oh . . . we've got a green one.

MR. JONES: Well . . . I guess the first thing is to take the role. I haven't the official role sheet yet, so . . . please print your names clearly on this sheet of paper and pass it around so you'll get credit for being here tonight.

BILL: Question!

MR. JONES: Yes . . . you did have a question, didn't you?

BILL: Yeah . . . How will we be graded?

SUE: Oh . . . how square!

MR. JONES, *smiling:* I'm glad you asked that.

MISS MOSKOWITZ: So am I.

LENARD: You are?

MR. JONES: Well . . . as of now everybody is worth an "A." I see all students as "A" students until they prove otherwise . . .

MISS MOSKOWITZ: Oh, how nice.

MR. JONES: But tonight I'd like us to talk about story ideas. Since this is a writing class, we don't wish to waste too much of our time on matters other than writing. And it is my conclusion that a story isn't a story without a major inherent idea which gives it substance . . .

MISS MOSKOWITZ: How true.

MR. JONES: And, by the way, that is how you are to retain your "A"'s: By handing in all written assignments on time and doing the necessary outside work . . .

LENARD: Typewritten or in longhand, Mr. Jones?

MR. JONES: I am not a critic, so you will not be graded on how well you write but merely if you attempt to grow from the experience you have in this class . . . This class is not only to show you the fundamentals of fiction, drama, and poetry but aid your productivity, or should I say creativity . . . ha ha . . .

A.T. CARPENTIER, *admonishing:* You might say from the standpoint of grammar that fundamentals are essential but . . .

MR. JONES, *piqued:* Mr. Carpentier . . . I don't understand what point you are making!

A.T. CARPENTIER, *belligerent:* Why . . . why . . . you can say that without the basics of grammar, punctuation, spelling, etc. . . . . that these neophytes will be up the notorious creek without even the accommodation of a sieve.

SUE: Jesus!

LENARD, *scowling:* Up the where, buddy?

MISS MOSKOWITZ: I don't think we should . . .

BILL: It's fantastic what you . . .

MARTHA: Is this really English 22E?

MR. JONES: Now wait a minute, class. Since this is the first night, I want everyone to identify themselves before they speak. All of you know my name . . .

MARTHA: I don't, sir.

A.T. CARPENTIER: You might say they will come to grief . . . artistic calamity.

MR. JONES: Ohhh . . . It's Jones . . . Ray Jones.

LENARD: Didn't you just publish a novel, Mr. Jones?

MARTHA: Mine's Martha . . . Martha Butler.

MR. JONES: Oh, yes . . . yes, a first novel.

A.T. CARPENTIER, *mutters:* Cultural lag's the real culprit!

BILL, *to* SUE: I'm Bill . . . Bill Cooper.

SUE: Pleased . . . just call me Sue. Susan Gold.

MR. JONES: Now . . . where were we? . . .

A.T. CARPENTIER: In the time of classicism there wasn't this rampant commerce among Philistines . . .

MR. JONES: Does someone . . .

MISS MOSKOWITZ: Story ideas, Mr. Jones.

MR. JONES: Oh, yes.

(*Hands are raised.* LENARD *is pointed out.*)

LENARD: I have an idea for a play.

MR. JONES: Your name, please.

LENARD: Lenard . . . Lenard Getz. I have an idea for a lavish stage spectacle using just one character.

A.T. CARPENTIER: It won't work . . . it won't work!

SUE: How do you know?

MISS MOSKOWITZ: Let Lenard tell us, will ya?

A.T. CARPENTIER, *indignant:* Let him! Let him, you say!

MR. JONES, *annoyed:* Please, Mr. Carpentier . . . please be . . .

A.T. CARPENTIER, *glaring about the room:* But I didn't say it had to be done as parsimoniously as a Russian play. I mean only as beginners you people should delve into the simplicity of the varied techniques of the visual communicative media and processes.

MR. JONES: For the last time . . .

A.T. CARPENTIER: Now take for instance cinema . . . or a teledrama . . . some of the integrative shots set the mood and that takes technique as well as craft.

MR. JONES: I have my doubts about all that . . . but it doesn't have anything to do with Lenard's idea, as I see it.

A.T. CARPENTIER: I don't agree with you, sir.

MR. JONES: It's just as well that you don't. Lenard, will you go on, please?

LENARD: Ahhh . . . forget it.

MR. JONES: But, Lenard, won't you tell us your idea?

LENARD: No!

MISS MOSKOWITZ: Oh . . . Lenard.

A.T. CARPENTIER: There is a current theory about protein variation . . .

MR. JONES: Not again!

SUE, *cutting:* I have a story idea!

MISS MOSKOWITZ: Good!

MR. JONES: Can we hear it . . . Miss . . . Miss . . .?

SUE: Miss Gold. Susan Gold.

MR. JONES: Thank you.

SUE: Well, it's about a story that I have in my head. It ends with a girl or woman, standing or sitting alone and frightened. It's weird. I don't know where I got THAT theme from! . . . There is just something about one person, alone, that is moving to me. It's the same thing in movies or in photography. Don't you think if it's two or more persons, it loses a dramatic impact?

MR. JONES: Why, yes, I do.

MISS MOSKOWITZ: It sounds so psychologically pregnant!

LENARD: It's my story of the stupendous one-character extravaganza!

(A few in the class hesitantly clap.)

A.T. CARPENTIER, *in a deep, pontifical voice:* Loneliness! Estrangement! Alienation! The young lady's story should prove an interesting phenomena—it is a phenomena that we observe daily.

MISS MOSKOWITZ: Yes, it is one of the most wonderful things I've ever
heard.

MR. JONES, *irritated:* Well, now let's . . .

A.T. CARPENTIER: The gist of that matter . . .

MR. JONES: I will not have any more interruptions, man. Are you all there!

A.T. CARPENTIER: I mean only to say that it is strictly in a class of phenom-
enology in the classic ontonological sense.

MR. JONES: There are rules you must observe, Mr. Carpentier. Like our
society, this school too has rules.

A.T. CARPENTIER: Recidivism! Recidivism!

MARTHA: Re-sida-what?

A.T. CARPENTIER, *explaining:* Recidivism. A noted example of alienation in
our society. We have tape-recorded AA[3] meetings without the patients
knowing that they were being recorded. In prison we pick up everything . . . from a con pacing his cell . . . down to the fights in the yard
. . . and I can say that the milieu which creates loneliness is germane to
the topic of recidivism.

MR. JONES: What? . . . You're a wire-tapper, Mr. Carpentier?

A.T. CARPENTIER: Any method that deters crime in our society is most inad-
equate, old boy.

BILL: A goddamned fink!

LENARD: I thought I smelled somethin'.

A.T. CARPENTIER: Crime is a most repetitive theme these days. . . . The pri-
macy purpose of we law enforcement agents is to help stamp it out
whatever the method.

MR. JONES: Carpentier!

A.T. CARPENTIER: Let the courts worry about . . .

MR. JONES: But, sir, speaking man to man, how do you feel about your job?
Doesn't it make you uneasy knowing that your race, I mean, our peo-
ple, the negro, is the most victimized by the police in this country?
And you are using illegal and immoral methods to . . .

A.T. CARPENTIER: Well, if you must personalize, that's all right with me . . .
but, really, I thought this was a class in creative writing, not criminol-
ogy. I hesitate to say, Mr. Jones, that you are indeed out of your depth
when you engage me on my own grounds . . . ha ha . . .

---

3. AA: Alcoholics Anonymous.

(MR. JONES *has taken off his glasses and is looking at* MR. CARPENTIER *strangely.*)

MARTHA, *raising voice:* I have a story idea . . . it's about this great dark mass of dough . . .

BILL: Yeah . . . like a great rotten ham that strange rumbling and bubbling noises come out of . . .

SUE: And it stinks something awful!

LENARD: Like horseshit!

MISS MOSKOWITZ: Oh, my.

MR. JONES: Class! Class!

A.T. CARPENTIER, *oblivious:* The new technology doesn't allow for the weak tyranny of human attitudes.

MR. JONES: You are wrong, terribly wrong.

A.T. CARPENTIER: This is the age of the new intellectual assisted by his tool, the machine, I'll have you know!

MR. JONES, *furious:* Carpentier! . . . That is what we are here in this class-room to fight against . . . we are here to discover, to awaken, to search out human values through art!

A.T. CARPENTIER: Nonsense! Nonsense! Pure nonsense! All you pseudo-artistic types and humanists say the same things when confronted by truth. (*Prophetically*) This is an age of tele-symbology . . . phallic in nature, oral in appearance.

MR. JONES: Wha' . . . I don't believe I follow you. Are you serious, man?

A.T. CARPENTIER: I have had more experience with these things so I can say that the only function of cigarettes is to show the cigarette as a symbol of gratification for oral types . . . Tobacco, matches, Zig Zag papers, etc. are all barter items in prison. There you will encounter a higher incident of oral and anal specimens. I admit it is a liberal interpreta-tion, true, but I don't see how any other conclusion can be drawn!

MR. JONES: You are utterly ineducable. I suggest you withdraw from this class, Mr. Carpentier.

MISS MOSKOWITZ: Oh, how terrible.

BILL: Hit the road, Jack.

A.T. CARPENTIER: If I must call it to your attention . . . in a tax-supported institution . . . to whom does that institution belong?

LENARD: That won't save you, buddy.

MR. JONES: Enough of this! Are there any more story ideas, class?

A.T. CARPENTIER, *mumbling:* It's councilmatic . . . yes, councilmatic . . .

MISS MOSKOWITZ: My name is Moskowitz and I'd like to try a children's story.

A.T. CARPENTIER: Yes, yes, F.G. Peters once sold a story to the Hoodie Dowdie people on an adaptation of the *Cherry Orchard* theme . . . and Jamie Judson, a good friend of mine . . .[4]

MR. JONES: Mr. Carpentier . . . please. Allow someone else a chance.

A.T. CARPENTIER: Why, all they have to do is speak up, Mr. Jones.

MR. JONES: Maybe so . . . but please let Mrs. Moskowitz . . .

MISS MOSKOWITZ, *coyly:* That's Miss Moskowitz, Mr. Jones.

MR. JONES: Oh, I'm sorry, Miss Moskowitz.

MISS MOSKOWITZ: That's okay, Mr. Jones . . . Now my story has an historical background.

A.T. CARPENTIER: Which reminds me of a story I wrote which had a setting in colonial Boston . . .

LENARD: Not again. Not again, for chrissakes!

A.T. CARPENTIER: Christopher Attucks was the major character . . .[5]

SUE: Shhhhhh . . .

BILL: Shut up, fellow!

A.T. CARPENTIER, *ignoring them:* The whole thing was done in jest . . . the historical inaccuracies were most hilarious . . . ha ho ho . . .

MR. JONES: Mr. Carpentier!!! (MR. CARPENTIER *grumbles and glowers.*)

MISS MOSKOWITZ: Thank you, Mr. Jones.

MR. JONES: That's quite all right . . . go on, please.

MISS MOSKOWITZ: Yes, now this brother and sister are out in a park and they get separated from their mother and meet a lion escaped from the zoo and make friends with him.

LENARD: And they live happily ever afterwards.

MISS MOSKOWITZ: Why, no, not at all, Lenard. The National Guard comes to shoot the lion but the children hide him up a tree.

BILL, *to* SUE: I got the impression that it was a tall tale.

SUE: Not you, too?

LENARD: I thought it had a historical background.

MARTHA: Can you convince children that they can easily make friends out of lions and then hide them up trees?

LENARD: I got that it's pretty clear what motivated the lion to climb the tree. If you had a hunting party after you, wouldn't . . .

---

4. Hoodie Dowdie: *Howdy Doody:* A popular children's show of the 1950s featuring a marionette, a clown, and a cowboy.

5. Christopher Attucks: Presumably, Carpentier means Crispus Attucks (1723–70), the African-American patriot generally regarded as the first martyr to U.S. independence from Great Britain.

A.T. CARPENTIER, *cutting:* Unless you give the dear lady that liberty . . . you'll end up with merely thou's and thee's!

MR. JONES: What?

MISS MOSKOWITZ, *simpering:* Oh, thank you, Mr. Carpentier.

A.T. CARPENTIER, *Beau Brummel:*[6] Why, the pleasure is all mine, dear lady.

MR. JONES: Enough of this! Enough of this!

MISS MOSKOWITZ, *blushing:* Why, Mr. Carpentier . . . how you go on.

A.T. CARPENTIER: Not at all, my dear Miss Moskowitz . . .

MISS MOSKOWITZ: Call me Madge.

MR. JONES, *sarcastic:* I'm sorry to interrupt this . . .

A.T. CARPENTIER: A.T. to you . . . A.T. Booker Carpentier at your service.

MR. JONES: . . . This is a college classroom . . . not a French *boudoir.*

MISS MOSKOWITZ, *to* JONES: Watch your mouth, young man! There's ladies present.

MARTHA, *to* MOSKOWITZ: Don't let that bother you, dearie.

LENARD: What kind of attitude must you establish with this type of story and do you create initial attitudes through mood?

MR. JONES, *confused:* I beg your pardon?

A.T. CARPENTIER, *answering:* Why, young man, almost from the beginning, the central motif should plant the atmosphere of . . .

MR. JONES: Thank you, Mr. Carpentier!

A.T. CARPENTIER: But I wasn't . . .

BILL, *cutting:* To what audience is it addressed?

SUE: Good for you!

MISS MOSKOWITZ: Why, young people, of course. In fact, for children.

A.T. CARPENTIER: I hardly would think so!

MARTHA: Oh, what kinda stuff is this?

MISS MOSKOWITZ: Mr. Carpentier . . . I . . .

MR. JONES: Well, at least you're talking about something vaguely dealing with writing. Go on, Mr. Carpentier, try and develop your . . .

A.T. CARPENTIER: A question of intellectual levels is being probed here . . . The question is the adult or the child . . . hmm . . . *Robinson Crusoe, Gulliver's Travels, Alice in Wonderland, Animal Farm* can all be read by children, dear lady, but the works have added implication for the adult . . . in a word, they are potent!

MARTHA: You're talking about universality, man, not audience!

A.T. CARPENTIER: Do you know the difference?

---

6. Beau Brummel: In the style of George Bryan Brummell (1778–1840), that is to say, in elaborately dandified fashion.

LENARD, *challenges* CARPENTIER: What's the definition of audience?

A.T. CARPENTIER: Of course, I don't use myself as any type of criteria, but I don't see where that story would appeal to my sophisticated literary tastes, whereas . . .

MR. JONES: Now you are quite off the point, Mr. Carpentier.

BILL: He thinks we should all write like the Marquis de Sade.

SUE: Yeah, bedtime tales for tykes by Sade.

MISS MOSKOWITZ: I think you're trying to place an imposition of the adult world on the child's.

MR. JONES: The important thing is to write the story, class. To write the story!

A.T. CARPENTIER: Well, I think that the story was not at all that emphatic . . . it didn't emote . . . it didn't elicit my . . .

MISS MOSKOWITZ, *confused:* Why didn't it?

A.T. CARPENTIER: I don't think the child would have the range of actual patterns for his peer group in this circumstantial instance.

MARTHA: What, man?

LENARD: I got the impression that the protagonists are exempliar.

MR. JONES: Class, do you think this story line aids the writer in performing his functions? . . . The culture has values and the writer's duties are to . . .

A.T. CARPENTIER: No, I don't think this story does it!

SUE: Why not?

A.T. CARPENTIER: It is fallacious!

MISS MOSKOWITZ: But it's only a child's story, a fantasy, Mr. Carpentier!

MR. JONES: Yes, a child's story . . . for children, man!

A.T. CARPENTIER: But it doesn't ring true, dear lady. The only way one can get the naturalistic speech and peer group patterns and mores of children recorded accurately . . .

MR. JONES, *rising in volume until* MR. CARPENTIER *finishes his speech:* Oh God, Oh, God, Oh, God, Oh, God, OH, GOD!

A.T. CARPENTIER: . . . is to scientifically eavesdrop on their peer group with electronic listening devices and get the actual evidence for any realistic fictionalizing one wishes to achieve.

MR. JONES, *scream:* NO!!!

A.T. CARPENTIER, *query:* No?

MR. JONES, *in a tired voice:* Thomas Wolfe once said . . .

A.T. CARPENTIER, *ridicule:* Thomas Wolfe!

MR. JONES: "I believe that we are lost here in America, but I believe we shall be found." . . . Mr. Carpentier . . . let's hope that we Black Americans can first find ourselves and perhaps be equal to the task . . . the burdensome and sometimes evil task, by the way . . . that being an American calls for in these days.

A.T. CARPENTIER: Sir, I object!

MR. JONES: Does not the writer have some type of obligation to remove some of the intellectual as well as political, moral, and social tyranny that infects this culture? What does all the large words in creation serve you, my Black brother, if you are a complete whitewashed man?

A.T. CARPENTIER: Sir, I am not black nor your brother . . . There is a school of thought that is diametrically opposed to you and your black chauvinism . . . You preach bigotry, black nationalism, and fascism! . . . The idea . . . black brother . . . intellectual barbarism! . . . Your statements should be reported to the school board—as well as your permitting smoking in your classroom.

SUE: Shut up, you Uncle Tom bastard!

BILL, *pulls her back:* That's for me to do, not you, lady!

MR. JONES: Four hundred years . . . Four hundred . . .

LENARD: We'll picket any attempt to have Mr. Jones removed!

MARTHA, *disgust:* This is adult education?

MISS MOSKOWITZ, to MR. CARPENTIER: I bet George Bernard Shaw would have some answers for you!

A.T. CARPENTIER: Of course, when examining G.B. Shaw you will discover he is advancing Fabian Socialism.

BILL: Who would picket a vacuum?

LENARD: Your levity escapes me.

SUE: Your what, junior?

MR. JONES: Let's try and go on, class. If you'll . . .

A.T. CARPENTIER, *to* MISS MOSKOWITZ: Your story just isn't professional, miss. It doesn't follow the Hitchcock formula . . . it just doesn't follow . . .

MISS MOSKOWITZ: Do you really think so?

MR. JONES: Somehow, I do now believe that you are quite real, Mr. Carpentier.

LENARD, *to* MR. CARPENTIER: Have you read *The Invisible Man?*

BILL: Are you kidding?

A.T. CARPENTIER: Socio-Drama will be the new breakthrough in the theatrical-literary community.

MR. JONES: Oh, Lord . . . not again. This is madness.

A.T. CARPENTIER: Combined with the social psychologist's case study, and the daily experiences of some habitant of a socio-economically depressed area, is the genius of the intellectual and artistic craftsman.

MR. JONES: Madness!

MISS MOSKOWITZ: Socio-Drama . . . how thrilling.

MR. JONES: Don't listen to him, class . . . I'm the teacher, understand?

A.T. CARPENTIER: Yes, yes . . . let me tell you a not quite unique but nevertheless interesting phenomenon . . .

MR. JONES: Now we know that there is realism and naturalism and surrealism . . .

A.T. CARPENTIER: . . . an extremely interesting phenomenon . . . adolescent necrophilia!

MARTHA: Oh, shit!

MR. JONES: I have a degree . . . I've written a book . . . Please don't listen . . .

MISS MOSKOWITZ: It sounds fascinating, Mr. Carpentier.

A.T. CARPENTIER: Yes, tramps will freeze to death and kids, children, will punch holes in the corpses . . .

LENARD: Isn't that reaching rather far just to prove that truth is stranger than fiction?

SUE: I have a story about crud and filth and disease . . .

MR. JONES: And stupidity and ignorance and vulgarity and despair . . .

A.T. CARPENTIER: I go back to my original point . . . I go back to necrophilia!

BILL: And loneliness . . . and emptiness . . . and death.

A.T. CARPENTIER: Cadavers! Cadavers! Yes, I come back to that! . . . Those findings could almost be case studies of true cases, they are so true in themselves, and that's where the real truth lies . . . Verily, social case histories of social psychologists . . .

MISS MOSKOWITZ, *enraptured:* Never . . . never in all my experience has a class aroused such passionate response in my life!

LENARD: I don't believe it!

MR. JONES: But I have read Faulkner in his entirety . . .

A.T. CARPENTIER: These people in New York, Philadelphia, Boston, Chicago, San Francisco . . . and places like that . . .

MR. JONES: I cut my teeth on Hemingway . . .

A.T. CARPENTIER: . . . they just get drunk and die in the streets . . .

MR. JONES: *Leaves of Grass* is my Bible . . . and Emily Dickinson . . .

A.T. CARPENTIER: . . . and then they are prone to suffer adolescent and urchin necrophilia!

MR. JONES, *frustrated:* . . . Emily Dickinson has always been on my shelf beside *Mother Goose.*

A.T. CARPENTIER: It's curiosity . . . not a sickness . . . curiosity!

MR. JONES: I don't want much . . . just to learn the meaning of life.

MARTHA: Will you discover it here, Ray?

LENARD: But how can anybody be so sure?

A.T. CARPENTIER, *offhand:* We happen to own some mortuaries . . . my family, that is . . . and it is our experience that children will disarrange a corpse . . . and if we don't watch them closely . . .

MR. JONES: Booker T. Washington walked barefooted to school! Think of that! Barefooted!

A.T. CARPENTIER: Once, as a case study in experimental methods I placed a microphone in a cadaver and gave some juvenile necrophilics unwitting access to my tramp.

(JONES *almost doubles over and clutches his stomach; his hands and feet twitch.*)

MR. JONES: I'd like to adjourn class early tonight . . . will everyone please go home?

A.T. CARPENTIER: What I'm saying is this . . . With our present cybernetic generation it is psycho-politically relevant to engage our socio-philosophical existence on a quanitatum scale, which is, of course, pertinent to the outer-motivated migration of our inner-oriented social compact. Yes! Yes, indeed, I might add. A most visionary prognosis, as it were, but . . . ha ho ho . . . but we pioneers must look over our bifocals, I always say . . . ha ha ha . . . giving me added insight to perceive the political exiguousness of our true concomitant predicament. True, preclinical preconsciousness gives indication that our trivialization is vulva, but, owing to the press of the press our avowed aims are maleficent! True! Yes, true! And we are becoming more so. In areas of negative seeming communications probing our error factors are quite negligible . . . For instance . . . Senator Dodd getting a pension for someone who has gotten abducted and initiated at a Ku Klux meeting . . . well . . . It's poesy! . . . Monochromatic!

LENARD: What's our assignment for next week, Mr. Jones?

MISS MOSKOWITZ: I have something to show you, Mr. Jones.

MARTHA: Are you okay, Mr. Jones?

MR. JONES: Ray . . . just Ray . . . okay?

SUE: Do you have office hours, Mr. Ray?

MR. JONES: I just want everybody to go home now and think about what has happened tonight . . . and if you want to be writers after this, then please don't come back to this class. I've just published an unsuccessful novel, as you know, and I thought I'd teach a while and finish my second one and eat a bit . . . But I think I'd rather not, eat well, that is, so you won't see me next week, but if any of you'd like a good steady job, I could recommend you . . . Reading is the answer. It must be . . . cultivating the sensibilities . . . Plato . . . Aristotle . . . Homer . . . Descartes

... And Jones ... I've always wanted to carry the Jones banner high.

BILL, *to* SUE: Hey, I've got some pretty good grass that just came in from Mexico.

SUE: Yeah? You have, huh?

BILL: It's at my pad ... would you like to stop by?

SUE: How far?

BILL: A couple of blocks.

SUE: Okay. It might be interesting.

A.T. CARPENTIER, *to a student:* Ubiquitous! A form of reference which exposes ...

(BILL *and* SUE *exit. Students begin filing out.* MARTHA *walks over to* MR. JONES, *though the other students are gathered about* MR. CARPENTIER.)

MARTHA: You look tired, Ray.

MR. JONES: Yeah ... yeah ... I've been reading a lot. The classics are consuming.

MARTHA: Yes, I've heard. Why don't we stop by my place and I'll fix drinks and you can relax ...

MR. JONES: Okay ... okay ... but my ulcer's bothering me ... Mind if I drink milk?

MARTHA: It's not my stomach. (*She helps him off.*)

A.T. CARPENTIER: Who's that French poet ... Balu ...

LENARD: Bouvier?

A.T. CARPENTIER: ... Bali ... Blau? ... (MISS MOSKOWITZ *shows* MR. CARPENTIER *a bound manuscript as he deposits his own in his briefcase*)

MISS MOSKOWITZ: Will you please look at my few labors of love when you find time, Mr. Carpentier? (*He shoves it in the case beside his own.*)

LENARD, *gathering his books:* Mr. Carpentier?

A.T. CARPENTIER, *snapping clasps on his briefcase:* Yes, Lenard.

LENARD, *pushing himself between* CARPENTIER *and other students:* What weight does language have on the contemporary prevalence to act in existential terms?

A.T. CARPENTIER, *leads them off:* When the writer first named the crow "Caw Caw," it was onomatopoeia in practice, of course ... but, too, it became the Egyptian symbol of death.

LENARD: The crow.

(MISS MOSKOWITZ *giggles. They all exit, crowing,* "Caw caw caw caw caw ...")

BLACKNESS

Though incomplete, the Twentieth Century Cycle *stands as one of the monuments of African-American drama, its sweep and scope influencing, among others, August Wilson. Originally planned as a series of twenty plays, it traces the lives of an extended family of African Americans through the Cold War era. Like Wilson, Bullins intended these plays to engage broad historical questions facing African America—he once wrote that the plays were intended to help African Americans "consider the weight of their experience of having migrated from the North and the West, from an agricultural to an industrial center." However, they tell that history in a distinct way, by focusing on the everyday lives, conflicts, compromises, and decisions of the characters. Also distinct is the presence of music. In the Wine Time marks Bullins's first successful use of music as a truly dramatic element. The competing radios of the Dawson's (which plays rhythm 'n' blues) and Miss Minny Garrison (playing gospel) provide a sense of historical situatedness, clarify the deep moral and metaphysical issues at stake, and underscore the very different attitudes and expressive styles in conflict on this small side street of a large northern industrial city in the early 1950s. The play was first produced at the New Lafayette Theatre, New York, in 1968 and first published in* Five Plays, *edited Ed Bullins (New York: Bobbs-Merrill, 1969).*

In the Wine Time

(1968)

To Janet

THE PEOPLE:

CLIFF DAWSON

LOU DAWSON, *Cliff's wife*

RAY, *Lou's nephew*

MISS MINNY GARRISON

BUNNY GILLETTE

MRS. KRUMP

MR. KRUMP

EDDIE KRUMP

BEATRICE

TINY

SILLY WILLY CLARK

RED

BAMA

DORIS

POLICEMAN

The people in this play are black except for the KRUMPS *and the* POLICEMAN.

THE PROLOGUE

She passed the corner every evening during my last wine time, wearing a light summer dress with big pockets, in small ballerina slippers, swinging her head back and to the side all special-like, hearing a private melody singing in her head. I waited for her each dusk, and for this she granted me a smile, but on some days her selfish tune would drift out to me in a hum; we shared the smile and sad tune and met for a moment each day but one of that long-ago summer.

The times I would be late, she lingered in the sweating twilight at the corner in the barber shop doorway, ignoring the leers and coughs from within until she saw me hurrying along the tenement fronts. On these days, her yellows and pinks and whites would flash out from the smoked walls, beckoning me to hurry hurry to see the lights in her eyes before they fleeted away above the single smile, which would turn about and then down the street, hidden by the little pretty head. Then, afterwards, I would stand before the shop refusing to believe the slander from within.

"Ray . . . why do you act so stupid?" Lou asked each day I arose to await the rendezvous.

"I don't know . . . just do, that's all," I always explained.

"Well, if you know you're bein' a fool, why do you go on moonin' out there in the streets for *that?* . . ."

"She's a friend of mine, Lou . . . she's a friend."

August dragged in the wake of July in steaming sequence of sun and then hell and finally sweltering night. The nights found me awake with

Cliff and Lou and our bottles of port, all waiting for the sun to rise again and then to sleep in dozes during the miserable hours. And then for me to wake, hustling my liquor money, and then to wait on the corner for my friend to pass.

"What'd the hell you say to her, Ray?" Cliff asked.

"Nothin'."

"Nothing?"

"Nawh . . . nothin'."

"Do you ever try?"

"Nawh," I said.

"Why? She's probably just waiting for you to . . ."

"Nawh, she's not. We don't need to say anything to each other. We know all we want to find out."

And we would go on like that until we were so loaded, our voices would crack and break as fragile as eggs, and the subject would escape us, flapping off over the roofs like a fat pigeon.

Summer and Cliff and Lou and me together—all poured from the same brew, all hating each other and loving and consuming and never forgiving—but not letting go of the circle until the earth swung again into winter, bringing me closer to manhood and the freedom to do all the things that I had done for the past three summers.

We were the group, the gang. Cliff and Lou entangled within their union, soon to have Baby Man and Henrietta and Stinky and Debra and maybe who knows who by now. Summer and me wrapped in our embrace like lovers, accepting each as an inferior, continually finding faults and my weaknesses, pretending to forgive though never forgetting, always at each other's vitals . . . My coterie and my friend . . .

She with the swinging head and flat-footed stance and the single smile and private song for me. She was missing for a day in the last week of summer.

I waited on the corner until the night boiled up from the pavements and the wine time approached too uncomfortably.

Cliff didn't laugh when learning of my loss; Lou stole a half a glass more than I should have received. The night stewed us as we blocked the stoop fighting for air and more than our shares of the port, while the bandit patrol cruised by as sinister as gods.

She was there waiting next day, not smiling nor humming but waving me near. I approached and saw my very own smile.

"I love you, little boy," she said.

I nodded, trying to comprehend.

"You're my little boy, aren't you?" She took my hand. "I have to go away, but I wanted to tell you this before I left." She looked into my eyes and over my shaggy uncut hair. "I must be years older than you, but you look so much older than I. In two more years you won't be able to stop with only wine," she said.

"Do you have to do it?"

"I don't know . . . just do, that's all," I explained.

"I'm sorry, my dear," she said. "I must go now."

"Why?"

"I just must."

"Can I go with you?"

She let go of my hand and smiled for the last time.

"No, not now, but you can come find me when you're ready."

"But where?" I asked.

"Out in the world, little boy, out in the world. Remember, when you're ready, all you have to do is leave this place and come to me, I'll be waiting. All you'll need to do is search!" Her eyes lighted for the last time before hiding behind the pretty head, swinging then away from me, carrying our sorrowful, secret tune.

I stood listening to the barber shop taunts follow her into the darkness, watching her until the wicked city night captured her; then I turned back to meet autumn and Cliff and Lou in our last wine time, meeting the years which had to hurry hurry so I could begin the search that I have not completed.

ACT I

SCENE: *Derby Street. A small side street of a large northern American industrial city in the early 1950s.*

At left, the houses stand together on one side of the street in unbroken relief, except for a tunnel-like alley which opens between the KRUMPS *and the* GAR-RISONS' *houses, forming a low, two-storied canyon, the smoke-stained chimneys the pinnacles of the ridges. Four-letter words, arrow-pierced hearts, and slangy street-talk scrawled in haste, smear a wooden fence, painted green, across the narrow street. Tattered posters of political candidates wearing scribbled, smudged mustaches, circuses of seasons passed and fading, golden and orange snuff containers decorate the enclosure. Each building's front is dull red, not brick colored, but a grey- and violet-tinged red, the shade the paint becomes after successive seasons of assault by the city's smoke- and grit-laden atmosphere. Precise white lines, the older ones yellowing, outline each brick of the walls, and every house has a squat stoop of five white stone steps.*

A raised level, upstage right, between the fence and the houses, represents "The Avenue."

From within the DAWSONS' *house black music of the period—called rhythm 'n' blues by disc jockeys at that time—is heard not too loudly and continues throughout the play, interrupted only seldomly by amusing, jive-talking commercials for used cars, televisions, appliances, hair straighteners, and skin lighteners. Some of the recording stars of this season are King Pleasure, Johnnie Otis, Fats Domino, Little Esther, Ray Charles, and "The Queen," Miss Dinah Washington. When* MISS MINNY GARRISON *raises her window, gospel music can be heard.*

AT RISE: *It is a sultry evening in late August. All the steps are occupied by members of the various Derby Street households. At the end of the street, downstage, is a corner lighted by a streetlamp, the gas-burning variety found still then in some sections of Philadelphia, Baltimore, New York, and Boston.*

All lights are down but the corner streetlamp, though dim shadows of the people on the stoops can be seen carrying on their evening activities: talking, gossiping, playing checkers and cards, drinking sodas, wine, and beer.

MR. KRUMP *enters and stands at the streetlamp. He is very drunk. Lights on the* KRUMPS' *doorstoop, the nearer to the corner. The* KRUMPS' *front door opens and* MRS. KRUMP *leans out.*

THE RADIO: And here we are folks . . . on a black juicy, jammin' 'n' groovin' hot August night . . . yeah . . . one of them nights fo' bein' wit' tha one ya loves . . .

MRS. KRUMP, *strident, over the radio:* Krumpy! What cha doin' on da corner? Hey, Krumpy! Hey, Krumpy! . . . Krumpy . . . Get the hell on over here!

(*Light on third doorstoop*)

CLIFF: Heee . . . heee . . . look 'a ole man Krump work out.

(BUNNY *and* DORIS *enter Derby Street at the corner and see* MR. KRUMP.)

LOU: Hush up, Cliff.

CLIFF: Sheeet.

BUNNY GILLETTE: Look 'a there, Doris!

LOU: Be quiet, Cliff. Will ya, huh?

DORIS: Awww, shit, girl. That's nothin' . . . it just that goddamn Mr. Krump again . . . drunk out of his fucken' mind.

THE RADIO: It's eighty-two degrees . . . maaan, that's hot-oh-rooney . . . yeah, burnin' up this evenin' . . . red hot! . . . Ouch! . . . But we're cool on the Hep Harrison red-hot, uptight, out-a-sight weather lookout indicator. That's eighty-two degrees . . . that's eight two out there . . . And here's a cool number that will hit you right where you're at . . . for your listenin' pleasure . . .

(MRS. KRUMP *has stepped to the center of Derby Street and calls up to her second-floor window as the music begins.*)

MRS. KRUMP, *raspy, urban voice:* Hey, Edward . . . Hey, Edward! Hey, Edward . . . come on down here and get your fatha! Hey, Edward . . .

DORIS: Hey, lissen ta that cow yell.

BUNNY: Ain't it a shame, girl?

(BUNNY *starts off.*)

CLIFF, *disgust:* Goddammit . . . Lou. You always tellin' me to be quiet . . . I don't even make half the noise that some of our good neighbors do.

DORIS, *to* BUNNY: Where ya goin', broad?

LOU, *sitting beside* CLIFF: Awww . . . she should leave Mr. Krump alone. All he's doin' is peein' aside the pole . . . and then he's goin' in and go ta bed.

BUNNY: Up on "The Avenue."

DORIS: Where?

(EDDIE KRUMP *sticks his head from his upstairs window. He has dirty blond hair and a sharp, red nose. He is about eleven.*)

EDDIE: Ohhh, Christ, Ma . . . what'cha want?

BUNNY: "The Avenue," Doris.

MRS. KRUMP, *furious:* Don't you Christ me, Edward . . . Come down here right away, young man!

CLIFF, *to* LOU: I bet he ain't gonna do it.

DORIS: Ain't you gonna see Ray? That's what you come down this way for.

LOU: He might, Cliff. Besides . . . you the one that's always sayin' everybody here on Derby Street only does what they want to do most of the time, anyway.

BUNNY: He's up there on the step . . . he could see me if he wanted . . . C'mon, girl . . . let's split.

(*They exit.*)

CLIFF: 'Specially mindin' other people's business.

(RAY *sits between* CLIFF *and* LOU, *one step below them.*)

LOU: Wasn't that Bunny, Ray?

RAY: Think I should go and help Mr. Krump out, Cliff?

CLIFF: Nawh.

(*Pause*)

LOU: Why, Cliff?

CLIFF: You stay yo' ass here where ya belong, Ray.

LOU: Don't you talk like that, Cliff.

MRS. KRUMP, *to* EDDIE *in window:* Eddie . . . are you comin' down here?

EDDIE: Nawh.

CLIFF, *incredulous:* Did you hear that?

LOU: Remember, . . . we mind our own business.

(*From the upstairs window of the* GARRISONS' *house,* MISS MINNY GARRISON *pushes her head; she has a bandanna tied about her head, and she is a huge black woman.*)

MRS. KRUMP, *starting for her door:* I'm going to come up there and beat the hell out of you, Edward.

(EDDIE *ducks his head in the window as his mother enters the door below. Sounds of* MRS. KRUMP's *screams, the shouts of* EDDIE KRUMP *and of running feet. Silence. Rhythm 'n' blues and gospel music mingle softly.* RED *and* BAMA *enter at the corner. They see* MR. KRUMP *and nod to each other, then slowly, stiff-leggedly, stalk about the streetlamp, tightening the circle about* MR. KRUMP *on each full swing around.*)

MISS MINNY: Ray . . . wha don't you help Mr. Krump git home?

(RAY *stands and looks up at her.*)

RAY: Yas'sum.

CLIFF, *to* RAY: Wha' . . . you gonna go down there and help? . . .

(RAY *hesitates.*)

LOU: Awww, Cliff . . . there ain't no harm in it.

CLIFF: No harm?

LOU: Ray always does it.

CLIFF: Well, it's about time he stopped.

MISS MINNY: Go on, Ray. Go on and git Mr. Krump.

RAY: Yas'sum. (*He trots to the corner.*)

CLIFF, *mimics* RAY *in high falsetto:* Yas'sum.

LOU, *angry:* Stop that, Cliff!

CLIFF: Sheeet!

RED: Hey . . . Ray . . . is this lump ah shit a friend of yours?

RAY: Nawh.

LOU: Why don't you stop that stuff, Cliff? Ain't nothin' bein' hurt because Ray's helpin' out Mr. Krump.

BAMA: Maybe they're related.

RED, *chuckling:* Hey, man, cool it. I know Ray don't play that. Do you, Ray?

RAY, *trying to support* MR. KRUMP: Nawh, Red. Nawh.

RED, *to* BAMA: See, Bama, Ray don't play the dozens.[1] You better be careful.

BAMA: Shit.

(RAY *and* BAMA *exchange stares.* BAMA *is several years older than* RAY.)

RED: You seen Bunny and Doris, Ray?

RAY: Yeah . . . they headed for "The Avenue."

CLIFF: Nothin' bein' hurt? Just look at that. Look at that, Lou!

(RAY *has slung* MR. KRUMP *across his shoulder. He is husky and carries his load well.*)

CLIFF, *standing, shouting:* Hey, Ray! Make sure his pants fly is zipped up or you'll be a victim of a horrible calamity!

LOU: You think you so smart, Cliff.

BAMA, *to* RAY: Tote dat bar', boy . . . lift dat bale.

RED, *booting* RAY *in the seat of the pants:* Git along, little doggie.

(CLIFF *is pleased with himself but starts as* RED *kicks* RAY *and stands, but* LOU *tugs at his trouser leg and he sits back down, chuckling over his wit, though scowling at* RED *and* BAMA, *who turn, laughing, and exit.* RAY *carries his load to the* KRUMPs' *door.* CLIFF *lights a cigarette and takes a drink.* LOU *tries to ignore him.*)

MRS. KRUMP, *wearing a perpetual worried expression, at her door:* Why, thank you, Ray. Just bring him in here and put him on the couch. Thank you, Ray. That Edward is just . . .

(*They go in,* MRS. KRUMP *at the rear, peering at* MR. KRUMP's *head, which dangles down* RAY's *back.*)

CLIFF: That goddamn Miss Minny's always startin' some shit!

LOU: Shusss . . . Cliff. She'll hear you.

CLIFF, *bitter:* I don't care if the big sow does. Always pretendin' her ears are filled with nothin' but holy holy gospel music . . . when they're nothin' but brimmin' with Derby Street dirt. (*Mutters*) Ole bitch!

LOU, *uneasy:* Cliff!

CLIFF, *looks up at* MISS MINNY: Always startin' some trouble.

(MISS MINNY *closes her window. Her light goes off.*)

LOU: See, she did hear you!

CLIFF: I don't give a damn . . . who she thinks she is anyway?

---

1. Play the dozens: African-derived spoken-word game in which players work complicated verbal tricks to, say, cast doubt on the legitimacy of the opponent's birth or characterize his or her mother in an unflattering light. Superiority is judged by audience opinion or visibly shaking one's opponent.

LOU: Cliff, you just tryin' to start some trouble with Mr. Garrison. You wouldn't say those things if Homer were home.

CLIFF, *challenging:* Wouldn't I?

LOU: No, you wouldn't!

CLIFF: I would do anything I do now if ole four-eyed Homer was sittin' right over there on that step pickin' his big nose.

LOU: He don't pick his nose no more.

CLIFF: How do you know? Is that what Miss Minny told you?

LOU: No, Miss Minny didn't tell me a thing. His sister, Marigold, showed me a picture of him in his sergeant's uniform . . . and I know nobody in the United States Army who makes sergeant still picks their nose.

CLIFF: Sheeet!

(*Silence*)

LOU: Cliff?

CLIFF, *angry:* Look what you've done to that boy, Lou. Look what you and his mother . . .

LOU, *angry:* Now don't you start in talkin' 'bout my dead sister!

CLIFF, *angrier:* Shut up! (*Pause and stares*) Don't you see what all of you are tryin' to do . . . Miss Minny . . .

LOU: Who's tryin' to do what, Cliff?

CLIFF, *continues:* Miss Minny . . . you . . . all the so-called high-falutin' pussy on this block . . .

LOU, *indignant:* Now you watch your mouth . . .

CLIFF: Pussy! Cunt! Bitches! Always startin' some trouble.

LOU, *apologetic:* That was no trouble, Cliff.

CLIFF: It was so . . . Who the hell Miss Minny thinks she is anyway tellin' Ray to go down there an' get ole man Krump? And gettin' kicked by that punk Red . . . Ray's nearly a man . . . he shouldn't . . .

LOU, *cutting:* She didn't mean nothin' by it.

CLIFF: Just like she didn't mean nothin' the time she passed around that petition to have us run off a Derby Street when we first moved here.

LOU: She didn't know us then . . . we was strangers. Why don't you forget it?

CLIFF, *raising voice:* What's so strange about us, huh? What was so strange about us back then when we moved in? What was so strange? Was we strange because I was goin' ta school on the G.I. Bill[2] and not totin' a lunch pail like all these other asses? . . .

---

2. G.I. Bill: The Servicemen's Readjustment Act of 1944, better known as the G.I. Bill of Rights, has provided billions of dollars to U.S. veterans for vocational training and higher education.

LOU: Shusss . . . Cliff.

CLIFF: I will not shusss . . . that's what they are, aren't they? Asses! Mules! Donkeys!

LOU: I'm goin' in if you keep that up, Cliff.

THE RADIO: . . . and Fat Abe . . . your local honest used car dealer is now offering a custom bargain fo' one of you real swingers out there . . .

(CLIFF *reaches up and pulls the door shut with a slam, muffling the radio.*)

CLIFF: You ain't goin' nowhere just because you don't want to hear the truth. (*Silence.* LOU *sulks.*) Well, they are asses . . . (*Ridicule*) Derby Street Donkeys!

LOU, *apologetic:* Well, I was workin', Cliff. And . . .

CLIFF, *cutting:* And they made a hell of a noise about that, too. Always whisperin' how you work so hard all day in a laundry for no-'count me who goes around carryin' books. And gets home in the middle of the afternoon and jest lays around like a playboy . . .

LOU: They did see you with them girls all the time, Cliff.

CLIFF: I ain't been with no bitches.

LOU: Cliff . . .

CLIFF: They're lies! That's all . . . every one a lie . . . and don't you let me hear you tell me them lies again.

(*Silence*)

LOU: Never?

CLIFF: Never!

LOU: What should I say when I find lipstick on your shirt . . . shades I don't use? (*Silence*) What should I say when I see you flirtin' with the young girls on the street and with my friends?

(*Silence*)

CLIFF, *tired:* Light me a cigarette, will ya?

(*She does.*)

LOU: This street ain't so bad now.

CLIFF: Was we so strange because your nephew Ray stays with us . . . and don't have to work (*bitter*) like an ass or mule or fool . . . like a Derby Street Donkey!

LOU: Cliff!

CLIFF: Why was we so strange?

LOU: Nawh, we wasn't . . .

CLIFF: Who wasn't?

LOU: We wasn't!

CLIFF: Yes, we was!

LOU: Nawh . . . we seemed strange because we always drinkin' this . . . (*raising her glass*)

CLIFF: Everybody else drinks somethin' around here . . . ole man Garrison puts at least a pint of white lightnin' away a night . . . pure'dee cooked corn whisky!

LOU: But their ignorant oil don't make them yell and holler half the night like this wine makes us.

CLIFF, *yells:* Who yells?

LOU, *amused:* . . . and we sing and laugh and you cuss like a sailor.

CLIFF: Who sings and laughs? . . .

LOU: We do!

CLIFF: You a liar!

LOU: Nawh, I'm not, Cliff. (*He grabs her arm and twists it behind her back.*)

CLIFF: Say you a liar.

LOU: Nawh, Cliff . . . don't do that.

CLIFF, *twists it more:* Who's a liar?

LOU: I am, Cliff.

CLIFF, *a slight jerk:* Who?

LOU: I am, Cliff. I am! (*He releases her.*)

CLIFF: That's right . . . sing out when I want you to. Ha ha ha . . . (*He tries to caress her.*)

LOU, *rubs arm and shoves him:* Leave me alone.

CLIFF, *kisses her:* I'm glad you finally confessed . . . It'll do your soul some good.

LOU, *sulking:* You shouldn't do that, Cliff.

CLIFF: Do what?

LOU: You know what.

CLIFF: Give you spiritual comfort? . . . Apply some soul ointment?

LOU, *disgusted:* Awwww . . .

CLIFF: I don't know if you never tell me, hon.

LOU: You know, all right.

CLIFF: That I cuss like a sailor?

LOU, *remembering:* That's right . . . and . . .

CLIFF, *cutting:* Well, you didn't say that.

LOU: I didn't? (*Pause*) I did too, Cliff.

CLIFF: What?

LOU: Say that we yell and holler and sing and laugh and cuss like sailors half the night.

CLIFF, *toasts her:* Ohhh, Lou. To Lou Lou, my Hottentot queen.[3]

---

3. Hottentot queen: The Hottentots are a pastoral people of Namibia and South Africa whose women have been noted for their prominent buttocks. Saartjie Baartman (1790–1815), the

LOU: I'm not!

CLIFF: My queen?

LOU: Hottentot! . . . My features are more northern . . . more Ethiopian.

CLIFF, *ridicule:* Haaaah! (*Pause*) Haaaaah! More northern . . . more Ethiopian! That beak nose of yours comes from that shanty Irishman who screwed your grandmammy down on the plantation.

LOU: Watch your mouth, Cliff.

CLIFF: Watch my mouth?

LOU: Yeah, watch your mouth. Some things I just won't allow you to say.

CLIFF, *mocking:* "Some things I just won't allow you to say." (*Offended*) Watch my mouth? Well, take a look at yours. Yours comes from that Ubangi great granddaddy on your father's side . . . your "northern" nose, well, we've gone through its . . .

LOU, *warning:* Stop it, Cliff!

CLIFF: . . . but your build is pure Hottentot, darling . . . and that's why I shall forever love you . . . however the Derby Street Donkeys bray about me being with other girls . . . younger, prettier girls, mind you . . . But Lou, baby, you are married to an A-number-one ass man . . . and yours is one of the Hottentot greats of northern America.

LOU, *indignant:* Fuck you!

CLIFF, *fake dialect:* Wahl, hon-nee chile . . . I just wanted ta tell yawhl dat yo' husband is one ob dem connoisseurs of dem fleshy Hottentot parts which'n yous is wonderfully invested wit'.

LOU: Fuck you, Cliff! . . . Ohhh, just listen to that. You make me say bad things, man. You think you so smart and know all them big words since you been goin' to school. You still ain't nothin' but a lowdown bastard at heart as far as I'm concerned.

(*Silence.* CLIFF *takes a drink.* LOU *is wary but defiant.*)

CLIFF, *smiles:* We do cuss too much, don't we?

LOU, *smiles:* And we drink too much.

(*He pulls her over and fondles her. She kisses him but pushes him away.*)

CLIFF: Like sailors?

LOU: Yes!

CLIFF, *amused:* I thought we cussed like sailors.

LOU: We do.

CLIFF, *raises voice:* Make up yo' mind, broad. Now what is it . . . do we cuss and drink like sailors or cuss like sailors and drink like . . . like . . . like . . . what?

"Hottentot Venus," caused a sensation when brought to France in 1814, becoming an object of racist scientific and sexual speculation.

LOU: Like niggers.

(*At the last word, lights go up on other stoops, revealing the occupants looking at* CLIFF *and* LOU. *Then lights dim and come up on "The Avenue." The figures of* RED, BAMA, DORIS, *and* BUNNY *are seen.*)

BUNNY: Go on now, Red . . . stop messin' with me.

RED: Awww . . . woman . . . stop all your bullshit. You know you like me to feel your little ass . . . c'mere.

DORIS: Stop fucken' with that girl, Red.

RED: What's wrong, Doris? You jealous or somethin'?

DORIS: Man . . . if you melted and turned to water and ran down the gutter, I wouldn't even step over you.

RED: Why . . . scared I'd look up your dress and see your tonsils?

BUNNY, *giggling:* Ohhh . . . girl, ain't he bad?

BAMA: C'mere, Doris. I wanna talk to you.

DORIS: You ain't never wanted to talk to me before, Bama.

(RED *has his arm about* BUNNY's *waist.* BAMA *takes* DORIS's *hand.*)

RED: C'mon, Bunny . . . I'll buy you a fish sandwich. (*To* BAMA) Hey, Bamah-lam . . . do you think these broads deserve a fish sandwich?

BAMA: Nawh, man, they don't deserve shit.

DORIS: Hey, Bunny, we really hooked us some sports . . . you better make it back to Ray, girl.

(*Lights down on "The Avenue." Lights up on Derby Street.* CLIFF *and* LOU *laugh as* RAY *comes out of the* KRUMPS'. *The radio is muffled in the background.*)

MRS. KRUMP, *off:* You sure you don't want another slice of cake and a glass of milk, Raymond?

RAY: Nawh, thank you, Mrs. Krump.

EDDIE, *sticks his head out of his window:* Thanks a lot, Ray.

RAY: That's okay; why don't you come on down for a while?

EDDIE: Nawh . . . I can't . . . I gotta headache.

CLIFF, *to* RAY: Little white Eddie don't want to come down after you carry his pissy pukey drunk daddy in for him, huh?

LOU: Cliff!

RAY, *embarrassed:* Nawh.

LOU: Cliff . . . no wonder they sent around that petition. Just look how you act.

CLIFF, *angry:* Yeah, just look how I act . . . fuck how I act!

LOU: You got the dirtiest mouth, Cliff.

CLIFF, *angrier:* Fuck how I act . . . fuck it! (*Stands and glares about at his neighbors. They turn their heads and resume their activities.*)

LOU: Just like a sailor.

CLIFF, *satisfied:* Yup . . . just like I always said . . . folks on Derby Street sure know how to mind their own business.

LOU: Just like the no-'count sailor I met and married.

CLIFF: Well, I am a mathafukken shit-ass sailor. The same you met and married, Lou.

LOU: Not at any more.

CLIFF: Still! I still am. Once a sailor . . . always a sailor.

LOU: Not any more. Besides . . . you stayed most of your time in the guard-house.

CLIFF, *to* RAY: Listen to that . . . listen to that, Ray. Guardhouse.

LOU: That was the reason I married you. Felt sorry for you and knew your commanding officer would go light on you if he knew you had been married when you deserted and not put you in the guardhouse for so long.

CLIFF: Yeah?

LOU: Yeah!

CLIFF: Don't think you did me any favors, baby.

LOU: Well, who else did? I went to your ship and testified . . . I kept you from gettin' a bad discharge. In fact, I'm the one who made a man out of you even though your mother and the whole entire United States Navy failed.

CLIFF, *mutters:* Bitch.

LOU: Do you hear that? Failed . . . to make a man or a sailor of ya.

CLIFF, *ridicule:* Ray. This broad, pardon the expression, this woman named Lou. . . . Lou Ellen Margarita Crawford Dawson . . . who calls herself your aunt, by the way . . .

LOU: I am his aunt!

CLIFF: This bitch don't know what a sailor is.

LOU: I don't? . . . I don't? Then I guess you know even though you spent most of your navy time in the guardhouse.

RAY: Brig, Lou . . .

CLIFF: Thank you, son. Thank you.

LOU: What? . . .

RAY: Brig, Lou . . . not guardhouse.

CLIFF: That's right . . . that's fucken-A right . . .

LOU, *mutters and takes a drink:* Dirtiest mouth I ever heard.

CLIFF: That's a lie . . . your sister has the dirtiest mouth in north, south, west and all of this town. (*To* RAY) That's your play-aunt Doris I'm talkin' about, Ray, not your dear dead mother . . . may she rest in peace . . .

LOU: You two-faced bastard. Listen to you sound in' like one of them white missionaries . . . "May she rest in peace . . ." Dirty-mouthed liar!

CLIFF: Liar? About what? My not being in the guardhouse?

RAY: Brig.

LOU: You know that's not what I mean.

CLIFF: Pour yourself a drink, Ray. Put some hair on your . . . ding-a-ling. (*Begins humming*)

LOU: I pity the day you talked me into allowing Ray to take a drink.

CLIFF: Whatta ya mean? He was a lush when he came here. His mother and him both almost drank themselves to death.

LOU: Cliff!

CLIFF, *defensive:* Ain't that right, Ray?

RAY: Sorta. I did kinda drink along with Mamma for a while until they put her away.

CLIFF: Sorta? Stop jivin' . . . for a youngblood, you can really hide some port.

RAY, *flattered:* Yeah . . . I do my share.

LOU: Now, Ray, I want you to . . .

CLIFF, *loud:* Quiet! You heard him . . . he does his share. Here's a toast to you, youngblood. (*Lifts his glass*) To Ray, who does his share.

(*They drink, except for* LOU.)

RAY: Thanks, Cliff.

CLIFF: Don't mention it, Ray. Just don't mention it at all. It's your world, son. It's really your world. (*To* LOU) Well, isn't it? (*Silence*) You don't feel like toasting Ray? (*Silence*) Ray . . . you know, Lou is a lot like your mother used to be. Quiet, except that your mother usually had a glass up to her mouth instead of her mouth clamped tight.

LOU: You shouldn't've of said that, Cliff. You're goin'a pay for that.

CLIFF: Pay? Ray, it's your world . . . does your ole Uncle Cliff have to pay?

RAY: Well, I don't . . .

LOU, *cutting:* Stop it, Cliff. Ray, I'm sorry. Cliff gets too much to drink in him . . .

CLIFF, *loud, cutting:* Nice night we havin' out here on our white, well-scrubbed steps . . .

(*Both together*)

LOU: . . . and he runs off at the mouth somethin' terrible. I know you wasn't much past twelve when I came an' got you and kept them from puttin' you in a home. And

CLIFF: . . . with all of God's white stars shinin' above your black heads. Ain't that right, Lord? You old shyster. You pour white heat on these niggers, these Derby Street

you had already started in drinkin' 'n smokin' and foolin' around with girls . . . and I knew you drank too much for a growin' boy, much less a man. But I couldn't see you in a home—it would have messed you up . . . or sent down South to Cousin Frank's. I don't mean you so young you don't know what you want to do, Ray. I'm only six years older than you . . . but Cliff still shouldn't be givin' you so much wine and teachin' you bad habits. It ain't good for none of us, not even me. I hardly know where I'm at some of the times when I start in drinkin' after I come from work . . . but it sho' do relaxes me. And your mother is gonna call me to account for it when we meet up in heaven . . . I really know that. The devil's in Cliff, I know that, to do what he's doin' to us . . . And I ain't helpin' things much. Listen to what I say, Ray, and not to the devil. Listen to me, Ray.

Donkeys, in the daytime and roast and fry them while they shovel shit for nex' to nothin' and steam them at night like big black lobsters . . . ha ha . . . the Krumps are little red lobsters of Yourn . . . and they just drink an' screw in the dark and listen to jive talk an' jive music an' jive HOLY music . . . but they still think they have to face You in the mornin'. That's right, face You, You jive-ass sucker! They don't know they got to face Your jive-hot, blazin' face . . . simple niggers . . . but they do 'cause they believe in You and Your lies. Stupid donkeys! They only got to look my god in the face once and forget about You, You jive-time sucker . . . (*Remembering an old joke*) . . . ha ha . . . she's black as night and as cool and slick as a king snake . . . (*Singing*) . . . Yes, Lord, yes, Lord, yes, Lord, yes, Lord . . .

LOU: Stop it, Cliff! You're drunk 'n' crazy 'n' drivin' me out of my head!

(*Silence.* CLIFF *stares at her.*)

RAY, *to both:* It's all right. It's all right.

LOU: Ray, when I get to heaven, your mother's gonna have a lot to say to me.

CLIFF, *laughs:* Heaven?

LOU: Yeah, heaven. And you better get some of the fear of the Lord in you, Cliff.

CLIFF, *disgust:* Every night. Every goddamn night when you start in feelin' your juice.

LOU: 'Cause I know better, that's why.

CLIFF: Is that why when I get you in bed every night you holler (*whining falsetto*), "Yes, Lord. Yes, Lord. Ohhh . . . Jesus. . . one more time."

(RAY *giggles*.)

LOU: You're bad, Cliff. You're bad. Bad!

CLIFF: Sho' I'm bad, hon-nee chile. (*Singing*) I'm forty hands across mah chest . . . don't fear nothin' . . . not God nor death . . . I got a tombstone mind an' a graveyard disposition . . . I'm a bad mathafukker an' I don't mind . . . dyin'.

LOU, *cutting:* You're just a dirty-mouthed . . .

CLIFF, *cutting:* Yeah, I know . . . and I'll have you know that just because I spent one third of my navy time in various brigs, not just one, understand, baby girl, but at least an even dozen between here and Istanbul, that I was still one of the saltiest salt water sailors in the fleet . . . on dry land, in the fleet, or in some fucken marine brig!

LOU: You wasn't shit, Cliff . . . You know that, don't you?

CLIFF: Sticks 'n' stones, Lou . . . sticks 'n' stones.

LOU: Pour me a drink, Ray . . . and give your no-'count step-uncle one too.

(RAY *pours drinks for the three of them*.)

CLIFF: Step-uncle? Now how in Jesus's name did I get demoted from uncle to step?

LOU: You just did . . . suddenly you just stepped down.

RAY: Do you think I can get into the navy, Cliff?

CLIFF, *grabs* LOU's *arm:* Sometimes, Lou . . .

RAY: Huh, Cliff?

CLIFF, *recovering:* Navy? . . . Why, sure . . . sure, Ray. When you come of age, I'll sign the papers myself.

LOU: Steps can't, Cliff. But I can.

CLIFF: I can, Lou . . . I should know. (*Proudly*) I joined on my sixteenth birthday.

LOU: Steps can't.

CLIFF, *pinches her shoulder:* Bitch!

LOU, *feigning:* Owww, Cliff. Owww.

RAY: If I'm of age, then you won't have to sign, will ya?

CLIFF: No, I won't. Not if you're of age, Ray.

LOU: He can't sign anyway.

CLIFF: I can too, Ray. You just watch me when the time comes.

RAY: I'll be sixteen next week, Cliff.

CLIFF: You will?

RAY: Yeah.

CLIFF: Already?

RAY: Yeah.

CLIFF, *to* LOU: He will?

LOU: If that's what he says.

CLIFF: Damn . . . so soon.

LOU: Sixteen ain't old enough. You have to be seventeen before they'll even let me sign for you, Ray.

CLIFF: I went when I was sixteen . . . my sixteenth birthday.

LOU, *peeved:* That's because you were down in Virginia in the woods . . . fool! They don't even have birth certificates down there . . . you could've went when you were thirteen if your mother had'a sworn you was old enough.

CLIFF: I was too old enough!

LOU: No, you wasn't. And Ray ain't, either. He's got to wait until he's seventeen. And then I might sign for him.

RAY: I got to wait? But Uncle Cliff said I could go.

CLIFF: Yeah, you can go, Ray. I'll sign the papers myself. You're goin' to the navy and see how real men live.

LOU, *angry:* He's not goin' . . . he's not old enough . . . and you ain't signin' no papers for him, Cliff. His mother wouldn't . . .

CLIFF: I'll sign anything I want fo' him. I'm his guardian . . .

LOU, *ridicule:* Guardian? How? With what? You ain't never had a job in your life over six months. What you raise him with . . . the few lousy bucks you don't drink up from your government check? You somebody's guardian . . . I . . .

(CLIFF *slaps her violently.*)

CLIFF, *low, menacing:* You talk too much, Lou.

LOU, *defiant:* It's my responsibility, Cliff. Mine. Mine. My responsibility. I'm not going to sign or let you sign. His mother . . .

CLIFF: Damn that! Damn it! I don't care what his dead mother wants. Who the hell cares what the dead want? It's what Ray wants that counts. He's got to get out of here . . . don't you, Ray? . . . Off'a Derby Street and away from here so he can grow up to be his own man.

LOU, *crying:* Like you?

CLIFF: No, not like me . . . not tied down to a half-grown, scared, childish bitch!

LOU: You don't have to be.

CLIFF: But I love you.

(*Lights down, up on "The Avenue."* RED *slaps* BUNNY.)

DORIS: RED . . . YOU MATHAFUKKER . . . STOP THAT!

BUNNY, *crying:* Go on now, Red. Leave me alone . . .

RED: Bitch! Who you think you tellin' to kiss your ass? You want me to kiss your nasty ass?

BAMA, *reaching for him:* Hey, lighten up, Red.

DORIS: Leave her alone!

RED, *being held by* BAMA: You want me to kiss your . . .

BUNNY: Nawh, Red. Nawh.

DORIS, *a short knife in her hand:* You better not touch her again . . . you better not. You goin'a be sorry for this.

(*Lights down on "The Avenue" and up on Derby Street*)

RAY: I'm sorry, Lou.

LOU: It's all right, Ray. We've fought before . . . I'm just sorry you have to see us act like this.

CLIFF: Awww, honey . . . I'll forget it if you do.

LOU: You beat on me and I'm supposed to forget it? In my condition.

CLIFF: You got nearly six months before the baby. He can't get hurt by just a little . . .

LOU: You know the doctor told you not to be hittin' on me no mo'. You did it on purpose 'cause you don't want it.

CLIFF: I'm sorry, Lou.

LOU: It's a wonder you didn't hit me in the stomach.

CLIFF: Well, it's a wonder I didn't.

LOU: See there. You don't want it.

CLIFF: Nawh, I don't want a baby I can't take care of . . . do you?

LOU: You can get a job.

CLIFF: At a dollar an hour? Dollar-an-Hour Dawson, that's me. Nawh, I don't want any kids until I can afford them. That's why I'm goin' ta school.

LOU: You studying business so you can take care of me an' your kids? What kind of job can you get in business? You got money to open you a business?

CLIFF: Lou, we've gone over this before. I'll manage.

LOU: Like you have gettin' a job?

CLIFF: Well, you want me to get a job in the laundry? Like all your cousins?

LOU: And me!

CLIFF: Startin' at a buck an hour. Hell no, I won't work!

LOU, *scared:* But what are we goin'a do when your checks run out, Cliff?

CLIFF: Me? I'll do the best I can. Maybe ship out again.

LOU: No, Cliff!

CLIFF: If I can't turn up anything . . . well, you and the kid can get on relief.

(*Silence*)

LOU: Where's your pride? A big strong man like . . .

CLIFF: A dollar an hour don't buy that much pride, Lou. There's a big rich world out there . . . I'm goin'a get me part of it or not at all.

(*Both together*)

LOU: You ain't no man. My daddy, he worked twenty years with his hands . . . his poor hands are hard and rough with corns and callouses. He was a man . . . he worked and brought us up to take pride in ourselves and to fear God. What did I marry? I thought you was a man, Cliff. I thought because you was loud and was always fightin' and drinkin' and was so big and strong that you was a man . . . but you ain't nothin' but a lowdown and less than nothin'!

CLIFF: I'm goin'ta get me part of that world or stare your God in the eye and scream, WHY! I am not a beast . . . an animal to be used for the plows of the world. But if I am, then I'll act like one. I'll be one and turn this fucken' world of dreams and lies and fairytales into a jungle or a desert. And I don't give much of a happy fuck which. There's a world out there, woman. Just beyond that lamppost . . . just across "The Avenue," and it'll be mine and Ray's.

LOU, *screams:* YOU'RE NOTHIN'!

CLIFF: In the navy, Ray can travel and see things and learn and meet lots of different . . .

LOU: NO!!!

CLIFF: . . . girls and make somethin' . . .

LOU: IS THAT WHAT IT DID FOR YOU?

CLIFF: Yeah, that's what it did for me!

LOU: Well, I don't want him to be like you.

CLIFF: How would you want him to be like . . . one of the Derby Street Donkeys? Or one of the ditty boppers or an avenue hype . . . or . . . a drug addict . . . or what?

LOU, *standing:* He ain't turned out so bad so far. (*Determined*) He's not goin', Cliff. (*Pause*) Ray, just get it out of your mind. I'm not signin' no navy papers . . . you're too young. (*She enters the house as the lights fade to blackness.*)

Curtain.

Mythic blues plays. Lights up on "The Avenue." The couples are in embrace.

BUNNY, *to* RED: I like you a lot . . . really I do . . . but what will Ray say?

RED: Fuck that little punk!

DORIS, *to* RED: What you say 'bout my nephew?

BAMA: He wasn't talkin' to you, Doris.

BUNNY: You ain't gonna fight me anymo' . . . are ya, Red?

DORIS: I'd cut that nigger's nut off if he had'a hit me like that, Bunny!

BAMA: You wouldn'a do nothin', Doris . . . you just . . .

DORIS: Yeah, I would . . . and that goes double for any jive nigger who lays a finger on me or mine!

RED, *places his hands on* BUNNY's *rear:* Why don't all you mathafukkers shut up! Can't you see I'm concentratin'?

(*Lights down, up on Derby Street.* CLIFF *and* RAY *sit upon their stoop. The remainder of the street is in shadow. Silence. From the last stoop up the street* BEATRICE *detaches herself from the shadows and walks toward the corner. She is a buxom brown girl and carries herself proudly. She speaks as she passes each shadowy group of forms upon the stoops.*)

THE RADIO: It's seventy-eight degrees . . . that's seven . . . eight . . .

BEATRICE, *passing:* Hello, Mr. Cooper. Miz Cooper.

SHADOWS: Hello, Beatrice. How you doin' tonight?

BEATRICE, *passing:* Hello, Miss Francis.

SHADOWS: Why, hello, Bea. How ya doin', girl?

BEATRICE, *passing:* Hello, Mr. Roy.

SHADOWS: Howdy, Beatrice. How's your folks?

BEATRICE: Just fine. (*She passes on.* MISS MINNY *puts her head out her window.*

BEATRICE *passes* CLIFF *and* RAY *without speaking, her pug nose up, her head sighting on something upon the Derby Street fence, on the far side of the street.* BEATRICE *comes abreast the Garrisons' house and looks up.*) Hello, Miss Minny.

MISS MINNY: Hello, Beatrice . . . how y'all?

BEATRICE, *stops:* Just fine, Miss Minny. How's Marigold and Ruth?

MISS MINNY: Awww . . . they're fine, Beatrice. They off visitin' mah sister this week.

BEATRICE: That's nice, Miss Minny. Tell them I asked about them, will ya?

MISS MINNY: All right, dear. Did you know that Homer asked about you in his last letter?

BEATRICE: No, I didn't. Is he still in Korea?[4]

---

4. Is he still in Korea?: The Korean War (1950–53) was a "police action" called for by the United Nations Security Council in response to the invasion of South Korea by Commu-

MISS MINNY: Yeah, he's still over there. They done made him a sergeant.

BEATRICE: Yes, I know. Marigold told me. He's doing okay, isn't he?

MISS MINNY: Oh, yes, he's just doin' fine and everything. Says he likes it over there.

BEATRICE: Tell him I asked about him, will you?

MISS MINNY: All right, Beatrice.

(BEATRICE *continues, and reaching the corner, she exits.* MISS MINNY *withdraws and shuts her window.*)

THE RADIO: . . . And now the genius of the great . . .

(*Music plays, softly.*)

CLIFF: Sheeet.

RAY: What'cha say, Cliff?

(*Silence. Both together.*)

CLIFF: I said that . . .   RAY: I wonder if . . .

(*Silence. Both together.*)

CLIFF, *annoyed:* Go on!   RAY, *embarrassed:* Excuse me.

(*Lengthy silence. Both take drinks and drag upon their cigarettes.*)

CLIFF, *hurriedly:* How old's that broad?

RAY: How old? . . .

CLIFF: Yeah.

RAY: Oh, Bea? . . . About my age, I guess.

CLIFF: She's certainly a snotty little stuck-up heifer, ain't she?

RAY: Yeah, I guess so.

(*Silence. Both together.*)

CLIFF, *almost leering:* I wonder what . . .   RAY, *explaining:* She's always . . .

(*Both halt.* CLIFF *stubs out his cigarette.*)

CLIFF, *yells over his shoulder:* Hey, Lou! (*No answer. To* RAY) Guess she's out back in the kitchen or the john.

RAY: Yeah.

CLIFF: Ray?

RAY: Huh?

CLIFF: Did you ever get any ah that?

RAY: Beatrice?

CLIFF: Yeah.

RAY: Nawh.

CLIFF: What she doin', savin' it for Homer?

---

nist Chinese and North Koreans. It was the first war in which the United States used fully integrated military units.

RAY: Homer? (*Laughing*) She can't stand Homer. Calls him "Ole Country."

CLIFF: What'cha waitin' on, boy?

RAY: Nothin'.

CLIFF: When I was yo' age, I'd ah had every little pussy on Derby Street all to myself.

RAY: You'd have them all sewed up, huh?

CLIFF, *not perceiving* RAY'*s humor:* Yeah, sho' would.

RAY: Ahhhuh.

CLIFF: How 'bout Marigold and Ruth?

RAY: What about them?

CLIFF: You ain't gettin' none of that, either?

RAY: Nawh.

CLIFF: Why not, boy? What's the matter with you?

RAY: Nothin'.

CLIFF: Nothing?

RAY: Nawh, nothin'.

CLIFF: With all this good stuff runnin' 'round here, you lettin' the chance of a lifetime slip by . . .

RAY: Yeah, I guess I am.

CLIFF: . . . always over there on Thirteenth Street messin' round with li'l Bunny when you should be takin' care of business back home.

RAY: I don't like any of the girls round here.

CLIFF: What's wrong with them? A girl's a girl . . . well, most of them are anyway.

RAY, *embarrassed:* Well, I like Bunny. Me and her's in love.

CLIFF: In love? In love? (*Cracking the door and over the music*) Hey, Lou Ellen . . . Your nephew's in love! (*No answer. Muttering*) Must'a fell in. (*Looking at* RAY) Boy . . . you got a lot to learn.

RAY: I can't help it, Cliff. And she loves me, too.

CLIFF: Ohhh, yeah . . . you really got a lot to learn.

RAY: Cliff . . . I . . .

CLIFF: Just because she comes down here with you on the nights that me and Lou are out don't make you be in love. You didn't think I knew, huh? Well, who the hell you think been turnin' those pillows on the couch over an' wipin' them off? Not your Aunt Lou . . . nawh, nawh, she'd damn near die if she knew you were doin' what comes naturally.

RAY: I'm sorry, Cliff.

CLIFF: Forget it. Oh yeah, now that reminds me. Clean up your own mess from now on. You're big enough.

RAY: Okay.

CLIFF: Bunny's the first girl you've had?

RAY: Nawh.

CLIFF: How many?

RAY: 'Bout half a dozen.

(*Silence*)

CLIFF: Well . . . you ain't exactly backward . . . but still when I was your age . . . but let's forget about that.

RAY: Okay.

CLIFF: Now what about Marigold and Ruth, don't they like you?

RAY: All the girls on the street like me, I guess . . . 'cept'n Beatrice 'n' she used to let me kiss her . . .

CLIFF: She did, huh? Well, what happened?

RAY: I don't know.

CLIFF: Well, why don't you get one of the girls next door? Screw one of Homer's sisters. (*Chuckling*) Get some of his stuff while he's away.

RAY: Yeah . . . yeah, Marigold likes me a lot. Homer even wants me to get Marigold so I might have to marry her and he'd have a brother-in-law he'd like, but she don't want it, not like that, and I don't see the sense of goin' with a girl if I can't do it to her.

CLIFF: You showin' some sense there, Ray. An' forget about that marriage stuff, too.

RAY: Yeah, and Ruth wants to get married too bad. I'm scared as hell of her.

(*Silence*)

CLIFF: Yeah, you better stick with fast little Bunny. Gettin' you in the service is gonna be hard enough . . . If your aunt knew that anyone was thinkin' about you and marriage . . . we'd really have a case on our hands. She'd probably lock you up in the cellar.

RAY, *contemplating:* And Beatrice thinks she's better than anybody else.

CLIFF: Yeah. I guess you do know what you're doin', stickin' with Bunny. But you'll be gone in a month, anyway.

RAY: In a week.

CLIFF: Yeah, that's right . . . in a week . . . And things will be different then for you.

(*Pause*) Hey, do you know what, Ray?

RAY, *slowly:* I met a girl the other day.

CLIFF: Do you know what, Ray?

RAY: I met a girl the other day, Cliff.

CLIFF: You did?

RAY, *more sure:* Yeah, I met her the other day . . . she's almost a woman.

CLIFF: She is?

RAY: A pretty girl.

CLIFF: You met her where, Ray?

(*Lights down and up on "The Avenue." The* GIRL *appears and stands under soft light. She has huge eyes and her skin is a soft black. The couples are fixed in tableau, but* RED *and* BAMA *pull away from* BUNNY GILLETTE *and* DORIS *and dance about the* GIRL *in a seduction dance, until the two girls break their position and dance against the attraction of the girl, in a symbolic castration of the boys. Lights down to fantasy hues on "The Avenue" and up on* CLIFF *and* RAY.)

RAY: I met her over on "The Avenue."

CLIFF: Yeah, and she was pretty?

RAY: Yeah.

CLIFF: That's good. But you better not get stuck on her.

RAY: Why? Why, Cliff?

CLIFF: 'Cause you goin' away in a month. You goin' to the navy, remember?

RAY: But she can wait for me.

CLIFF: Well . . . most women are funny. They don't wait around too long. They get anxious . . . you know, nervous that they won't get something that they think belongs to them. Never could understand what that somethin' was, but most of them are on the lookout for it, whinin' for it all the time, demandin' it. And I guess some of them even get it.

RAY: She'll wait.

CLIFF: Don't be too sure, son. Most of them don't.

RAY: Lou waited for you, didn't she? (*Silence*) Didn't she?

(*Silence*)

CLIFF: Yeah . . . but that was a little different.

RAY: How?

CLIFF: It was just different . . . that's all.

RAY: But how would it be different for you and Lou and not for me and my girl?

CLIFF: Well, for one, I don't know your girl, so I can't say positively just how she'd act . . . And, two, and you better not breathe a word of this to your aunt . . . you hear? (*Pause*) Well, Lou Ellen is different because . . . well, because she's got character.

RAY: My girl . . .

CLIFF, *cutting:* And your aunt's got principle and conviction, and you have to be awfully special for that.

RAY: But, Cliff . . .

CLIFF, *continuing:* . . . Now don't tell her, your aunt, I said these things, but she's special in that way.

RAY: I won't tell her.

CLIFF: For someone to have all of them qualities in these times is close to bein' insane. She's either got to be hopelessly ignorant or have the faith of an angel . . . and she's neither.

RAY: Nawh, I don't guess she is.

CLIFF: I don't deserve her, I know.

RAY: You two pretty happy together, aren't you?

CLIFF: Ray?

RAY: Yeah.

CLIFF: Don't think about her too much.

RAY: Lou?

CLIFF: Nawh . . . you know. Your girl.

RAY: Oh.

CLIFF: Yeah.

RAY, *distant:* Yeah, I guess so.

CLIFF: Why do you say it like that?

RAY: Awww, I was just thinkin'. Lou says I can't go . . . and . . . and this girl . . . she . . . well, I see her every day now and . . .

CLIFF: Have you . . .

RAY, *upset, cutting:* Nawh! We don't . . . we don't need to do anything. We just look at each other and smile . . . that's all.

CLIFF: Smile?

RAY: Yeah.

CLIFF: What else?

RAY: That's all. I just wait on the corner for her every afternoon, and she comes dancing along with her little funny walk and sometimes she hums or sings to me a while . . . then smiles some more and goes away . . . (*Lights down on "The Avenue" and the dancers*)

CLIFF: Boy, you better git yourself another drink.

RAY: I won't see her no more if I go to the navy, Cliff.

CLIFF: There's other things to see. Get her out of your head, Ray. There's a lot more fish in the ocean . . . ha ha . . . and a lot more girls where she came from. Girls all sizes and shapes . . .

RAY, *protesting:* You don't know where she came from!

CLIFF: Why don't I? I just need to take one look at any girl and I know all about her. And with yours . . . well, your just tellin' me about her makes me know. I know all about her, Ray. And let me give you some advice . . . Now you trust me, don't you? (*Pause*) Good. I want you to stay away from her. There's all kinds of girls on this stinkin' planet . . . speakin' all kinds of tongues you never would think of, comin' in all kinds of shades and colors and everything. When you become a swabby, the world will open up to you. Say, maybe you'll go to France

... to Nice or Marseilles ... the Riviera. Lie out in the hot sun ... You won't need a suntan, but you can lie out there anyway so those tourists and Frenchmen can see you and envy you. And you'll see all those sexy French broads in their handkerchief bathin' suits. Yeah, I can see you now, Ray, out there in your bright red trunks with sunglasses on, peekin' at those girls. Or maybe you'll go to Italy and git you some of that dago stuff. Ha ha ha ... best damn poontang in the world, boy. (*He ruffles* RAY's *woolly head and takes a good-sized drink.*) Ha ha ha ... put hair on your tonsils. (*Pause. Laughing*) Yeah, there's nothin' like walkin' down a street in your navy blues. You know ... you know ... you should get tailor-made, skin tights, Ray, with buttons up both sides, and have your wallet slung around back of your pants ... I can see you now. Your wallet will be fat as a Bible. And ... and the pretty little broads will be callin' out to you. "Hey, Yankee! Hey, sailor! Hey, Joe! Fucky fucky ... two American dollah!" Ha ha ha ha ... yeah! Yeah, that's livin', Ray. That's livin'.

RAY, *enthused:* Is it, Cliff? Is it?

CLIFF: In some ports you can get a quart of the best imported whiskey for two bucks and in some ports you can get the best brandy for only a buck or so. And the nights ... ahhh ... the nights at sea, boy. Ain't nothin' like it. To be on watch on a summer night in the South Atlantic or the Mediterranean when the moon is full is enough to give a year of your life for, Ray. The moon comes from away off and is all silvery, slidin' across the rollin' ocean like a path of cold, wet, white fire, straight into your eye. Nothin' like it. Nothin' like it to be at sea ... unless it's to be in port with a good broad and some mellow booze.

RAY: Do you think I can get in, Cliff?

CLIFF: Sure you can. Sure. Don't worry none about what your Aunt Lou says ... I've got her number. I'll fix it up.

RAY: I sure hope you can.

CLIFF: Sure I can. As long as I tell your aunt I'm fixin' to ship out she'll sell you, herself, and probably her soul to keep me with her.

RAY, *frowning:* You goin'a ship out, Cliff?

CLIFF: Nawh ... nawh ... I had my crack at the world ... and I've made it worse, if anything ... you youngbloods own the future ... remember that ... I had my chance. All I can do now is sit back and raise fat babies. It's your world now, boy. (TINY *rounds the corner.*) Well, here comes Tiny. (*Knocks on door behind him with his elbow.*) Lou. Lou. Here comes little Tiny.

(*It has gotten darker and the shadowy figures have disappeared from the other stoops into the doors of the houses one after another.*)

LOU, *off:* What'cha want, Cliff? I just washed my hair.

CLIFF: It's Tiny . . . she's comin' down the street.

(TINY *is a small, attractive girl in her late teens. As she comes abreast of the alley, a large man in wide-brimmed hat jumps out at her and shouts.*)

CLARK: Boo!

TINY: Aaaaaiieeeeeee ! ! !

(*After the scream, there is recognition between the two, and* CLARK *laughs, nearly hysterically, and begins trotting first in a circle about* TINY, *who looks furious enough to cry, then across the street to the fence where he leans and laughs, pounding the boards with his fists. Windows go up.*)

MRS. KRUMP: Is anything wrong?

MISS MINNY: What's all dat noise out dere?

LOU, *at door, her hair disheveled:* Clark, you shouldn't go round scarin' people like that!

(*The* POLICEMAN *passes the corner and stops and looks over the scene.*)

TINY, *regains breath:* You ole stupid mathafukker!

MRS. KRUMP: Is anyone hurt?

CLIFF, *stands, his arm around* TINY's *shoulder:* Nawh, Krumpy . . . the goddamn natives are restless, that's all.

MRS. KRUMP: Ohhhh . . . I'm sorry . . . I just wanted to help. (*Her window closes.*)

MISS MINNY: You and your friends shouldn't all the time be usin' that kinda language, Cliff . . . gives the street a bad name. We got enough bad streets and boys around here without you makin' it worse.

CLIFF: If you kept your head in where it belongs, you wouldn't hear so much, Miss Minny. Now would you?

MISS MINNY: I'm gonna talk to somebody 'bout you, Cliff. Somethin' should be done about you. (*Her window closes.*)

POLICEMAN: Is everything okay, Cliff?

CLIFF: Yeah, Officer Murphy. Everything's great.

POLICEMAN: Well keep it that way. I want it quiet around here, Cliff. (*Turns the corner*)

RAY: His name's not "Murphy," Cliff.[5]

CLIFF: To me it is . . . If he doesn't know to call my right name, I don't know his.

RAY: He said "Cliff."

---

5. Murphy: A stereotypical name for a presumably Irish, definitely white cop.

CLIFF: Yeah, he said "Cliff" like he was sayin' "boy." He didn't say "Mr. Dawson."

LOU, *ridicule:* Mr. Dawson . . . and his mob.

TINY: I'm sorry, Cliff. I didn't mean to make all that noise . . . but that stupid ole Clarkie over there . . .

CLIFF: That's okay, Tiny. It's not your fault. Old nose for news up there has been after us as long as I can remember. (*To* CLARK) Hey, Silly Willy . . . come the hell on over here and stop tryin' to tear down those people's fence . . . besides, it wasn't that funny, anyway.

RAY: You sho' can holler, Tiny.

TINY: I was afraid, man. Some big old stupid thing like that jumps out at you. Damn, man . . . I'm just a little thing . . . he makes two of me.

LOU: From the way you holler, sister, I know they'll have to want you really bad to get you.

TINY: Fucken-A baby. If they want mah little ass they gonna have to bring ass.

CLIFF: With Clark's big bad feet he couldn't catch a cold.

TINY: I should'a known better than to be walkin' along beside some alley, anyway. If I hadn't seen you folks up here on the steps I would'a been out in the middle of the street with runnin' 'n' hollerin' room all around.

RAY: You still didn't do so bad.

CLARK, *comes over, snuffling and wheezing. He has a large moon face and is in his early thirties. Giggles:* I'm sorry, Tiny . . . ha ha ha . . . but I couldn't help myself when I saw you over on Ninth Street turn the corner.

TINY, *peeved:* You been following me that long, man?

CLARK, *nearly convulsed:* Heee heee . . . yeah, I ran through the alley and waited . . . and . . . heee heee . . . and when . . . heee heee . . . I heard your walk, I jumped out.

LOU, *angry:* Somebody's goin'a shoot you, you old dumb nut.

RAY: Wow, Tiny, you almost scared me. You sure can holler.

TINY: Yeah, man, I really can when somethin's after me.

LOU: C'mon, girl. C'mon in while I fix my hair.

(LOU's *hair is long and bushy, just having been washed. It covers her head like a gigantic crown.*)

TINY, *steps across* RAY: Okay, girl. Hey, Ray, don't cha look up my dress.

RAY, *jest:* Why not, Tiny?

TINY: You must think you're gettin' big, boy.

RAY, *drawl:* I is.

LOU: Not that big, boy.

CLIFF: Why do you keep pesterin' the boy, Lou? If he didn't try and look, I'd be wonderin' what's wrong with him.

LOU: Is that what you do, look?

CLIFF: What do you think?

(*Silence.* CLARK *begins snuffling.*)

LOU: The only thing that's wrong with Ray is you, Cliff. I know some of those nasty things you been tellin' him.

(*Silence.* LOU *and* CLIFF *stare at each other.*)

TINY: I saw Doris and Bunny, Lou. (*Pause*) They said they'd be over. Said they had some business to take care of.

(*Pause*)

CLARK: Doris comin' over?

TINY, *to* CLARK: Yeah . . . yeah, stupid ass. She said she'd be down. And Ray, Bunny said you'd better keep yo' ass home, too. She wants to ask you some questions about that girl you been seein' out on "The Avenue."

RAY: What did she say?

CLIFF, *grinning:* So, it's finally got back home.

LOU, *hostile:* Yeah, it's gotten back. You don't like it?

TINY: She said you'd better keep yo' black ass home, Ray. That's what she said.

CLIFF, *weary:* Awww . . . Lou . . . please.

LOU: Followin' after you the way he does, it's a wonder he ain't always in some trouble.

CLIFF, *caressing her leg:* But, baby . . . (*She pulls her leg back.*)

RAY, *angry:* What she mean, I better keep mah black ass home? I'll go where I want . . . with who I want. She better watch it . . . or I won't be lettin' her come down here.

CLARK: Hey, listen to Tiger.

LOU: I ain't gonna let you start anything with little Bunny, you hear, Ray? Don't be hittin' on that little girl.

RAY: Awwww . . . sheeet.

LOU: What'd you say?

CLIFF: What'd it sound like he said?

LOU: Now you keep out of this, Cliff.

CLARK: You women folks are sho somethin' else.

TINY: You shut your mouth and mind your business, Clark.

LOU: Now listen here, Ray. Don't you talk to me like that, frownin' up your face an' rollin' yo' eyes. You gittin' too mannish 'round here. You hear? (RAY *doesn't answer, but gives a deep sigh.*) Don't you bother that girl.

CLIFF: Ray?

RAY: Yeah?

CLIFF: If Bunny fucks with you . . . you knock her on her ass, ya hear?

RAY: Yeah, that's what I'm aimin' ta do, Cliff. Right on her ass.

(LOU *and* TINY *go in.*)

CLARK: Hey, how 'bout pourin' me some of that wine you hidin' down there?

RAY: We ain't hidin' no wine.

CLIFF: Pour your own troubles, garbage gut.

CLARK: Why, hell, you ain't got nothin' here 'cept enough for maybe Ray, here.

CLIFF: "Ray, here?" What do you mean, "Ray, here?" Why this youngblood nephew of mine will drink you underneath the table and into the middle of nex' week, ole Silly Willy Clark.

CLARK: Sheeet.

CLIFF: Can't you, Ray?

RAY, *proudly:* Sure as hell can.

CLARK: Well, we'll see . . . come on, let's go on up to the store and get us a big man.

RAY: A big man?

CLARK: That's right . . . a whole gallon.

(CLIFF *stands and beckons* RAY.)

CLIFF: Never stand in the way of a man who wants to part with some coins . . . and buy ya a drink at the same time, I say.

CLARK: Yeah, c'mon . . . (*As an afterthought*) . . . I'm buyin'.

CLIFF, *humming:* Hummmm hummm hummm . . . don't mind if I do get a little refreshing night air . . . C'mon, Ray, let's take a stroll.

CLARK: Well, which liquor store we goin' to? The one up on "The Avenue" or the one down by the bridge?

CLIFF: Let's go up on "The Avenue." (*Pause*) That's okay with you, Ray?

RAY: Yeah, fine with me.

CLARK: Boy, we gonna get pissy pukey fallin' down drunk tonight.

CLIFF: If you see your girl up on "The Avenue," you'll point her out to me, Ray, won'tcha?

RAY: Yeah, Cliff. Yeah.

(They exit. The street is clear. Music plays, then a commercial begins. And lights down.)

Curtain.

ACT III

TIME: *Forty-five minutes later.*

SCENE: *Derby Street.* LOU, TINY, DORIS, BUNNY GILLETTE, RED, *and* BAMA *sit upon the* DAWSONs' *stoop. A gallon jug of red wine is on the pavement beside the steps, and everyone except* RED *and* LOU *has a paper cup in hand.* LOU *has her hair in curlers.* DORIS *is a small girl, not as small as* TINY, *and has a full figure.* RED *looks like a hungry wolf, and* BAMA *seems to be mostly elbows and knees.*

LOU: I don't see how you folks drink that nasty ole muscatel wine.

DORIS, *demonstrating:* There's nothin' to it, baby sis.

RED: That's about the only goddamn thing we got in common, Lou. I don't drink that fucken' hawgwash, neither.

LOU, *primly:* If you must sit on my steps this late at night, Red, I wish you'd respect me and the other girls here by not bein' so foul mouthed.

RED, *indignant:* Shit, woman, talk to your ole man, Cliff . . . I'm usin' Mr. Dawson's rule book.

LOU: Don't blame Cliff!

BAMA, *to* RED: Forget it, huh?

RED: You sometimes forget who your husband is, don't you, woman?

TINY: Yeah . . . knock it off, you guys.

RED, *to* TINY: Fuck you, bitch!

LOU, *to* RED: I got a good memory, little red nigger.

RED: So use it . . . and don't bug me.

BUNNY: If you fools gonna keep this up all night, I'm goin'a go home!

BAMA: Bye!

LOU: But I got to live with Cliff, Red, . . . not you . . . hear?

DORIS, *in high voice, nearly drunk:* Do y'all want a hot dog? Do y'all want a hot dog?

TINY: Why don't we all stop arguing? I knew this would happen if you bought more wine, Bama.

BUNNY: You been drinkin' much as anybody.

BAMA: Ahhh, don't blame me. If I didn't get it, somebody else would.

BUNNY: They up on "The Avenue" gettin' some more now.

LOU: Cliff and Ray's probably out lookin' for some ole funky bitches.

TINY: That's the way those punk-ass men are, girl.

BUNNY: Sho' is!

LOU: Who you callin', "punk-ass"?

TINY: Not anybody . . . well, I don't mean, "punk," . . . it's just that all men are messed up.

BAMA: What chou talkin' 'bout, broad?

RED: Hey, Bama, you better straighten your ole lady out before I have to do it.

DORIS: Do y'all want a hot dog?

BUNNY: Yeah, who's this girl Ray's been seein', Lou?

LOU: Don't ask me, chile. Don't even let him know I said anything.

RED: Tell Ray I want to meet her, Bunny.

(BUNNY *threatens to pour her wine on him.*)

TINY: When will Cliff be back?

DORIS: I said, do y'all want a hot dog?

LOU: You waitin' for Cliff now, Tiny?

TINY: Yeah . . . Doris, I want one . . . but give them time to cook, will . . .

LOU: I asked you a question, Tiny.

TINY: Nawh . . . nawh . . . can't you see I'm with Bama? Ain't I, Bama?

RED, *mutters:* Goddamn . . . what a collection of cop-outs.

BAMA: Hey, get me a hot dog, too.

DORIS: The mathafukkers should be done by now.

TINY, *nervous laugh:* Woman, stop usin' all that bad language. You know Lou don't like it.

DORIS: Shit on you and Lou both, it's my mouth.

LOU: Now, I ain't gonna warn none of you no longer . . . Next one says one bad word has got to go home.

BAMA: Will you listen to this, now?

RED: Hey, Doris, get me one of those fucken' hot dogs, will ya?

LOU: That did it, Red . . . Go home!

RED: Okay.

TINY: Doris, you can't say two words without cussin' . . . Don't you know any better?

RED, *stands:* But before I go, Lou, tell me what did I say that was so bad?

LOU: I don't have to repeat it.

DORIS: I wouldn't be talkin' bout people so fucken much if I was you, Tiny. Remember, I know somethin' . . . now, don't I?

LOU: That goes for you, too, Doris.

TINY, *frightened:* Whatta ya mean, Doris?

BUNNY: Uuuhhh uhhh . . . y'all sure do act funny when you start in drinkin' this mess.

BAMA: Yeah . . . whatta ya mean, Doris?

DORIS: I ain't talkin' ta you, Bama.

BAMA: I'm talkin' ta you. (*To* TINY) What she got on you, Mamma?

TINY: Whatta ya mean?

DORIS, *drunk:* Whatta ya think I mean?

BAMA: That's what I'm tryin' to find out . . . what ya mean.

RED: Shall we go . . . children?

TINY: That's what I'm askin' ya . . . whatta ya mean?

LOU: Now look. You broads can take that business back where you got it.

BAMA, *amused:* That's tellin' them, Lou.

TINY: Don't you be callin' me a broad!

BUNNY, *to* RED: Red . . . don't you think . . .

RED: Shut up, woman!

LOU, *amazed:* Wha' . . . I didn't . . .

BAMA, *joking:* Yeah, you did. I hear you.

DORIS, *jest:* Don't be talkin' to mah baby sister like that.

TINY, *scared and belligerent:* What you gonna do 'bout it, bitch! You gonna tell her 'bout Cliff and me?

BAMA: Hey, cool it, baby.

LOU: What did you say?

BUNNY: Now, Lou . . . don't get mad . . .

LOU, *disgust:* Okay, let's forget about it. You guys don't have to go home . . . I want you to wait on Cliff.

RED, *sitting:* Wasn't plannin' on goin', anyway.

LOU: Now, looka hare, Red.

RED, *angry:* Goddammit! Make up your mind!

DORIS, *to* TINY: You tryin' to be bad, ain't you, you li'l sawed-off heifer?

TINY, *rising:* "Little heifer!"

(CLIFF, RAY, *and* CLARK *turn the corner. They have a gallon jug of wine, half-emptied, which they pass between themselves and take large draughts. They visibly feel their drinks and stop under the streetlamp and drink and talk.*)

CLIFF: Ray . . . just learn this one thing in life . . . When the time comes . . . be a man . . . however you've lived up till then . . . throw it out of your mind . . . Just do what you have to do as a man.

RAY, *not sober:* Sure, Cliff . . . sure.

CLARK, *still drunker:* That sho is right, Dawson . . . that's right . . . but why can't we be men all the time, Dawson?

CLIFF, *annoyed:* You don't know what I'm talkin' 'bout, silly ass, do you . . . do you, now?

BUNNY: Here comes Cliff, Ray, and Silly Willy Clark.

DORIS, *moving toward* TINY: I'm tired of your little ass jumpin' bad around here, Tiny.

TINY, *scared, but standing her ground:* You are?

BAMA, *between them:* Hey, knock off the bullshit . . . ya hear?

RED: Nawh, Bama . . . let them get it on and see who's the best.

TINY, *crying:* Bama, why you always takin' somebody's side against me?

LOU: Shut up, all of you!

BAMA: I'm not takin' nobody's side against you, baby.

DORIS: You ain't takin' my side, Bama? And what you callin' her "baby" fo'?

TINY, *to* BAMA: Y'are!

BAMA: I ain't. We all just out to have a good time . . . that's all . . . a good time, huh?

(*He pulls* DORIS *down beside him and puts his arm about her.*)

TINY, *scratching at his face:* You bastard . . . I thought you was comin' down here to see me.

(DORIS *pulls her small knife.*)

LOU: Doris, stop!

DORIS: What the fuck's wrong with you, bitch! (CLIFF *comes up and sees* DORIS's *knife but doesn't appear to notice. She puts it away.*) I'm goin' in an' get a hot dog. (*Same high voice*) Y'all want a hot dog?

(*No answer. She enters the house.* BAMA, TINY, *and* LOU *glare at each other.* RED *and* BUNNY *sit together.*)

RED: Well, if it ain't Mr. Dawson and nephew . . . the Derby Street killjoys. And hello, Mr. Silly Willy Clark . . . you simple mathafukker.

CLARK: Hey, everybody . . . (*passing them the bottle*) . . . knock yourselves out.

BAMA: We got ours.

(LOU *silently stands, looks at* CLIFF *and the drunken* RAY, *and enters the house.*)

RED, *hugs* BUNNY, *looks at* RAY: Hey, what'cha mathafukkers doin'? Why don't you all have a sit down?

CLARK: Don't mind if I do, Red . . . Hey, Cliff, is it okay if I sit down on your steps?

CLIFF: Be my guest . . . you know me, don't you?

BUNNY, *pulls away from* RED: C'mon now, Red . . . stop all that stuff, man.

RED: You like it. (*He feels her breasts as they break.*)

LOU, *looking out the door:* I don't want to hear any more of that nasty shit from your mouth tonight, Red. And watch how you act!

RED: Watch how I act?

CLIFF: Yeah, that's what she said . . . watch how you act.

LOU: Yeah, you keep your hands to yourself. I saw that.

RED: Hey, what's wrong with you goddamn people tonight? Is there a full moon or somethin'?

BAMA: Hey, Red, let's split.

RED: Mr. and Mrs. Dawson . . . and nephew . . . I'm sorry. Forgive me. Will you please accept my humble-ass apology, huh? Will you Dawsons do that? (RED *places his hand upon* LOU's *leg; she pulls away.*) Now what have I done?

BUNNY: What's wrong with you, Ray?

DORIS, *sticks head out of door:* Do y'all want a hot dog?

TINY: Ray's gone off somewhere behind that wine . . . look at him slobber spit . . . probably with his . . .

BUNNY: With his what?

TINY: Nothin', hon . . . I was just kiddin' . . . (*shakes* RAY) . . . Wasn't I, Ray?

RAY: Yeah . . . yeah.

BAMA, *mimics* DORIS: "Do yawhl wants a hot dawg?"

TINY: Don't be so mean, Bama.

DORIS: Y'all can kiss mah ass.

LOU, *caricature:* "Don't be so mean, Bama."

BAMA, *furious:* Who you tellin' to kiss your ass, woman? I thought you saw what Bunny got tonight up on "The Avenue" for . . .

(MISS MINNY's *window goes up.*)

TINY: Don't be so noisy, baby.

RED: I thought you was gonna get me one ah those mathafukkin' hot dogs, woman.

MISS MINNY: Cliff . . . Cliff . . . I see you out there . . . I'm callin' the police right now about all this disturbance! (*Her window goes down.*)

DORIS: You better watch your little self, Tiny.

LOU: I told you about your mouth, Red.

TINY: Watch myself?

RED: My mouth . . . awww . . . Lou. You can't be serious.

CLIFF: Well, children, it's time that Daddy got to bed . . . I suggest that everyone goes home to bed or just home. Good night, all.

LOU: Ain't you gonna stay out here and wait for the cops, Cliff?

CLIFF: Good night, my love. Don't be too long . . . I think your hair's sexy.

(*He goes in, followed by* DORIS.)

DORIS, *off:* Do y'all wants a hot dog, Cliff?

RED: If I hadn't seen Cliff beat so many bad niggers' asses, I would think he's a chicken-hearted punk.

LOU: There's more than one way to be a coward.

BAMA: You better not let him hear you say that, lady.

CLARK: It's been a hard night, heh, Bunny?

BUNNY: Honey, these wine times is somethin' else.

RAY, *mumbling:* Sho is, baby. Sho is.

DORIS, *back again, peering bleary-eyed at each one:* Do y'all want a hot dog? Do y'all want a hot dog? If y'all don't, speak up . . . dese here hot dogs gonna be all gone, cause I'm eatin' them fast as I can.

RED: Shove 'em up your ass . . . you silly bitch.

LOU: Okay, you all have to go now!

(RED *rises and is followed by the rest, except* RAY, *who snores on the step.* LOU *goes back into the house, and her fussing with* CLIFF *about* RAY's *condition, his friends, and* TINY *can be more sensed than heard.*)

BUNNY: Ray . . . Ray?

RAY: Yeah?

BUNNY: I gotta tell you somethin' . . . Ray? . . . Ray? . . . I got somethin' to tell ya.

BAMA: Leave him alone, Bunny.

TINY: Yeah, let him sleep. He'll find out.

RAY: Yeah . . . what is it?

BUNNY: I'm Red's girl now. (CLARK *gets up and enters the house.*) Did you hear me, Ray? Did you hear me?

(RED *faces the building, and urinates in one of the wine bottles.*)

RAY, *groggy:* Yeah . . . I heard you, Bunny. You're Red's girl now.

BAMA, *giggling:* I guess Ray's really got himself a new girl, Bunny.

RED, *hands* RAY *the wine bottle he has just finished with:* Let's toast to that, Ray.

(*Blindly,* RAY *lifts the jug to his lips as* BAMA *and* TINY *gasp.*)

BUNNY: No! . . . No, Raayyy ! ! !

(*She knocks the jug out of his grasp, smashing it upon the pavement.* RAY *wakes instantly, perceives her action, and lashes out at her face. He lands a solid punch that knocks her sprawling in the street.* RED *rushes* RAY *and hits him with a hay-maker aside the head.* RAY *grabs him for support, and the two fall to the pavement, grappling.* TINY *screams, and* MISS MINNY's *window goes up. There are shouts and noise of running feet. The fighters roll about the pavement and* BAMA *reaches down and pulls* RAY *off* RED *and holds him as the older boy smashes him in the face.* CLARK *rushes from the house and grabs* BAMA *from behind. Upon his release from* BAMA, RAY *butts* RED *in the midriff and staggers him to the entrance of the alley.*)

RED *pulls a bone-handled switch-blade;* RAY *grabs his arm, and they fight their way into the alley.* DORIS *comes out of the house holding her small knife.*)

DORIS, *to* BUNNY: Where's Ray . . . Where's Ray?

(BUNNY, *dazed, points to the alley.* DORIS *enters the alley as* CLIFF *runs out of the door in pants only in time to see her disappear in the tunnel. The street is lit; the* KRUMPs' *upper windows are open.*)

EDDIE: Kill 'em . . . Kill 'em!

MRS. KRUMP: Keep back, Edward . . . there may be stray bullets!

(CLARK *has choked* BAMA *into surrender.*)

RED, *from the alley, muffled:* All right . . . all right . . .

(*As* CLIFF *runs into the alley there is a sharp sigh, then noise of more struggle and a groan.* LOU, TINY, BUNNY, *and Derby Street residents crowd around the alley entrance.*)

MISS MINNY: Oh, Lord . . . what's happened . . . what's happened?

MRS. KRUMP: Close the window, Edward . . . Close the window!

(*The* KRUMPs' *window closes. The* POLICEMAN *turns the corner at a run.*)

RESIDENT, *to another resident:* Did you see what happen, Mr. Roy?

MR. ROY: Nawh, Miz Cooper . . . but I knew somethin' had to happen with all this goin' on down here.

(RAY *emerges from the alley, blood on his shirt.* DORIS *follows him, her dress splotched with blood.*)

POLICEMAN, *running up with hand on pistol:* What's happened here?

CLIFF, *steps out of the alley, holding* RED's *knife. Hands knife to* POLICEMAN *and points in alley:* I killed him.

LOU, *incredulous:* You killed him . . .

(CLIFF *nods.*)

RESIDENT: Did you hear that?

MISS MINNY: What happened? What happened, Miss Francis?

RESIDENT: Cliff Dawson's done killed a boy.

MISS MINNY: Ohhh . . . my Lord.

TINY, *disbelief:* You killed him?

POLICEMAN, *leads* CLIFF *to stoop:* Okay, everybody . . . get back and don't nobody leave. By the looks of most of you . . . we'll want to talk to you. Get back . . . Will somebody call an ambulance and wagon?

MISS MINNY: I already did.

(BAMA *has revived; he looks sick and sits beside the alley entrance.* BUNNY, CLARK, *and* DORIS *support* RAY, *who looks to be in shock.*)

LOU: Cliff . . . Cliff . . . don't do it . . . don't leave me! Tell the truth.

CLIFF, *caresses her:* It won't be for long . . . I was protectin' my family . . . our family.

(LOU *cries, joining* TINY, BUNNY, *and one of the neighbors.* DORIS *appears resigned to the situation.*)

RAY: She's gone . . . she's gone . . .

(*A siren is heard.*)

DORIS: Who's gone, Ray? Who?

RAY: She is . . . my girl . . . my girl on "The Avenue."

DORIS: She'll be back.

RAY: No, she's not. She won't be back.

THE POLICEMAN: I have to warn you, Mr. Dawson, that anything you say can be used against you.[6]

CLIFF, *genuine:* Yes, sir.

(BEATRICE *turns the corner.*)

RAY: Never . . . she'll never be back.

CLIFF: Lou . . . Lou, I want one thing from you . . .

(LOU *looks at him, then at* RAY.)

LOU: He's all I got left, Cliff . . . He's all the family I got left.

(*He looks at her until she places her head upon his chest and sobs uncontrollably.*)

BEATRICE, *walking up, to* MISS MINNY *in her window:* What's the trouble, Miss Minny?

MISS MINNY: Ohhh, somethin' terrible, girl . . . I can't tell you now.

CLIFF, *handcuffed to the* POLICEMAN: It's your world, Ray . . . It's yours, boy . . . Go on out there and claim it.

(*Sirens nearer. Lights down and music rises.*)

MISS MINNY: Come down tomorrow for tea, Beatrice, dear, and I'll tell you all about it.

BEATRICE: All right, Miss Minny. The Lord bless you tonight.

MISS MINNY: He will, dear . . . 'cause he works in mysterious ways.

BEATRICE, *starting off:* Amen!

(*Lights down to blackness and a commercial begins on the radio.*)

Curtain.

---

6. Anything you say can be used against you: This phrasing is an anachronism, as the Supreme Court case that mandated informing a criminal suspect of his or her rights (the so-called Miranda rights) wasn't decided until 1966.

This is arguably Bullins's greatest work, one that bears comparison to Anton Chekhov's The Cherry Orchard. *Like Chekhov, Bullins is interested in how love can be expressed in a "cemetery of human failure and class arrogance" (as he puts it in "Should Black Actors Play Chekhov?" reprinted in this volume). With this play, part of his* Twentieth Century Cycle, *Bullins perfected a dramatic structure that he had been working on since* The Electronic Nigger, *a structure also found in* In the Wine Time, Goin' a Buffalo, *and* The Taking of Miss Janie. *The seemingly disjointed encounters; interrupted conversations; bawdy humor; sudden, sharp violence; self-search soliloquies and moments of intense intimacy are typical any time a group of longtime hard partyers gather together—and it's captured perfectly here. However, the apparent chaos of this "party play" is only superficial. This is a "conscious party," where one finds both meticulously crafted emotional movement and elegantly propulsive verbal structure.* The Fabulous Miss Marie *builds dramatic tension not from plot or significant events but from moments, gestures, and words arranged with the rhythmic aplomb of a Nina Simone or Big Joe Williams. It was first produced at the New Lafayette Theatre, New York, in 1968 and first published in* The New Lafayette Theatre Presents, *edited by Ed Bullins (New York: Anchor, 1974).*

The Fabulous Miss Marie

(1971)

The people in this play are Black.

TIME: *Early 1960s; the past, etc.*

PLACE: MARIE HORTON's *house—a single-story, two-bedroom bungalow in Los Angeles, near Pico and Western.*[1]

---

1. Los Angeles, near Pico and Western: The author explains: "The 'Wilshire' was a haven for 'wannabe' upscale working-class blacks . . . though in the late 60s it was very mixed."

Stage black. Slowly, a bizarre Christmas tree lights up. Its bulbs wink and glare colorfully in contrast to the shadows and blackness of the rest of the stage. A small dog yaps abruptly offstage, then quiets. The tree commands the area for some moments, then a Rhythm 'n' Blues number of the period rises from a cheap, portable, imitation-alligator-covered phonograph.[2] A television set lights up without sound, its picture out of focus at first, then clearing to show a white face smiling and speaking wordlessly. Giggles in the dark. The dog sounds offstage.

A VOICE: Damn! (*Silence except for the music*)

(*Lights of the tree and television show figures on stage*)

MARIE'S VOICE, *impatient:* C'mon, Bud!

(*More giggles and the whirring sound of a film projector*)

TONI'S VOICE: Damn, Bud . . . Little-ass Whitie could have done better than you.

(*Dog yaps*)

RUTH'S VOICE: You hear her tellin' you to let her in so she can take care of business, can't ya?

(*A screen lights up feebly, at first, then the film begins. It is apparent from the start that it is a pornographic film. There is a sound track of heavy lovemaking pervading the space, mixed with the other mechanical and human sounds. If the technology of the cinema proves too difficult to negotiate for the Black Theatre group that does the play, then a framed scrim, lighted from behind, can serve as the movie screen, with actors playing there, their silhouettes simulating the lewd and obscene performances. Female laughter and giggles of delight.*)

MARIE, *giggles:* Ohhh . . . gawd, Horton! . . . Ohhh . . . this is awful, Bill. Heee heeee . . . ha ha ha . . . Hey, Mr. Horton! . . . this the best you can find, huh? . . . This old sad thing is as about as sexy as my grand-mammy's drawers.

RUTH: Shhh . . . quiet, Marie . . . I can't hear the slurpin' . . .

(MARIE *goes into a fit of giggling.*)

BILL, *drunk, stretched out upon the floor:* Hey, Marie . . . Hey, stuff . . . I brought you back a dirty movie . . . didn't I? . . . Heeyyyy . . . that's a dirty movie, ain't it?

MARIE, *giggles:* Oh, stop it . . . Bill. Ha ha . . . you're killing me.

RUTH: Slurp . . . slurp. . . slurp . . .

MARIE, *screams and laughs:* Oh . . . Ruthie . . . Ha ha ha . . . hee hee . . .

---

2. Phonograph: Machine that plays music recorded on vinyl disks.

(*As the television glare lowers to blackness and the music from the phonograph drifts away to silence, the lights rise to show* MARIE HORTON's *Christmas party.*)

TONI: I don't know what you're laughin' at, Marie. That's the vulgarest thing that I've ever seen.

BUD: You're just sayin' that, baby . . . (*Winks*) Wait till I get you home tonight and try out some of that French kissin' stuff on ya.

TONI: Bud! . . . Have you lost your mind? . . . Man . . . you better kiss me like you civilized or don't even get to the first pucker.

(MARIE *is sprawled upon a couch.* BILL HORTON *lies drunkenly upon the floor.* ART GARRISON *is in an alcoholic stupor upon the floor, his back propped up by the couch.* RUTH *and* TONI *stand, peering at the movie screen.* BUD *operates the projector.*)

MARIE: Awww . . . Toni, girl . . . You so crazy.

RUTH: Sho is.

TONI: Why, Ruth . . . I would never say anything like that to you.

RUTH: Well, you know I was kiddin', Toni.

TONI: But you said it anyway.

RUTH: Well it wasn't nothin' . . . Marie says far worse things to you than . . .

TONI, *cuts:* Now, I wasn't talkin' about . . .

MARIE, *cuts:* Hey . . . you two ole hens! . . . Stop all that cacklin'.

BILL, *slurs:* Damn . . . Marie . . . nobody can say anything . . .

MARIE, *jovial:* Shut up, Horton . . . man . . . you so drunk. Get up from there and fix me a drink.

BILL, *groggy:* When I fix you a drink, I'll be fixin' us a drink.

TONI: You gonna let him talk to you like that, Marie?

RUTH: Sho she is.

BUD: I thought you folks were gonna look at this movie?

MARIE, *shrugs:* Well . . . Mr. Horton pays the bills . . . and if he don't want to get me a drink . . . well . . . the ole red nigger don't have to do nothin' for yours truly . . . Nawh . . . nobody don't have to do nary a thing for Miss Marie . . . Miss Marie is quite independent . . . Hummp!

BILL, *groans:* Ohhhh . . . Marie . . .

MARIE: Shit! . . . I still want me a Scotch on the rocks, man.

TONI: Turn that filthy thing off, Bud! Nobody wants to look at that.

(*Dog yaps.*)

MARIE: Awww . . . c'mon, Toni . . . Let's look at the old dull thing.

TONI: You should turn that filthy shit off, Marie. Look at it.

RUTH: You lookin' at it so hard yourself, Toni . . . Why you want it off?

TONI: Now, Ruthie . . . you can't say that I'm lookin' at that junk seriously . . . can you?

BUD: Yeah.

TONI: Oh, keep quiet, Bud! (*Pulls out the power cord to the movie projector. It grinds to a stop with a mechanical groan. If actors are used behind a scrim, they make the noise of their being unplugged. Lights change. The dog yaps.*)

TONI, *ladylike:* Marie, honey . . . why don't you let that goddamn dog in?

RUTH: She can't . . .

BUD: Can't?

TONI: Bud!

MARIE: Nawh . . . she's in heat. She's gotta keep her little white ass out in the back yard.

BILL: Ha ha ha . . . and she pees on Marie's new rugs.

TONI: Gawd . . . leave the little bitch out then. I wouldn't have her wetting on my new nylon carpets.

(*Lights change. Sprawled upon the couch,* MARIE *slips her slipper from her foot, lets it drop to the carpet, and, with her stockinged toe, nudges* ART's *head, leaning beside the end of the couch.*)

MARIE, *teases* ART: Hey, you . . .

RUTH: Hey, Marie . . . let him sleep.

BUD: Ha ha . . . don't wake him . . . let him slept . . . ha ha . . .

TONI: Damn . . . I forgot that guy was still here.

MARIE, *pulls her leg back:* Hey . . . don't you hear what I'm sayin' to you? . . . I want you to get me a drink . . . Scotch on the rocks, baby. Ambassador Scotch . . . my brand . . . you know where it is, don't you? . . . And take out your coffee cup on your way out.

BUD: He knows the Scotch's out in the kitchen . . . Ha ha . . . out in the kitchen . . . to your right . . . beside the 'frigerator . . . Hey . . . remember when everybody thought that Frigidaire meant all 'frigerators?

MARIE, *rises:* Hey . . . Art . . . hey! You gonna get me my drink, huh?

BILL, *groggy, half conscious:* I'll take a V.O. and water . . . champ.

(ART *stirs. Bleary-eyed, he looks up at* MARIE *standing over him and he smiles drunkenly.*)

MARIE: Oh, now you're awake . . . 'bout time. Man . . . you were snoring to beat the band.

(BILL *falls asleep and begins snoring.* TONI *giggles as* BUD *whispers into her ear and tries to feel her butt. The lights change, and sensual melody comes from the phonograph, and the TV comes dimly on as the lights change color. The dog yaps outside. All figures drift into the shadows except for* ART, MARIE, *and* BILL, *who snores upon the floor just beyond the spill of the confined light.*)

MARIE: You've slept so long . . . baby. And you've missed the movie and my guests have gone an' everything. Look at ole Bill over there . . . drunk to the world . . . and it's so quiet except for our breathing . . . I want me a Scotch on the rocks, baby. Ambassador . . . Scotch . . . my brand . . . And while you're up, honey . . . ha ha ha . . . see how the V.O. and the ale is holdin' out. Bill will be thirsty when he wakes up . . . and Ruth'll be wantin' her ale when she comes over.

ART, *drowsy:* Huh?

MARIE: Now . . . Art . . . (*She stands, moves around in front of him, reaches down, and pulls her fingers through his shaggy head of hair. He takes her hand, climbs to his feet, and kisses* MARIE *passionately for a long moment. Catches breath.*) Oh . . . Art . . . not here, baby. (*He kisses her again.*) Let's go into the bedroom, Art . . . Yes, I know that Bill is stone-cold drunk and it's impossible to wake him . . . but let's go in the bedroom anyway . . . Doin' it in front of him makes me feel creepy . . . Uhhggg . . . Oh . . . don't kiss me so hard, baby . . . Remember . . . I'm a soft, tender woman . . . ha ha . . . well taken care of . . . not plump, ya understand . . . ha ha . . . not even pleasingly . . . but first you have to get me a drink, Art. My motor won't turn over too tough with a dry battery, honey . . . You know what I drink, don't you? . . . Ambassador . . . Ambassador Scotch . . . top shelf . . . imported . . . yeah, that's what I drink . . . yeah . . . that's what you have to bring Marie Horton to clean her pipes . . . umhmmmm . . . Miss Marie . . . takes it on the rocks, honey . . . that's right . . . you better believe it! (ART *withdraws into the shadows. The music plays, and the lights and TV's glare throw strange patterns across the stage.*) Whatchou say? . . . I been drinkin' Scotch for quite some time now . . . ever since I got accustomed to tryin' to live like I would like to become accustomed to . . . ha ha . . . damn right, I do. I used to live in Buffalo, ya know . . . I'm really from Pittsburgh, you understand . . . but I used to live in Buffalo with my granny . . . just like Wanda lives here with me . . . but God knows I wasn't stupid like Wandie . . . God knows I wasn't. Damn . . . I was a slick little chick. That's when I started bein' called "Miss Marie." . . . It used to snow real deep up in Buffalo and I had my little red boots that I used to tip 'round in . . . and everybody used to say: "There goes little cute Miss Marie . . . down to get a bucket of beer for her Granny." And that's where I'd be on my way to . . . and I'd get there and get inside where it was warm by the coal stove and blow my breath into my hands and take my bucket around to the back end of the bar . . . that's where they filled your bucket . . . back 'round the side there . . . back in those days. And it ain't had nothin' to do with discrimination . . . I'm from the

North . . . and I ain't never known anything 'bout no discrimination . . . I always did have my freedom . . . Yes, sir . . . Miss Marie will tell you . . . I want to thank you. (*During the remainder of* MARIE's *speech,* BILL *rises from the shadows and enters a lighted area, opposite* MARIE, *and begins a shuffling dance.* BILL *does the dance of a 1930s negro showman, the Black Bottom, the Soft-Shoe, the Buck 'n' Wing; he appears a young man at the start of his dance but toward the end of* MARIE's *monologue, he becomes the man he is on Christmas Day, 1961. Meanwhile, the Christmas tree glows and pulsates dimly to the rhythm of the scene, as the television casts its mute image outward and the phonograph plays softly.*) If I couldn't have my Scotch every day, honey . . . I'd quit! I'd just give it up, baby. Nawh . . . I ain't kiddin' . . . Hummp. And it better be Ambassador, too. Those old cows in my clubs would swear that I was slippin' if they saw me sippin' a Miller's High Life . . . Wouldn't they? . . . Yeah . . . sure would. Bad as me havin' no fur coat. Marie Horton . . . without even a stole. Ohhh . . . that Bill . . . he says I don't need a fur in Los Angeles. Sheet . . . I've had a fur ever since my granny gave me my first one when I was nine . . . 'cept now that we out here. You know I'm president of three negro women's clubs . . . really the founder as well as president. And I have to keep myself together . . . or what would the girls say? Hell, I know what they'd say . . . They'd say, "Who does Miss Marie" . . . that's what they call me . . . "Miss Marie" . . . "Who does Miss Marie think she is?" they'd say. . . "She hasn't even got a fur coat," they'd say . . . "Every time you see her she's in that old red print dress . . . with her fat gut stickin' out so far it looks like the middle button's gonna pop off," they would say. "Probably needs to wear her house dress, poor dear, with that little bit of money Bill brings in," they would say . . . If I stood for them 'n let them . . . Shoot . . . I ain't never gonna let them say nothin' about Marie Horton. Nawh suh! That's for somebody else to tolerate . . . not Miss Marie. We been out here in L.A. for twelve years now . . . Bill and me. Came out a couple years after the war. And it's groovy, baby . . . nothin' but high life. Bill makes three times as much . . . maybe four . . . as he made back East. He used to dance . . . before he went out and had to get a job. Yeah. I don't know how anybody can stay back there in the cold. Give me L.A. any day, baby. It's got everything . . . And the men . . . the men . . . makes a girl like me drool all over her cocktail frock . . . 'cause this is the place to keep an old hen scratchin' like a spring bird. Ooooo . . . yeah. In the warm California sun. (*She does a large bump and grind, snaps her fingers, and humps the audience as* WANDA *enters* BILL's *area of light and is snatched by the hand and is made to reluctantly dance with the now drunk man.* MARIE *grinds, grimacing as if during orgasm.*) You can take it if you can make it . . . 'cause you ain't gonna break it . . . yeah. Miss Marie wants to thank you.

BILL *and* MARIE, *stop still in their pools of light and speak together:* Bill brings home two hundred stone cold dollars a week . . . to me, Miss Marie . . . and puts it in my hand. And the tips he makes parkin' cars out to the studio in Beverly Hills is more than that. We make almost as much as some colored doctors make . . . 'n we spend it too. 'Cause it's party time every day at Miss Marie's house.

WANDA, *tries to pull away from* BILL; *he pulls her back:* Ahhh . . . Uncle Bill . . . I'm tired.

(*Lights come up. Christmas tree lights dim and dissolve into the background with the TV. The dog yaps outside.*)

BILL, *dances:* Heeyy . . . Wandie . . . you ain't gonna let your ole uncle out-dance you . . . are ya? (*Does high kick and step.*) Whheee . . . swing it, girl . . . Oeeeee . . . yeah . . .

(*Lights up on* RUTH, TONI, *and* BUD.)

WANDA, *dancing:* Ahhh . . . Uncle Bill . . .

MARIE: Bill! . . . Hey, Bill . . . leave that broken-down little broad alone. She ain't nothin' but a young girl . . . hummmp . . . but she acts like she's got an iceberg up her twat . . .

(WANDA *holds down her skirt as she is flung about by* BILL.)

WANDA: Ohh . . . Aunt Marie . . .

TONI: Bill . . . why don't you leave that child alone . . . You can see that she don't want to dance with you.

BUD: Well, I don't care if she don't want to dance with ole Bill . . . as long as I got nex' dance. (BUD *begins to do the Twist and moves into* BILL *and* WANDA's *area and dances with* WANDA.)

MARIE: Do it, Bud . . . What's that new dance that you and Wandie does so good?

RUTH: It's called the Twist . . . Marie.

MARIE: Ohh . . . well . . . Bud sho can do it . . .

TONI: Sho can . . . chile . . . (*The telephone begins to ring.* MARIE *dances a fast rumble to the phone, while* BUD *and* WANDA *do the Twist and* BILL *Soft-shoes and Buck 'n' Wings almost in the shadows.* TONI *watches, tapping her foot. The dog yaps.* ART *enters, carrying a tray of drinks.*) Well . . . here's our boy . . . Art.

(*On her way to the telephone,* MARIE *sweeps a drink from the tray, almost upsetting the mess in* ART's *hands.*)

ART, *catching balance:* Hey! . . .

MARIE, *answers phone, a high, false, young voice:* Hey . . . what's happenin'?

TONI, *to* ART: Did you bring my Southern Comfort?

MARIE: Oh, Bea . . . how ya doin', girl?

ART, *to* TONI: Ahuh . . . (*He hands her a drink.*)

BILL: Mine's V.O. and water, Art. That's Canadian . . . ya know . . .

(*The television lights up.* ART *serves* BILL *and* BUD, *and is politely refused by* WANDA. *The dog yaps outside. In a lighted area at back, an actor pantomimes what is supposed to be happening on the television screen. There is the negro evening news announcer, in bow tie and serious face, wordlessly mouthing about the dreary events of the day.*)

MARIE, *on phone:* Yeah, girl . . . we still partyin' . . . yeah, this is some Christmas. Yeah . . . really, Bea. We started at Shadow's place two days ago, girl. I really wanted to wait to at least Christmas Eve, honey . . . but those niggers couldn't wait to swill some liquor and call themselves having a good time . . . Sure she's with him! . . . yeah! . . . Ruth's still with that nigger, child . . . Ahuhnnn . . . it should have been somethin' . . . Ahuhnnn . . . would be still over to Shadow's, but you know how he is . . . wouldn't give Ruth a moment, girl . . . Ha ha . . . that man is the biggest cockhound in town . . . Gawd! . . . Didn't give anybody a chance . . . ha ha . . . bad enough for Ruthie it was her old man who forever had a sweaty . . . and I mean sweaty! . . . wet palm on her booty . . . but we other girls had to suffer the consequences . . . NO! . . . Nawh, whore . . . don't put that off on me . . . he ain't my type . . . none of ours . . . ha ha . . . not even Ruth's . . . Heee ha ha ha . . . I want to thank you, chick . . . him and Bill . . . ha ha ha . . . Toni calls them the Gold Dust Twins, honey . . . Yeah! . . . Bill's still fucken' that funky ole white bitch, girl. Yeah . . . sho is corny . . . He swears to me that it's all a product of my imagination . . . Yes, he does . . . but he don't know I know he's got that little old red baby by her . . . I hear tell it looks like a wrinkled-up pink baboon . . . yeah . . . Ha! . . . Iris tell me that (*whiny voice*) "Maybe you should have a baby for Bill." . . . WHOOP! . . . hee ha ha ha . . . ain't that the limit, Bea? . . . The only thing Bill Horton's gettin' from me is a hard time if he don't bring some money in here, and I mean some money . . . Ha! . . . The Gold Dust Twins[3] . . . but

---

3. Gold Dust Twins: Characters created by E. W. Kemble in 1902 for Fairbank's Gold Dust Washing Powder. The tutu-clad, coal-black twin toddlers are one of the most popular trade images in U.S. history. In general use, the phrase refers to an inseparable pair that achieves miraculous success.

Bill's the drunky half, girl. Shadow's dizzy . . . an' Bill's drunky, honey
. . . I want to thank ya. (*She snaps her fingers and wiggles to the music and
the rhythm of her voice.*) . . . Yeah, preach, baby. Tell it like it is . . . ha
ha ha . . . ooooeee . . . you a wicked heifer, woman . . . Geezus! . . . what
Ruth and I got to go through, girl . . .

WANDA: But you should do somethin' . . . somethin' . . . anything not to fall
into a grave of middle-age remorse . . .

BILL: What you say, Wandie?

MARIE, *to* WANDA: Get out of that spotlight, broad . . . this is my story,
understand?

WANDA: Oh, nothin' . . . Uncle Bill . . . nothin' . . . and I'm sorry, Aunt
Marie.

BILL, *cutting a fancy step:* Wheee! . . . See that, Marie! . . . See that!

MARIE: Child . . . Bill's here really cuttin' the fool now . . . ha ha . . . you
should just see him with his ole timey self.

(*The TV news announcer has disappeared and has been replaced by figures simulating a non-violent civil rights demonstration of early sixties' vintage. They pray,
they kneel, they appeal, they sing "We Shall Overcome" respectfully, then they are
beaten mercilessly.*)

WANDA: Oh . . . look . . . look y'all . . . the civil righters.

TONI: The civil who? . . .

BUD: Rights, sweet cake . . . rights.

RUTH, *in her cups:* What they rightin' about?

BILL, *dancing:* Hey, Marie . . . looka here, stuff . . . watch this one . . . wheee
. . . C'mon, Wandie . . .

WANDA: Nawh, Uncle Bill . . . Nawh . . . I want to watch the Freedom
Marchers.

MARIE: Bea . . . they got some fools on this television that ain't got no sense,
girl . . . They gettin' their natural ass kicked by some crackers, chile
. . . big ugly-lookin' rednecks.

(ART *returns with more drinks, sets them down, and takes one. He stands apart
from the group, watching.* GAFNEY *enters.*)

ART: Niggers always look so cool because they don't want anybody to know
how bad things are.

GAFNEY: Just as I thought. These people are drinking and carousing.

WANDA: He's in my class, Art . . . I know you and Aunt Marie and Uncle
Bill don't like Gafney, but try to be nice to him, huh?

MARIE, *still on telephone:* Shucks, child . . . Freedom Marchers . . . huhnnn
. . . I already got my freedom . . . have always had it. I don't need no

raggedy-ass niggers beggin' and moanin' and gettin' their behinds whipped for my freedom, honey . . . Nawh, sir, Miss Marie got what she's got . . . and that spells "freedom," baby.

WANDA: But you don't understand . . . Aunt Marie, you don't understand. It's not about what you have or what I have, but what we all have, need, and want as Black people.

GAFNEY: Teach, sister! . . . Tell 'em where it's at!

(*The dog yaps. Lights change. The TV images fade, and all on stage disappear into shadows except* BILL.)

BILL: It ain't been a bad life. Hell no, not a bad one. It could have been worse, ya know . . . Yeah, chief . . . it could have been a buster . . . wow . . . But I met Marie, see . . . and . . . (*in dim, tinted light,* MARIE *appears, swaying and humming to soft music, cradling an imaginary bundle in her arms as if it were a baby*) it started straightenin' out for me from then on. Until now. Which ain't so bad, actually . . . Me and Marie been makin' it close to sixteen years. We make it pretty well together. Yeah, that's my ole lady, Marie . . . Hardly ever get hassled by the world. She keeps the kinda house I like to live in . . . and we drink and party together and like some of the same people . . . It could have been worse . . . I coulda stayed in Pittsburgh and kept on pluggin' away at nuttin' . . . but me and Marie came out here. Out here where the sun almost never stops shining, where palms wag above the dog-days boulevards . . . yeah . . . it coulda been worse . . . We coulda broken up . . . yeah . . . we coulda, but we stuck it out. I guess our most serious hassle was when we was three-four years into our thing. (*The lights dim on* MARIE.) I usta run numbers some back in Pittsburgh[4] . . . and I got busted. Yeah, I got busted. Got sixty days . . . which wasn't so bad, ya understand . . . but bad enough. And I got out in thirty-three. Don't know how. Wasn't good time or nothin' like that. I forget now. Probably my boss, Big Time, gave somebody some juice downtown. (MARIE's *face is seen— startled, apprehensive.*) I was one of his best boys. And I come home to where Marie and I were stayin' . . .

MARIE, *nervous, angry:* Big Time! . . . nigger, why didn't you tell me that you put in a fix for Bill? He's home and here we are—caught! Damn! I don't care if you thought he wasn't gettin' out until after the weekend. Gon' man, you got a second to get out the back door before he sees

---

4. Run numbers: The "numbers" was a lottery-style game, illegal though popular. The "runner" took customer picks, ran those picks back to headquarters for processing, and delivered to winners. It was replaced by state-run lotteries starting in the late 1960s.

you. I can handle him . . . Don't worry . . . I can take care of Bill Horton . . . Just get your ass out of here, ya hear?

BILL: . . . and I was so happy I hollared out, "HEY, STUFF . . . HEY, MARIE!"
. . .

MARIE, *aside:* Which saved my dark behind . . .

BILL: . . . and I came through my front door . . . A dim light was on in the
back . . . (*A black figure is portrayed upon the movie screen: it is seen tiptoe-
ing with clothes and shoes in hand, then sneaking with exaggerated movements, then disappears from the screen.*) I saw a shadow. "Marie?" I called.
Then there was some movement and noise. The bathroom door opening and closing. Footsteps in the kitchen and then the soft slam of the
back door . . . After Marie came out of the bathroom, we had our worse
argument . . . We nearly busted up right then and there . . . The bitterness lasted in our lives for over a year . . . She never did tell me who
it was. Said it was my dirty mind, my nasty, jailbird imagination and
the drinks I had had before I got home . . . But I know my woman . . .
and now I don't blame her too much. There are just some things about
a woman that you understand if you've been together long enough and
are tryin' to make it. But that was an argument we had . . . whew . . . I
almost hit her . . . Yeah, I almost tore her head off . . . But I didn't.
There's something about hitting a woman that means the end. When
you raise your hand to a woman that you love and hurt her that way
. . . well, somethin' just goes out of the relationship . . . Do you understand what I mean?

MARIE: Yeah . . . you mean that you better not think of crackin' your
knuckles too close to Miss Marie . . . if you know what's good for your
weather-beaten buns.

BILL: Now, if I were to strike Marie . . . well, there'd be an awful row . . .
She's spoiled, you know. But it would blow over . . . on the surface . . .
after a while. But something would be gone . . . it would be long gone
. . . and perhaps that's the thing that has made this thing between us
work, ya know. And I don't want to lose that . . . Nawh . . . it ain't been
a bad life . . . and I ain't about to mess it up, if I can help it. Not for love
or hate or a white woman . . . or nuthin'. HEY, MARIE! . . . HEY,
STUFF! . . . FILL UP MY GLASS AGAIN. YOU KNOW MY DRINK,
BABY. YOU KNOW IT!

(BILL *and* MARIE *fade away; lights alter.* ART *steps forward as the dog yaps, then
quiets.*)

ART: I can dig where you comin' from, chief, but you're wastin' your
breath.

GAFNEY: You would think so, wouldn't you? For you, this is the best environment that you could have?

WANDA, *from the shadows:* Can't you two try and understand one another?

ART: Hey . . . Gafney . . . if you gonna be talkin' to me, friend, you gonna have to start talkin' like the rest of us. Some of those words you use are too much, man.

GAFNEY: Yes . . . that's what you say but you can't fool me none, Art Garrison. You make out like you don't know nothin', that you're just a nigger off the streets like everybody else . . . or like lots of people would like to be like . . .

ART: No kiddin' . . . tell me more.

GAFNEY: But I got you down pat, you . . . you . . .

WANDA, *from the shadows:* Please don't say it . . .

GAFNEY: . . . YOU CON MAN! You just do that dumb act to fool people. You just around here waitin' to take advantage of these poor Black people . . . Why . . . why I've even seen you taking night courses at City College!

ART: You know it all, don't you, Gafney?

GAFNEY: Yes, I know all about you . . . and you know what? (*Pause*) You know what? (*Pause*) You know . . . I could tell you something?

ART: You could, huh?

GAFNEY: Yes, I could. (*Pause*) I could tell you something that you wouldn't even believe. That hardly no person . . . Black or white . . . would believe.

ART: You can, huh?

GAFNEY: Yes, I can tell you something about me, Art Garrison . . . If I really thought for a moment that you could understand.

ART: I might.

WANDA, *from the shadows:* So would I. Gafney . . . try me.

GAFNEY: Now nobody knows this . . . that means nobody . . . except people who don't matter to me anymore.

ART: Ummhmmmm . . .

GAFNEY: Now nobody knows this, Art.

WANDA, *from the shadows:* Nobody knows . . .

ART: Yeah, man . . . nobody knows it.

GAFNEY, *proudly, after deep breath:* I come from the streets, too . . . I wasn't born in a well-to-do colored neighborhood in Atlanta, Georgia . . . and was brought to L.A. when I was a baby . . . No, brother . . . I come from East Saint Louis.

ART: No kiddin'.

GAFNEY: Yes, brother Art . . . I am a Soul Brother, too.

ART: Well . . . this is really news . . . HEY, WANDIE! . . . HEY! GAFNEY
SAYS THAT HE'S A STREET NIGGER! . . . HEY, WANDA, DID YOU
HEAR THAT? . . . GAFNEY SAYS THAT HE'S A STREET NIGGER!

GAFNEY, *venomous:* Art Garrison . . . you're nothing! You're nothing, Art
Garrison. Nothing!

MARIE, *off:* Art . . . don't just leave your empty coffee cup around my house,
nigger . . . pick it up . . . try and help me keep my place nice.

(*Lights and shadow and music alter;* ART, *alone, speaks.*)

ART: I'm on my ass, man. Down, down down . . . I mean down, brother.
And my spirit is down. Way down. Down so low I can't fly . . . not
right now. So I'm layin' . . . yeah . . . with this bitch and her ole man.
It sure is somethin' else. Wouldn't have believed it if I hadn't seen it
. . . Whew . . . but I'm takin' care of business, ah little taste. Got this
ole sister, Marie, jacked up. And she's keepin' her ole man cool. She
tells him that I'm suffering from a bad situation. And I am. Just got out
of the slam. Just gettin' myself together. I stay here and eat and sleep
and do whatever they want me to do, which is mainly gettin' drinks for
them and drivin' them around in their car. Just light work . . . except
for the action I give the ole girl when her daddy Bill is out of sight or
out like a light . . . (MARIE *appears.*) Oh oh . . . here she comes again.
(*To music, they kiss, embrace, and dance intimately, then break. She leaves.*)
See what I mean? She's got heavy and hot, hot pants for me . . . if she
wore them. Nawh . . . she doesn't . . . nawh, nawh . . . I'm not kiddin'.
Swear I'm not. Marie Horton don't wear no drawers. Not one stitch
. . . Says they slow her down, yeah. She's a pistol, man. But it was lucky
I hooked up with her and her ole man, Bill. 'Specially now that I can't
do nothin' for me. Wow . . . a broad can really get you down. I'm
comin' off one of those bad broad trips myself . . . but that's another
play, right, sport? But I got to get my ass up off the ground. Yeah, I got
to make it. I got places to go, things to do, people to see and myself to
be, yeah. Gotta clear my head. Get this pain in my brain in gear. Gotta
get Garrison in gear. And this is the place to make it for the moment.
Good grease, man.[5] More drinks than I can stand to drink. And then
there's Miss Marie . . . and maybe there's her little niece . . . Wanda.

(*Lights alter. Dog yaps off.* MARIE *and* BILL *are seen.*)

MARIE: Did you have to take her around our friends, Bill? Did you have to
take that white woman where we go?

---

5. Grease: Food.

BILL: I was drunk, Marie . . . High as a kite . . . It shouldn't have happened, I know, but I just couldn't help it.

MARIE, *resigned:* No . . . I guess you couldn't . . . You done so much to me over the years . . . I guess doin' just one more thing like this don't really matter.

BILL: But, baby, if we could . . . if we could . . .

MARIE: Well, I can't . . . you saw to that, didn't you?

BILL: . . . If we could have only had kids, Marie.

MARIE: It was the abortion that did it. It was that . . . that damn quack that you got me that messed me up for life.

BILL: I never wanted you to do it, Marie.

MARIE: It was your fault, Bill Horton! It was your fault! You got me pregnant!

BILL: But I never wanted you to get that operation. I never wanted you to get rid of the baby.

MARIE: But the other one went okay . . . Nothing happened to the first one.

BILL: Your grandmother saw to that.

MARIE: Granny had her place in the community . . . Granny couldn't have me do something terrible like that and ruin our good family name.

BILL: But you should have never gotten rid of our baby, Marie.

MARIE: But I could have never had a baby by that ole nigger from The Hill[6] . . . I couldn't do that to Granny, Bill . . .

BILL: It would have been so nice if . . .

MARIE: If you just hadn't told our friends . . . I would have let you keep her quietly . . . as long as you kept up my house.

BILL: I was drunk . . . drunk as a skunk . . . and I wanted the world to know that I could have kids . . . even if she was white.

MARIE: You shouldn't have gotten me pregnant . . . You shouldn't have been younger than me and got me pregnant . . . and give in to me and gotten the operation for me like Granny had . . . and married me 'cause you ruined me . . . That's right, Bill, we wouldn't have been married now . . . and out of love.

BILL: Sometimes when I get drunk, I'm sorry afterwards . . . sometimes . . .

(*Lights and shapes alter; the Christmas tree glows from the darkness. The dog yaps outside.*)

---

6. The Hill: Pittsburgh's Hill District was one of the most dynamic, powerful black communities in the United States from the 1930s to the 1950s. This "Crossroads of the World" was noted for its bustling club scene, its Negro League baseball team, its newspaper (the *Courier*), and the stylish dress and manners of its residents and visitors.

TONI, *off:* Why don't that damn mutt keep quiet?

RUTH, *off:* Whitie just wants something to eat . . . Marie'll feed her soon.

TONI, *off:* I sure as hell hope so, honey . . . that's a noisy little bitch.

RUTH, *off:* Marie's gotta wait until Bill gives her some shoppin' money . . . she only feeds her dog steak.

TONI, *off:* Sheet . . .

MARCO: You don't know me. I just got here . . . My name's Marco . . . Marco Polo Henderson . . . now ain't that a handle? My folks really hung one on me . . . I sure won't get confused with a lot of other niggers. 'Cause my name is strange. And I'm a pretty yellow nigger, anyway, with curly curly hair that all the little black mamas like to run their hands over. And the white bitches speak to me in my tongue, too, baby . . . and it ain't forked, dig? Nor is it cold, hmmm . . . ha ha ha . . . Yeah, man, if I only had that piece of paper. If I only had that degree . . . (*During* MARCO's *speech,* BILL, ART, STEVE BENSON, *and* BUD *swing and sway together, harmonizing Christmas carols.* GAFNEY *stands to one side with folded arms and impatiently taps his foot until* WANDA *comes near enough for him to corner and wordlessly exhort to her his truths. She patiently hangs on his every word while attempting to listen to* MARCO) . . . Damn . . . I could get out of this chickenshit level of existence . . . Man, my ass is on the ground . . . Wow, my ass eats grass if this ain't a bad scene for me, Jim. All I got to show for nothin' is a little-ass chickenshit government check to go to school on . . . If it wasn't for my gettin' disability from the VA[7] for my asthma, I would really be up shit creek without proper means of locomotion . . . Wow, my dick would be in the sand, man. I'd just be humping along, my balls draggin' . . . if I wasn't a fuckin' invalid. Yeah! That's right, boss. Couldn't do nothin'. Now they expect me to finish this last year on my degree with no dough. The court's after me. My ole lady's screamin' for support . . . Support, shit! . . . She knows I can't pay no support for Adrienne and Keith. I gotta finish school. Why did she wait till now to start this shit? Been outta the service for almost three years. No word from her. She was doin' alright . . . and the kids were so much hers that I couldn't even see them if I wanted to. Didn't even know where she was for a while. Then, bam! . . . Before I knew it, I was in court. She wants all kinds of money, even back money for the times she didn't get no money when I didn't have no money after my service checks stopped. Sheet . . . she's at the other end of the state and got me sneakin' around

---

7. VA: Veterans Administration.

like Robert F. Williams[8] . . . Yeah, there might be a nab behind every bush, man. What if they bust me at school? And this dizzy-ass bitch I'm messin' with, Wanda, ain't nothin' but a drag . . . Damn . . . how chickenshit . . . what kinda goddamn luck do I have, anyway? If I only had that piece of paper, man. I could split and get me a job somewhere . . . but, man, I dig California . . . I really dig it . . . yeah yeah yeah . . . in the warm California sun.

(*As the carolers disintegrate into shadowy figures,* ART *steps away from the forms and joins* WANDA *and* GAFNEY.)

ART: What cha doin' these days, Wandie?

WANDA: Nothin' . . . I was goin' to school . . . but I'm not even doin' that now. Aunt Marie's on me to get a job.

MARIE, *momentarily appears:* You better believe it! She's gonna get a job or my name ain't what yawhl know it to be. Wandie! . . . You gonna stop your funky ass from comin' in here with a wet twat after stayin' out all night . . . layin' up with Marco!

WANDA: Ohhh . . . Aunt Marie.

(MARIE *disappears.*)

GAFNEY, *to* ART: Yes . . . I was just informing the sister here that there was many positive things she could be doing with herself . . .

ART, *ignores* GAFNEY: I know of a little job that you can have, Wandie.

GAFNEY: Day care centers are always in need of young, energetic, and sensitive people to work with the children.

ART: You could bring home maybe two . . . three hundred bucks a week, Wandie.

WANDA: I could?

GAFNEY: And there are tutorial programs . . . in the ghetto . . . mainly voluntary, of course . . .

ART: I got a buddy who's got this masseur parlor over on Crenshaw.

WANDA: But, Art . . . I don't know.

GAFNEY: Wanda! I believe that would be completely wrong for you.

ART: Easy man . . . I'm talkin' to the girl, okay . . . Listen, Wanda, you don't know how to massage nobody . . . and you don't need to know. My friend needs somebody straight-lookin' to front for his business in the

---

8. Robert F. Williams (1925–96): African-American Civil Rights and Black Power activist. He advocated armed resistance and international solidarity against white racism and was forced into exile after being framed for kidnapping.

back. All you'd have to do is welcome the chumps, check them out, and refer them to the people in the back . . . Oh, yeah . . . and answer the phone.

WANDA: Art, you couldn't think . . .

ART: But he'd dig your nicey style, baby . . . You could get almost anything you'd ask for.

WANDA: Ohhh . . . Art.

(MARIE *laughs in the background.*)

GAFNEY, *stutters:* Mmmmmmmaaannn . . . tttthhh . . . ttthhhhis this is terrible! . . . Ttthhiisss this is the mmmo . . . oooss . . . stt disgusting, fff . . . fffoouuulll act that I-I-I-I . . . ttthhhaattt I-I-I-I've evvvver seen!

WANDA, *hurt:* Art . . . how could you?

ART: Take it easy . . . think it over . . . two-three hundred bucks a week could mean a lot to you right now . . . Why don't you think about it, Wanda.

(*In tears,* WANDA *exits.* MARIE *and* MARCO *appear.* MARIE *still laughs.*)

MARIE: Ha ha ha . . . ha hee hee . . . Art . . . ha . . . Art, you're too much. Ha ha . . . tryin' to put Wandie's stiff ole corny butt on the block.

GAFNEY: It's disgusting.

MARCO: Look . . . Marie . . . she's your niece, not mine. I got my own problems. You take care of her. She ain't movin' in with me . . . umm umm . . . If she ain't got no place to stay, that's her problem.

ART: Maybe I can find somethin' else for her to do.

MARIE: Well, she's gonna have to do somethin'. Draggin' herself in here every night like some ole mangy dawg. Thinks because she hardly eats here and sneaks herself into my bathroom to wash her ole funky drawers, that she's not takin' up space. Well, soap costs, you know. And every towel in this house is my towel . . . I've got them counted. And two women in one house is two women too many.

GAFNEY: This is just too awful . . . I have to get out!

(*He exits. The lights grow dim on the figures. The dog yaps.*)

MARCO: I don't care if the broad stays with me now and then . . . Sure she wants to move in with me . . . and she's got a pretty nice little box . . . but man, I'm tryin' to make it . . . and she ain't in my program at the moment.

ART: I was just trying to be helpful . . . people.

(MARIE *whoops with laughter and clutches* ART. *They kiss hard and go off together. Black. Lights up on* STEVE BENSON.)

STEVE: Well, I'm really not in this one. I just eased through the door. Came in behind Marc. Kinda by accident. And Art's my cousin . . . and I know some of the rest of these people. So I guess I just get pulled into the middle of this. Things haven't been going too well with me. I've had some bad problems lately . . . yeah . . . women. Yeah. You can bet on it. Was goin' with this married broad. Yeah. She has a husband . . . and a lot of problems. And somehow I got myself into the middle of it. Sure was scary for a minute . . . but it's over now. We had several hassles, then she took a shot at him, and he realized that she was in love with him . . . and the memory of me hanging around them screwin' up their new-found love affair was too much for them. They up and moved back to the sticks where they came from. And what made it so cold was that they were my landlords . . . and I had to find a new place to stay . . . and the whole thing's messed with me, ya understand. I started hittin' the jug again. Quit my job, dropped out of school . . . and started staying by myself again . . . sittin' in the library, browsing in bookstores, driving around with no place to go . . . Yeah, I got a little car now. Sports car. Nawh, didn't cost me much. I got it with my severance pay from work. Now all I got to worry about is puttin' gas in it and paying my room rent. But this town is gettin' me down. Time for gettin' my hat. Maybe I'll head north. Or even get out of this damn country. Who knows. I'm just makin' it, that's all and I'm here to see my buddy buddy Marco Polo Henderson . . . and my cousin . . . Art Garrison . . . and maybe throw a quick so-long to Miss Marie.

(MARCO and ART enter. Seeing STEVE, they greet him: slap hands ["Gimme five"], Eastern embrace ["Salaam, brother"], and good-natured put-downs ["Hey, where'd you find this chump?"]. Off to one side, MARIE looks on, smiling, until BILL joins her and grabs her thoughts. The dog yaps.)

BILL: I don't know how they could do that, Marie . . . I just really don't know.

MARIE: Did they tell you that they were going to fire you?

BILL: No.

MARIE: You didn't know anything?

BILL: Nawh . . . I don't know how . . .

MARIE: Oh, God! . . . the car payment is already past due . . . the rent has to . . . Ohhh, Bill . . . how could this have happened to us?

BILL: I don't know, baby . . . I don't know . . .

MARIE: Well we have to do something. We can't just lay down and die. Have you spoken to your boss again? . . . Have you spoken to Izzy?

BILL: Nawh . . . nawh . . . Izzy sez he don't want to see me no mo'.

MARIE: Not see you! But you built his business . . . When I got you that job, all he had was that little parkin' lot down off the Main Street . . . with his bein' down at the race track more than anything . . . Now he's in Beverly Hills . . . and Silky Sullivan didn't put him there.

BILL: Marie.

MARIE, *angry:* I worked at Izzy's house. I cleaned his house and took care of his brats. And he won't talk to you? I was down too low and have rose up by covering up his shit and patchin' his ass together . . . 'cause his woman ain't woman enough to do it . . . and now he won't talk to you? . . . I've come too long aways to go back to nothin'!

BILL: Marie.

MARIE: Well, if he won't talk to you, then he'll talk to me. We've stuck by that man . . . what's he going to do now that he doin' good . . . just shove us aside? That's just like a Jew!

BILL: Marie!

MARIE: Yes, Bill . . . what is it? What is it, baby?

BILL: There's been some money missing from the till . . . at least that's what Izzy said. He said he kept quiet about it and only hinted around for a while . . . but he said it got out of hand.

MARIE: But you make a good salary, Bill . . . and your tips are more than your check.

BILL: And Marie . . . Marie, he said he didn't like what I was doin' with my life.

(*Pause*)

MARIE: Bill . . . you didn't take her on your job, too, did ya?

BILL: I was drunk, Marie . . . drunk. I dreamed of how it would be for me to drive out along Sunset Strip in my convertible with my top down with a white woman next to me . . . close, ya know? Right under me . . . Baby, I'm sorry . . . I was drunk . . . her, too . . . and then when we got out to the lot and she met Izzy, she said somethin' to him that I didn't like, and I hit her.

MARIE: You did?

BILL: Yes, I did, baby . . . right in front of everybody.

(*Pause*)

MARIE: How much does her apartment cost you, Bill?

BILL: A lot, baby . . . a lot . . . I didn't mean to get into this . . . I really didn't, baby . . . but . . .

MARIE, *realistic:* Well, I got to call Izzy's ole lady . . . I didn't wipe the shit from her little bastards' behinds for nothin'. She owes me what's mine . . . and Izzy does, too . . .

BILL: Izzy said that you were a good, hard-workin' woman, baby . . . and that he liked and respect you . . .

MARIE: Bill . . .

BILL: Huh, baby?

MARIE: Fix me a drink will ya?

BILL: Yeah, baby . . . yeah . . . but Izzy wished you all the best.

MARIE, *gentle:* Shhss . . . shhhsss . . . Bill . . . I have to get back your job. Fix me a drink, honey.

BILL: You're too good to me, Marie . . . Baby, I'm sorry.

MARIE: Shhsss shhssss . . . Bill . . . stop being sorry. (*Bright*) You know there's no despair in Miss Marie's house. Hey, what's our theme song, lover?

BILL and MARIE, *fall into a brief show routine and Buck 'n' Wing and sing together:* Bill brings home two hundred stone-cold dollars a week . . . to me, Miss Marie . . . and puts it in my hand. And the tips he makes parkin' cars out to the studio in Beverly Hills is more than that. We make almost as much as some colored doctors make . . . 'n we spend it, too. 'Cause it's party time every day at Miss Marie's house.

(*They dance and sing into the darkness. The dog yaps. Lights up on* GAFNEY *and* ART.)

GAFNEY: Man, you're nothin'.

ART, *casual:* I'm not?

GAFNEY: No, you're nothin' . . . Just a nothin' nigger . . . You haven't got any ethics, any values, or morals.

ART: Nawh . . . I guess I haven't.

GAFNEY: You'd do anything to get what you want, no matter what.

ART: Well . . . not anything.

GAFNEY: What make you be like you are?

ART: Be like I am? . . . I don't know . . . maybe I was just raised properly. Maybe 'cause I was born with a tin spoon in my mouth.

GAFNEY: You can treat it like that, brother, if you want. But lighthearted-ness concerning your evil nature won't make it.

ART: Tell me more . . . brother.

GAFNEY, *preaching:* There are a lot more things . . . yes, a lot more things that you could be doin' . . . doin' in the service of the Black man . . . than draggin' down your brothers and sisters . . . leading them down the crooked path in this vile "wilderness of North America."[9] . . . Yes,

---

9. Wilderness of North America: Phrase coined by Nation of Islam founder Master Wallace Fard Muhammad (1877–1934?) to describe the spiritual and geographical conditions of African Americans. Popularized by the Honorable Elijah Muhammad (1897–1975) in speeches and publications during the 1960s.

there are a lot more things that you could be doin' than draggin' down your brothers and sisters for your own advantage.

ART: Like what?

(*Lights change.* BUD *stands in the movie screen area. He plays out his scene as though he were acting in a documentary film.*)

BUD: Sure I'm here . . . And I don't mind it much. Marie and Bill are good sports. We get along good . . . And they come from my ole home town, though they come from up on "The Hill" . . . where all the nitty gritty folks are . . . which is okay, ya know. But they're some crazy niggers . . . Marie and Bill . . . sometimes. And they make good buddies. I like them . . . Yeah, I'm sure of that. And they don't know none of the niggers I work with, which is a treat. I'm a schoolteacher. Math. Junior high school. Nothin' heavy, but somethin' nice and steady . . . and the district where I teach is not in the ghetto, if you know what I mean. Where I teach, the kids know how to act. They've had some home guidance.

(*Lights on* BUD *fade; the Christmas tree winks; and* ART *and* MARCO *appear somewhere in the space. They pass a small brown cigarette between them.*)

ART: Hey, man . . . hope you didn't get mad about Wanda.

MARCO, *supercool:* Nawh, baby . . . everything's everything . . . Look, Jim, I want the broad to get out of here and get some coins too, dig? Then she can throw me some change.

(*In the background, off,* WANDA *is heard crying quietly alone throughout the remainder of this segment.*)

ART: I hear ya.

MARCO: If she were makin' enough I might even let her move in with me and take care of things while I finish school, dig?

ART: You got it all figured out . . . You're pretty hip.

MARCO, *sucks deeply:* Well . . . you know . . . I gotta take care of myself.

ART: Yeah . . . I know what you mean, champ . . . My cousin Steve's pretty quiet . . . and kinda slow, ya know . . . I didn't think he was associating with real operators like you. (*They pass the cigarette.*)

MARIE, *off:* DON'T SMOKE MORE THAN A COUPLE OF THEM DOPE THINGS IN HERE . . . STUFF GET IN MY CURTAINS AND MY FRIENDS'LL THINK I'M HAVIN' AN OPIUM DEN IN HERE!

(*The last drags are taken and the cigarette is stamped out.*)

BUD: Toni and I don't have any kids. But if we did . . . we would see that he or she got proper home guidance . . . And I guess I'd take a crack at being assistant principal. You know . . . get up in the world . . . but with Toni working, together, we do okay, so why work up a sweat? I always say. We have a nice home, the car's a fairly new "T" bird[10] . . . and I can get in a couple holes of golf whenever I get the mood. And my ole lady, Toni . . . she's kinda foxy, huh? Bet you'd like to get a little taste of that, wouldn't cha? Yeah, I know you would. But I don't think that's likely.

(*Lights and music change.* ART *and* MARCO *appear again.*)

ART: Since we both hustlin' men, Marco . . . I can talk to you, can't I?

MARCO, *suspicious:* Yeah . . . sure . . . you can talk to me.

ART: Well I was thinkin', man . . . since we both playin' this Marie Horton scene, that we shouldn't kill the goose that lays them good eggs . . . you know what I mean, man?

MARIE, *off; young, seductive:* Oh, Art . . .

MARCO: Nawh . . . No I don't.

ART: Well, as I see it, man. There's only so much to be had here, ya understand? A few chicks at best, some drinks, a little chow, and a warm bed, if things are right . . . see what I'm gettin' to?

MARCO: Well . . . not exactly.

ART: It's like this, man . . . you take care of your own side of the street, dig? . . . I'm here already . . . and I don't need that much company.

MARIE, *nearer, soft, sweet:* Oh, Art . . .

MARCO: You tryin' to tell me somethin', man?

ART: Yeah . . . Like I don't want to see you around here that much more. All you out here for is to put Wandie through some changes for your own kicks[11] . . . then screw her a little and browbeat her a lot . . . I'm tryin' to get my groceries together, fellow, and you holdin' up the action . . . See what I mean?

MARIE, *almost on top of them; strange:* I'm here, Art.

MARCO: Yeah, man . . . I see what you mean.

(*Lights change.*)

BUD: Don't get me wrong about your not bein' able to hit strong on chicks. It's just where my ole lady, Toni, is concerned, that's all. See, I'm not saying that you can't hit harder than me or anything or that she's got cast-iron drawers or somethin'. It's just that Toni don't go for bedwork too strong, if you know what I mean. Not that she's frigid or anything. She'll get into it if she's in the mood. But she's always holdin' back, ya know. Says she don't want any kids, ever. Says that the world is ugly and she doesn't want to bring her kids into it. I say that the

---

10. "T" bird = Ford Thunderbird.

11. Put . . . through changes: In the jazz jam, the competitive movement through chord progressions intended to challenge another musician's skills. In more general use, forcing another person through unpleasant issues and emotions.

world is the world; it'll take care of itself like we're takin' care of ourselves. But she says, no. And that's the way it is. So, she takes the pill.
And before that, it was jelly or grease or somethin'. And when I get
affectionate . . . she acts bothered . . . I don't mind not havin' kids too
much or the pills she takes . . . but her always pushin' me off . . . damn
. . . I can understand why some cats drink, ya know . . . Hey, Marie . . .
how's the booze holdin' out?

(BUD *fades out*; BILL *and* WANDA *appear. The music is low.* BILL *and* WANDA *act
as lovers.*)

WANDA: But Uncle Bill . . . I told you I couldn't do this.

BILL: Look, Wandie . . . you like me, don't ya? . . . And I like you, too.

WANDA: But Uncle Bill . . . I can't . . .

BILL: Just call me Bill, baby . . . Just call me Bill. You're Marie's niece . . .
not mine.

(ART *walks through, observes* BILL *and* WANDA, *and continues out, unseen by
them.*)

WANDA: But you know this is wrong, Bill.

BILL, *takes her in his arms:* I've loved you for so long, Wandie, baby.

WANDA, *responding:* You shouldn't do this Uncle . . . I mean, Bill.

BILL, *feeling her give in:* Just relax, baby . . . you need some love, don't ya?
Just relax and let me love you.

WANDA: Take care of me, please . . . see that no one hurts me anymore,
Bill.

BILL: You're my little girl, baby . . . my own little girl.

(*The Christmas tree lights wink, the couple fades from sight, and* MARIE *saunters
in with a half-filled glass in her hand.*)

MARIE: Each glass I raise to my lips, with every drop of Scotch I drain from
my mug, the moments pass, my life goes, and I am an old woman. No
regrets . . . no, no regrets. A few missed parties. Some spent dollar
bills. A mistake or two, but hell, that's life, ain't it, honey? So, no tears
here . . . just keep the good times keep on keepin' on. Don't let the
music stop. Yeah . . . poppa stoppa . . . go it one again. That's my song
. . . yeah . . . play it, yeah . . . go it one again. I'm a good Catholic . . . I
go to confession . . . whenever I have to . . . and get up in time. So I
ain't studden[12] 'bout a thing . . . I just tell that cute young priest that
Miss Marie's takin' care of business . . . and everybody's cool . . . if the
Lawd don't mind, you better believe Miss Marie don't give a
hummmmp hummmmp hummmmp . . . right, peaches? Say it again, my
liddle puttie cat . . . wheeee . . . Miss Marie will tell you . . . ha ha ha . . .

12. "Studden": Studying.

(GAFNEY *and* ART *appear*.)

GAFNEY: We've come a long way, brother Art . . . and you ain't helpin' us Black people any with your niggerish ways.

ART: Yeah, I know I've come a long ways . . . from all way inside my mama.

GAFNEY: I'm talking about slavery, brother . . . please, don't be facetious . . .

ART: Don't be what?

GAFNEY: You know what I'm talking about.

ART: Do I?

GAFNEY: Yes, you do! You know I'm talking about your being a nigger pimp!

ART: Hey . . . watch your foul language, prophet.

GAFNEY: To communicate with you and your kind, I find that I must sink to your level.

ART: Level? . . . Then you're on a higher level than me?

GAFNEY: Someone has to lead, my brother.

ART: So niggers like me get out of slavery . . . then they find that niggers like you think they're leading us. Nigger . . . we've been led and misled for four hundred years . . . why don't you leave us alone and let us find our own way for a while?

GAFNEY: I'm not a nigger, Art . . . I'm a Black man!

ART: Yeah . . . I guess we have come a long way.

(*They fade as* MARIE *winks and blows them kisses*.)

MARIE: Why do I like young boys? Didn't think you'd ever ask, sweetie. My my . . . but the things you want to get into . . . ha ha . . . you mean Art, don't you? . . . Yeah? . . . shusssssh . . . ummm mmm . . . yeah, I know what you mean. He's a young boy, or man, if you want to get into that . . . and I like him all right. Oh, I like Art. He makes me feel so good . . . so good . . . you know what I mean, honey? Yeah, I'm sure you do. That's why. 'Cause he makes me feel the way I like to feel. That's all there is to it, baby . . . I'd jump over forty old men's pooties to get to a young man. You hip to that, honey? Miss Marie is together . . . but she likes her good times, too . . .

GAFNEY, *off*: You're decadent . . . you're indecent . . . you're counterrevolutionary . . .

MARIE: . . . I wanna thank ya . . .

(*She fades out of sight. Lights on* RUTH *and* BUD. RUTH *is straightening her clothes.* BUD, *his back to the audience, is fixing himself.*)

RUTH: What if Toni finds out?

BUD: Take it easy, baby . . . take it easy.

RUTH: But Toni's one of my best friend-girls.

BUD, *turns to her:* There's nothin' to worry about.

RUTH: Ohhh . . . this is all a mistake. I musta drank too much . . . how could I? . . . Oh, I know what it was now . . . it was that dirty movie of Marie and Bill's . . .

BUD, *chuckles:* Ruth, baby . . . ha ha . . . baby.

RUTH: Get away from me! Don't put your nasty hands on me. What if Shadow knows?

BUD, *incredulous:* The Shadow knows?[13]

RUTH: Shadow! My man . . . Oh, Jesus; how did I get my black ass into this? . . . Oh, please don't tell Marie . . . Please . . . that damn woman can't keep a thing to herself, 'cept'n her own business.

BUD: Relax . . . relax . . . everything's gonna . . .

RUTH: Please don't tell Toni . . . please . . . Ohh, those dirty movies.

BUD: Well, I wouldn't tell my ole lady, Toni, would I? Not even I'm that dumb.

RUTH: Oh, god, I need a drink . . . Now Bud, don't you tell anybody anything, ya hear? . . . If you do, man, you'll be sorry!

(*She rushes off. Light fades on* BUD, *then up on* WANDA.)

WANDA: Ahhh . . . this is such a miserable, mean existence. Men grabbing at you, grabbing what's yours and what they think is or should be theirs. Oldness and death around the corners. In the corners of their aspiring middle-class, middle-aged souls. To drink the drink of youth they think is to buy a fifth of 100-proof oblivion. Here I am just starting out on this thing called life and from what I see so far I can't get up enough enthusiasm to smile about it any longer. When I came from Pittsburgh, I thought I was coming to a better place. Not a better life, really, but a better place. I could have gone to the university back there, but I wanted to get away. I knew I could stay with my aunt . . . ha ha ha ha . . . Thought I was comin' to a little ole lady's house who had cats and maybe a budgie, which is a stinky little bird, and certainly potted plants. No one's seen Aunt Marie back in Pittsburgh, Buffalo, or Brooklyn, where our family's from, for a long time. She had quite a

---

13. The Shadow knows: Catchphrase of the popular Columbia Broadcasting Service radio show *The Shadow* (1930–54). It answers the question: "Who knows what evil lurks in the hearts of men?" The Shadow possessed the ability to cloud the perceptions of others, allowing him to observe or escape them.

reputation for being wild . . . My, my, the stories that they still tell. They said that her mother died in childbirth, she being the child and nobody knowing who was the daddy . . . Aunt Marie's mother was said to have conceived in college. It was quite a scandal of the day . . . since not many black girls went to college, daughters of undertakers or not. And Aunt Marie was brought up by her mother's mother . . . who was one of the first colored teachers in Pottstown, PA. And they said that Aunt Marie was very spoiled from receiving almost anything that she wanted, even when there was a depression going on in those days . . .

BILL, *off:* Wandie . . .

WANDA: They say that Aunt Marie used to drink corn whiskey and smoke cigarettes in public and cuss and race in cars with their tops rolled back and she wouldn't go to school . . .

BILL, *nearer:* Wandie, baby . . .

WANDA: "Look at what school did for my poor little mamma," she would say. And she was a showgirl and went to Philly and New York . . . and somethin' happened that nobody ever talks about and she ended up out here with Bill.

(BILL *enters.*)

BILL: Wanda . . . there you are. I've been looking all over for you.

WANDA: I've been here, Bill . . . just here.

(*He clutches her, holds her close.*)

BILL: Baby, you worried me for a while . . . You're not sick, are you?

WANDA: Yes, Bill . . . I'm a little sick.

BILL: You are? . . . Oh. I know a man shouldn't ask about a lady's illnesses . . . but . . .

WANDA: I'm pregnant, Bill.

BILL: Oh . . .

WANDA: Yes.

BILL: By me?

WANDA: Maybe.

BILL, *breathes deeply:* Ahhhhhh . . . I see.

WANDA: I'm leaving soon.

BILL: You are?

WANDA: Yes. I'm going to go stay with Marco.

BILL: You are?

WANDA: Yes. He doesn't want me or love me . . . but he is all I need and care about.

BILL: Will he let you?

WANDA: I love him . . . and I'm pregnant . . . it doesn't matter now what he wants.

BILL: I see . . . you know, I might be able to help you out some.

WANDA: Thanks.

BILL: You know I love you too, Wandie . . . but I couldn't live without your Aunt Marie.

WANDA: I know . . . well, I have to go now.

BILL: Yeah . . . I know . . . Wandie?

WANDA: Huh?

BILL: What are you going to name the baby?

(*She kisses him, he holds her for a second, then they part.* WANDA *exits.* BUD *joins* BILL. *They hold drinks in their hands.*)

BUD: Hey . . . how's it goin', Capt'n?

BILL: Can't complain, Chief . . . How's it go with you?

BUD: Just another Christmas . . . A few of the girls are just a bit younger . . . or seem that way.

BILL: Yeah . . . they're all the same . . . too much food . . . too much to drink . . . too much heartburn.

BUD: Thanks for havin' us over.

BILL, *slightly drunk:* But we always have you and Toni over . . .

BUD: The kids act different.

BILL: Different? . . . Yeah . . . I guess they do . . . You know . . . these young people are confused . . . they're lost.

BUD: But things were different when we were kids.

BILL: Sure was . . . but I don't want to go back to the good ole days.

BUD: But these kids . . . I dunno . . . maybe it's the revolution.

BILL: What you mean?

BUD: Well, I'm around them all the time, ya understand . . . I know them.

BILL: Yeah.

BUD: And they're just different.

BILL: Oh.

BUD: Hey . . . that's strange.

BILL: What is?

BUD: None of us have kids . . . not me and Toni or you and Marie . . . nor Ruthie . . . or almost anybody that we hang out with.

BILL, *chuckles:* Havin' kids must be out of style.

BUD: For some people, at least . . . for us. Hummm . . . maybe we're dying off. Maybe we're a vanishing breed.

BILL: Yeah . . . last of the big-time dodos . . . ha ha . . .

BUD: But we've had some good times.

BILL: Yeah . . . we've had a ball.

BUD: Ha ha . . . but if I can have a choice, I'll take a woman any day . . . with no strings attached . . .

BILL: Yeah . . . no strings.

BUD: And no history . . . and no future . . . with me, at least.

BILL: Yeah . . . at least.

BUD: Happy New Year, Bossman! . . . May all your troubles be as fleeting as youth.

BILL: Ha ha . . . well said, Professor. You ready for a fresh one?

BUD: Why not, Maestro?

(*They fade away.* RUTH *appears.*)

RUTH: Ha ha . . . Marie is crazy . . . We have a lot of fun. She thinks I'm crazy, but she's the one. I'm not like Marie's other friends. I'm a real friend. Me and Toni, though Toni's not like me at all . . . Most of Marie's friends are those ole bags that are in her clubs or are too stuck-up to be in them and have clubs of their own that Marie would like to be in . . . I'm from Texas . . . a high-top-boot-wearin', ten-gallon-hat, dusky queen of the wide-open spaces, that's me. Yippeee! . . . I run a power machine over on Sepulveda Boulevard. We make costumes for TV. That's how I make my money, friend. None of that waitin' for some man to give me what I deserve stuff. I'm a gal to get her own. Sure, the guys I go with give me what they want to give me. But I got better sense than to start dependin' on them, and get let down, ya understand? I'm independent. And I drink beer. And I keep Marie company. 'Cause Bill is out more than he's in, so we two lonesome gals have a lot to talk about. We talk about Marie's poker parties. And her pot luck suppers . . . and other socials. And we kid about my boy friends and about Bill's girl friends and about Wanda bein' so dumb . . . and lots of things like that. We good friends, Marie and I. But I don't understand her none. Not one bit . . . But we good friends just the same.

(*She exits.* ART *and* GAFNEY *appear.*)

ART: Well, I don't know, man . . . All that stuff you tellin' me sounds okay . . . but I don't see how it's gonna get me any money . . . and that's my problem right now.

GAFNEY: That is the least of your problems, brother . . . You're an African and . . .

ART: I'm a what?

GAFNEY: African, my brother . . . In these days of the early sixties with so many newly emerged African states coming to the fore in world influence . . . the fact of your Black birth, even in this spiritually desolate place known as North America . . .

ART: Look, man . . . I got a lot of things to do . . . Why don't you save that . . .

GAFNEY: You can't continue avoiding the truth, Art.

ART: Well, man . . . my truth right now is that I need some dough. Big dough would be best . . . then I'd feel more like a man, African or not.

GAFNEY: We Black people are in a fight for liberation, brother. That is our manhood! And Africa is at the center of our struggle.

ART: Look, Gafney . . . I say let the Africans struggle for what they want . . . and I'll liberate some green here . . . My fight is right here . . . and this is where I stand or fall.

GAFNEY: You just don't understand . . . It's not about the white man's money . . . you just don't understand.

ART: Give me a gun, Freedom Fighter . . . and I'll liberate some dough-ray-mee . . . dig?

GAFNEY: You'd more than likely take it from some helpless Black people.

ART, *annoyed:* Maybe . . . but then I could go to Africa or jump down to see Brother Castro . . . or smoke some good opium with the master . . . Mao.[14]

GAFNEY, *indignant:* The great Chairman Mao has no use for drugs!

ART, *angry:* CAN'T YOU EVER TAKE A JOKE . . . NIGGER!

(*They fade from sight.*)

TONI: I'm Toni. I'm a social worker . . . not that that matters. But I am that, among other things. I'm kinda fine, as well. And I know it. Yes, I know it . . . but I go for it as well. And that's cool. 'Cause Toni's fine . . . you can believe that, baby. I'm Marie's friend. Her home girl, Toni. We grew up together, though I'm at least fifteen years younger than her. We really didn't grow up together, ya know. Came from the same neighborhood. Though my folks had more money than Marie's. This is a true story, ya know. But you can't always believe what you see . . . or hear. (ART *reappears, a drink in his hand. He stares at* TONI *a long moment. She tries to ignore him. He hands her the drink. She nods a nervous "thank you," sips drink, clears throat.*) We met out here, Marie and I, and having known some of our same families, mutually, and friends, per-

14. Brother Castro . . . Mao: Fidel Castro (1926–) and Mao Zedong (1893–1976), both successful leaders of communist revolutions, are popular heroes for Black Nationalists, Mao for his theory of "cultural revolution," which advocates social transformation through interaction between intellectuals and the masses.

sonally, we have been fast friends ever since, always having someone near and dear close at hand to reminisce over the good ole days. And our relationship has deepened. I know Marie more than I know my ole man, Bud. And she thinks she knows me. (ART *stands behind her, holding her close about the waist, kissing the back of her neck and whispering in her ear. She is quite perturbed, but continues to speak and hold onto her self-control.*) We remain dear friends. Even though she has problems . . . Like Bill . . . now that's a real problem. A grade "A" all-American problem . . . Whew . . . nigger drink more than the law allow . . . And his runnin' round with that white bitch. IN FRONT OF HER FRIENDS! L.A.'s a big place . . . stretches moocho miles . . . yeah . . . wide open spaces for days . . . and this nigger, when he gets drunk, takes his ole skinny white heifer to his hangouts. Nigger pretends that they ain't Marie's places to play, either . . . Last time the nigger came through with her, he was loud . . . yeah, LOUD . . . claimed that she was going to have his baby, bought drinks for the house . . . isn't that disgusting? . . . this was at the Sportsman's Inn . . . and then got belligerent with the whore and ended up slappin' her and takin' her out to the parkin' lot and beatin' her ass in his car. Niggers are somethin' else, chile. Let me tell you . . . (*Though maintaining her discipline, she begins to respond visibly to* ART.) I hang out with some of the simplest-behinded Negroes there is. You can believe that . . . Toni'll tell ya. Sheet . . . make me act vulgar sometimes . . . I wouldn't just let one of these niggers use me. Come suckin' round me and got a white woman on the side. I'm takin' care of Toni, that's who . . . and Toni is precious, special, and cold as January in the North Pole.

(*She pushes* ART *away. He takes her arm and pulls her. Reluctantly at first, she goes with him. They dissolve into the shadows.*)

WANDA, *appears and sings:* It's little enough / to love / and need. / It's little enough / to be / for real./ It's little enough / to keep / my man, / but can / I be myself? / It's more than enough / to have / you near / (the dark packed muscle / the desperate / meat). / It's more than enough / to wet / your lips / with the / taste of / me, myself. / It's enough / to have you. / It's enough / to be yours. / It's enough / to keep you / if you're / really mine. / So, here I am. / Take what's yours. / So, have me. / Now, / don't pass / the chance. / So, love me / while / I am hot / and know / my name / was Wanda.[15]

(*Lights on* MARIE *and* STEVE *standing, drinking, and flirting. The dog yaps.*)

15. "Woman's Song": Ed Bullins, lyrics; Pat Patrick, music. Downpat Music Co. (BMI), 1971.

RUTH, *off:* Shoot the niggers . . . shoot the niggers . . .

MARIE: God . . . what's that?

STEVE: I dunno.

RUTH, *off:* We got our right . . . we got 'em . . . shoot the niggers . . .

(ART *and* TONI *enter.*)

MARIE: Damn . . . Toni . . . Art . . . what's happening? (*She starts toward the noise.*)

TONI, *restrains* MARIE: No, sister . . . no . . . don't go back there.

MARIE: What's going on?

RUTH, *off, sobs:* Shoot 'em . . . it's not fair . . . I got my rights . . . I ain't never had no trouble out of white folks . . .

TONI: It's Ruth . . .

MARIE: I know . . . that's Ruth's voice.

STEVE: What's she sayin' that for? Shouldn't somebody . . .

ART: Ruth's cracked up . . . she's havin' a fit back there.

MARIE, *struggles:* Oh, my God . . . let me go to her.

TONI, *holds her:* Bud's with her . . . he'll do all he can for her.

MARIE: But it should be me . . . or you, Toni. She needs us.

TONI: No . . . she's got who she needs . . . she's with her man.

RUTH, *off:* Shoot 'em . . . oh, Lawd have mercy . . . I already got my civil rights . . . I'm free as a white lady . . . yes, I am . . .

MARIE: She's with her man? Bud?

ART: Yeah . . . Bud.

(MARIE *begins laughing slowly, picking up to near hysteria, then weeps. They stand about her, soothing her, not looking at each other.*)

MARIE, *finally:* Ruth and Bud?

TONI: Yes, they were having a little thing . . . like Art and I . . .

ART: Hey, kid . . . I ain't in it.

TONI, *pursues subject:* Like Art and I were having a little thing . . . and somehow we . . .

MARIE, *resigned:* You and Art . . .

ART: It wasn't nothin', baby . . . I had a few drinks . . . and I got bored . . .

STEVE: Has this something to do with Wanda's splittin'?

TONI: Wanda's gone?

ART, *disgust:* Awww . . . she's gone with that jive-ass nigger of hers . . . Marco.

STEVE: Hey, man . . . that's my friend.

MARIE, *tired:* No . . . no . . . I think I know why Wanda left . . . Art . . .

ART: Huh?

MARIE: You haven't left any dirty coffee cups around, have you?

(*With great halloing,* BILL *enters. He has Christmas-gift-wrapped bottles of liquor and a pink box under his arms.*)

BILL: Hey, baby . . . Marie, baby . . . I'm home . . . Dry the tears from your eyes, swweeeet cake . . . I've kicked the wolf in his tail . . . He won't be sniffin' round our door no mo' . . . Daddy's done brought home the goose.

TONI: Bill . . . quiet . . .

MARIE, *regaining composure:* Take it easy, Toni, dear . . . HORTON, YOU OLE PIRATE . . . WHAT YOU BEEN UP TO, NIGGER?

(*They laugh and clutch one another.*)

RUTH, *off, lower:* I got all I need, yes, indeed . . . Yes, indeed, I got all I need . . .

BILL: You lookin' at a workin' man, mamma . . . Not only a workin' man . . . but one with a substantial raise . . . AND listen to this . . .

MARIE: Sock it to me, sweetie . . .

BILL, *plays it for all it's worth:* AND A MANAGERIAL POSITION! . . .

RUTH, *off:* Ohh ohh ohhh . . . ohh oooooohhhhhh . . .

TONI: You . . . you're managing the parking lot now?

BILL: No, my dear . . . I am manager to the entire garage beneath the Beverly Hills Motor Spa . . . and I've already spent my bonus.

MARIE: Leave it to my Bill.

STEVE: Damn. (*The TV comes on. A Black man is shown exhorting a ghetto crowd. Then flashes of rioting, looting, police, National Guard, etc. The TV personality looks larger.*) Look . . . they've started the revolution . . . Those civil rights brothers are really taking care of business.

MARIE: Hummp . . . most of them niggers ain't nothin' but cops . . . tryin' to find out what they can get Black people to do . . . You should know how sneaky white people is . . . honey. And how they use the Black man against the Black man . . . Hummp, better than to be that kinda fool.

(ART *has withdrawn to the side. He smokes and looks on as they unwrap the liquor and* MARIE *tears open her box.*)

TONI, *squeals of delight:* OH . . . MARIE . . . YOU LUCKY OLE BITCH!

(MARIE *pulls a fur stole from the paper and cardboard.*)

BILL, *expansive:* Not quite ermine . . . but not dog either . . .

TONI, *envy:* Oh, that's just adorable . . . I'm going to have to push Bud into administration . . . I see that now . . . there's just no future in being at the bottom.

(MARIE *models the stole, swaggering about the stage.*)

BILL: I don't know what you told Izzy, baby . . . or Izzy's ole lady . . . but . . .

MARIE: The past is the past, Bill . . .

BILL, *dances:* If you say so, sweetheart . . . Hey, watch this step . . . got that? Art . . . get old Billy Boy his regular.

MARIE: No, no . . . I'll do it, baby . . . Art was just leavin' . . . for good.

TONI: He is?

ART: Seems like I've heard this somewhere before.

GAFNEY, *enters:* Art, there you are. Have you seen Wandie? Have you, huh? I see you're still standing around. What are you going to be doing when the revolution comes?

ART, *softly:* Gafney . . . without me, you won't have a revolution.

GAFNEY: Oh, man . . . (GAFNEY *looks at* ART. ART *feints then jabs him sharply in the nose.*)

BILL: Art . . . damn . . . what's going on here?

GAFNEY: Owww . . . you shouldn't have done that . . . Don't you know I'm non-violent . . . you stupid, ignorant nigger! (GAFNEY *rushes off, holding his bleeding nose.*)

BILL: Say, Art . . . we can't have any of that in here. This is our home.

MARIE, *laughing:* Cool down, Poppa Horton . . . Art's just leaving . . . He was just giving us his calling card . . . weren't you, lover?

ART: See you folks . . .

TONI: See you, Art . . . Call me sometime . . . we're in the book.

STEVE: Guess I'll be leaving with you, man.

MARIE, *takes* STEVE's *arm; seductive:* No, you can't go now, Steve . . . My party's just starting . . . besides . . . I want you to do something for me later on.

RUTH, *off, low:* I've got everything I need . . . everything, everything, everything.

TONI, *nervous:* I'm going back here and talk to Bud about his promotion . . . maybe Ruthie needs me now . . . (*She exits.*)

ART: Why don't you lay . . . cousin Steve . . . I generally travel alone.

STEVE: Okay . . . see you around.

ART: Next time you hear from the folks . . . give 'em my best.

STEVE: I'll do that.

ART: Hey . . . remember how we'd fight all the time when we were kids? Who usta win, huh? . . . I wonder who was the best?

STEVE: We'll never know now . . . will we?

(ART *exits.*)

BILL, *dances:* Hey, Marie . . . Hey, stuff . . . get me a drink . . . Hey, sweet stuff . . . get me a drink, will ya?

MARIE: What you think you got around here, Mr. Horton? . . . Brownskin service? . . Oh, Steve . . . will you fix us some drinks, please, honey? . . the usual.

STEVE, *shrugs:* Oh . . . sure . . . why not? (*He goes to get drinks.*)

MARIE: Fur or no fur, Bill Horton . . . you got to keep on gettin' out of here and gettin' me some money . . . Miss Marie is used to havin' what she wants.

BILL: Watch this step, baby . . . remember this one . . . C'mon, let me see if you can still do it.

BILL *and* MARIE, *do their brief routine and sing together:* Bill brings home two hundred seventy-five stone-cold dollars a week . . . to me, Miss Marie . . . and puts it in my hand. And the tips he makes parkin' cars out to the studio in Beverly Hills is more than that. We make almost as much as some colored doctors make . . . 'n we spend it too. 'Cause it's party time every day at Miss Marie's house.

(*They dance off. The stage is left dark with the Christmas tree shining and the TV flickering on. The dog yaps outside. The telephone begins to ring.*)

Blackness.

A number of Bullins's plays attempt to politicize the material conditions of drama and theater. They are best described by the oxymoron "agitprop closet dramas" because they are at once rallying calls to action as well as opportunities for readerly contemplation of the underlying conditions of consciousness and communication. In this case, the play highlights the material conditions of Afrocentric scholarship. Published in slightly different form in the journal The Black Scholar *in 1975, the play effectively draws attention to the way "Blackness" can be domesticated by white-controlled publication interests—and revolutionary action and identity transformed into inert objects. At the same time, it asks us to consider the kinds of actions that a reader might take to extend the simple action of its protagonist into the realm of scholarship and criticism.*

Malcolm: '71, or *Publishing Blackness*

Based upon a Real Experience

(1971)

Lights up: A BLACKMAN *sits at a literary/looking desk. Books of Blackness, revolution, nation/building, Black poetry, drama, literature, music, How-to-be-Black, etc. The phone rings. The* MAN *pauses in his reading, meditation, coffee drinking/gazing into cup/space and lifts receiver.*

BLACKMAN: Black Aesthetics Limited . . . Go on . . . run it on down.

(*Lights up: A whitegirl holds phone. Wears glasses and is in a mini mini etc. Has pencil and chart on which* SHE *takes notes. Sound of dog barking comes from* HER *side of reality.*)[1]

WHITEGIRL, *innocent, girlish:* Hello. Is this Bossblack . . . the Blackrevolutionarysoulnationtimeliberator poet?

(*Dog barks.*)

BLACKMAN, *tired:* Yeah.

WHITEGIRL: Oh, goodie . . . Professor Hack gave me your name . . . Professor Jack Hack . . . you know him don't you?

---

1. This archival version of the play differs somewhat from the version published in *The Black Scholar*. In the latter, Whitegirl does not appear onstage.

BLACKMAN: Yeah . . . I know Hack.

WHITEGIRL: Yes. The white professor who teaches Black poetry and aesthetics at the new Black Revolutionary Third World City University in their Black Academics department. You know him . . . he was the Black Students' victory for burning down the administration building during that dreadful hassle over Black Studies?

(*Dog barks.*)

BLACKMAN: Yeah . . . I said I knew him.

WHITEGIRL: Well . . . my name is Sharon Stover and I'm editing a book on Radical/Protest/People's Poetry . . . and I could just not not include you, Mr. Bossblack.

(*The dog barks.*)

BLACKMAN: Ahuhn . . .

WHITEGIRL: I am starting my anthology back at the radical beginnings of this century . . . with the anarchists, wobblies, nihilists, etc. . . . and coming up through the colored peoples' struggle . . . and up to the Black revolutionary . . . (*Dog barks.*) Quiet, Malcolm! . . . and up through the Black revolutionary Panther communalism Now generation.

BLACKMAN: Ummmmm . . . hmmmmm . . .

WHITEGIRL: I have an old radical poet /socialist/communist of the thirties . . . who is now strangely a Zionist . . . to do the intro . . . and it's going to be really wild . . . (*Dog barks.*) Hush, Malcolm! . . . you wouldn't imagine how terribly, terribly radical and revolutionary this book is going to be! . . . And I was hoping that, if you could collect a section for the Blacks . . . I mean the Black poets, of course, well I could meet with you . . . anywhere you'd say . . . and . . .

BLACKMAN: Hey . . . could I ask you a question?

WHITEGIRL, *beaming:* Oh . . . why surely.

BLACKMAN: Is your dog named "Malcolm"?

WHITEGIRL: Yes.

BLACKMAN: Who is it named after?

(*Pause. Dog barks.*)

WHITEGIRL, *hesitant:* After Malcolm X.

(*The* BLACKMAN *gently hangs the phone up.*)

Lights down.

Blackness.

Early in the morning of August 11, 1975, white jailer Clarence T. Alligood was found dead on a bunk in the cell of Joan Little, his pants around his ankles, semen stains on his thighs, an ice pick in his hand, seven puncture wounds in his chest. Little herself was gone. Bullins paid close attention to the subsequent murder trial—even writing an open letter to Little warning her to avoid those who would exploit her cause. Erika Munk's 1976 review of the Theatre of the Riverside Church's production of Jo Anne!!!, *directed by Berliner Ensemble veteran Carl Weber, accused it of misogyny, apoliticism, and crude antiwhiteness. Featuring four versions of the murder, repeatedly shifting theatrical styles, and some rather lurid sexual spectacle and language—including a woman playing a dog on a leash and a "feminist" ripping off her clothes and proclaiming "Power to the Bitches"—it is undeniably a scandalous play. Regardless of how one interprets these matters, it is important that we recognize the play as a meditation on the possibility of judicial truth and justice in a racist, sexist society intent on turning every act of violence into entertainment. Though its presentation is troubling, the fact remains that both Little's attorney and political activists did exploit her for fame and profit; whether Bullins does the same is an open question. The play was first published in* New/Lost Plays by Ed Bullins: An Anthology, *edited by Ethel Pitts Walker (Aiea, HI: That New Publishing Company, 1993).*

Jo Anne!!!

(1976)

THE PEOPLE

JO ANNE, *young blackwoman, 20.*

GUARD ALL GOODE, *southern working class man, 60.*

LAWYER SCOTT, *blackwoman, beautiful, quietly determined, intelligent, 28.*

LAWYER CANE, *whiteman, astute, efficient, and level-headed, mid-thirties.*

DIXIE THE DOG, *an actress who wears a menacing-looking black leather and metal costume.*

WHITE ACTIVISTS, *sometimes male, sometimes female and sometimes a townsperson.*

BLACK ACTIVISTS, *sometimes male, sometimes female and sometimes a townsperson.*

BLACK REPORTER, *a city person, mostly an observer, early middle-age.*

EXTRAS (4), *black and white, used as needed.*

VOICES

Except for JO ANNE *and* ALL GOODE, *most of the other characters can double. Actually, less extras can be used. And the voices come from the ranks of the company who are not on the stage at the time or are taped previously and broadcast over the system.*

THE MUSIC: *The music is an integral component of this play. The instrumentation should allow the musicians to shift and slide easily through rural and urban blues, gospel, jazz, hillbilly, bluegrass, and other city, country, and western forms.*

JO ANNE *has a theme, which is played at times during her speeches and scenes, or when she is off-stage and being talked about. This music should reveal her character and emphasize her origins, but should have the underlying strength and heroic qualities of her Taurian[1] nature—stamina, eagerness for experience, holds own in any situation, patient, holds steadfast to ideals—though this music has a sensitive feminine lyricism about it.*

ALL GOODE's *theme is heavy, mocking, boozy, and threatening, but it should keep its "down home" quality. A funny, "folksy" line runs through this music to denote* ALL GOODE's *character, which is that of a "good ole boy" but with a guilty, moralistically paranoid, and psychotic Christian alcoholic bent.*

The overall musical feel should be that of dynamic action. It should push the form of the play and bridge any gaps through continual sheets of sound, which are wedded to the action of the production. During lulls in the music, contrapuntal beats and rhythms are blended through the scenes to give tension, tone, and emphasis to the thematic drama of the play.

THE SETTING: *First, each entrance to the theater auditorium should have an electronic weapons detector, the type used at airline terminals to search passengers before boarding. These devices should be monitored, and the audience should be controlled individually when passing through them. The machines should be functional and turned on, and if heavy objects are detected upon audience members, nothing should be made of it by the theater staff and the person should be passed through without incident.*

---

1. Taurian: Possessing the characteristics of the astrological sign of Taurus the bull.

Second, each staff member at the entrances should have a portable metal detector, and when an audience member passes through the large electronic weapons detector, they should be gone over quickly by the hand-held machine, exactly as airline security teams do. But if a warning buzzer goes off, indicating large concealed metal objects, the operator is to take no notice and pass the audience member through without incident.

Third, in the first three rows, center, of the theater are forty-two seats set aside, fourteen seats in each row. These seats are special—they will serve as the spectator section for the symbolic trial and play within the play and as a symbolic jury box made up of audience members. When anyone from the stage addresses the audience, these will be the people they concentrate on.

Fourth, the stage settings are minimal. This is a play of the mind and spirit; it doesn't need to be pinned down by huge, heavy scenery. The major settings: the cell area, the cabin interior, the guard's office, the witness chair for JO ANNE, which will resemble a throne, and the swamp and countryside and town. But all these places can be created out of the actor's imagery and with lights and several portable pieces and props.

Five, lighting is crucial to this production. It should be thought out to completely blend with the action of the play and have its own character, which should be special and unique. This is not a realistic play, and the lighting should make the audience aware of this strange nightmare vision they are experiencing.

Six, the audience in the special forty-two-seat spectator section will be seated last, after the others take their seats. They should be held together as a group, in a special place, not seen, if possible, and let into the auditorium last to begin the play. (ALL GOODE will seat them, and the play begins.)

House lights down. ALL GOODE's *theme is heard. Light on* ALL GOODE *seating the spectators in their special section.*

ALL GOODE, *enjoys authority:* Awww rite, folks . . . now these are the ground rules: yeah, I been doin' this for a while now . . . so I know what works . . . and what don't. Now, this is a murder story . . . right, and you all are the spectators . . . Now, there's only so many seats for ya. Forty-two, to be exact. That's three rows of fourteen seats each. Now don't be complainin' about extra spaces on the bench beside ya, an' there bein' enough room for ya friends. Don't be puttin' ya purses and your hands on the place next to you, sayin' you're savin' it for somebody. In this court, first come, first served. That's all there is to it. I got mah orders from headquarters, now. And you all are new around here, so listen to what I tell ya. Now anybody gettin' up an' leavin' has got to stay out 'till after the recess. No talkin', no smokin'. An' ya better act like good Americans! (*Sees a* TOWNSMAN, *a small, elderly blackman, seated in the audience, speaks to spectators.*) 'Scuse me, y'all. (*To* TOWNSMAN, *patronizing*) Hey there . . . ole uncle . . . . You can't sit over there like that. What ya think is goin' on around hare? Ya got to get in line with these here other folks.

TOWNSMAN: I'm lookin' fo' the claim office, suh.

ALL GOODE, *smiling widely:* Claim office? What you want to claim, Amos? Ha ha ha. Now this is the third floor of the court where the trial's bein' held. Claims are taken on another floor, Sunshine. Now you got to go downstairs, boy.

(*The* TOWNSMAN *rises silently and shuffles up the aisle toward the exit.*)

ALL GOODE, *hearty, resuming:* Now, ladies and gents . . . let's get back to the ground rules: No packages, cameras, tape recorders, etc., allowed inside. Yeah, this may not suit your ideas, but that's what the rules are. Don't change rows once you get in court and are assigned a seat . . . There'll be no guns, knives, or books allowed inside this court of America. So everybody get ready for what's goin'a happen. This is Wade County Court in the Carolinas, U.S. of A., and ya better not forget it, ole buddy.

(MATRONLY WHITE WOMAN SPECTATOR *stands and addresses* ALL GOODE.)

SPECTATOR, *dignified:* Pardon me? Pardon me, sir? What's going on here? Who's on trial?

ALL GOODE, *indignant:* Who's on trial? Why that black nigrah gal—Jo Anne!

SPECTATOR: But . . . but . . . but who got killed?

ALL GOODE, *amazed:* Who got killed? Need ya ask? Why, yours truly . . . (*He takes a deep bow.*) Me! (*Proud*) One of the good ole boys . . . GUARD ALL GOODE!

SPECTATOR: Excuse me . . . I thought this was Radio City Music Hall.

(*The* SPECTATOR *leaves her seat and exits.* ALL GOODE *follows her with his eyes as she exits up the aisle. Her seat can be taken by someone else. Lights change as* ALL GOODE *turns and exits. A special light shows the spectator section. If they still are being seated, the light holds, then slips down.* JO ANNE's *theme comes over top of* ALL GOODE's *music. The sounds become bolder. Heavy drumming begins. Noise of struggle in the dark of the stage. Lights up dimly on a scrimlike arrangement. Two oversized silhouettes are seen fighting—a large male and a smallish female. The male is getting the best of the female figure. He has a weapon in his hand. He raises his arm to plunge the weapon in her, but he slips on something wet upon the deck and falls. The two silhouettes freeze and lights shift. Under a special light, the* REPORTER *and a* TOWNSWOMAN *appear. The* TOWNSWOMAN *is black and wears a maid's costume; she is making a bed.*)

REPORTER, *interviewing with tape recorder:* And what do you think happened to Jo Anne that night?

MAID, *shrugs:* I dunno. But his shoes were outside the cell. HE had the key, not Jo Anne. She did not let HIM in.

REPORTER: Do you believe that this will be out in her trial?

MAID: It better be! These hare young black and white people around hare will tear up this town if they don't let Jo Anne free!

VOICES (*Lights off them. The figures behind the scrim begin their struggle anew. The female figure grabs the weapon away from the fallen man and backs off. The male figure lunges at her. As he closes on her, the female strikes out at the male in fear, desperation, and hate. As the weapon pierces* ALL GOODE): JO ANNE!!!

(*The male fights to kill her with bestial energy. He knocks her down and kicks and stomps her. She strikes again and again with the weapon and slows him down by hitting his legs. She fights her way to her feet and plunges the weapon into the man again, as he rushes her.*)

VOICES: JO ANNE!!!

(*Like a wounded animal, the man beats and pummels the woman. He is about to kill her with his brute strength, except that she strikes once more.*)

VOICES: JO ANNE!!!

(*Lights down slowly as the struggle continues. Silence. Lights up on jail cell. The scrim fixture has been pulled into the flies and* ALL GOODE *can be seen leaning on the cell door, without pants, his bloody undershirt covering his private parts.* JO ANNE *is frozen in tableau.* ALL GOODE *pulls an ice pick from his bleeding chest and tries to get to* JO ANNE. *He freezes before he touches her.* JO ANNE *stirs.*)

JO ANNE, *prays:* Oh, Lord in heaven . . . what have you brought me to? Why have you chosen this to be my fate?

VOICES, *rhythmic:* RUN, JO ANNE! ESCAPE, SISTER! RUN, JO ANNE! GET AWAY FROM THIS EVIL, VIOLENT PLACE!

JO ANNE: Oh, please, God, show me the way. Help me, Lord. Give me the strength to be free.

(JO ANNE *rushes off. Lights change slightly.* GUARD ALL GOODE *stirs.*)

ALL GOODE, *half-drunk, wild-eyed:* She killed me! . . . That nigger bitch killed me. Do ya hear that! A nigger bitch killed me!!! Ya hear that, brothers? Killed. Me. Guard All Goode—a whiteman . . . a Southern whiteman, in a Southern town. Now ain't that the limit? . . . Gawd damn! What in tarnation is this world comin' to? What is happenin' 'round hare?

(*Lights change. Lights down on* ALL GOODE. *Lights up on* BLACK REPORTER *and* FOUR ACTIVISTS. *As action moves on, the* PREACHER *gives a benediction.*)

BLACK PREACHER, *oratory:* Lord . . . give us the strength to carry out your will in this fight to free young Sister Jo Anne. In your wisdom, grant us the will and bless us with your might to turn back the devil and his helpers in this great battle between good and evil.

BLACK REPORTER: Do you think that the Klu Klux Klan will take an active role in this case? This is Klan country, isn't it?

BLACK ACTIVIST #1: Well, the white robes of the Klan have been replaced by the black robes of the Southern judicial system.

BLACK REPORTER: In such a court, do you believe that the facts will come out?

BLACK ACTIVIST #2: Now look . . . I've been sayin' that All Goode committed suicide, that's right, a modern day form of Hari-Kari.[2]

BLACK PREACHER: Give us the lips to speak the truth, oh, Lord. Lips that never lie. Give us the brain to think, Lord. Thoughts that do not betray our lack of knowledge and our ignorance. Give us your guidance, Lord. Show us the way to the promised land.

BLACK REPORTER: So you see this as, first of all, a women's issue?

BLACK ACTIVIST #3, *female:* What? Well, men do not usually have to be confronted with rape!

WHITE ACTIVIST, *female:* What we are talking about is Jo Anne being the symbol of the women's struggle in this nation. What we are talking about is that white, fat, gutted-pig guard coming into that black girl's . . . I mean woman's cell and raping her. What we are talking about is that fat, old cracker, All Goode, being the symbol of the old South— white surpremacy, racism, sexism, male chauvinism . . .

BLACK PREACHER: Amen, Lord. Amen, Lord. Show us the way, Jesus.

(*Lights down. Up on the cell.* ALL GOODE *is drunk. Now cleaned up, he hangs on the bars outside of* JO ANNE's *cell. He has an ice pick in his hand, which he pokes through the bars, and a plate of chicken in the other hand.* JO ANNE, *her back to him, pretends that she is asleep.*)

ALL GOODE: Jo Anne . . . Jo Anne . . . it's me, lover boy. Guard All Goode. I got somethin' for you, gal.

———————————

2. Hari-Kari: Also called seppuku; ritual suicide by disembowelment, at one time practiced in Japan.

(JO ANNE *doesn't stir*. ALL GOODE *sticks his ice pick into a piece of chicken, takes it off the plate, and pushes it toward* JO ANNE.)

ALL GOODE: Don't ya want none of this chicken, honey? It's golden brown and . . . ummm ummm . . . is it delicious. Makes ya want ta smack ya lips. Jo Anne? . . . I done ate myself full already. Ole Cookie over in the commissary don't mind none. With you bein' the only one in jail here, he got to throw lots of the food away, anyhow. So I eats lots of it up. And this hare chicken and stuff I brought you. Jo Anne? . . . Jo Anne? . . . why ain't you talkin' to me, honey? Ya mad at me? Awww . . . don't be mad at ole Goody. I don't mean no harm. Heee heee . . . that ole Cooky got some good moonshine up there. Yeah, I got me a little snort. Shucks. I downed me nearly a pint of his best. And on top of what I had me before I got here, well, that's what I call quite a load to carry. But that don't make much nevermind to me. Nawh, sir. Hey . . . ya mad at me for what I said to you yesterday, Jo Anne? Awww . . . I didn't mean much of nothin' by it . . . ole Goody wouldn't hurt his sweet lil Jo Anne. I like ya, ya know. Now all I said was . . .

JO ANNE, *turns:* I know what you said! Just go away and leave me alone.

ALL GOODE: Ahhh . . . you ain't sleepin'. So ya do remember what I said? Now all I said was . . .

JO ANNE: LEAVE ME ALONE!

ALL GOODE, *leering:* All I said was that I'd like to screw you so long and hard that you'd scream out to me that your pee hole was sore.

JO ANNE, *disgust:* You filthy beast!

ALL GOODE, *waves chicken around:* Filthy beast! Now, looka here, gal. I treat you good. This goddamn chicken is the best ya can get here. What's wrong? Your black ass is too good to appreciate some good treatment? Is it, huh? Is it? What! You ain't goin'a answer me, bitch? (*He throws the chicken at her and holds the ice pick menacingly. Furious.*) I'll show you, you black whore! (*He takes out his keys and unlocks her door. He is so drunk that he staggers against it, preventing himself from opening it to get inside. Muttering.*) I'll show you, you nigger bitch. I'll show you.

JO ANNE, *scared, but defiant:* You better stay out of here, man! You better not come in here if you know what's good for you.

ALL GOODE, *hesitates, scratches his head, and tries to remember where he is at and what he is doing there. Remembers:* You talkin' to me like that? Why let me tell ya, gal. I'm the bossman here. I'm your lord and master back here in this corner of hell, ya understand? When I tell you to squat, you better ask me what color. Ya understand? When I tell ya to spread open ya legs, gal, you better open up like a goddamn bloomin' rose just kissed by the sun. Ya understand that, gal?

JO ANNE, *angry:* I understand that you ain't gonna walk out of here, if you come in this cell and try and mess with me, man!

ALL GOODE, *too drunk to open door. His large stomach gets in his way, and he fumbles with the keys and locks the door back:* One of these days, gal. One of these days. I got all the time I need. You ain't goin' nowheres.

JO ANNE: You leave me alone, you hear? Or I'm reportin' you.

ALL GOODE: Report me? You black niggers still don't believe that you're in America. Ha ha . . . report me? What's the word of a black nigger bitch like you against my word, the word of a whiteman down here? Whew . . . if I wasn't so tired tonight, I'd give you really somethin' to report. Now I'm gonna go up hare to my office and get me a wink, but if ya want anything, honey babe, just give me a little call. Ole Goody'll come lick and suck your thing fo' ya 'till ya hollars mah name, ha ha!

JO ANNE, *winces:* You filthy pig!

ALL GOODE: Huhn . . . ya pretendin' none of them big black bucks ain't done hung you on the end of their tongue yet? . . . Shucks . . . you don't know the facts of life yet, gal. Let ole Goody show ya . . . . Ya know, I really likes you a lot, Jo Anne. Ya reminds me of a gal they had back here a good while ago. Hot dog! Did we have ourselves a time. That gal was really good to me. Uummm uummm. And you remind me of her, Jo Anne . . . only she was white trash and not even as good as you. Ya know . . . I loves you . . . . Yeah . . . I loves ya even though you is black. And I only loves two other things more than you on this god's little green acre we stand . . . That's mah bitch dog, Dixie, and mah ma's hot apple deep-dish cobbler. Yeah I loves ya ah whole lot, Jo Anne. Almost as much as Dixie. But Dixie's one dog that's got aholt of mah heart. You two should meet some day. Gee, willikers! That bitch is in heat now. A coal-black doberman, she is. A mean bitch. Chew up any ole dog that gets a hardon for her . . . Yeah, I really loves ya, JoAnne. And I can't do without you much longer, gal. I dream about you every night. And even when I wash up before I come to work . . . hee hee . . . I play with myself and daydream of you . . . . (*Makes masturbation movements*) . . . "Jo Anne," I whisper. "Jo Anne, give it to me, gal. Give ole All Goode what he needs, gal. Let me have it, baby. Give ole All Goode what he needs, gal. (*Humps the bars and has a sex fantasy.*) Just a little bit to the left, sweety. That's it! . . . That's it. You ain't nothin' but sweet black sugar, honey. That's it . . . black sugar . . . huhn . . . black sugar . . . hump . . . black suuuugaaar . . . Oh, Jo Anne, gal!"

(JO ANNE *has turned her head. She cries in lonely terror as* ALL GOODE *comes out of his sexual reverie.*)

ALL GOODE, *finishing:* Good night, mah little black sugar honey. I'll never forget you.

(*He exits to his office.* JO ANNE *is alone.*)

JO ANNE, *whispers:* You sick animal . . . if you ever come back here, I'll shove that pig sticker of yours in a place you'll never find it.

(*Lights down. Lights up on* BLACK REPORTER, LAWYER SCOTT, *an* ATTRACTIVE BLACKWOMAN, *and* TWO BLACK LADIES.)

SCOTT, *to* BLACK LADIES: I advise you not to say a word.

BLACK REPORTER, *to tape recorder:* Testing . . . testing . . . testing . . .

BLACK LADY #1: I'm so worried about Jo Anne.

BLACK LADY #2: God's with her. Remember, Jo Anne has always been strong and able to take care of herself.

BLACK LADY #1: Yes, I know, but I worry still.

SCOTT, *to* BLACK LADIES: It is important that you remain completely silent.

BLACK REPORTER: Testing . . . one, two, three . . . testing . . .

BLACK LADY #1: She's not a bad girl. Just been so unlucky, so far.

BLACK LADY #2: Yes, indeed, but those days may be over, praise the Lord. There's good people all over the world who are for Jo Anne now.

BLACK REPORTER'S TAPE RECORDER, *plays back:* Testing . . . one, two, three . . . testing . . .

SCOTT, *to* REPORTER: I'll speak to you in the court room.

REPORTER: Yes, I understand.

SCOTT: Good. I'll speak to you in court.

REPORTER, *into tape recorder:* Jo Anne, age twenty . . . a black woman . . . is a heroine . . . whether she likes it or not . . . . whether she realizes the impact she has made on contemporary history . . . But the question remains whether a female, whether a woman or girl, has the right to protect her body, her sexual self, from predatory acts by . . . by anyone . . . that is, up to and beyond the door of death.

(*Lights down. Lights up on courtroom.*)

BAILIFF: Hear ye! Hear ye! Court of the County of Wade, State of Carolina, is now in session. All rise for Judge All Goode Hopgoode, better known as Hoppy.

(ALL GOODE, *dressed as judge, enters and takes seat behind judge's bench.* CANE, *a white civil rights attorney, represents the defense.*)

JUDGE HOPPY: Be seated . . . Ladies and gents of the jury . . . How yawhl this mornin'? Good? Good. Well, we got ourselves a little piece of business cut out for us, a little piece indeed . . . Ha ha . . . As I was sayin' to my lil she-pup, Dixie, this mornin' before I sashayed down here, dixie," I said to her as I pulled her ears, "there's more than one way to skin a polecat in these hare parts . . . 'specially when the critter's black and white. Dixie, I said, there's a critter in the woodpile . . . an' there's more than one way to root him or HER out. More than one way indeed" . . . . Ha ha ha. Lawyers for the defense and prosecution, are ya ready?

PROSECUTION: Ready, your honor.

DEFENSE: Yes, your honor.

PROSECUTION: I object:

JUDGE HOPPY: Sustained.

DEFENSE: Your honor:

PROSECUTION: I object:

JUDGE HOPPY: Sustained!

DEFENSE: But! . . . But! . . .

PROSECUTION: Contempt of court!

JUDGE HOPPY: Sustained!

(GUARDS *start to drag* CANE *off.*)

CANE, *rhetorical:* Is this the quality of justice you call justice in these parts? Is this justice? Is it? . . .

(CANE *is carried off.*)

JUDGE HOPPY: Now it may not be justice to him, folks, but this is Klan country. And any white, Christian, loyal American will know what I mean by justice bein' justice, southern style.

(*Lights change. Lights on* JO ANNE.)

JO ANNE, *shy at first:* My momma always told me I'd make it. She always told me I had what it takes and could make it no matter what. And I've always believed momma. But this situation I'm in now has almost got the best of me. And all I ever wanted to do was get away from this place and see some of life and travel. But now I'm locked up here, in jail, with this crazy cracker who will probably do me in if I don't get mighty lucky . . . Ohhh . . . I sure hope you're with me, Lord. I sure hope so. You know I can take almost anything, right Lord? I'm tough, or that's what some people have told me. But I ain't bad or mean. I believe in givin' anything a try, at least once, if there ain't no harm in it to nobody. I ain't never hurt nobody really bad. I only seem to hurt myself, that's all, Lord. But I'm game to see what life holds for me. If I got to work hard and do men's work, I ain't afraid of that. Whatever life throws at me, I can scoop it up, Lord. 'Cause I ain't afraid of much. And I don't believe in takin' no stuff.

(*Lights change.* JO ANNE *is in the girl's toilet of a big city school.*)

STREET GIRL #1, *to* JO ANNE: Hey . . . you new here . . . give me a quarter.

JO ANNE, *shy:* Oh, you need a quarter? . . . Let me look in my purse . . .

STREET GIRL #2, *crowds* JO ANNE: Hey, ya country bitch! You just got to the city. This school's our turf (*snatches purse from* JO ANNE) Here! Give me your fucken' money, bitch!

JO ANNE, *resists:* Don't do that, please. That's all my carfare and lunch . . .

STREET GIRL #1, *pushes* JO ANNE: Shut up, shorty! You belong to me now.

JO ANNE: What are you talkin' about? Give me my money back.

STREET GIRL #2: You're in our gang, now. We run things around here.

JO ANNE: Nobody runs my life. I'm free!

STREET GIRL #1: You better shut your mouth, little bitch. Or we gonna do it for ya.

JO ANNE: Look, you two . . . I been patient with you. Now, give me back my things and leave me alone and I'll forget this.

STREET GIRL #2, *tries to hit* JO ANNE: I'll show you who . . .

(JO ANNE *punches* GIRL #2 *in face. Then* GIRL #1 *rushes* JO ANNE, *and the three girls fight hard in the lavatory.*)

STREET GIRLS, *together:* Bitch! Just you wait! Owww! Hold still, damn you! Owww, damn it! Little bitch, just wait 'till we get you! Ouch!

(*The* TWO STREET GIRLS *almost get the best of* JO ANNE, *until she pulls an Afro pick from her hairdo and stabs one girl on the hand and rakes the other's shoulder.*)

STREET GIRL #1: We give! We give. Please don't hurt us, sister.

STREET GIRL #2: Stop! Stop! We'll be your friend. We'll be your ace boon girls. Just don't hurt us.

JO ANNE, *rests:* My name's Jo Anne. I guess I'm in your gang now. Just remember, I don't take no stuff from nobody.

(*Lights up on* REPORTER *and elderly black* TOWNSMAN.)

REPORTER: Is that all you can remember, sir?

TOWNSMAN: Wahl, I hear tell that when Jo Anne left here for that little bit of time and went up North, wahl, she fell in with some fast company.

REPORTER: Oh?

TOWNSMAN: They weren't really bad kids, ya understand, they was just kinda fast. I hear tell that Jo Anne was sent back down here 'cause she was gettin' mighty independent up there . . . Not bad, just hardheaded.

But my my . . . wasn't that a mistake now! Sendin' that poor chile back down here.

REPORTER: Yes, sir, it appears to have been a mistake.

TOWNSMAN: Wahl, I got to get along, sonny boy. Before this play's over, I's still gotta find me the claim office.

(*The* MATRONLY WHITE WOMAN *wanders on.*)

WOMAN: Excuse me, gentlemen. But do either of you know the way out of here?

TOWNSMAN, *rising:* Wahl, ma'am . . . just stay close to me. I'm sure we can help each other.

(*The* COUPLE *exits. The reporter writes in his notebook. Lights alter and up on* JUDGE HOPPY, CANE, *and the* PROSECUTOR.)

JUDGE HOPPY: Now the rules of evidence, as I see it, is as clear as the day is long.

CANE: Your honor. . . .

PROSECUTOR: I object.

JUDGE: Sustained.

CANE: BUT SEMEN WAS DRIPPING FROM THE END OF THE DEAD MAN'S PENIS!!!

PROSECUTOR: I object!

JUDGE: Contempt of court!

(GUARDS *rush in and drag* CANE *off.*)

JUDGE HOPPY: Now the rules of evidence, as I see 'em, don't deal with nary a hypothetical question. Evidence is evidence. And when you can't find none, you invent it. And when you discover some, you obscure it . . . My Gawd! . . . Why everybody knows that. It's the foundation of Carolina justice.

(*Lights change. Up on* JO ANNE *in her cell area.*)

JO ANNE: I don't represent the old South . . . but the new. That's right. I'm of the new South. The young, new, black South. And we part of the old, too, but are really new . . . Now, I love my momma. More than anything else outside my own life. But I don't want the life that my momma had to accept, because she was poor, black, and female here in America, for myself. No. Those days are over. Forever. We children of the new South won't allow them to return. But it is those people of the older generation, our mothers and fathers, who have taught us to seek out a better life than they had. They taught us to demand and fight for a better way of life. And that's what we are doing, even those of us who have to leave here to get ourselves together before we come back and take this whole thing on. You see, I love to travel. Always have. By car, by train, or any other way. Ha ha . . . Yeah! This little woman, Jo Anne, sure likes to be gettin' up. Ya know . . . I believe what they be sayin' about travel being educational and stuff like that. Ya know . . . it gives you something to compare your past by. When you travel, you feel that you're not being held back by your old self, by old ways. It makes you proud that you got on out and did something fo' yourself. You see, there's two things I believe in . . . that's God and Love. Yes, but you got to find yourself before you can really discover God or Love. And that's where travel comes in, sometimes. Yeah, I know this might sound kinda heavy, but listen for a moment . . . please? Now, there's two things I really want out of this life I love so much: that's to be somebody, somebody important, and I want my people to be proud of me. But I ain't gonna take no stuff from nobody. I'm just tryin' to make it and don't mean nobody no harm, unless they mean me some. I'm no trouble, really, I'm just passin' through, ya know. At least that's how I felt before this "incident" happened. Yeah, I've heard all that stuff about what was supposed to have happened in that jail cell and what did happen and all kinda stuff. But take it from my point of view: What if the worse had happened to ME, not to Guard All Goode, but to me, a little black Southern girl? I don't know . . . but I think that I would have been swept under the rug like so much embarrassing dirt. Now what if a huge, drunken, depraved monster had come to where you were sleeping and had made you suck his . . . his PENIS, that's right, give him up some "head" or have him drive his ice pick into your eye. Would you have fought? Nawh. You'd probably have cried a lot and spit some . . . and swallowed the whole mess with your pride like we black women been doing for hundreds of years. But all of us ain't gonna be takin' that kinda shit no more. No more, I saw to that! But what if I had put up a fight and he had gotten the best of me and had done what he wanted anyhow, then turned me over to the other guards? Or the men prisoners down in the pit? Ya know, some prisoners have been made such animals by this living hell called "jail" that they don't have much human values. That's right! I'm here to testify, yawhl . . . Unbelievable? Not if you in a dark, cold, Southern jail on a night when your jailer's passion is cruel and hot and there's only this little black ass, Jo Anne, between him and satisfaction. Look! I didn't have time to kill myself because of that human outrage forced upon me; he was the only one in striking distance, so I had to off him for survival's sake, but I wouldn't have killed myself, neither. That's just not in me . . . and I'm not the enemy . . . he is.

(*Light up on* ALL GOODE *reclining in his office chair. He rises and walks down toward* JO ANNE.)

ALL GOODE: Cut the crap, Jo Anne, gal . . . you might get some of these hare people to go along with you . . . but they ain't heard my side of the story, yet.

JO ANNE: And they ain't gonna hear it, ole buddy. Remember . . . I killed you.

ALL GOODE, *accusing:* You foully murdered me when I was unawares and had been seduced into physical rapture through the ecstasy of passionate lust.

JO ANNE: Say wha? . . . Guard All Goode . . . are you talking to me?

ALL GOODE: You can hear, niggah! Now don't you start gettin' cute with me. Just give the people the facts.

JO ANNE: The fact is . . . I killed you, man. And if you don't watch how you talk to me. I'm gonna take care of what's left of you.

ALL GOODE, *apprehensive:* Now . . . now, Jo Anne, honey. Now don't get . . .

JO ANNE: I'm not your honey, man. Never been . . . and don't you forget it.

ALL GOODE, *ornery:* Awww, Jo Anne . . . you know that just ain't right. You know I always did treat you good, gal. You special to me. Now, you should come off that nasty stuff you talkin' about and what I was supposed to have did.

JO ANNE, *puzzled:* "Supposed to have did"? What you mean?

ALL GOODE: You know what I mean, Jo Anne. You know I'm your jail house man.

(*Furious,* JO ANNE *rushes him and strikes out.* ALL GOODE *slips out of her reach, like the spirit he is.*)

JO ANNE, *fights shadows:* Lying cracker bastard! Liar! Faggot! You nasty punk, you!

ALL GOODE, *worried:* Now . . . Now, Jo Anne . . . don't get yourself worked up, gal. I'm only trying ta get what's fairly mine.

JO ANNE, *still angry:* What's that, pig! A state funeral?

ALL GOODE, *reacting:* No, bitch: My good name!

JO ANNE: Your good name? Your good name? Now you have really lost contact with this world. Your name is shit, man. Has always been. But now you done got caught with your pants down. You hip? Your name? Hah! It will really be remembered for what it stands for—SHIT!

ALL GOODE: I demand justice!

JO ANNE: You screwed justice, All Goode, remember? You raped the old bitch the night I had to take you off this planet.

ALL GOODE, *pleads:* Look . . . look . . . I only want you to be a little fair.

JO ANNE: Fair? I been fair. I've listened to you this long. What do you think you're doing? Haunting me or something? Listen, man . . . if you mess with me any more, I'll kill your memory by never mentioning you again and destroy your image by creating curse poems about your deeds. Listen, ole buddy, I'll eliminate your soul the same as I did your greasy body.

ALL GOODE, *on knees:* Jo Anne . . . Jo Anne . . . please . . . please, Jo Anne . . .

JO ANNE, *terrible temper:* What is it! What do you want!

ALL GOODE: Give me my moment in the true spotlight of history . . . men's minds. Allow me my chance on the stage of truth . . .

JO ANNE, *annoyed:* Ohhh . . . you so corny, man. Say . . . why should I allow you anything?

ALL GOODE: Because you're fair, Jo Anne.

JO ANNE: No I'm not. I don't even want you to think that, All Goode.

ALL GOODE: But you got a good Christian heart, Jo. Just give me a pinch of Christian charity, please.

JO ANNE, *softens:* Nawh . . . I can't. I'm sorry, but I can't.

ALL GOODE: But why?

JO ANNE: Well, people wouldn't understand. They'd look at your lying images and think there's some truth in your story.

ALL GOODE: But it is true!

JO ANNE: So you say! So you say there is, you sonna bitch! What you did to me is the only truth there is, motherfucker! And you paid for that. *I* made you pay. And if you don't watch yourself now, you gonna pay for the rest of eternity in that hot hole of hell.

ALL GOODE: But I can't go, don't you understand? I can't go nowhere. I'm not at peace. I'm a goddamn restless spirit trying to get my say. Give me my chance, gal. In the name of God . . . (*Thundering rumbles are heard.*) . . . let the chips fall where they may, but as a Christian . . . extend me grace, sister.

JO ANNE, *cold:* Whether you have the ear of God . . . or the devil . . . I'm deaf to you, All Goode.

ALL GOODE: What do you have to be afraid of?

JO ANNE: Me, afraid? Hey, I'm not afraid of a living . . or dead . . . ass. Especially you.

ALL GOODE: Well, I know that. I know that. But you won't give what's due me?

JO ANNE: There's nothin' due you, not even this conversation.

ALL GOODE, *threatens:* Do you want me to haunt you the rest of your days?

JO ANNE, *stalks him:* Haunt me! Nothing like you better think they hauntin' me. I wasn't studden³ nothin' bout you when you was alive and stinkin' up the world . . . and you less than a shadow now. You just a bad memory that's fast disappearing. In the morning, you'll be gone with my bad dreams. Disappear, All Goode, don't forget you're dead.

ALL GOODE: Give me three minutes, Jo Anne.

JO ANNE: No!

ALL GOODE, *appeals:* One? . . . Awww . . . it's not for me, gal. Not for me . . . but for the ones I left behind holding the bag of my finished reputation.

JO ANNE: They heard the facts. Everyone did. The trial took care of that. The whole world knows of your moments on earth.

ALL GOODE, *anguish:* No . . . no . . . not that way. Not from my lips. Not in my words. Oh, Jo Anne, give this old, dead, stupid man this last wish. Oh, Jo Anne. . . you're strong and bright and sexy and everything . . . I'm nothing. Oh, please be kind and generous, as well. Time . . . it's getting away from me. I don't have long to be here to plead my case. And . . . and it's too soon to appeal to Satan . . . and too late to ask God . . . I can only turn to you, honey. Please allow this ole peckerwood his chance to redeem his place in the minds and hearts of his kind.

JO ANNE, *almost silent:* All right . . . all right . . . I'm gonna give you what you tried to take from me . . . a chance to retain your soul. But I don't want no stuff, now.

ALL GOODE, *cries at her feet:* Oh, Jo Anne, gal . . . Jo Anne . . . bless you . . . bless you . . .

(*Lights down. Music is heard. Lights up on* SCOTT *and* TWO FEMALE ACTIVISTS, *a black and a white.*)

TWO FEMALE ACTIVISTS, *together:* WE ARE THE CONCERNED BITCHES FOR FEMALE FREEDOM, INC. WE ADVOCATE TOTAL WOMEN'S JUSTICE AND LIBERATION!

SCOTT, *rational:* Sure . . . sure . . . I hear what you all are saying . . . but I have to concern myself with Jo Anne's best interests.

BLACK ACTIVIST, *rhetoric:* There are nearly a hundred people on death row here. Jo Anne is only one case among many. Don't forget the thousands of other oppressed black and other female prisoners. It's one more step in the political process of oppression of black people, yes. But it's only one case. And what I'd like to see . . .

SCOTT, *tired:* I know that . . . I know that . . . but Jo Anne . . .

---

3. "Studden": Not caring about.

WHITE ACTIVIST, *militant:* Women's Rights is the main issue here! If it had been a white woman in this position, she may not have been brought to trial, true, but nonetheless, the Women's Rights issue is the supreme . . .

BLACK ACTIVIST, *speechmaking:* The rape of the black female and its national political justification are tied to the image of the portrayal of the nigger man as a bestial animal raping and taking white meat!

WHITE ACTIVIST: Amen!

SCOTT: I understand all that . . . but I have to concern myself with Jo Anne. She's fragile and all this type of . . .

WHITE ACTIVIST, *saluting:* Power to the Bitches!

BLACK ACTIVIST, *saluting:* Right on!

SCOTT, *concerned:* Please keep Jo Anne's welfare at heart. Don't lose this special person among your issues.

WHITE ACTIVIST, *swaggering:* This is the biggest thing we power bitches been into in a long time, and we gonna make the most of it. Jo Anne is only one woman—we're out to free all women!

BLACK ACTIVIST: Sock it to 'em, sister!

WHITE ACTIVIST: Power to the Bitches! Off with your bra and drawers! Pink Pussy Power!

(The TWO ACTIVISTS *begin disrobing and demonstrating. They cover their well-proportioned bodies with stick-on labels which read:* DON'T SCREW JO ANNE AGAIN! PAWS OFF OF JOANNE! MOTHERFUCKER!, *etc. They do a contemporary female dance. The* BLACK ACTIVIST *rips off her bra, glasses, and pants and gives a power salute.*)

BLACK ACTIVIST: Black Power! Bitches Power! Power!

SCOTT: Please, sisters . . . please . . . we have to use our heads in this . . . we . . .

WHITE ACTIVIST: This is our chance, sisters. We have a real test case named Jo Anne . . . Bitches have the right to defend themselves from male pigs!

BLACK ACTIVIST: Right on! Off the men!

WHITE ACTIVIST *speechmaking:* Not only is Jo Anne on trial here—it is the long-neglected rights of blacks and women to get equal justice in the South . . . the rights of prisoners to dignified treatment, often abused and misused in this state . . . the rights of women to defend themselves with violence, if necessary, against sexual assault . . . plus the system of capital punishment, still maintained here . . . and which is intolerable!

(*Cheers and applause are heard from the wings.*)

SCOTT: Please, sisters, please . . . just remember Jo Anne . . . right? . . .

Remember Jo Anne . . . she's not only a symbol . . . . she's real . . . she's human . . . she's feminine . . .

(*Lights down on the demonstration.*)

BLACK ACTIVIST: OFF THE MEN!

(*Lights up on bare stage—the countryside. The baying of hounds are heard; torches are seen in the distance. The setting is the countryside: woods, swamps, and bayous of Southern nightmares, where black rape, murder, lynching, and maiming are never forgotten memories. Enter* ALL GOODE *with* DIXIE THE DOG, *and several* HENCHMEN *carrying torches, shot guns, clubs, and ropes. The stage lighting should throw the thug-like posse's shadows into huge patterns over the stage. The coloring of the scene should be crimson and rich, bloody shades. A couple of the men wear the white costume of the Ku Klux Klan. Among them, unhooded and recognizable, is the* PROSECUTOR. DIXIE THE DOG, *is an actress who wears a menacing-looking black leather and metal costume. Spikes jut out of her huge collar and a chain is used as a leash by* ALL GOODE *to hold back the terrible beast. Arching her spine at the waist,* DIXIE *walks on her hands and the balls of her feet like a squat monster. She does not crawl on her knees nor stop her hungry, predatory movements and ferocious sounds while onstage.* DIXIE *is muzzled, for she barks fiercely at the spectators while dripping saliva and showing her fangs as she lunges for victims.*)

ALL GOODE, *charging the audience:* At 'em, Dixie! At 'em, girl! Hunt the niggah, Jo Anne! We must have her dead!

HENCHMEN: WE MUST HAVE HER DEAD!

ALL GOODE: Git her, Dixie! Search her out in her lair! She killed me, a whiteman! And we must take her head!

HENCHMEN: WE MUST TAKE HER HEAD!

(DIXIE *howls and lunges against her chain.*)

ALL GOODE: Howl, Dixie! Show your sharp white teeth! We got Jo Anne to kill before we git to bed and sleep!

HENCHMEN: WE GOT JO ANNE TO KILL BEFORE WE GET TO BED AND SLEEP!

(*The* LYNCH PARTY *makes several awesome sweeps of the stage, then disappears into the wings.* DIXIE's *baying and howls are heard off. Lights change. Up on* JO ANNE *in cabin, crouched in a rocking chair. The distant sounds of the search party worry* JO ANNE).

JO ANNE, *frightened:* When they catch me, I wonder if they'll kill me quick . . . or slow . . . What if they ALL rape me before they kill me, including the dog? It's possible. It's been known to happen 'round hare. I know my Southern history. And what if they torture me long and then burn me alive? . . . . Oh . . . what if they gouge out my eyes . . . or force a fiery torch down my throat . . . (*gasp*) . . . or up between my thighs? I know my Southern history . . . and anything could possibly happen to little me . . . . Oh God! . . . please help me, Lord. Please send me a sign that you haven't abandoned me, Lord. I'm in your hands . . . .

(*Lights up on* CABIN DWELLER, *a young, self-assured blackman.*)

CABIN DWELLER: Don't worry, sister Jo Anne. No devils will get you tonight, nor any others, as long as you believe in yourself and the freedom of black people.

JO ANNE: But it's so hard to think of anything with those dreadful avengers stalking me. Or to believe in anyone, even myself. My body and brain are paralyzed by numb fear and hopeless panic.

CABIN DWELLER: That's natural, sister. But everything will be all right one day soon. Believe me.

JO ANNE, *puzzled:* Who are you?

CABIN DWELLER: I live here in this cabin.

JO ANNE, *starting:* I should go! I saw your light when I was stumbling through the swamp. I just couldn't go any farther . . .

CABIN DWELLER: Don't worry . . . don't worry, sister Jo Anne. Everything will be okay.

JO ANNE: How do you know my name?

CABIN DWELLER: I hear it broadcast over my radio every ten minutes. I don't have electric here, but my radio has fresh batteries.

JO ANNE, *wistful:* Oh . . . you know . . . I almost thought . . . (*She pauses.*)

CABIN DWELLER: What did you think, sister?

JO ANNE, *hurried:* Nothin' . . . Ah . . . but if they catch me here in your place . . .

CABIN DWELLER, *hypnotic:* Relax . . . please . . . rest yourself . . . nobody's going to find you here.

JO ANNE, *sleepy:* I'm so tired . . . . If I could only rest a minute. This is like some terrible nightmare that I've fallen . . . say . . . brother . . . what's . . . what's your name?

(JO ANNE *falls asleep. The* CABIN DWELLER *lifts her from the rocking chair and places her gently in the large, old-fashioned bed. He pulls a quilt over her. Then he turns the light down, reaches under a pillow and takes out a revolver, places it beneath his shirt, walks back to the rocker, and sits, facing the door. The* SEARCH PARTY's *sounds fade in the background. Lights alter. Lights up on* ALL GOODE. *He is in the jail area.*)

ALL GOODE: Now . . . it's time . . . for mah story. It's time for you to get the real truth, from me . . . All Goode's truth. Now is the time you been waiting for.

(*Light on* JO ANNE, *coming into jail*)

JO ANNE: Okay . . . get on with it, man. You don't have that much time to tell your lies.

ALL GOODE: Lies, you say . . . Well, we'll see about that.

JO ANNE, *taunts:* Okay, we'll see . . . We'll see, huh?

ALL GOODE: Let me begin . . . I was sitting back in my office there. The night was dark. The hour was dead as a grave yard. And I hear this noise.

JO ANNE, *suspicious:* What noise?

ALL GOODE: I'm gettin' to that. Just be patient. I'm the one whose time is running out, not you . . .

JO ANNE: Well, go on.

ALL GOODE: I intend to.

JO ANNE: Well, do it!

ALL GOODE: Okay. Okay . . . . Well, I hear this noise . . . It's strange and somethin' I wasn't used to. Go on, gal, make that noise you was making that night I died.

JO ANNE: Me makin' noise? Are you out of your mind, man?

ALL GOODE: Yeah, it was you, Jo Anne. You was sleepin' and makin' all kinds of noises . . . ya know, sexy-like.

JO ANNE: Now I told you, man, if you started tellin' lies, that I wouldn't . . .

ALL GOODE: Aww, stop ya bitchin', woman! First, you say I can tell mah story the way I know it . . . Now you jumpin' on me every chance you get. Look! You got the upper hand. You livin' and I'm dead. I know they say dead men have no tales and other kinds of things like that, but you gave me your word that I'd be heard out. Now what's it gonna be?

JO ANNE: All right. Go on. I'll try and keep quiet.

ALL GOODE: Good! . . . So I heard these noises. It was almost like a baby whining for milk. I couldn't make out what it was.

(*The sound that* ALL GOODE *describes comes from off-stage or through the sound system.* ALL GOODE *plays out the scene.*)

ALL GOODE: Now, that noise raised the hair on the back of my neck. It was strange, ya know, female-like and sexy. I was all alone there by myself, except for you, Jo Anne.

JO ANNE: Ahuh.

ALL GOODE: I didn't know what to do. I couldn't see what was makin' the noise over the closed-circuit TV from where I was sittin'. And I was scared to come back to the cells. And if I called up to the main building and got the chief night guard back there, and if he heard and found nothin', well, he'd probably laugh at me or get mad and write me up and say I was drinkin' too much on the job. But I couldn't ignore that noise. It was gettin' louder. And it was gettin' to me. Mah ole johnson was as hard as a yard dawg's dick in the mornin'. But I didn't have no weapon back there. They wasn't allowed. Ya know, one of you desperate criminals might use it to escape, Jo Anne.

JO ANNE: Oh, cut the corn, All Goode.

ALL GOODE: So, I remembered the ice pick in my desk and got it. Then I snuck back into the cell area . . . and ya know what I found?

JO ANNE: No, I don't know what you found.

ALL GOODE: I found you back there in your cell dreamin'.

JO ANNE: Dreaming?

ALL GOODE: Yeah, you must of been, 'cause you was makin' the sexiest sounds, gal. You should'a heard yourself. You probably was dreamin' of some giant niggah stud just humpin' and bumpin' it to you.

JO ANNE: Oh, shut your filthy mouth, pig!

ALL GOODE: But let me finish . . . let me . . . We just now getting to the good part. Now, Jo Anne . . . I want you to make that sound.

JO ANNE: You what?

ALL GOODE: Make that sound. You know, the one you was makin' that night. Go on . . . it goes like this . . . (*Imitates the sound*)

JO ANNE: Now, I know you outta your mind.

ALL GOODE: Now, that's the sound. That's the sound. You was layin' over there in your cell and makin' it. And when I come up, I accidently kicked your tin drinkin' cup layin' outside your door, and you rose up. Go ahead, gal, get over there on that bunk and rise up the way you did that night.

JO ANNE: All Goode . . . don't you realize it now? You were the one dreamin', not me. You were in a drunken stupor and dreamed all this.

ALL GOODE: Listen hare . . . listen hare . . . You rose and looked at me, yes, looked at me with unseeing eyes, as if you wasn't human, 'cause, dammit, you was still asleep, like a sleepwalker. And you said . . .

(*Now in the cell,* JO ANNE *says the words and plays out the part.*)

JO ANNE, *in unearthly voice:* Darling . . . I been waitin' for you. Come. Come to me, my love.

ALL GOODE, *excited:* Ooooeeeee . . . woman! There you was. Like I always wanted. Just waitin' and wantin' me!

JO ANNE, *normal:* It was your dream, fool! Your dream.

ALL GOODE: Nawh . . . nawh . . . nawh nawh nawh . . . it was YOUR dream, Jo Anne, and you was dreamin' I was some black superstud, and that was okay with me, 'cause whether you was dreamin' or not . . . I was your man then and I was gonna have you like you wanted me to. Then you said . . .

JO ANNE, *disrobes in sensual voice and manner:* I'm yours, baby. I'm all yours. Come and get me, daddy. Look what you get when you're lucky.

(*The scrim begins to slowly descend from above.*)

ALL GOODE: I couldn't control myself. I tore off my shoes in the hallway . . .

JO ANNE, *normal:* No one's gonna believe this lying dream of yours, All Goode. You know that, don't you?

ALL GOODE, *sexually aroused:* Don't interrupt . . . don't interrupt . . . . Now I didn't damage your dreams, did I? I didn't stomp all over your fantasies and illusions, did I? Sex dreams are real, gal, let me show you . . .

(*The scrim is in place and shows* JO ANNE *and* ALL GOODE's *silhouettes inside the cell.*)

ALL GOODE: You know how ya did me, gal.

JO ANNE, *normal, defensive:* Did you? What you talkin' about?

ALL GOODE: You know what you said. You said . . .

JO ANNE, *dreamlike:* Take off your pants, daddy. Take 'em off. I want ta kiss your little thing.

(*They are in sexual embrace behind the scrim.*)

ALL GOODE: It ain't too little . . . it ain't too little for you, Jo Anne, honey.

JO ANNE, *dreamlike:* Come here, Goody. Let me suck your brains out through your toes.

ALL GOODE: Oooeeee, hot dawg! I knew I was into somethang deep then. I pulled my pants off, then mah drawers and my sport shirt that they got for evidence now. I was clean, bare-assed buck-naked except for mah tee shirt. Then you was undressin', throwin' your bra over the cell door and kickin' your panties under the bunk, and your hands . . . Gawd . . . your hands was doin' things to mah pecker that I can't even describe, much less imagine . . .

(JO ANNE *and* ALL GOODE *play out the action of the narrative.*)

ALL GOODE: I had forgotten that I still held the ice pick in mah left hand. All I could do was place mah right one on the top of your head as you went down on me . . . aahhhh . . . and close my eyes and hold on. Oooohhh, Jo Anne . . . gal, you loved me so much that night. So much.

(JO ANNE *rises up and struggles. The spell is broken.*)

JO ANNE, *normal voice:* You liar! You lyin' dog!

ALL GOODE, *hurried:* Then, just as I came floodin' out into you, you musta woke up, cause you screamed!

JO ANNE: Aaaahhhhhh . . . I'll kill you for this! I'll kill you!

(JO ANNE *throws herself on* ALL GOODE. *The two oversized* SILHOUETTES *fight.*)

ALL GOODE: Nawh, Jo . . . nawh, gal. Don't do this to me. Don't!

(JO ANNE *scratches and tears at* ALL GOODE's *eyes. He becomes angered and punches her. The fight rages all over the small cell, behind the scrim.* ALL GOODE *is getting the best of* JO ANNE. *He has the icepick in his hand. Suddenly aware of it, he raises his arm to plunge the weapon in her, but he slips on something wet upon the deck and falls. The two* SILHOUETTES *freeze and lights shift. Under a special light, the* REPORTER *and a* WOMAN TRAVELER *appear. The* WOMAN TRAVELER *is white and wears a smart looking white pants suit. She holds a cocktail.*)

REPORTER: And what do you think happened to Jo Anne that night?

WOMAN TRAVELER: Do you believe she's innocent?

REPORTER: Personally, I do. But what do you believe?

WOMAN TRAVELER: Well . . . there seems to be too many holes in the case . . . pardon the pun. But I'm suspicious over the legal justice system down here, and I'm suspicious of the media and the coverage they're giving this case, and I'm suspicious of all the politics involved. I'm a Southerner . . . really a Westerner, from East Texas, but even so . . . I can't imagine them convicting that girl, Jo Anne.

(*Lights off them. The figures behind the scrim begin their struggle anew. The* FEMALE FIGURE *grabs the weapon away from the fallen man and backs off. The* MALE FIGURE *lunges at her. As he closes on her, the* FEMALE *strikes out at the* MALE *in fear, desperation, and hate.*)

VOICES, *as the weapon pierces* ALL GOODE: JO ANNE!!!

(*Lights change. The scrim disappears.* ALL GOODE *can be seen leaning on the cell door, without pants, his bloody undershirt covering his private parts.* JO ANNE *looks on in wonderment.*)

ALL GOODE: And that's how it happened, honey. That's my story.

JO ANNE: No. No. It wasn't anything like that. I had total justification for what I did to defend myself from you. You're tellin' it wrong. You're still lyin'. But just you wait, the truth will come out. It will, you'll see!

Lights down.

ACT II

From this point on, the audience and spectators are not treated specially: They become one. All barriers are removed and the audience is allowed to become a regular theater audience, in the usual sense. Lights alter. ALL GOODE *and the* PROSECUTOR *are seen standing on the moors. They both wear white robes with the hoods thrown back. They carry brilliant torches that burn with the intensity of highway flares and cast strange shadows.* DIXIE THE DOG *hunkers at their feet, looking restless and fierce, occasionally growling and baring her fangs. The* PROSECUTOR *fashions an efficient noose from the large rope carried on his shoulders.*

PROSECUTOR: We have to git that nigger, Jo Anne. She killed you, Goody ... And we can't let niggers, female or not, do our people in and plead that they had some kind of ah defense. That bitch is as good as dead. Your soul can rest on that, All Goode.

ALL GOODE: Friends, friends ... where would a man be without his friends, whether on this earth or not?

PROSECUTOR: But there's ah lot of questions that I could ask you, ole buddy. You know that, don't you?

ALL GOODE, *embarrassed:* Sure ... sure ... I know ... but ask away, anyway. What have I got to lose that I haven't already? She took my life .... What do you want from me? My balls?

PROSECUTOR: Now ... now ... settle down, ole buddy. It's just if I have to face her on the witness stand ... you're dead ... hers is the only version we got to deal with ... Times ain't like they used ta be, ya know. We can't fake but so much stuff against her.

ALL GOODE: Yeah ... yeah ... you can believe that. I remember when that length of hemp in a whiteman's hands was the only justice or evidence a niggah needed to know about in these hare parts.

PROSECUTOR: And it still is, All Goode, dear dead friend. 'Cause that little black bitch ain't gonna get no nearer the court room than the cemetery, if we can help it. But tell me, ole buddy, how did you get yourself in a predicament like that?

ALL GOODE, *wary:* Predicament?

PROSECUTOR, *laughs:* Sure ... ha ha ... you know, you gettin' caught with your pants down.

ALL GOODE: Oh, that.

PROSECUTOR: Ha ha ... yeah, Goody, man ... C'mon ... tell me all about that ... ha ha ... Remember now ... I'm an officer of justice and I'm only seeking the ... ha ha ... the. . . ha ... the facts!

ALL GOODE: Well now, from my point of view . . . there wasn't much funny about the whole thing.

PROSECUTOR, *serious:* But to get caught like that, man. If you had only seen the pictures. My Gawd! We tried to obliterate the facts as much as we could, but with the whole goddamn country and half the world lookin' over our shoulders . . . Well, there's only so much you can do. But tell me now . . . how did it all happen?

ALL GOODE, *subdued:* To tell the truth, I don't know.

PROSECUTOR: You don't know? But what about that story about dreams and all that? I never did believe that, but what are ya tryin' to tell me now?

ALL GOODE: I'm tryin' to tell you that I was drunk that night . . . drunk as a skunk thet ate reefer weed by mistake. Heck, man, doggone it all! . . . I don't remember nary a thing except mah johnson gittin' hard, me wantin' some of that black gal . . . and then wakin' up dead.

PROSECUTOR: But why did you tell that lie about yours and Jo Anne's dream?

ALL GOODE: Well . . . it's kinda like this . . . It seems at this point that everybody's lyin', right?

PROSECUTOR: Damn right!

ALL GOODE: Wahl . . . I'm stuck here in this story for some reason, right? I can't go to heaven or hell right now, as I sees it.

PROSECUTOR: That's right. We got to clear this case up before you can go where you supposed to.

ALL GOODE: Right . . . right . . . Now, since I don't know what really happened and that anything that I say might be used against me when I come up for judgement, wahl, I believe it's better to tell some tiny fibs and not a big big lie. 'Cause if I'm responsible for lyin' against Jo Anne and distortin' people's minds and gettin' her done in, well, the Lord might not look too favorably on that . . . and I'm still hopin' to get some kinda reprieve from him.

PROSECUTOR, *disgust:* Ya know, Goody . . . you been around jailhouses too long. You soundin' like one of them jailhouse lawyers.

(*The* PROSECUTOR *starts off.*)

ALL GOODE: Hey . . . where ya goin'?

PROSECUTOR: Home! . . . When you ready to do some serious nigger huntin', let me know. You got too much on your weak mind, All Goode. Your soul? Bah!

(*The* PROSECUTOR *disappears as* ALL GOODE *stands watching him exit.* DIXIE THE DOG *watches the* PROSECUTOR *leave, then becomes alert, growls, and turns her attention in another direction. She rises, growls more, then begins whining and cowering.*)

ALL GOODE: What's wrong, girl? What do ya see? Huh? Huh? Dixie?

(*Suddenly,* DIXIE *breaks away and bolts off in the direction that the* PROSECUTOR *took, yapping like a terrified puppy.* ALL GOODE *stands, looking mystified, using his torch to search in the shadows. Noise is heard.* ALL GOODE *looks uneasy. The* BLACK TOWNSMAN *enters from the direction that* ALL GOODE *is looking, leading the* MATRONLY WHITE WOMAN. *She wears dark glasses and uses a white cane; her mannerisms are those of the blind. The couple is intent upon where they are going.*)

ALL GOODE: Wahl now, you're a long way from home, ain't cha, shine?

TOWNSMAN: Excuse me, suh. Is this the way to the claim office?

ALL GOODE: Claim office? Boy . . . you've lost your way. Turn around now. The claim office is back in the court house building. It's downstairs, next to the jail.

TOWNSMAN, *smiles and scratches head:* Why thank ya, suh.

ALL GOODE, *grins widely:* Why not at all, lightnin'.

(*The* TOWNSMAN *turns and leads the* WOMAN *off.*)

WOMAN: Are we going in the right direction now?

TOWNSMAN: Yas'um.

WOMAN: Good . . . then we'll get there in time.

(*They exit.* ALL GOODE *watches them go.*)

ALL GOODE: If I wasn't in such a hurry to track down that gal, Jo Anne, I'd ask those two what they know.

(*He starts off.*)

ALL GOODE: Dixie! Here, girl! C'mon, dawg. We got work to do. We got to ketch and kill ah niggah, ya hare? Hey, Dixie!

(*Lights down. Lights up on* JO ANNE *in cabin. She reads a book in the dim light from the window. Her jail clothes are gone, and she wears a man's overlarge bathrobe. The sleeves fall over her hands and she pushes them back. A sound at the door. Frightened,* JO ANNE *puts the book in a pocket of the robe and quickly crawls behind and under the large mattress upon the bed. When she is in place, no sign of her can be seen. Enter the* CABIN DWELLER.)

CABIN DWELLER: Jo Anne? Jo Anne? I'm back.

(*Surprised, he searches through the cabin—in closets, under the bed, behind furniture, etc.*)

CABIN DWELLER, *finally, sadly:* She's gone . . .

(*At that moment,* JO ANNE *pops out from under the mattress.*)

JO ANNE, *brightly:* Hey, man . . . you got to do better than that to get me.

CABIN DWELLER, *happy:* Hey . . . I thought you were gone.

JO ANNE: What would you have done if I were gone?

CABIN DWELLER: Done? Nothing. I guess.

JO ANNE: How would you have felt?

CABIN DWELLER: I would have worried about you.

JO ANNE: Worried? But wouldn't you have missed me?

CABIN DWELLER: Of course, I would miss you. Having you here this past week has filled my life so much.

JO ANNE: But you have such a full life now. You have your books . . . and you're always busy . . .

CABIN DWELLER: But it's not like having you near.

(*The* CABIN DWELLER *sits on the bed near* JO ANNE *and looks into her eyes. She gets up and walks about the cabin.*)

JO ANNE: I guess I've already upset your life, haven't I?

CABIN DWELLER: No, not at all. You know . . . you've really brought purpose to my life.

JO ANNE: How's that?

CABIN DWELLER: I didn't know why I was here . . . Now you've come . . . and that question has been answered for me.

JO ANNE: You say things so beautifully.

(CABIN DWELLER *takes* JO ANNE *in his arms and kisses her. She breaks away from him.*)

JO ANNE: Please, don't do that.

CABIN DWELLER: Okay . . . if you don't want me to.

JO ANNE, *shudders:* I'm not tryin' to act funny or be ungrateful to you . . . but the last time a man touched me . . . it was so awful.

CABIN DWELLER: I see . . .

JO ANNE: Oh . . . and that's not the only thing. I'm not good for you. I've already put you in trouble. They're still looking for me. I can hear their dogs across the swamps and their helicopters and their posses . . . If you start liking me too much, you can lose your life like I'll probably lose mine.

CABIN DWELLER: Don't worry about those things. We're in this together. If they come, you hide under that mattress there.

JO ANNE: But that's a death trap.

CABIN DWELLER: I don't think so . . . I still have some tricks left for them. Just do as I say, please.

JO ANNE: My life is yours.

CABIN DWELLER: Thank you. But it's your heart I'm after.

(*He pulls her to him and kisses her again. She pulls away.*)

JO ANNE: No . . . please . . .

CABIN DWELLER: Okay . . . but . . . just give me one more kiss for luck. (*He kisses her.*)

JO ANNE: I'm unlucky right now.

CABIN DWELLER: Then let me give you one more for myself. (*He kisses her again.*)

JO ANNE: No . . . don't do that . . . please . . .

CABIN DWELLER: Okay . . . so, if I can't kiss you . . . let me hold you . . .

JO ANNE, *smiles and snuggles close to him:* All right . . . for a little while . . . But remember . . . you might be holdin' a soon-dead woman, so don't lose your head over me, ya hare?

CABIN DWELLER: You know what?

JO ANNE: What?

CABIN DWELLER: I'm going to protect you with my life.

JO ANNE: I bet you are . . . You know what?

CABIN DWELLER: What?

JO ANNE, *country sweet:* I bet cha goin'a get lots of chances to prove all that.

(*Lights dim on cabin. Light up on* CANE. *The white liberal is being accosted by two* BLACK ACTIVISTS, *a male and a female.*)

MALE ACTIVIST: We know there's all kinds of hanky panky goin' on here. We want our fair share . . .

CANE: Look, we've worked together for years . . . What do you mean by "fair share."

FEMALE ACTIVIST: Why are you, a whiteman, a Southern whiteman, heading this case?

MALE ACTIVIST: By "fair share" I mean of the monies that this Jo Anne "thang" is bringin' in. Ya hip to that, Chuck?[4]

CANE: The name's Cane. And I don't follow you about "monies." What do you mean?

FEMALE ACTIVIST: I know you have that sister frontin'[5] for you, but that's only window dressing. We're saying that we don't like the way this whole thing is being handled. And if it doesn't change, radically and

---

4. Chuck: Short for "Charlie" or "Mister Charlie," a generic name for white men who exploit and oppress Blacks, possibly derived from the name of an infamous Mississippi labor contractor of the 1920s, Charles Lowrence.

5. Frontin': To put on appearances.

soon, that steps are going to be taken. We demand action! By any means necessary.[6]

CANE: Now, come on . . . We don't have to resort to the dead rhetoric of the sixties, do we?

MALE ACTIVIST: We want our forty acres and the mule that got away, whitie![7]

FEMALE ACTIVIST: There are those who are consciously aware of the implications of this case.

MALE ACTIVIST: The judicial system stinks down here. You're part of it, like a fat, white maggot on a rotten porkchop.

CANE: Look a hare . . . I'm not so liberal that I won't punch you in the nose, brother! This is all a waste of your and my time.

MALE ACTIVIST: Now hear me out, all right?

FEMALE ACTIVIST: In terms of strategy, in terms of being effective . . . we activists have been mighty effective.

MALE ACTIVIST: This case goes to the very heart of the question of whether a black woman has the right to protect herself from a whiteman.

CANE: Exactly! I've been saying that all along.

FEMALE ACTIVIST: This is a very racist system, you know.

CANE: I know! I know!

MALE ACTIVIST: The real killer should stand up.

CANE: The real killer?

MALE ACTIVIST: Yes, the real killer.

CANE: What do you mean by "the real killer"?

MALE ACTIVIST: It's my theory that All Goode committed suicide . . .

CANE: How's that again?

FEMALE ACTIVIST: I totally resent the appearances of . . .

CANE: Quiet! I want to hear this theory.

MALE ACTIVIST: It's my theory that . . .

FEMALE ACTIVIST: Don't you tell me to be quiet!

CANE: Now, don't take it personally, Ms.

MALE ACTIVIST: Please, sister.

FEMALE ACTIVIST: What you think this is, some plantation or somethin'?

---

6. By any means necessary: Phrase coined by Malcolm X (1925–65): "We want freedom by any means necessary. We want justice by any means necessary. We want equality by any means necessary."

7. Forty acres and the mule that got away: Forty acres and a mule were promised to newly liberated African-American slaves by Union General William T. Sherman in a special field order in 1865. The phrase is commonly associated with the land-for-slavery reparations movement.

MALE ACTIVIST: Sister! Be your natural beautiful, queen-like, gentle black self. We men are talking about important things.

(*The* FEMALE ACTIVIST *storms out.*)

FEMALE ACTIVIST: CHAUVINISTS!!!

(*They look after her.*)

CANE: It looks like your women are acting more like our women every day.

MALE ACTIVIST: Yeah . . . this Jo Anne "thang" has really got them riled up. I just hope that they don't ever confuse me with All Goode and the Power Structure.

CANE: Why you think I'm workin' so hard? And now your theory . . .

MALE ACTIVIST: Oh, yeah . . . Well, it's my opinion that the real killer should stand up.

CANE: "The real killer?" Hey, you said that before, didn't you?

MALE ACTIVIST: Yeah, there was some other hanky panky goin' on in that jail besides with All Goode and Jo Anne. You been lookin' at the so-called evidence. Well, wasn't his body moved, wasn't the position changed in the later photos from that in the early photos?

CANE: It looks that way.

MALE ACTIVIST: And wasn't lots of blood wiped up after he was supposed to be dead and then his pants got missing and his shirt was washed out . . . ?

CANE: Yeah . . . yeah . . . but the authorities always try to cover up the evidence when they or some of their own are involved.

MALE ACTIVIST: See there! See there! You said it, not me. "When they or some of their own." Man . . . this was a modern Hari-Kari!

CANE: Hari-Kari!

MALE ACTIVIST: Yeah . . . All Goode died from just one stab wound. All that other stuff was just window dressin' and Jo Anne's scratches and nicks. Someone snuck in there after Jo Anne had fled and delivered the *coup de grace* . . . or either, out of remorse, when he found himself a degenerate disgrace, All Goode did himself in!

CANE: You don't expect me to get up in front of a court of law in the Carolinas and make my case on that?

MALE ACTIVIST: There's too many on death row now because there was less of a defense made by their attorneys. Our women, in jail, are being beaten and raped everyday. We are not getting our freedom of expression.

CANE: Now . . . now . . .

MALE ACTIVIST: We need to go into the 21st Century really free . . . the men as men . . . the women with their freedom . . .

CANE: What can I do to help? Tell me! What can I do?

MALE ACTIVIST: Well, a third of all the money you solicit will do for starters. We'll talk later about the film, stage, and publication rights.

CANE: "Money," "solicit," "publication rights" . . . hmmm . . . would you kindly define your terms?

(*Lights down. Lights up on the cabin.* JO ANNE *washes dishes and cleans up. She hums a song about Freedom. She hears the barking of dogs and the sound of running feet. The* CABIN DWELLER *bursts into the room.*)

CABIN DWELLER: Jo Anne! Quick! Hide in your place!

ALL GOODE, *off:* At 'em, Dixie! Get her, gal!

HENCHMEN, *off:* String her up! Hang her up! Burn her up! Jo Anne killed a whiteman and, for that, death she'll earn!

JO ANNE, *hesitates:* But if they find me here, you'll die like me.

CABIN DWELLER: Get in your place, quick, darling, and stop questioning our plan.

JO ANNE: You called me "darling."

CABIN DWELLER: Get in your place!

JO ANNE: I've time to run out the back way.

CABIN DWELLER: They'd have you within a mile . . .

(*He pats her on the rear and pushes her under the mattress. Seeing that she is fully hidden, the* CABIN DWELLER *smoothes out the covers, then he takes his gun out of the table drawer and puts it in his large bib overall pocket. After that, he goes to his kitchen shelf and takes a can of red pepper and sprinkles it generously about his bed. The terrifying sounds of the lynch mob are outside. As the* CABIN DWELLER *puts the pepper back, his door is torn asunder from the frame and hinges, and* DIXIE THE DOG *charges through, knocking over the table and savagely menacing the* CABIN DWELLER. ALL GOODE, *the* PROSECUTOR, *and their* HENCHMEN *follow* DIXIE *with drawn and ready shotguns, whips, firebrands, and ropes.* DIXIE *sniffs, snuffs, and slobbers over the* CABIN DWELLER, *then attacks the area of the bed and receives a snout full of red pepper. She sneezes, howls, stops to drink from the dishwater-filled sink, and bounds, whimpering, from the cabin, her tongue lolling out.* ALL GOODE *panics and follows her.*)

ALL GOODE, *off:* Dixie, honey? Baby, what's wrong? Come back here, gal!

PROSECUTOR: Why that dog actin' up? What you give her, boy?

CABIN DWELLER, *country dumb:* Wahl, suh, that hound of yourns musta got into the roach powder I got spread around here.

HENCHMEN: Roaches? Poison! GAWDDAMN THESE FILTHY-ASS NIGGERS! Hey, this place is too small for that black bitch to hide in. We'll be outside when you wants us, chief.

(*They exit in a disorderly rush.*)

PROSECUTOR, *looks around cabin:* You out hare all by yourself, boy?

CABIN DWELLER: Yassuh.

PROSECUTOR, *looks in pots:* This sho looks like a lot of food for just you, boy.

CABIN DWELLER: I cooks for more than one day at a time, suh.

PROSECUTOR, *looks at dishes upon the floor:* It sho looks like you use lots of plates for yourself, boy.

CABIN DWELLER: I got a habit of dirtying up all my dishes before I have ta give' em a washin', suh. It's what the roaches come for.

PROSECUTOR, *starts to scratch:* Yeah . . . roaches . . . (*The* PROSECUTOR *sits down on the bed.*)

PROSECUTOR: You ain't seen nobody sniffin' around hare, have ya, Sam?

CABIN DWELLER, *scratches head:* Nawh suh. There ain't nobody here but this chicken.

PROSECUTOR: If you see a black nigra gal 'round hare, what ya goin'a do, Smokey?

CABIN DWELLER, *bucks eyes and mouth hangs open:*[8] Why that's an easy one, Captin! . . .

(*The* CABIN DWELLER *suddenly lifts the ax beside the fireplace and buries it with a mighty chop between the feet of the* PROSECUTOR.)

CABIN DWELLER: GAWDDAMN ROACHES!!!

(*As the ax strikes the floor, the* PROSECUTOR, *holding his shotgun pointed barrel up, with his finger upon the trigger, flinches and fires into the roof. The* PROSECUTOR *is scared almost witless. He drops his gun and whip and feels his vital parts. At first, he isn't sure whether his head, genitalia, and limbs are all intact.*)

PROSECUTOR: But . . . but . . . ROACHES, YOU SAY!!! GAWD! . . . HOW CAN YOU NIGGERS STAND . . .

(*The* PROSECUTOR *gathers up his things and hurriedly exits. Sound of a motorcycle gang revving up. The posse varooms off into the night. The* CABIN DWELLER *looks out the window and listens. Then he walks over to the bed.*)

CABIN DWELLER: Jo Anne, honey. C'mon out. We done beat 'em again.

(*Lights alter. Lights on the* LAWYERS SCOTT *and* CANE.)

CANE, *nervous:* How do I look? Do you think everything will be all right?

SCOTT: I think so . . . I've already met and talked to her. She's agreed to give herself up under our scrutiny and we will defend her. That's a lot of money we have to get raised to handle this case properly.

CANE: I know . . . but the Senator's on our side. And this is a dream case

---

8. Bucks eyes: Opens eyes as wide as possible in mock fear and surprise.

with every major women's issue you can imagine . . . But it's so fantastic. I can hardly believe that something like this could happen.

SCOTT: It might seem fantastic to you, but it happens to black women year in and year out.

CANE: Oh, I'm sorry. I'm so uninformed about . . .

SCOTT: Let's not go into Southern white liberal remorse. She really needs your help. Mine, yes, but she really needs your help.

CANE: Of course . . . of course . . .

(*Lights alter. Up on* JO ANNE. *She wears a dress.*)

JO ANNE: Hello . . . are you the lawyers who said they would help me?

(JO ANNE *sees* CANE *and is scared.* CANE, *sensing something wrong, moves toward* JO ANNE.)

JO ANNE: Don't you touch me! Don't you come near me, whiteman! I'll kill you if you try and make me do that again!

SCOTT, *understanding:* Jo Anne, dear . . . everything's all right. This is Attorney Cane. We work together. We'll be handling your case together. Please trust both of us and the people we assign to your defense team. Trust nobody else, except your mother, and try to talk as little as you can.

JO ANNE: He's not going to hurt me, is he?

SCOTT: No. I swear upon my life and soul that nobody will harm you.

CANE: And I swear on mine, too. As a Southern gentleman . . . before they touch a hair of your head to harm you, Jo Anne, I'll overthrow this corrupt, evil system that sexually enslaves women, defeats and destroys their men, and oppresses all dissent.

JO ANNE: Oh, thank you . . . I'm not afraid now. Not of anything. If you friends stick with me, and if the people of this great land learn my story and stand with me . . . What have I to fear?

(*Lights alter. Up on the* PROSECUTOR.)

PROSECUTOR, *sure of his case:* Ha ha ha . . . I'm not here to save no souls . . . . Nawh, in Southern justice it's plain to see the law. . . . Ha ha . . . the law is the law. Ya know what I mean? It's always been the way it is. From my father to his to way way back, and now down to me, here. From the first to the last. If ah nigger kill ah whiteman . . . for any reason whatsoever . . . that nigger is dead. No matter if he's a man, no matter if he's ah woman . . . no matter who that nigger is, they dead, dead, dead! And that's Southern justice. That's right! Jo Anne killed white folks. Her penalty is death. This is the South. Our ways are old and lasting. Remember, nothin' of value really changes. And the death of this niggah gal will prove our system is right and just . . . by our ways and standards, ya understand?

(*Light up on the courtroom.* ALL GOODE *presides, drinks from a bottle, and gets drunk as he speaks. He wears black robes.*)

ALL GOODE: Fellow white Americans . . . tragedies happen to all of us. Even those of us who live and work in this great land. Hic! This land over which the great stars and stripes wave forever . . . I want ta thank ya for the faith and sympathy that you've shown me. Yes, shown this guilty ole fool. Hic! I'm sorry I got caught. I'm sorry that things turned out the way they did. But what have I really to be sorry about? That gal is a nigger. White folks have always been better than them. We've always had the right to do what we wanted with them. So what's all the fuss about now? I'm a Christian. Hic! I pay mah taxes. So why's everybody against me? Why ya lookin' at me like that? I'm white. And when ya white, ya right, right? Hee ha ha . . . Boy, I bet cha would really have liked to have been with me when I got to her that night . . . (*Giggles. He is now in the jail area. The scrim slowly descends.*) I knew I was goin'a get her that night. I was goin'a get her . . . yeah, have her suck mah johnson off . . . then fuck her 'till I couldn't no more. Then I was goin'a punch my ice pick dead in the top of her nappy head . . . and pull it out, so nobody could see the wound. Folks 'round hare would say she died from pneumonia. Nobody cares if a nigger dies in jail . . . 'cept the nigger's family . . . but they can't do nothin'. They ain't got no power. Not like I thought I had that night.

(*Lights alter. Light on* JO ANNE, *who sits on witness stand.*)

JO ANNE: He was all the time after me. All Goode. He'd make nasty remarks and try to touch my private places when he could get close enough to me. I warned him to stay away from me. I pleaded with him to let me alone. But every chance he got, he was after me.

CANE: And why didn't you tell the authorities? Why didn't you report him?

JO ANNE: I was afraid. The word of a black woman in jail is no good against a whiteman's word. I was afraid that they'd just ignore it like they ignore everything else they want to . . . and then he would really have me where he wanted. But he already knew he had me where he wanted. Ohhhh . . . ohhhh . . . it's so horrible to tell.

CANE: Take your time. Don't worry. Nobody's gonna hurt you, now.

SCOTT: Be calm, dear. Be calm. Take your time. Just tell the truth and nothing but.

JO ANNE: And that night I awoke, and he was in my cell, standing over me like . . . like . . .

CANE: Like what, Jo Anne?

(*The scrim is in place.* ALL GOODE's *form is seen, with a figure that looks like* JO ANNE. *They play out* JO ANNE's *words as she testifies.*)

JO ANNE: . . . like an evil spirit.

(*Sound of* DIXIE THE DOG *howling offstage*)

JO ANNE: He grabbed me by the throat, strangling me, and said . . .

ALL GOODE (*over the theater's sound system*): Don't give me no trouble, bitch! Get your clothes off . . .

JO ANNE: . . . he said. He said for me to take my clothes off. I started to say somethin', but he punched me hard and put the ice pick up against my eye and said . . .

ALL GOODE, *voiceover:* I'll dig your eyes out with this pig sticker if you give me the slightest bit of trouble, ya black bitch!

JO ANNE: Then I undressed like he told me. He wasn't but inches away from me, so I couldn't do anything. After I took off my bra and hung it up . . . I . . . I didn't want to . . . oh, I can't go on, I can't!

CANE: You have to, Jo Anne. The story has to be told.

SCOTT: We're with you, Jo Anne. We're here.

JO ANNE: Then he told me . . .

ALL GOODE, *voiceover:* Get down on your knees, black bitch!

JO ANNE: My knees got weak. I almost fainted, but I became clear-headed, somehow, and knew what I had to do. But he stopped me before I was all the way down and said . . .

ALL GOODE, *voiceover:* You ain't got your drawers off yet? Here! Let me help ya!

(*Behind the scrim,* ALL GOODE *tears off the silhouette's panties, throws them to the floor, and kicks them under the bunk.*)

JO ANNE: And then he pushed me down. He took his hand and put it on top of my head and pushed me down. He had that ice pick at my eye and throat all the way down. HE TOOK MY HEAD AND PUSHED IT DOWN!!! AAHHHHH . . .

CANE: Recess! Your honor! Where are ya? I request a recess for my client! In the name of mercy and justice, we plead for time to compose our client, Jo Anne!

(*Lights to black. Pause. Lights up on* JO ANNE *and* ALL GOODE *on the moors.*)

JO ANNE: Well, All Goode, that's my story. It's out now and on record.

ALL GOODE: Yeah. Nothin' can be done about that. My goose is cooked. When you dead, anything can be said about you, and that's what it has to be.

JO ANNE: My version was the truth, man. I was there, remember?

ALL GOODE: So was I there, but it's just that I don't rightly know all the time what happens when I'm drunk or dead. But you know, you coulda painted a better picture of me.

JO ANNE: I dealt with the truth. What else could I do? Sure . . . now you're dead and sober you don't seem such a bad person. But that ignorant oil you usta drink, and your freaky sex hangups, well, they were your undoing, All Goode. I even kinda liked your sense of humor some-times, when you wasn't bein' nasty. But tell me somethin' . . . When you had your chance, why didn't you lie more? Why didn't you make me out to be what the prosecutor and other bigots think of me?

ALL GOODE: Wahl, it's a long story, gal.

JO ANNE: I'm not your gal! Address me properly, if you're gonna say any-thing to me at all.

ALL GOODE, *mocking:* Why, yes, Ms. Jo Anne.

JO ANNE: I won, All Goode. Won completely. And my victory is a victory for all oppressed women in this land.

(*Light on the* PROSECUTOR)

PROSECUTOR: This case may not be won on the flimsy evidence we have, ladies and gentlemen of the South. But we Southerners, we old guard, we good ole boys know the real story, don't we now?

(ALL GOODE *and* JO ANNE *are back in the cell area.*)

PROSECUTOR: Now let us construct the scene as it really probably hap-pened, sons and daughters of Dixie. That woman, that murderess, Jo Anne, lured our neighbor, our co-worker, and friend to his death. Let us go back to that dark, bloody night.

(JO ANNE *and* ALL GOODE *play out the scene.*)

JO ANNE, *from cell:* Goody . . . oh, Mr. All Goode, sir?

ALL GOODE, *reads paper:* Huh . . . What you want, Jo Anne?

JO ANNE: Could you come back here? I want to tell ya somethin'.

ALL GOODE: Tell me what ya want. Ain't nobody here but us. What is it?

JO ANNE: Come here, Mr. All Goode. It won't take too long.

ALL GOODE, *drains his bottle:* Okay, but it better be good. (*He walks back to her cell.*)

ALL GOODE: Now what is it?

JO ANNE, *sexy:* Mah back itches . . . would you scratch it for me?

ALL GOODE: Is that all you want?

JO ANNE: Yes. Could you do it for me please, Mr. Goody?

(*Lights lower.* ALL GOODE *has his arms through the bars, scratching* JO ANNE's *back.*)

ALL GOODE: Wahl now, I'm not supposed to be this close to you women prisoners. You ain't gonna tell nobody now, are ya?

JO ANNE: Tee hee . . . do you think I'm crazy? Hey, Goody, why don't you open the cell door and come in?

PROSECUTOR: And this wanton hussy enticed and lured this southern whiteman into her black widow's nest.

ALL GOODE: I can't do that, gal.

JO ANNE: Ah, yes you can, Goody. If you do . . . I'll give you some of the best stuff you ever had. Ah, c'mon, I'm so hot for you, daddy.

(ALL GOODE *smirks and takes out his keys.*)

ALL GOODE: Now you ain't gonna try no funny stuff, are ya, Jo?

JO ANNE: Why no, Goody . . . I'm just lonesome for you, that's all.

(ALL GOODE *opens the door and enters the cell. The lights dim so that their bodies hardly can be seen. As soon as the lights dim, the couple embraces and pulls their clothes off hastily.* ALL GOODE *takes her in his arms again and eases her down upon the bunk after they kiss passionately. They begin to make love.*)

PROSECUTOR: And this temptress, this Jezebel, this Delilah, this Pandora, this siren seduced this weak, good man, and in his weakest moment of desire and passion, she committed upon him the act of MURDER!

(*Sounds of love-making*)

JO ANNE: Oh, Goody. Oh, daddy. You gonna let me get out? You gonna let your little Jo Jo get away?

ALL GOODE: Oh, baby. Oh, Jo Anne . . . this is so good.

JO ANNE: You gonna open the door to freedom for me, daddy?

ALL GOODE: Freedom? Oh, this is so good! What you know about freedom, gal?

(JO ANNE *pushes him off.*)

JO ANNE: What you think I know about freedom, punk! You're my one-way ticket, what you mean by that shit?

ALL GOODE: I'm keepin' you hare, gal, as long as I can. You the best jail cunt I could ever imagine. Open your legs up now!

(JO ANNE *reaches under her pillow and brings out an ice pick.*)

ALL GOODE: What the hell? Where's that one come from?

JO ANNE: Don't you recognize it, sucker? I took it out of your desk drawer and kept it for you.

ALL GOODE: Black bitch!

(*He lashes out and knocks the weapon from her hand. He grabs the weapon and rises to plunge the ice pick in her, but he slips on something wet upon the deck and falls.* JO ANNE *grabs the weapon away from the fallen* ALL GOODE *and backs off. He lunges at her. As he closes on her, she strikes out at him.*)

VOICES: JO ANNE!!!

(ALL GOODE *tries to kill her. He knocks her down and kicks and stomps her. She strikes again and again with the weapon, and slows him down by hitting his legs. She fights her way to her feet and plunges the weapon into* ALL GOODE *again.*)

VOICES: JO ANNE!!!

(*Like a wounded animal,* ALL GOODE *beats and pummels her. He is about to kill her with his brute strength, except that she strikes once more.*)

VOICES: JO ANNE!!!

(ALL GOODE *staggers and falls.* JO ANNE *jumps up and dresses hurriedly. She escapes as* ALL GOODE *weakly reaches for her.* ALL GOODE *leans upon the cell door, without pants, his bloody undershirt covering his private parts. He holds the ice pick, but dazed, he pitches forward upon his face, burying the weapon in his chest. Finally, he stirs, pulls the ice pick from his chest.*)

ALL GOODE, *mutters, dazed:* This is terrible . . . . This can't happen on my shift. I've got to clean this mess up.

(*He stumbles to the wash basin and tries to wash the blood from himself, but he merely manages to wet himself up. Then, pitifully, he drops to the floor with a wet paper towel and wipes at the blood. Footsteps are heard.*)

ALL GOODE: She's comin' back. (*Coughs*) She know better than to try any- thing 'round here. Things could really go bad for her. (*Coughs*) Jo Anne? Jo Anne . . . c'mon in, gal. You know the way . . . (*coughs*)

(*The elderly black* TOWNSMAN *enters, carrying a noose and followed by the* MATRONLY WHITE WOMAN. *The* WHITE WOMAN *is costumed as* JUSTICE— *gowned in white, blindfolded, with the other paraphernalia of the character— scales, sword, etc.*)

ALL GOODE: What's this, Sambo?[9] You done lost your way to the costume ball?

TOWNSMAN: Is this the claim office?

ALL GOODE: You must be kiddin', boy. (*Coughs*) The claim office opens in the mornin'.

---

9. Sambo: A reference to *The Story of Little Black Sambo* (1899), by Helen Bannerman. It is beloved and racist.

TOWNSMAN: Is your name All Goode?

ALL GOODE: Yeah . . . but . . .

(*The* TOWNSMAN *slips the noose over* ALL GOODE's *head.*)

TOWNSMAN: The time is now, for you, Mr. All Goode. I was sent to claim you. Sorry I'm late.

JUSTICE: Justice is blind, true, and I sometimes lose my way . . . Especially in these Southern regions. But I usually get to where I'm going, in the end.

ALL GOODE: Is this true? Is this happening? Ah, have a little mercy, fellah.

TOWNSMAN, *pulls noose:* Shhh . . . just follow me, Mr. All Goode. We ain't got far to go. And there's no escape for you. We already underground a bit. Now watch your step, lady, and keep close to me. Here we go now.

(*The* TOWNSMAN *leads* ALL GOODE *away, followed by* LADY JUSTICE *bringing up the rear. Lights alter. Up on* JO ANNE *making a speech.*)

JO ANNE: And it's the people who create and keep just laws. Together we can have a land where all women, all men, all children can be free and live under the benefits of a just and fair government. But it's the people who must demand this! Me, I'm just one little ole lucky woman. Don't make me a symbol; I'm really not no hero, or nothin'. I'm one of y'all. One of the people. So remember . . . Power to the People! Power forever and ever! . . .

(*Lights down. Up on the* REPORTER *and the* CABIN DWELLER.)

CABIN DWELLER: We cannot allow this to happen again. We blackmen cannot let our women be raped and nearly murdered in the prisons of America. It must end here. And we are the ones to make it end!

REPORTER, *into tape recorder:* I am now signing off. This is living historical theater of the mind. This was really imagined and believed . . . this was lived and done.

Blackness.

Bullins's most recent play, Harlem Diva *possesses many of the features of his post-1976 work: an interest in the history of African-American artists, a magical-realist style dramaturgy, and a desire to put on a truly entertaining show. But one also finds aspects here that extend back to the earliest work, particularly his interest in the family as a carrier of both historical consciousness and blindness, an idea he has been working with since* In the Wine Time; *his willingness to stage truly silly events, as one sees here in a scene of miraculous healing inspired by some very good fried chicken; and his affection for female characters with big personalities.* Harlem Diva *was read in 2006 at the Hibernian Hall Ballroom in the Roxbury Center for the Arts building in Dudley Square, Boston.*

Harlem Diva

(2005)

THE PEOPLE:

GERI HARREL, *An actress fighting for a better day, black, 60–70.*

CHANAL, *A private middle school teacher,* GERI's *daughter, 38.*

MAXWELL, *A wannabe Hip Hop mogul, etc.,* GERI's *son, 32.*

STAGEHAND, *"Caretaker" of* GERI's *dream, 65.*

BALLARD/MIRROR FIGURE, *Property manager of* GERI's *apartment complex, 55.*

TIME: *Now*

SETTING: *The set should be semi-representational, but strongly indicative of a theater space and a living area in a different building. Lights up on the dimly lit stage of the old, abandoned Langston Theatre in Harlem. We see some of the backstage area of the theater and a part of the stage. The scene appears empty of life. Then, from "outside," behind a door which must have been the original stage door, banging is heard, and* CHANAL's *voice cries out.*

---

*Concept by Bill Latham.

CHANAL: Mother! . . . Mother! . . . It's me, Chanal, Mother! . . . It's me . . . Ohhh . . . I know you're in there, Mother, come out . . . Please . . . Open up this door . . . I've something to tell you, Mother. Please! . . .

(*On one side of the theatrical stage, a pup tent is seen, and soon* STAGEHAND *crawls slowly from the opening in front of the tent.*)

CHANAL: Mother! . . . I'm not going away . . . I have to talk to you . . . Maxwell is coming to visit, I mean, see you, Mommy (*she cringes at the word "Mommy"*) . . . Oh, please, don't make me have to go through this on the other side of this door, mother! I need to talk to you before Maxwell does . . . I have to . . . (STAGEHAND *shakily pulls himself erect and marches proudly to the door.*)

CHANAL: Mother! . . . Mother! . . . (*Almost childlike*) Don't do this to me, Mommy! . . . Don't, Mommy . . . (*Threatens*) Look . . . I'm not the one! I'm not the one you should be messing with like this. (*Angry*) I was raised in Harlem by you, just like your mother, who we called Mum (*she cringes again*), raised you. I'm not the. . . (STAGEHAND *opens the door and confronts* CHANAL.)

STAGEHAND, *tough voice:* What you doin' bangin' on my door and screamin' like you're dizzy or somethin'?

CHANAL: Stagehand! . . . If that's what you're calling yourself this year . . .

STAGEHAND: *This year!* . . . Hey, don't try and play me, kid. You've known me as long as you've known your mama!

CHANAL: See . . . I know you have my mother in there. . . (*gestures*) . . .

STAGEHAND: In my tent! Hmmp! No such thing. I haven't seen . . .

CHANAL: Stop! Don't lie to me. (*Moves forward*) Let me in there!

STAGEHAND: Now you wait a minute! You fresh little . . .

(CHANAL *pushes the door against* STAGEHAND's *extended hand.*)

CHANAL, *ready to fight:* You . . . you get out of my way or I'll . . .

STAGEHAND, *shrugs and waves her in:* I haven't seen your mother since this morning, Miss Chanal.

CHANAL, *inside theater:* Don't you call me *Miss* Chanal. I don't need your phony bohemian Harlem patronizing to catch me off-guard like you have my mother. My plain name, Chanal, is good enough for me where you're concerned. And what was she doing here with you this morning?

STAGEHAND: If I can be discreet (*goads her*), I'll just say she was *taking care of business*, which she was, *Chanal.*

CHANAL, *raises voice:* Oouuu! And what do you mean by that, you dirty little *man!* My mother . . .

STAGEHAND, *cuts in:* I must urge you not to lower yourself, dear, by way of your speech. You are a princess in a royal Harlem theater family . . . Your mother, Madame Geri . . .

CHANAL, *angry:* Can that crap, man! . . .

STAGEHAND: Haven't you started going to church? That mouth! Shame on you!

CHANAL: That's none of your business, man.

STAGEHAND: Chanal, you sound so *past tense* . . . "Man?" You know your mother told you I'm called *Stagehand.*

CHANAL, *angry:* Keep my mother out of this!

STAGEHAND: But I thought you were looking for her, chile. And you've known since your baby crib days that I'm *Stagehand,* a name bestowed upon me by your great father, Milford Thomas Harrel III, a true black matinee idol of the Chitlin' Circuit[1] . . . You say you don't remember . . . You're so in denial.

CHANAL: So you say. I don't remember any of that. And keep my father's name off of your lips . . . *Stagehand.*

STAGEHAND: Truly, I have no motive to make myth. And you know that I babysat you in the dressing rooms back yonder while your folks were on this stage, bringing down the house.

CHANAL: Every theater in the Western World and other parts of the universe has stagehands, and . . .

STAGEHAND: I did not achieve my name through a title of lackeyism . . . My name was given to me as an acknowledgment that I was the ultimate *real deal* stage roustabout. I was and am the stagehand that few others can touch! And even though I've changed your diapers . . .

CHANAL: You're crazy! . . . My father was a minstrel show spook, that's all. Learned his acting craft from his father . . . So that's how you enchant my mother? With your phony, old-timey stories?

STAGEHAND: But she is part of the stories. Still is. Perhaps the greatest part. Behold! The magic of our Harlem Diva! . . . (*He raises his arms outward and upward and upon his toes turns in circles with awe, reaching out and flicking on light switches as he goes. The Langston Theatre is fully revealed.*) Behold! The world that Madame Geri Harrel helped conceive!

CHANAL: Stop it! Stop! I know she's under your spell in this scam of yours, whatever it is. Where is she? Where?

STAGEHAND, *stops turning, gestures:* Go on! Look in every nook and crooked

---

1. Chitlin' Circuit: Name given to theatrical venues throughout the southern and eastern United States catering primarily to African-American audiences and promoting popular material.

cranny of this wonderful place . . . In fact, my child, I suggest that you should spend as much time here as you possibly . . .

CHANAL: No way! Get out of my face . . . you scam artist! You trash dump guru!

STAGEHAND, *fatherly:* Chanal.

CHANAL, *shouts:* Scam artist! Scam artist! Scam artist!

STAGEHAND: My, my . . . at least you recognize that I am an artist, even while you misperceive that your mother, Madame Geri Harrel, is a great and mighty one, too, in her own right . . . And she and I, humbly, have a grand vision. A vision that you believe is a hoax, a con game, a bunko bit . . . but in fact will shake the theater art world to its flat feet. (*With flourish*) Yes, in this time and place . . . I see it here! I see it! The Vision! The Vision! . . . Given to me by that magic lady . . . your mother.

CHANAL, *starts off, turns wearily:* Tell . . . tell my mother that I must see her. Please give her that message and nothing else. I . . . I . . . can't stay here in this awful place any longer.

STAGEHAND: You mean you can't accept your destiny.

CHANAL, *turns back:* Oh, so now you think you're humoring me with more of your lies.

STAGEHAND: My minor skills cannot do that for you, child.

CHANAL: You know what you can do with that *child* stuff . . .

STAGEHAND: For a school teacher, even an elementary school one, you have . . .

CHANAL, *angry:* Talk like a man, you precious little sleaze! You can't even go to bed like a man . . . Crawling into that pup tent at night to go off to sleep, and claiming that you're security for this old dump. You're too pathetic to make me even laugh. Hah! Before I go, I should slap your face.

STAGEHAND, *coldly:* Chanal . . . I'll let your mother know that I saw you.

CHANAL, *plays a youngster:* Sir? Please kind, sir . . . Tell me about your tent that cannot even hide your feet. Nor my mother.

STAGEHAND: Madame Geri told me that you wouldn't take up an acting career, one that was offered you on a golden platter.

CHANAL: Hump. I guess I just didn't take to it . . . Say, old man. Tell me the story of the tent!

STAGEHAND: What is there to know?

CHANAL: Just play the game, please.

STAGEHAND, *sighs:* The tent . . . the tent is one of the borders to the world, nothing less. It contains me in this place. And outside . . .

CHANAL: Outside of this theater?

STAGEHAND: No, my dear . . .

CHANAL: I'm not your *dear*!

STAGEHAND: I know that, but I'm not talking about the smoggy atmosphere outside these windows, or the clouds above even. Or the heavens and planets and constellations, even, and all of it. The Universe.

CHANAL: The universe?

STAGEHAND: All the universes! All the universes that ever were and are. Everything! Heaven! Hell! And the impossibility of knowing anything! Through theater . . . through artful spell making . . . through . . .

CHANAL, *annoyed:* Shut up! Shut up, you black fool! . . . I give you a second, and you waste my precious minutes. I'm leaving. And I'm telling you this: Stay the hell away from my mother. And keep your so-called ideas to yourself . . . My eleven-year-olds at school have better things, much more and better things, to say than you.

(*She storms out. He walks over to his tent and pulls an umbrella from it and opens the umbrella above his head. Lights change.* CHANAL *is captured in a spotlight in front of the door that she entered from the alley.*)

CHANAL, *tears in eyes:* Lord. Lord. Lord . . . Help me find my mother. Please help me, Lord. (*She sings a moving gospel solo.*)

(*Lights change. A kitchen dining room in a Harlem apartment is revealed. The building it is in has a tarnished but still respectable history and overlooks the Harlem River valley and Yankee Stadium. Babe Ruth is said to have lived nearby during the roaring twenties.* GERI HARREL *enters from the bathroom in a costume which subliminally shouts Apollo Theatre Amateur Night. She moves to a mantel above which is a large framed photo of Milford Thomas Harrel III. Music begins, as if it comes from* GERI'S *head as she gazes at the picture . . . She sings a couple of bars, in her rendition of an obscure Ethel Waters tune from the 1930s or '40s. She looks up at the photo, blows it a kiss, and impishly smiles.*)

GERI: *Milford . . . Milford Thomas Harrel . . .* what a husband and lover you were . . . Ahhh . . . what a lover! They don't make studs like you today, Viagra or not. The times we had and the shows we did . . . Remember? Remember, darling?

(*Her hips sway slowly. She puts down the photo and bumps up the tempo excitedly, giving her version of a red-hot Burlesque Queen. She shouts gleefully and does a cute little dance to her mental music in the slightly dim light. She goes to a CD player and turns it on. The music is loud, and she becomes lost in a gleeful hallucination. She shouts at a wall as if there is a presence there that only she can see. Then in the background, as if in a mirror, the picture figure materializes and*) *dances silently behind the unknowing* GERI. *She dances with the air, showing nifty steps from a bygone era to her unseen partner. Soon, banging comes from the pipes, muffled shouts of "Quiet down!" "Stop the racket!" and "Turn it off!" seep through the walls. Then somebody outside bangs on her door. The mirrorlike figure disappears.* GERI *stops her dancing suddenly. She puts a hand over her heart and looks tuckered out. She drags her feet but reaches the sofa and collapses in a faint as the door flies open and* CHANAL *storms in and goes to her.*)

CHANAL, *angry:* Mother! What in God's name have you been doing! I don't know what I'm going to do with you!

(BALLARD *enters. He goes and turns off the CD player, then moves toward the sofa.*)

CHANAL, *continued:* Look at what you're wearing? Where are you going? And where have you been all day? Mother! Are you listening to me? Are you?

BALLARD: It looks like she's knocked out, Chanal.

CHANAL: Knocked out! . . . You mean . . . you mean . . . (*Frightened*) Oh, God! Mama . . . Mama. Oh, God!

(BALLARD *pulls out his cell phone.*)

BALLARD: Chanal, I'm calling 911 . . .

(*Lights change. Sirens screech and wail in the dark. Lights come up on the Langston Theatre door.* MAXWELL HARREL *walks briskly up to the door and knocks. On the third series of knocks,* STAGEHAND *appears at the interior side of door and opens it.*)

STAGEHAND: Wha' tha'! . . . (*Throws up hands*) MAXWELL!!! . . . Lawd! . . . (*Hugs* MAXWELL, *who gently struggles*) The prodigal has returned!

MAXWELL: Easy, Unc . . . Easy! Dag . . . you's as bad as a Mount Morris Park mugging.

STAGEHAND, *unloosens hold:* I knew it! I knew you were comin'. (*Playing psychic*) A vision in the night shone with the clarity of day . . .

MAXWELL: Hold on, old man . . . you've lost your dialect.

STAGEHAND: Lost? My dialect?

MAXWELL: Yea, the phony one.

STAGEHAND, *mildly miffed:* Now looka here, little negro!

MAXWELL: Well, you haven't changed. But I tried.

STAGEHAND: Tried what, college kid?

MAXWELL: Matriculated college man to you, old timer, in whatever dialect you can use.

STAGEHAND: Now, watch how far you want to go, Mr. Max-sharp-as-an-ax. I use ta change your diapers not so long ago.

MAXWELL: Whoa . . . cap on me now? Where have I heard that one before?

STAGEHAND: Let's not bring your mom into this game.

MAXWELL: Why not? YOU got her goin' again. Ha. You and she are the co-chairs of the development committee to restore this legendary Langston Theatre. Right?

STAGEHAND: I see that you get your mail. Your sister tried to keep Geri from sending you our newsletter.

MAXWELL: I guess I have been away for a while. Ha ha . . . Say, why do I call you "Unc," and Chanal hasn't a good word to say about you?

STAGEHAND: That's easy . . . Geri and me have always been close enough to be sister and brother.

MAXWELL: With my dad right in the middle, huh?

STAGEHAND, *suspicious:* What are you getting at, Maxwell? I told you that Geri and I have always . . .

MAXWELL: "Always?" You always say "always."

STAGEHAND: Yes, we've long had a special bond.

MAXWELL: Special bond? While dad was out there in front, you and mom took care of things . . . backstage.

STAGEHAND: That's nearly right. Your dad was our leader and Geri's husband. She was his partner . . . and I . . .

MAXWELL: And you?

STAGEHAND: And I did *everything* backstage, including taking care of you kids, little Chanal and young Master Maxwell. And your beloved father, Milford Thomas Harrell III, *always* knew he could depend upon me to look after Geri and his interests.

MAXWELL: I started calling you "uncle" after you began taking me out to the Apollo Theatre and other places. What was that about?

STAGEHAND: Other places? You mean down to Philly to play with my kids? What was what about? You and your sister grew up in theater dressing rooms. Your parents and I had to get you out into the sun and the open world. "Stagehand, Stagehand," they would say. "Get these kids out of this dark place. They need air! They need life! They're growing old too soon."

MAXWELL: "They're growing old too soon" . . . Yes, but not entirely. Chanal and I saw half naked showgirls all the time. And silly men cavorting in fluorescent-hued pajamas in that circus-like atmosphere. But that's not the whole story.

STAGEHAND: It isn't? Why not?

MAXWELL: Hummm. Let me think . . . and remember . . . I was allowed to go anywhere you wanted to take me, but Chanal couldn't even go near the outside door with you.

STAGEHAND: Oh, I had almost forgotten that . . . Well, Maxwell, you can understand that it was practically a post-Victorian age. Certain decorum was kept at that time.

MAXWELL: That's bullshit, man. It was the mid-'60s. In the Black Arts days. Almost anything and everything went down back then.

STAGEHAND, *shakes head vigorously:* Not anything! Not . . .

MAXWELL: Why were my parents fighting so hard to keep you away from my sister?

STAGEHAND, *serious:* What are you trying to say, Maxwell? Do you have a dirty mind?

MAXWELL: Ya know, there's *always* another story behind the front story. Don't play that choir boy game with me.

STAGEHAND, *angry:* What do you want in here! You're not looking for your mother. You came here to make me a nervous nelly. If any of the sons of my children were here, they'd slap the shit out of you, mister.

MAXWELL: Uncle Stagehand . . . you were dressing queer before queer came into fashion . . . But you know I'd dare any of those sweetly raised-up offspring of yours to even look at me . . . cross-eyed!

STAGEHAND: Get out! Get out! . . . What are you here for?

MAXWELL, *sinister:* I'm here to tear down this Langston Theatre legend dump. This decadent pig sty of pretense.

STAGEHAND, *apoplectic:* What are you saying! Are you mad, *nigger!*

MAXWELL: School has done a great deal for me, Unc. I've been able to do research. And my research among other things has proven that the trust fund of my father, the old timey Milford Thomas Harrel III, was left exclusively to my mother, Geri Harrel, not any of it to his daughter, Chanal, or his only son, me . . .

STAGEHAND, *wheezing whisper:* I knew it! I *always* knew it!

MAXWELL: You *always* knew what, Mr. Stuck-on-Stupid?

STAGEHAND: I always knew that there was a reason why your father didn't name you Milford Thomas Harrel IV . . . That man had great vision.

MAXWELL: Talk all the trash you want . . . I've critically thought this through. My mother is mentally on the edge, so I'm getting her confined to a well-appointed psychiatric elderly retreat to end her days and, as for the estate, I'm offering Chanal a split of 70–30, the 70 for me, of course, and the balance of our trust after we liquidate this co-op building and the archival treasures of the Black Arts and Black Renaissance periods . . .

STAGEHAND: Talk English, not madness . . . English!

MAXWELL: Get to this, old folks. It's Gangster Time! The Hip Hop Revolution has landed! I'm taking and using this swag to build the greatest

Hip Hop digital radio station in the midwest! YA SEE WHAT I'M SAYIN', BOSSMAN!!!

STAGEHAND, *falls kicking and screaming:* NNNOOOOOOOOOOO!!!!!!
. . .

(MAXWELL *turns and exits.* STAGEHAND *halts his fit and looks after him until he disappears, then reaches and picks up his umbrella, not opening it, but holding it with both hands. Then he cries mournfully. The lights rise in* GERI's *kitchen. She sits in her favorite chair, drinking her favorite cup of tea. Standing over* GERI, CHANAL *watches her intently. Near* CHANAL, *seated in another chair, is* MR. BALLARD. *In the dining room, next to the kitchen, is a large, imposing poster of the deceased Milford Harrel III.*)

GERI: So what do you want me to say, Chanal? I had an episode. It was a short one . . . What's the problem, dear? I've had them before.

CHANAL: But you have these so-called episodes almost all the time now, mother. You can't keep ignoring them. Admit it, your mind is going. You need help.

GERI: I have a doctor. I have a good medical plan . . . Your father saw to that
. . .

CHANAL: Mother, you need to be in a secure, supervised place where you'll be cared for!

GERI: I'm in my own place. And I'm perfectly happy here. Have been for a good while.

MR. BALLARD: For lots of years, in fact.

CHANAL: Mr. Ballard! I'm talking to my mother. I don't need you butting in when . . .

GERI: Watch how you speak to Mr. Ballard, Chanal! Have some respect for him. And have some respect for me!

CHANAL: I have all the respect in the world for you, mother. But I don't need . . .

MR. BALLARD: Look, I'll be going.

GERI: No, you won't, Mr. Ballard. Not until I finish my tea here and leave for my appointment.

CHANAL: Appointment!

MR. BALLARD: In that case, Miss Geri, I'm at your service.

CHANAL: Where do you think you're going, mother?

GERI: None of your business . . . Now listen to me. You're not my parent. I'm your parent. So get away from me with your bossy mouth.

CHANAL: Mother, I can't . . . I can't let you . . .

GERI: Shut up, Chanal.

CHANAL: Please, Mommy . . .

GERI: SHUT YOUR MOUTH, GIRL!!!

(MR. BALLARD *rises to his feet.*)

MR. BALLARD: Easy, Geri, you can't put this stress on yourself.

GERI: I'm not putting anything on myself, Mr. Ballard. It's people who won't stop what they want to do, and not listen to me. Both you and Chanal, sit down and listen to me. I need to have my say. (MR. BALLARD *and* CHANAL *sit down.*) All right . . . My story begins in the 1930s . . .

CHANAL, *surprise:* The 1930s!

GERI, *softly/ intently:* For the last time, Chanal, *dear* . . . Close your mouth and listen.

(CHANAL *nods with understanding.*)

(GERI continues) . . . Okay . . . I was born in the mid-1930s. No, I'm not ashamed to admit that. I lived my life and didn't take time to throw too much of it away. You see, I was the child of show business performers . . . My husband's grandfather was the first of a line, the Harrel singers, dancers and show folk. My grandparents on my father's side joined the Harrel Troupe when they were young, and our families have been together ever since, until my mom and poppa crossed over and the rest of my blood family followed them . . . But before then, we did our share of pushing black show business forward. First, before we came along, there were slave-time entertainers on the plantations. Even before emancipation when the slaves were set free, there were the minstrels that were invented by that white clown Daddy "Jim Crow" Rice. A white man who saw a dancing street corner performer and then made-up a jig-a-boo show called minstrels, and he made a killing. He and his white, racist bozos disgraced and disrespected a whole race of black people here in these United States. But in about thirty years, we black performers flipped the script and turned the colored white black-imitators to really black by refusing to use blackface cosmetics any more. They did this so that they and their children would survive. It's hard to get up in this place called "America" if you don't have any money. And the Harrels were among the best at making money from their God-given talents, amen. That's why my parents' folks joined them. And in the 1890s they had the rebellion. Don't look at me like that! Learn something! Remember, the rebellion was when black performers here in America refused to put on blackface and did their acting, dancing, and singing on stage in their real, natural black faces. And that's when this country's black theater really became black . . .

CHANAL: Mother, please . . . You're tiring yourself.

MR. BALLARD: Not to mention us.

GERI: WHAT DID YOU TWO SAY???

(CHANAL *moves toward* GERI.)

CHANAL, *caring:* Take my hand, mother . . . We'll sit and talk for a while.

MR. BALLARD, *warning:* Chanal!

GERI: No! I have to go! I have an appointment. (*Turns to Milford's picture*) Mr. Milford Harrel . . . Tell our guests that I must leave for my appointment. Some very generous rich people wish to help me with my cause . . .

CHANAL: Mother! There are no rich people. In here or outside. There's only Mr. Ballard, me, your daughter, but someone is coming . . . to visit you, mother. I want to tell you about . . .

GERI: No! You're trying to take me away. Whoever you are, you're trying to put me away, take my money and the Langston Theatre from me.

MR. BALLARD: Uh oh, I was afraid of this. (*To* GERI) Relax, Geri, it's only us.

CHANAL: It's your fault she's like this, Mr. Ballard.

MR. BALLARD, *ignores* CHANAL: Geri, everything's going to be all right. You're going to stay here with me. And I'm going to take care of you and everything else. (*Encircles* GERI's *waist with one of his arms*)

CHANAL, *shock:* What are you saying! . . . Take your arm from around my mother!

GERI, *aside:* Do you see that, Mr. Milford Harrel? Mr. Ballard has everything under control, like he has always had. He's strong like you, Milford, dear.

(*The hall door flies open and* STAGEHAND *rushes in.*)

STAGEHAND, *out of breath:* Madame Geri . . . Chanal . . . (*puff puff*) . . .

GERI, *clearheaded:* Stagehand . . . What are you doing here? I told you to never leave the theater and come here.

STAGEHAND, *stutters, agitated:* I . . . I . . . I know . . . Madame . . . Ger . . . Ger . . .

GERI: Geri's my name. I know that!

CHANAL: Now look, Mr. Ballard and Stagehand have ruined everything.

STAGEHAND, *blurts:* Maxwell has been stabbed! Stabbed in the spine! Maxwell has been stabbed outside of Starbucks!

GERI: Starbucks! I knew it . . .

(GERI *faints.* MR. BALLARD *holds her.*)

CHANAL: Precious Lord, save us!

(*Lights change. They come up on* MAXWELL *asleep in a hospital-like bed set-up in* GERI's *dining room. Standing over him are* CHANAL *and* STAGEHAND.)

CHANAL, *continued, near whisper:* Oh, look at my poor brother . . . He looks so sweet and untroubled as an angel from above. How could anyone try to take his life away? . . . Please, Mr. Stagehand, explain this mystery to me.

STAGEHAND: Well, I wasn't there, Chanal, but my homey Turik the Terror . . .

CHANAL: Turik! You mean that ole crackhead Oliver Smith who used to play three-card monte down in Times Square and chess up here on a Hundred and Twenty-fifth Street before and after his Black Revolutionary I.D. change and then became a Harlem Jazz and Gospel Club guide for Asian, European, and South African tourists?

STAGEHAND: My, my . . . you know almost everybody uptown, Chanal.

CHANAL: I wouldn't believe anything that . . .

STAGEHAND: I know. I know. Turik hardly tells the truth even when you pay him. But he was there. Sissy Willy saw him. And Sissy never lies. I swear it.

CHANAL: Says who?

STAGEHAND: Now do you want to hear what I heard, Chanal?

CHANAL, *sighs:* Go 'head. Change the channel . . . if you want to.

STAGEHAND: Well, to hear Sissy Willy tell it, it was somethin' else. Now Sissy's a man, a real man, even though he's got effeminate ways about hisself, but that don't matter much . . .

CHANAL: Tell the story, Stagehand.

STAGEHAND: All right. Now this come straight out of the mouth of Sissy Willy, as told by Turik the Terror . . .

CHANAL: Then this has got to be a lie. Turik, a.k.a Oliver Smith, a.k.a Black Brother Doom, short for Bro Doom, cannot tell the truth under any circumstances.

STAGEHAND: Listen. Listen to what I know.

CHANAL: To what you know? . . . Go on. Let me hear what you *think* you know.

STAGEHAND: Maxwell stepped into Magic Johnson's Starbucks Coffee Shop on 125th Street and Frederick Douglass Boulevard . . . In my day, that big beautiful street was . . .

CHANAL, *correcting:* Boulevard!

STAGEHAND: You said it! Boulevard . . . Maxwell was there. And when he came in, Sissy Willy and Turik were drinking latte and tea . . . it is all part of their new intellectual I.D. thang, ya dig? So, since your brother Maxwell knows them, he goes over and hung a while. Did you know that Maxwell drinks dark roast without anything?

CHANAL: You must be kidding now. That's not my brother you talking about. He . . .

STAGEHAND: Then Maxwell left by the back door and got stabbed.

CHANAL: Not so fast! Stabbed? . . . MAXWELL DON'T EVEN DRINK NO DAMN COFFEE!!!

STAGEHAND: But it happened. That's what I said. And I got witnesses . . . Sissy Willy and Turik the Terror were there.

CHANAL: Now listen to me. I almost married that Oliver Smith before he took that Turik name. He was a Black Studies major at City College. That's before he lost his cool, or should I say, lost his mind . . . Either way, he started smoking the wrong stuff and went down to the ground. But he's not likely to be stabbing anybody, especially my brother, Maxie.

STAGEHAND: It was Junior Loco who stabbed Maxwell in the back . . .

CHANAL: Junior Loco! Oh, lord! . . . He's Turik's younger brother.

STAGEHAND, *calmly:* Now that's a known fact in Harlem.

CHANAL: That fool was in that angry rage thang when we were demonstrating back then so much. Loco, as we named him, got so enraged at *anything* that it seemed beautiful at the time.

STAGEHAND: I hear you. I was there too.

CHANAL, *agitated:* Bu-bu-bu . . . but . . . how did it . . . ?

STAGEHAND: You see, Maxwell stepped on his left sandal with Junior's foot still in it.

CHANAL: *No!*

STAGEHAND: Yes! Maxwell and Junior Loco had had a beef back in the day when they thought they were both handball aces of the little handball court over by Riverside Drive off of West End Avenue.

CHANAL: That's not what I was talking about.

STAGEHAND, *ignores her remark:* To Junior, that was nearly the deepest disrespect that Maxwell could pay him by treading on his left foot.

CHANAL, *unconvinced:* Stagehand, let's go into the living room and sit down and calmly talk about this crazy mess like sane people. Maxwell will be all right.

STAGEHAND: Okay. Just wait until I get some cookies from the bowl off of the table. I talk and think better when my sweet tooth isn't worrying me.

(*Lights change. In his hospital bed in* GERI's *living room,* MAXWELL *emerges from his medication-induced coma by opening his eyes in a hypnotic stare. He can see, but he cannot talk. He can breathe, but he cannot move his body. His face has little movement or expression. He tries to cry out. No sound comes from him.*

According to his face, he is fighting with all his might to get up and leave his bed, though nothing happens except that his mind can be heard.)

MAXWELL, *in his mind:* Oh shit! What the hell is this! God! . . . If there is a
   God. Have you kicked me to the curb? Have you thrown me down
   into purgatory or hell? . . . Oh damn! . . . Who but the devil could be
   so cruel as to bring me back here in this condition? How could I have
   landed in this place. My mom's place. In her dining room even . . . I
   bet they ran out of beds at Harlem Hospital and my mom volunteered
   to take me off their hands. I can imagine what she said: "I'll take him.
   I'll take my son, Maxwell. I can cure him with mother's love and home
   cooking. He loves my fried chicken. And I'll give him tender, loving
   care . . ." This is terrible. To be helpless and trapped in my crazy
   mom's domain. I can't even cry. If I could, I would cry until I got tired,
   then commit suicide. I wake up like this in the seat of ignorance. At the
   center of stupidity. Off the end of idiocy. Who in the hell is mocking
   me? God or the Devil? Or have they double-teamed me? Shit shit shit!
   I have to get out of this . . . or at least die . . . To be given oblivion
   which might be like an eternal drunken stupor. I can see, I can smell, I
   can hear . . . But can I fart? . . . Or can I . . . no . . . I can't move or feel
   anything below my chin . . . What was that asshole Junior Loco thinking? He thinks he's cool. But he doesn't know dick! I beat his ass out
   of green bucks every time he got on the court with me. He thought he
   was so good. But then why did I kick his no-hand-ball-playing ass
   every time I saw the sucker? . . . Yeah, I know. Because I was the
   sucker. I shoulda thrown him a scrap of fat every once-in-a-while. But,
   no, ole bad Maxie had to take it all . . . all the bread. All his coins. Son
   of a bitch! . . . Look at the position I'm in! Didn't Mom and Pop know
   that their entertainment-life delusion was a total distortion of how to
   resist the white power structure in this country? Mom! Pop! Didn't
   you know you can't wrest power away from the power broker with
   puckered lips? You attacked the master race with smiles, lies, and
   kisses . . . Yeah, I know, I said "master race." Well these so-called
   Black people are still playing the slave game, ain't you, Mom? You
   sang for the white folks . . . You danced and acted contented. How idi-
   otic could you be? . . . But how could I know all this? College? Not
   entirely . . . It was because I've been to hell and back these last few
   hours or days or weeks. I've sat in purgatory, or at least floated through
   the stories of outer-body death and reclamation. It's just like the stories of those like me who were claimed by death but somehow was
   thrown or slipped back into this world . . . And me! If I'm back from

the other side, why didn't I get my body back to bring with me? GIVE ME BACK MY BODY, WHOEVER HAS GOT IT! GIVE IT BACK! GIVE IT BACK! . . . Please, Lord . . . who I don't believe in much. Or please, Satan . . . who I refuse to believe in at all. Cut me some slack. Just this once. I'll go quietly when my time comes. But this can't be that time. I've got plans. This can't be my destiny. I must have another fate . . . When I went over to your side. Ya know, through the tunnel, with the music and lights, meeting family and friends who have gone before or were from other times, I met people who knew me and I kinda knew them, and they showed me the way back here . . . but . . . but . . . wasn't my dad one of them? Maybe, I guess. It's so hard remembering. And it just seems to have happened some moments ago. But this can't be all there is. Oh, I'm so tired. I've never been this tired in my . . . my . . . life. Tired and mixed up . . . Tired . . .

(*Lights change. Enter* CHANAL. *She goes to* MAXWELL, *feels his forehead, and sees that he is comfortable. His eyes are closed. Then she exits into her room.* STAGE-HAND *enters.*)

STAGEHAND: Can I have some more cookies, Chanal? They really . . .

CHANAL: No, Mother is coming home. She got to her meeting on time, in spite of her falling out like a flake. And she and Mr. Ballard are shopping for dinner. We're all going to have dinner here, according to Mommy, including you, Mr. Stagehand.

STAGEHAND: What? Why I never . . .

CHANAL: We have a lot to talk about. And a lot to do. And, Mr. Stagehand, you're needed here . . . badly.

STAGEHAND: Badly?

CHANAL: Very badly.

(*Lights change. Music.* STAGEHAND *does a soft shoe dance in a shadowy, empty area of the dining room where* MAXWELL's *bed stood, while* GERI *and* CHANAL *prepare the table for the evening meal.*)

GERI, *happy:* Stagehand . . . Stagehand! Bravo. (*To* CHANAL) Sister, isn't Stagehand a wonder? A wonderful dancer? A dream figure in classic black form . . . Yo, Stagehand . . . after you finish your bit, fix a plate for Chanal and me . . . and don't forget about Maxwell . . . (*To* CHANAL) My, what a talented performer he is!

CHANAL, *dryly:* People don't dance like that anymore, mother.

GERI, *sighs:* Yes, I know . . . That's why we have to bring back the *best* . . .

CHANAL/GERI, *together:* . . . of the Good Old Days.

GERI: Now, now, sister . . . have patience.

CHANAL: Mother, I have nothing but patience . . . Dealing with *these* people everyday.

GERI, *looks at* CHANAL: Is this all that bad?

CHANAL, *watches* STAGEHAND *cavort:* Mother . . . why does Stagehand have to do that behind-the-times shuffle? He's sawing on my nerves like a beaver. He can't be thinking he's entertaining us?

GERI: Oh, Stagehand is just happy. He sees the Langston Theatre rising as he dances.

CHANAL: Dances? . . . Hump . . . That's probably some old stuff he lifted from that clown at the Apollo Theatre that used to bring out the hook on Talent Contest Night.

GERI: My Goodness . . . don't call Sandman Sims "that old clown." He was nearly an institution in himself.

CHANAL: He'd be perfect for your Langston Theatre now, right?

GERI, *coyly:* No, he wouldn't, sister. We have our own Mr. Stagehand here. In all due respect, he's greater than even Sandman. And nearly as versatile as Sammy Davis Jr. was.[2]

CHANAL, *intense:* Mommy! I wasn't being serious about all this nonsense.

(CHANAL *and* GERI *have a song competition. First,* CHANAL *sings a gospel song. Then* GERI, *accompanied by the nifty dancing of* MR. STAGEHAND, *answers her daughter with a Billie Holiday song.* MR. BALLARD *enters before* GERI *and* MR. STAGEHAND *complete their number and watches until they are finished. The number ends with them gathering in the kitchen.)*

MR. BALLARD, *applauding:* Geri . . . Stagehand . . . You still can bring down the house.

CHANAL: I beg your pardon, Mr. Ballard. You're not capable of judging a performance of that kind.

STAGEHAND: What? Am I hearing things right?

GERI: Relax, everyone . . . Take it easy. Cool down, all of you. And fix our plates, Stagehand.

CHANAL: Mommy . . . Stagehand . . . you two are so classically boring. In a negro way, I mean.

MR. BALLARD: What the hell is she . . . ?

GERI: Easy, take it easy. Take it easy. Sister, I've already asked you to watch your mouth.

CHANAL: Well, Mr. Ballard's only the janitor of this building. He can't profane our . . .

---

2. Sammy Davis Jr. (1925–90): African-American dancer, singer, comic, actor, and musician; member of the so-called Rat Pack surrounding singer Frank Sinatra.

GERI, *rises:* Chanal "Sister" Harrel! Let me remind you that this is my home, not yours! . . .

CHANAL: Mommy!

GERI: Sister! I want you to go into the other room and wheel your brother in here in that new chair I got for him to eat with us.

MR. BALLARD: Geri . . . Geri . . . It's okay. It's okay.

MR. STAGEHAND: Right . . . right. No reason to snap. I can go and get Maxwell while . . .

CHANAL: Why does a janitor have more say-so here than me?

GERI: Because he's not a janitor now. He's the Property Manager since I invested enough in this place.

MR. BALLARD: Harry Belafonte had a job something like this when he was a youngster and worked across the way . . .[3]

CHANAL, *correcting:* AVENUE!

GERI: "SISTER," GO GET YOUR BROTHER! AND EVERYONE ELSE, PLEASE KEEP QUIET!

CHANAL, *mutters:* As God is my witness, I am . . .

GERI, *quietly to* CHANAL: Go!

(*Sulking,* CHANAL *goes into the next room. Lights change.* CHANAL *rolls out the comatose* MAXWELL *sitting strapped in his wheelchair.* MAXWELL *is being fed intravenously. Upon the dining room table, there are plates and utensils for* GERI, CHANAL, STAGEHAND, *and* MR. BALLARD, *but none for* MAXWELL.)

CHANAL, *from center of the room:* Since there are so many nonbelievers here, I'll just say, dinner's ready. Help yourself. In God's name, amen.

GERI: And amen to that! Sister, you're too long-winded with all that preachy stuff. I'm glad you made a wise choice and got this show on the road. Nobody wants their food getting cold . . . Help yourselves, everybody.

CHANAL: Mother, you don't understand. I wish I could make you . . .

GERI, *impatient:* Just go and eat, girl!

(GERI *and* CHANAL *are handed filled plates by* STAGEHAND. MR. BALLARD *serves himself, likewise* STAGEHAND. *All eat, except for* MAXWELL, *who sits across the room, strapped silently into his wheelchair.* STAGEHAND *looks sorrowfully at* MAXWELL *and steps into a light, while in the background the others create a visual of slow-motion action.*)

STAGEHAND: What a life I have lived. And here I am after more than fifty years serving the person who I have most adored. Geri Harrel. The wonderful one. The Sugar Hill Diva . . . She has talent, she has history,

---

3. Harry Belafonte (1927–): Jamaican-American singer, Tony Award–winning actor, and political activist.

she has vision and brains. And she's not a bad looker for her age. And now it all comes together with Geri at the true center of her show business saga. How do I fit in? . . . Well, Geri and her husband, Milford Harrel, the III, found me . . . Or maybe it was that I found them. It was somewhere around 1950. In Wilmington, Delaware. I had just been kicked out of my wife's house with nothing but an old duffle bag. I had recently been honorably discharged from the US Navy and had my separation check in my wallet. Word was that my wife was gunning for me, and I was dead certain that she wasn't going to get any of my last check. So I went to somewhere where I suspected that she wouldn't be. That's how I got to Club Society, in Wilmington, a little colored club off of the main drag where small shows on the traveling circuit would come through town . . . That night at Club Society, an act new to me was featured—the Harrels, which were Milford Harrel III and Geri . . . I soon found out they were really married. And I discovered that they were there for me. You see, they changed my life, so I knew it had to happen the way it did. I don't know what they did, but it worked on me. That was Thursday, and the next two nights I was in my usual spot, soaking up whatever I could of their performances. To me, Geri was, if not as good as Ruth Brown,[4] she'd at least give her something to think about. And that meant the world to me, 'cause before Geri, Ruth Brown I thought would be my favorite 'til death do we part. Then Milford and Geri were gone. In the early morning hours they disappeared . . . Oh, where was my great love, Geri. It was no way we could remain separated. Almost crazed by the loss, I asked the club's staff and regulars where had the Harrels gone. "They probably went to Atlantic City. There's a lot of dives they appear at over there," someone offered. "Oh, I bet they down in Cape May. That's one of their spots this time of year," another one confided in me. But I got no definite answer until I pumped up my nerves and asked Bully, the owner of the club, where had Geri Harrel gone. "In five days they gonna open in Philly at the Blue Note over on Ridge Avenue, or at Pep's or the Showboat down near Broad and South Streets," he let me know. And five days later, I was at a little table next to the little stage in Philadelphia watching my dream unfold . . .

(*Lights heighten.* MR. BALLARD *points at* MAXWELL *and shouts.*)

MR. BALLARD, *excited:* Look, y'all! Maxwell's trying to say something!

MAXWELL, *straining:* Chi . . . chi . . . chic . . .

---

4. Ruth Brown (1928–): African-American recording star in the mid-1950s for Atlantic Records, member of the Rock and Roll Hall of Fame, noted supper club performer, and Tony Award winner for *Black and Blue* (1989).

(GERI *and* CHANAL *rush over to* MAXWELL.)

GERI: Maxwell, son . . . I hear you. Mommy hears your beautiful words, baby.

CHANAL: Maxie's been touched by the Lord! HALLELUJAH!!! Hallelujah! Bless his name!

GERI: QUIET, SISTER!!! We must listen to your brother . . . Go on, son. Speak your words.

MAXWELL: Chic . . . chic . . . chic . . .

MR. BALLARD: Is that all, man?

(*A volcanic force within* MAXWELL *forces him to his feet, causing him to break the bonds that tie him to his wheelchair* . . .)

GERI/CHANAL/MR. BALLARD/STAGEHAND, *together:* OOUUUUUUUUU . . .

MAXWELL, *screams:* CHICKEN!!! CHICKEN!!! . . . I HAVE TO HAVE SOME OF MY MOM'S CHICKEN!!!

(MAXWELL *lumbers forward to the table and grabs a chicken drumstick in each hand and escapes out the hallway door.* CHANAL *has a holy fit—wiggling, gyrating, almost foaming at the mouth, and talking in a strange language.*)

CHANAL: Ah root ah roota zoot te . . . ah yeayeayea . . . ah ah . . .

(GERI *comes to center stage and looks around the room.*)

STAGEHAND, *looks as well:* Damn.

GERI: You know . . . I can always count on Maxwell to mess up the joint.

(*Lights down.*)

ACT II

Lights up on STAGEHAND's *tent, set up in the middle of* GERI's *dining room. Snoring sounds come from inside the small tent, which has someone's feet sticking out at one end. A couple of knocks beat on the hall door. The feet from the tent twitch, and, when the knocking increases, the snoring stops, and* STAGEHAND *pushes himself feet first from the tent.* STAGEHAND *is dressed in flamboyant night clothes, reminiscent of a by-gone movie era of Arabian matinee idol rogues and mechanized winged horses. For a moment,* STAGEHAND *listens to the knock and wipes the sleep from his eyes with the hem of his sleeping gown.*

BALLARD's VOICE, *off-stage:* HELLO IN THERE! . . . STAGEHAND . . . STAGEHAND. I CAN'T HEAR YOU . . . SO I KNOW YOU'VE STOPPED SNORING. GET THE HELL UP, MAN, AND COME OPEN THIS DOOR!

STAGEHAND, *calls out:* Who's there? What do you want?

BALLARD: I want to see Geri. Tell her I'm out here.

STAGEHAND: She's not here, Ballard . . . Call her on her cell phone.

BALLARD: Cell phone! (*Mutters*) Somebody must be kidding . . . I don't have any use for that kinda stuff.

(*Sound of key in lock on apartment side of door.* STAGEHAND *acts perplexed.*)

STAGEHAND: Ballard! What in almighty hell are you doing! . . . Christ! You're making me lose my cultured self, man.

BALLARD, *entering:* I've used my key . . . I'm the Property Manager of this building complex.

STAGEHAND: You have no right to barge in here . . . like . . . like . . .

BALLARD: Like I'm looking for suspicious activities. Right! I am looking . . .

STAGEHAND: Fool! You know there's nothing suspicious going on in Madame Geri's apartment.

BALLARD: How do I know? I haven't seen her in a couple of days.

STAGEHAND: Well, she's out trying to catch up to Maxwell and straighten him out.

BALLARD: Yeah, like Maxie's lost. He's down on 125th Street with a big Poland Spring Water Cooler bottle collecting money for Geri's and yours pet project . . . the Langston Theatre.

STAGEHAND: He must have taken a turn for the worse and completely lost his mind . . . I heard he was doing some wild things.

BALLARD: You heard something! Where? In your tent?

STAGEHAND, *superior tone:* Why, yes, Mr. Ballard . . . My cell phone works very well from there.

BALLARD: You don't say?

STAGEHAND, *insufferably smug:* And my little community grapevine is . . . how should I say it? . . . *On the money.*

BALLARD: Well blow it out your ear, Einstein! What I'm talking about is that boy Maxwell Harrel destroying everything his momma has built these last twenty years . . . and you, her so-called right-hand man, ain't doing nothin' but layin' in his little tent and . . .

STAGEHAND: And . . .

BALLARD: And snoring!

STAGEHAND: I know that Maxwell calls himself starting a street corner charity for Geri and declaring the Langston Theatre an international shrine . . . Hump! Doesn't make sense to me for him to do all that, but what can I do? Geri gave me instructions when she left for me not to do anything until she tells me.

BALLARD: You're such a good . . . *boy*, Stagehand . . .

STAGEHAND, *shrugs:* And since Chanal's gotten engaged to Junior Loco, who's back in Riker's for breaking his parole by stabbing Maxwell near the nerve close to his rear end that almost paralyzed him for life . . .

BALLARD: I know. We all know. But we thought that Maxwell's spinal cord had been cut, but it was only slightly scratched . . .

STAGEHAND: Right! And Maxie sprang back on his feet like our own miracle, and the fool has now lost his mind completely for mistaking Junior Loco's bad aim for the hand of God.

BALLARD: Ha! It's probably just an act. The only miracle that I saw was some of Geri's southern soul-fried chicken ripped-off . . . But wait a minute . . . I almost forgot to ask you . . .

STAGEHAND: What?

BALLARD: How did our church-going, educated Chanal get engaged to Junior Loco, the dizzy chump who stabbed her brother?

STAGEHAND: Oh . . . ya see, Chanal's a very special person. She has forgiveness in her heart and soul. And Junior Loco is one of them pretty boys.

BALLARD: Nawh . . . nawh . . . I'm not going to believe this.

STAGEHAND: She's almost like a jailhouse missionary, ya know. Somehow, she saw Junior Loco's predicament after she visited him once to cuss him out for what he did to Maxwell, so she visited him some more in the lockup, and since Maxwell was almost miraculously recovered, she saw this as a sign that she was on the right path.

BALLARD, *dubious:* To glory?

STAGEHAND: Something like that.

(BALLARD *turns to leave.*)

BALLARD, *shakes head:* Maxwell could have been paralyzed for life.

STAGEHAND: But, he was soon out of his wheelchair and taking on the world again.

BALLARD, *faces* STAGEHAND: It was really only a day and a night that Maxwell was paralyzed. But this doesn't give Chanal any excuse to get in bed with . . .

STAGEHAND: So much has happened recently . . . Loco's still in jail. Nobody's been in bed with anybody as far as I know.

BALLARD: But you moved in here with your kiddie tent and . . .

STAGEHAND: I'm Madame Geri's Security. I have to be . . . wait! . . . Did you say kiddie tent?

BALLARD: For a grown man, you seem kind of strange sleeping in there with your feet out? Are all you show people really so mixed up?

STAGEHAND: You do not know what you're talking about, Ballard.

BALLARD: Next thing we'll see is you cuddling up with a big ole Teddy bear, if you don't do it already.

STAGEHAND, *threatens:* Watch what you say, ignorant one. I'll have you know that I am versed in the secret Tibetan Warrior Art of the Finger Death Stroke.

BALLARD: Ignorant! You reject from the circus . . .

(STAGEHAND *does a short, ludicrous warrior drill.*)

STAGEHAND, *demonstrating:* YAAAYEEEE . . .

(BALLARD *jumps back, quickly puts on brass knuckles, and assumes a boxer's fighting pose.* STAGEHAND *calmly walks up to* BALLARD *and slaps him in his very surprised face.* BALLARD *forgets his brass knuckles and grabs* STAGEHAND's *throat and begins squeezing.* STAGEHAND *almost reaches unconsciousness when* GERI *enters.*)

BALLARD, *adulation upon seeing* GERI: WELL, KISS MY WRIST!

(GERI *has gotten a complete makeover. She turns heads by merely appearing.* STAGEHAND *tries to crawl to* GERI, *but collapses, gasping for air.*)

GERI: What's this? Part of my world is collapsing, and you two, my so-called support team, act like you're down at the street basketball court.

BALLARD, *near awe:* Geri . . . you look divine, baby.

STAGEHAND, *nearly choking:* Ger . . . (*coughs*) . . . Geri . . . You look like yourself . . . back in the day.

GERI: Hold it! . . . I appreciate your comments, especially you're being staff, but seriously, nothing has happened to me that millions of women worldwide don't make happen every morning in front of their mirrors.

(BALLARD *and* STAGEHAND *shake their heads negatively.*)

BALLARD: No way!

GERI: All one needs is the know how . . . and to have the Benjamins[5] to maintain yourself. And you both know I own a part of this co-op dream we're standing in the middle of, bought forty years ago at 1950's prices. So, you both can probably count on your fingers and toes what it's likely worth in today's money. And you'd be probably wrong. It's even worth much more. And also, I've religiously, but on the quiet side, invested in this building's realty corp.

BALLARD: Okay, so you're rich . . . But where have you been, Geri?

STAGEHAND, *recovered:* That's "Madame Geri" to you, bully!

---

5. Benjamins: As in Benjamin Franklin, the face on the hundred-dollar bill.

BALLARD: Bully? So what happened to your Tibetan Death Finger?

STAGEHAND: Dang! I forgot the incantation.

GERI: Stagehand . . . You're so gallant to throw yourself in front of Ballard's rage . . . for me.

BALLARD: Hummp! . . . Blowin' smoke his way, huh?

GERI: And my own Harlem friend, Mr. Ballard. How debonair you are today.

BALLARD, *confused:* What you call me that for?

GERI: Listen to this, guys: I've been on a short retreat with some wealthy board members of the foundations I've been meeting with for the past year. We look to be dead on course with our dream.

STAGEHAND, *modulated:* Yea.

BALLARD: And with everything else?

GERI, *crestfallen:* You mean my children . . . my children . . . Ballard? . . .

BALLARD: Yes, Geri . . .

GERI: Stagehand . . .

STAGEHAND: Madame?

GERI: Are my children on the wrong path?

(*Silence.* STAGEHAND *and* BALLARD *look at one another and shrug.*)

BALLARD: Well, Geri, by the way they act sometimes, you might think that they need some guidance.

GERI, *frustrated:* But they're grown now. And they haven't listened to me since I can remember.

STAGEHAND: Geri . . . Ballard and I don't have any answers we can give you that matter.

(GERI *looks at them, then she feels dizziness coming on. She reaches out for the couch as both men fall over one another to catch her. They all lay still. The shadow of the figure in the mirror appears, unseen by them, then disappears. A rap of knuckles at the door, and* MAXWELL *enters. He wears a Nehru-type outfit.*)[6]

MAXWELL, *beatific:* Welcome, family and friends. I am here to share the truth with you.

(GERI *sits up.*)

STAGEHAND, *startled:* Madame Geri!

BALLARD, *apprehensive:* Geri . . .

---

6. Nehru-type outfit: Lacking lapels and conventional collar, the Nehru jacket was popularized by India's first prime minister, Jawaharlal Nehru. Quite fashionable in the 1960s, it enjoyed something of a comeback in the 1990s.

MAXWELL, *beatific:* Mom.

GERI, *to herself:* I was sinking. Sinking to a deep place, among dark clouds . . . and I heard my son's voice. And my willpower brought me back here. For I have work to do . . . work that is in the future, not in the past. (*To* MAXWELL) Hello, Maxwell . . . you've come to see me?

MAXWELL, *happy:* Yes . . .

BALLARD: Let your mother rest, Maxwell.

STAGEHAND: Maxie . . . why don't you . . .

GERI: Ballard . . . Stagehand . . . please go down and take the car for servicing. A good washing and tune-up should do. I'll see you later. (BALLARD *and* STAGEHAND *pause.*) I've been to see a new doctor . . . who gave me a new prescription. It will allow me to go forward, not live in the past . . . I should be all right now that my son's here.

(BALLARD *and* STAGEHAND *silently leave.* MAXWELL *appears even more happy.*)

MAXWELL, *phony accent:* Mum, dear . . .You're looking so with it today.

GERI: Son, did you know that my mother called her mother "Mum," and I in turn called my mother "Mum"?

MAXWELL: Does it matter so much now, Mo-ther?

GERI: There hasn't been anyone in our family called Mum in quite a while, perhaps more than fifty years.

MAXWELL: Well look, I'm here to talk to you about your future and mine.

GERI: Maxwell, I hope you haven't lost your mind. All I plan for now is my own future, and perhaps a bit of planning for yours and your sister's as well . . .

MAXWELL: It's so wonderful how you can still handle those men. I just don't see you ever handling me that way, anymore.

GERI: There's almost nothing that you can see at the moment, Maxwell.

MAXWELL: Did I hear you correctly, Mother?

GERI: Yes, you have . . . I raised you to be a precious jewel . . . and now, you're practically worthless. You seem permanently spoiled, son.

MAXWELL: Oh, your language is so gauche. Does its sour tone come from your diet? Have you had your heavy helping of cabbage today, Mother?

GERI: That's coleslaw to you. Why do you have so little respect for me, son?

MAXWELL: Ahhh . . . really . . . I came here today to discuss business, not diets.

GERI: Exactly.

MAXWELL, *pulls document from pocket:* I have here something I want you to read . . . Do you have your eyeglasses handy?

GERI, *calmly:* Your father and I raised you to be civil to your elders, to have manners.

MAXWELL, *hotly:* Don't give me your phony pretensions! How did you think I felt when I was a young boy and walked around Harlem with my friends and we saw pictures of you, Mo-ther, in skimpy tasseled costumes or those with only feathers and your smile to hide your breasts?

GERI, *surprised:* You were embarrassed?

MAXWELL: They laughed at me!

GERI: You were raised in the theater, son, not the church. Don't you understand that?

MAXWELL: They laughed at me and made my life miserable . . . Sometimes you went around practically naked. Hah! The whores on the avenues worked under the cover of night, not selling their wares in the open like fish dinners.

GERI: Don't go over the top, Maxwell. Your father created the shows, and I was his co-star, and my assets were never privately sold.

(MAXWELL *shoves document at* GERI.)

MAXWELL: Sign this! . . . I'm taking over the Langston Theatre project . . . Did you know it's a nonprofit gold mine? . . . Why didn't I think of this before? . . . But I had to go to hell and return to find out what's really important in this life.

GERI: Are your two sons important to you? You've proven your wife isn't.

MAXWELL, *near tantrum:* Oh, snap! Why did you send them away where I can't find them? Jerome and Little Milford are mine! And you gave that worthless piece of a wife of mine more money than she's ever seen so she could run off with them. How dare you, you traitor!

GERI, *calmly:* Whatever you're on, it's eating up your brain, son.

MAXWELL: You know where you can go, old woman, with that *son* shit!

GERI, *hurt:* I dared to do what I did before it was too late because I couldn't allow you to beat the life out of my grandsons and their mother.

(MAXWELL *advances on* GERI.)

MAXWELL, *losing it:* You! . . . You! . . .

(GERI *pulls a hand gun from under the pillow of the couch she sits on. She points the gun toward* MAXWELL's *face.*)

GERI: Stop!

(MAXWELL *halts.*)

GERI, *continued:* This is a pearl-handled pistol, one of a pair. Your ex-wife has the mate . . . Don't worry, I taught her how to use it . . . Your father, who you probably thought was a dancing Uncle Tom, was always armed when we went through KKK country on our Chitlin' Circuit tours. Yes, Milford Harrel III taught me how to handle and use this tool. And if need be, I'll blow you away, *son.*

MAXWELL, *incredulous:* You've . . . you've what?

GERI, *orders:* Sit down . . . on the floor . . . there.

(He hesitantly sits on the floor.)

GERI, *continued:* Now. Why are you messing with my Langston Theatre? . . . Answer me!

MAXWELL, *mutters:* Well . . . it . . .

GERI: Speak up. We haven't all day.

MAXWELL, *clears throat:* Uumph . . . The Langston just fits in with my plans. My plans to be powerful and rich . . . like you.

GERI: Your plans to be powerful and rich? . . . Do you see me killing my brain with whatever you're using? . . . But before you got this habit, why did you drop out of all the colleges and universities I paid for you to go to?

MAXWELL: Mom . . . I don't have time to waste on that stuff. I'm smarter than those professors and students. They just holding me back . . . like you're doing.

GERI: I gave you lots of money . . . and it all disappears like you do when it suits you. Your wife gets nothing . . . your children . . .

MAXWELL: I don't have time for this! I don't have TIME FOR THIS!

GERI: Tell me how you're going to get what you say you want out of life?

MAXWELL: And then you'll give me what I need?

GERI: No, I'm not going to give you what you think you need. But I'll strongly consider it if you successfully go through a rehab program that I approve of. C'mon, tell me.

MAXWELL: Have you heard of the Digital Tech Explosion? . . . (*Excited*) With the billion dollar Hip Hop World jammin' forward, there's only one way to go with this now new thang . . . trillions are on the horizon. Yea! Monee, honee!

GERI: Wait a minute . . . me and the theater are about as low tech as you can go . . . a few boards and some money . . . but what else?

MAXWELL: Well, you see, it's a place to start. With a place to produce, there's no telling where I can take it. And it's eligible to get grants and donations . . . worldwide. Ooweee! Money's mammy! . . . Mom! You gotta give me a stake in the Langston.

GERI: First, your rehab program.

MAXWELL: Look, you don't know anything about any programs. You just holding me back like you always have. You've never been there for me when I needed you. You'd be off following dad with your skimpy, laughable costumes. You're not a real mother.

GERI: Maxwell, listen to me. Whatever you say, it doesn't matter. I'm not letting you counterfeit my dream of a theater and arts and culture place for the people. For the people and our family. Not to make some fast money, not even to be a community celebrity. The Langston Theatre is for the future, after I'm gone, after we all are gone.

MAXWELL: Why don't you take all your money and build this white elephant?

GERI: Because if it were mostly my money, the institution would collapse as soon as I'm gone. You and Chanal would go for each other's throats over the money. A digital Hip Hop mess for you, missionary madness in the near and far corners of the world for Chanal.

GERI: Everything would soon be gone . . . But with a nonprofit reservoir for black and world theater and dance that . . .

(MAXWELL *stands up.*)

MAXWELL: I'm leaving. I've heard more than I can stand.

(GERI *puts gun away.*)

GERI: I feel sorry for you, son. A man, like an entire people, who turns against themselves and fights themselves from succeeding because they refuse to believe in the correct dream is hopeless, and will remain hopeless unless they begin to see how empty hopelessness is . . . I'm sorry . . . So your friends teased and hurt you because of me? They must have bullied you, too. I wish I was closer to you to help you through your hurt. Do you know that hurt little boys and girls can grow up to really hurt grownups and children too? . . . And can destroy their own lives . . . and those lives of those near them.

MAXWELL, *aggressive:* Shut up, old woman.

(BALLARD *appears in the doorway and hears and sees* MAXWELL *from behind.*)

MAXWELL, *moves toward* GERI: You . . . you . . . (BALLARD *jumps at* MAXWELL, *grabbing the back of his collar and the seat of his pants, and turns* MAXWELL *toward the outside doorway.*)

BALLARD, *angry:* You lousy punk!

MAXWELL: Hey, man! . . . My back! . . . Leggo! Leggo! . . . It hurts! Aahhh!!! Ma . . . Ma . . . Mama!!!

(BALLARD *bum rushes* MAXWELL *out of the apartment. The sound of* BALLARD *beating* MAXWELL *comes from outside as* GERI *stands and walks into her bedroom. Lights change. Lights up on* GERI's *place. She sits in the wheelchair in front of her bedroom doorway.* BALLARD *stands beside her.* STAGEHAND *enters.*)

STAGEHAND, *uneasy:* Madame Geri, what's wrong?

BALLARD: Geri's okay. Don't sweat it.

STAGEHAND: But when I came up the street just now, I saw medics walking Maxwell into their ambulance. And now you're sitting in that . . .

GERI: Hold up! Don't get excited. Everything's fine . . . (*Sighs*) I'm fine. Just a bit tired. I felt like sitting down and found out this chair's comfortable. I'm perfectly all right.

STAGEHAND: Good! Then we're taking you to the Langston.

GERI: The Langston Theatre?

BALLARD: Right! Chanal demanded that I come and get you two.

GERI: I don't understand . . . I didn't give any orders for . . .

BALLARD: It's all right. Just sit back and we'll take care of everything.

(BALLARD *begins guiding* GERI *in the wheel chair. Lights change. In the dimness, gospel music rises.* CHANAL's *voice is heard and she is seen singing a spiritual. Lights change . . .* CHANAL *is on the Langston Theatre stage. Soon, on the other side of the stage,* GERI *is wheeled in by* BALLARD *and* STAGEHAND. *They watch* CHANAL *perform. She is in a new mood, a mood that is loving and upbeat. The new arrivals are moved to clap, pick up and play tambourines, and join in the singing. After* CHANAL *finishes her number,* GERI *steps out of the wheelchair and sings an Ella Fitzgerald signature scat song.* GERI, CHANAL, STAGEHAND, *and* BALLARD *rock the house. When the number is completed, they all hug, and* CHANAL *acts as emcee.*)

CHANAL: Hi, mom. Thank you. And thank you, Stagehand and Mr. Ballard, for making this a special night at the Langston Theatre of Harlem . . . You may not know, but this is the Langston Theatre's birthday . . . and we're going to have a birthday party. This date was chosen for the Langston's party because one of its founders has her birthday today also . . . Give a great big Happy Birthday to a real Harlem Diva . . . the one and only Sugar Hill Divine Lady . . . my mother, Geri Harrel!

VOICE: Happy Birthday, Geri! . . . Happy Birthday! . . . Party Time! Party Time!!!

(*They all sing the "Happy Birthday" song in the modern black way. Then the food and refreshments are uncovered.*)

CHANAL: Okay, party people . . . It's not all over until it's over. We have a couple more things on our agenda before we open the doors and invite our audience and friends in. Right now, we're all family in here, so I want to tell you that I heard from my brother, Maxwell, a little while ago. Check this! By now, Maxie is on a plane, going back to enter a program that will help him with his problem so that he can peacefully and lovingly join his family.

GERI: Thank God!

(*Applause from all*)

CHANAL: And I have a report about yours truly.

GERI: You're not going to embarrass me, are you, Chanal?

CHANAL: Not on your life, Mom. No way.

GERI: And thank you for this party, Chanal. You're so good at this kind of thing.

CHANAL: Is that a job offer I'm hearing, Mo-ther?

BALLARD: Careful, Chanal . . . You know Geri has delicate health.

(*Everybody laughs.*)

CHANAL: So, speaking of jobs . . . I'm on my way back to graduate school. Raaayyy! . . .

GERI: See there? I knew we were all survivors. Look and see what we've done? This place we're celebrating tonight. The hundreds of places like this that have come, gone, or stayed in the last several decades. And what about the schools and their students which have moved things along? And what about the movements and struggles that have helped make us free, independent, and strong . . .?

STAGEHAND: Geri . . . like most of the time, you're right! . . . You're right! Hey, yawhl! Geri's right, as usual . . . C'mon, get up here, everybody. We're going to have a line dance to end all line dances. Just follow Geri here.

(*They start their special line dance as the lights of the Langston Theatre go dim. Suddenly,* GERI *looks up and screams.*)

GERI: Fire! Fire! . . . I smell smoke.

CHANAL, *uneasy:* Easy, Mama . . . Don't be upsetting these folks. There's possibly nothing . . .

GERI: I smell smoke! (*Looks, screams*) EEEEEEEE! . . . There's some flames!

BALLARD: I see 'em! I see 'em!

STAGEHAND: Somebody on the avenue told me that Junior Loco was out! . . .

CHANAL: NO, LAWD!!!

STAGEHAND: They said Junior Loco was out and was goin' to get revenge.

CHANAL: Revenge, hell! For what?

GERI: Watch your mouth now, daughter!

CHANAL: Chill, Mo-ther!

(GERI *draws back her hand as if to strike* CHANAL, *but* CHANAL *nods her head affirmatively.*)

CHANAL, *continued:* Yes, mom . . . I see your point . . . (*To audience*) Everybody, go to an exit!

GERI: Everybody stay calm. There's exits galore!

(*Lights dim. A smoke machine pushes clouds of colored smoke across the stage. Lasers pick up cherry-, orange-, and violet-hued highlights . . . Figures are seen within the smoke.*)

GERI: Stagehand! Is that you? . . . What do you think you're doing?

STAGEHAND: I'm beating out this damn fire, Geri . . . Ahh, I mean Madame . . . Ouch!

GERI: It looks so out-of-con . . .

(STAGEHAND *screams and thrashes around. He jerks, obviously burnt.*)

STAGEHAND, *screams:* THE FIRE! IT'S GOT ME! EEEEE! PUT IT OUT! PUT IT THE HELL OUT!

CHANAL: HELP HIM! HELP STAGEHAND!

(*The silhouetted figures of* GERI, CHANAL, *and* BALLARD *are seen against the smoke, lights, and action, beating around the frantic* STAGEHAND *with tablecloths and towels.*)

GERI, *a revelation:* KOOL AID! THE KOOL AID! . . . WE'VE GOT A WHOLE PLASTIC TUB OF IT!

CHANAL: THAT'S RIGHT! THAT'S RIGHT! BALLARD! OVER HERE! HELP ME WITH THIS! . . . (*To* GERI) Get out of the way, Mom.

(CHANAL *and* BALLARD *carry the tub over to* STAGEHAND *and throw its contents on him. The fire is extinguished. Smoke blows away.*)

STAGEHAND: Heavens! Did you have to drown me in this ghastly stuff? . . . Kool Aid!

BALLARD: Say, Stage*ham!* . . . You should see the mess on this stage.

GERI: That's all right, Ballard. We're all together. We'll be all right.

STAGEHAND, *still on back:* Ooooo . . . but I'm not all right . . . Ooooo . . . is this what dying feels like?

(*Sounds of sirens outside*)

GERI: Well, here comes the 9–1–1 team. Chanal, offer the guys and girls some of these chicken wings and waffles when they finish with what they got to do.

(*Lights change. Samples of the music play for an interlude. Lights up on* STAGE-HAND *dancing in a splendid costume with broom in hand. With practiced Hip Hop steps, he sweeps the stage and tidies up.*)

STAGEHAND, *to audience:* It's a year later. And we have a new theater. In fact, we are now the New Langston Theatre. How about a round of applause for this great accomplishment! . . . And now, it is birthday time again for Geri Harrel, the New Langston Theatre, and its Players . . .

(*He picks up his colorful umbrella and opens it while dancing.*)

STAGEHAND, *calls out:* ENTRÉE ENSEMBLE!

(*In beautiful regalia,* GERI, CHANAL, MAXWELL, *and* BALLARD *dance on with unfurled parasols and umbrellas.* STAGEHAND *takes his place among them, and they dance a passionate, loving ritual expressing togetherness to music echoing Mardi Gras on modern Harlem sidewalks. If the performance space permits, a limited number of the audience can be led into the finale of the dance/ritual in a celebratory fashion.*)

The End

THEATER
PIECES

Deceptively complex, The Theme Is Blackness *recalls both the* serrate *of the Italian futurists (in which seats were triple booked, slathered with glue, or dusted with itching power) as well as the mystical tendencies of West African philosophy, which emphasizes a nonobjective, participatory approach. At its first production at San Francisco State College in 1966, Chebo Evans's Third World Three Black music trio improvised jazz against a sonic background of rattled chains, moans, and groans, while performers crept under the seats, grabbing ankles and such. This anticipates many of the techniques used in Amiri Baraka's* Slave Ship *(1968). The play was first published in* The Theme Is Blackness: The Corner and Other Plays, *edited by Ed Bullins (New York: Morrow, 1973).*

The Theme Is Blackness

A One-Act Play to be Given before Predominantly White Audiences

(1966)

SPEAKER: The theme of our drama tonight will be Blackness. Within Blackness, One may discover all the self-illuminating universes in creation. And now BLACKNESS—(*Lights go out for twenty minutes. Lights up.*)

SPEAKER: Will blackness please step out and take a curtain call?

(*Lights out.*)

Blackness.

Among the most provocative of Bullins's experimental works, It Bees Dat Way *is also among his most formally radical. The play draws attention to the ethics of staging revolutionary violence and the political potential of imagining it as a reader. In this case, Bullins asks five Black performers to improvise lines of action to the "most absurd conclusion," including beating, theft, and rape, until all the white spectators have exited. The last, exultant line of the play is not the one we would expect. Spoken by the quarrelsome, drunken Corny after a tirade of revolutionary slogans, it compels the reader to consider what survives the moment of stereotypical, absurd, race-based violence: The performer behind the performance? The stereotype? Or theatricality itself, impossible to ever completely banish from the encounter of mutual Others? The play was first produced at the Ambience Lunch-Hour Theatre Club, London, in 1970 and first published in* Four Dynamite Plays, *edited by Ed Bullins (New York: Morrow, 1972).*

It Bees Dat Way

(1970)

THE PEOPLE:

JACKIE: *Forty-five. A bleary-eyed, nappy-headed, drunken Blackwoman.*

POPPY: *Mid-twenties. A junkie. Black.*

OUTLAW: *Mid-teens or younger. Husky and athletic. Black.*

TRIGGER: *Late teens. About same size as* OUTLAW, *though thinner. Black.*

CORNY: *Early forties. Knows more than his appearance shows. Drunk. Black.*

SISTER: *Early twenties. A tender, lost look about her. Black.*

SCENE: *This ritual is to be given in a location that is frequented by a white audience.*

The room or space or playing area is one place. A four-sided enclosure with ceiling.

Painted black.

The single setting is a street-lamp, near the center of the space. The entire set or space represents a Harlem street corner, the street-lamp being the only illumination at the beginning of the ritual.

Musicians are concealed somewhere in the space behind a scrim or false wall so that they can view the action unmolested and play to the emotional tensions, but be invisible to the audience.

Only twenty-five people are allowed into the play during a performance. And these people must be predominantly white.

The people are let in. They are a regular theater audience and they look about for seats, try and distinguish the set from the real things in the room, and wait for the play to go on as they uncomfortably stand around and whisper to themselves. JACKIE, POPPY, OUTLAW, TRIGGER, CORNY, *and* SISTER *enter the same as the audience, not distinguished as being actors.*

JACKIE, *bumps white person; she is drunk:* Hey. . . do you know what's goin' on?

POPPY, *not far away:* Not so loud, baby . . . there's a show goin' on.

JACKIE: I wasn't talkin' to you, sucker!

POPPY: I was only tryin' to be helpful, baby.

JACKIE: I ain't your baby. Go be helpful someplace else, brother.

POPPY: Okay . . . if you deal it that way, sister. Square business.

OUTLAW, *to somebody white:* Hey, what's happenin'? What's goin' down?

(*Whenever the actors start a conversation with one of the audience they take it as far as it can possibly go in vocal and physical action. They follow the situation to its most absurd conclusion: being that* JACKIE *is drunk,* POPPY *is a junkie needing money for drugs,* OUTLAW *has made a career from mugging white people,* TRIGGER *does anything in the way of violence (mostly helping* OUTLAW*),* CORNY *is a quarreler and semi-drunk street-person, and* SISTER *will get into anything where she thinks she might score some cash. Whichever way the audience goes, the actors go counter to it or with it, whatever is most unlikely and threatening, even into physical abuse: scuffling, rape, strong-arming, and beating the audience.*)

TRIGGER, *to whites:* What's the matter? You lose somethin'?

CORNY: Ain't that a bitch?

SISTER: Sho is.

JACKIE: Yeah . . . I lost somethin' . . .You want to make somethin' of it?

POPPY: Ahhhh . . . chump!

OUTLAW: Kiss mah . . .

JACKIE: Shut up! . . . shut up your dirty fucken filthy mouf!

CORNY: Yo mamma.

JACKIE, *to white man:* You ain't got nothin' ta drink, honey? What's in yo pockets, chump! Awww . . . what kinda square are you . . . a corny square?[1]

CORNY: Hey . . . who said my name? Huh? Who said it?

POPPY: Yo mamma.

SISTER, *to white man:* Hey, baby . . . you want to have a nice time?

JACKIE: Yeah? Is that a fact?

TRIGGER: Do tell?

JACKIE: Don't be in mah mouf, sucker! Get yo own thing.

POPPY: I saw him. I saw him take it!

(OUTLAW *or* TRIGGER *has taken someone's wallet or purse.*)

CORNY: Shut up, punk! What's in it fo' you?

POPPY: He went over there. There he is, over there.

JACKIE: Shut up!

POPPY, *to white woman; confidential:* He ain't too far from here. I can find him . . . I can get back what you lost . . . What's in it for me?

SISTER: You like ta have a nice time, baby?

POPPY: What's in it for me?

OUTLAW: Take yo hands off me . . . I ain't got nothin'. Take your mahtha-fukkin' hands off me.

TRIGGER: Hey, Outlaw, you want me to go up side this mahthafukker's head?

JACKIE: DON'T HIT HIM! . . . PLEASE, GOD IN HEAVEN, DON'T LET ME WITNESS NO NOTHIN' LIKE DIS . . . OH, LORD, DON'T LET ME SEE DIS MAN GET KILLED!

POPPY, *to white man:* I saw him. I saw that nigger do it. What you want to give me, boss, to make me tell what I know? Huh? Huh? Huh, boss?

OUTLAW, *to white man:* It ain't me, it's that other nigger. He went that way.

TRIGGER, *scratching his head and shuffling:* Nawh, boss, it ain't me . . . but he ain't too far from here.

JACKIE: OH, LORD, BOOBIE, WHAT SAY NAYDEEN ON THE DRUNKEN BAGEL SIDE[2] . . .YESSIRREEEE . . . WOW! . . . But what did I do wrong to deserve dis, Lord?

SISTER: She's stone.[3]

---

1. Square: Into the latest thing, but too late to be respected.

2. Oh, Lord, boobie, what say naydeen on the drunken bagel side: Speaking in tongues is an ecstatic practice based on the biblical story of Pentecost, when the resurrected Messiah gave his followers the ability to speak across language barriers. Bullins also plays here with surrealist automatic writing and dadaist radical nonsense.

3. Stone: Stoned, intoxicated.

CORNY, *to white people:* Your mamma's stoned . . . you gray-assed, diseased-brained crackers.

JACKIE, *to white man:* I sho like to put mah shoes under your bed, mister. (*She belches.*) Burp! . . . 'Scuse me, sugar . . . I got a little gas.

CORNY: Yeah . . . I said it! . . . I said it! . . . What you gonna do about it?

JACKIE: Never mind him, folks. He ain't nothin' but a no-'count nigger.

POPPY, *to white people:* Don't make no never mind.

JACKIE: Don't pay no attention, ya hear?

OUTLAW, *to white girl, trying to feel her:* What's your name, baby?

TRIGGER, *to white girl's friend, be it man or woman:* We gonna try and help you, dig?

CORNY: Write your name on this piece of paper. If I'm lucky, I can save you yet.

JACKIE: DON'T PAY NO NEVER MIND TO DESE HERE NIGGERS!

CORNY: If I'm lucky, I can save you yet. But you gonna have to believe in me . . . you gonna have to believe in ole Corny.

JACKIE: PUT YO FAITH IN JESUS! . . . YES, LAWD . . . PUT YO FAITH IN HIM!

SISTER, *to white boy:* How much did you lose, sweetie? You gonna have to let me keep your money for you. (*She rubs his face and feels his crotch.*)

CORNY: Yeah . . . believe in Corny! Put your faith in Corny . . . 'cause I'll pull you through.

OUTLAW, *to white girl:* Hey, baby . . . why don't you let me help you step out of your drawers?

CORNY: Look'a hare . . . just write yo name and phone number down on this piece of paper.

JACKIE: Cryin' ain't gonna help ya.

POPPY: Nawh . . . you's in it now, mathafukker!

OUTLAW: Quiet now! Quiet. Now I don't want to hurt you . . . you too nice and all that for me to be hurtin' you . . . just relax, baby.

TRIGGER: Look in the halls . . . up the stairs.

SISTER: First time it happened to me was in a hall . . . in the stairwell really, honey.

CORNY: Yeah . . . sometimes when they take your money, they throw what's left in the halls.

SISTER: In Philly, we got alleys as well.

JACKIE: So why you tell me your problems? C'mon, you got a bottle or somethin'? Hey, boobie . . . you gonna buy this time? Huh? You buyin', baby?

SISTER: Stay outta the alleys in the summertime, sister. Stay outta the alleys . . . they usta tell me.

JACKIE: Cryin' ain't gonna help you, baby. It just ain't.

POPPY, *to white person:* Can I help you?

OUTLAW, *to white person:* You better stay away from him . . . you might lose somethin' you can't get back.

(*Lights change to alternating spots. Blinking lights and moving shadows, as if the room were moving. Sound of far-off sirens, muffled calls of police radios. Music changes in intensity, is more driving.*)

JACKIE: Yeah, that's right, baby. You let us take care of it.

POPPY: I'll let you know if anything goes down.

OUTLAW: Now, you better split, dig?

TRIGGER, *to white person:* You gonna call the police?

CORNY: No police!

SISTER: How much did you lose, baby?

CORNY: No police!

JACKIE: It matter to me. Yes, indeedy, Lawd. I care . . . Goddowmighty know I know . . . sho nuf!

POPPY: You goin'a remember the people who help you?

OUTLAW: Sheet . . . that wasn't shit.

TRIGGER: I only got eleven bucks, nigger. You got the rest!

CORNY, *to white woman:* Do I get somethin' if I find your pocketbook?

OUTLAW: You want me to find your drawers, bitch? . . . Damn . . . what more can I do for you?

CORNY: Let me tell you some deep shit.

JACKIE: You can't tell us nothin', nigger.

CORNY: You think you bad. Got a gun and all that shit. You out here shootin' the cops. Well, the cops ain't made dis shit.

SISTER: I just want to give somebody a good time. Just step right up and have your wallets ready.

CORNY: Cops ain't the ones to shoot . . . niggers . . . only if they git in your way. Dese hare people ain't the ones to get . . . they ain't got nothin' . . . just like you and me . . . they just work for them that made dis mess . . . The ones to shoot is who what made this mess.

SISTER: These people gonna mess you around, baby. Everybody's hustlin' dese hare days.

CORNY: SHOOT SOUTHERN CONGRESSMEN!

JACKIE, *to white people:* You better get out while you can, folks.

(*Audience is allowed to leave in twos and threes.*)

CORNY: SHOOT THE PRESIDENT . . . HE'S CUTTIN' OFF WELFARE AND PUTTIN' PEOPLE OUT OF WORK AND TRYIN' TO

DESTROY YOU WITH BIRTH CONTROL PILLS AND WORMS IN YO' WATER . . . AND SENDIN' YOUR BOY TO VIETNAM!

POPPY, *to whites:* Don't forget mah friends, sugar. And you better not forget me.

CORNY: SHOOT YOUR GOVERNMENT . . . THEY'S THE ONES MAKIN' WAR ON YOU!

OUTLAW, *to white girl:* Could I have somethin' to remember you by?

CORNY: GET YOUR GUN AND JOIN THE REVOLUTION, BROTHERS . . . AND CHANGE, CHANGE THIS SHIT! . . . AND CHANGE THIS SHIT!

TRIGGER: They was only lookin' fo' a good time . . .

SISTER: What else?

CORNY: GET YO GUN . . . IS DEATH ANY WORSE THAN THIS, BROTHERS? . . . CAN THEY KILL US ANY MORE THAN THEY HAVE ALREADY?

SISTER: For nex' to nothin' I can get me a fix, baby.⁴ So what if someone does have a little fun?

JACKIE, *to last white people:* Now be smart and get in the wind.

OUTLAW: Don't call me, baby . . . I'll call you.

(*Last white people go. Full of noise, sirens. Crowd sounds, gunfire, riot, revolution sounds. Energy music. Lights turning orange in flickering shadows.*)

CORNY: AIN'T DIS A BITCH, MAN. . . I'M STILL ALIVE!!!

---

4. Fix: Heroin, enough to get well intoxicated.

Among Bullins's more disturbing works, the shocking race-based violence of this work threatens to obscure for the reader its complexities and ironies. First, there is the matter of face paint. Inevitably, it recalls the rollicking brutality of blackface minstrelsy. However, it might also recall a tribal aesthetic, either authentic or improvised. Or it may be simply abstract. Whatever the case, Bullins uses the face— both of the performer and the audience member—to inject issues of race and racism into that most hallowed site of moral philosophy: the face-to-face meeting of mutual Others. The play was first published in The Theme Is Blackness: The Corner and Other Plays, *edited by Ed Bullins (New York: Morrow, 1973).*

A Short Play for a Small Theater

(1970)

Lights up on a "little" theater. The space should be painted black—stage, walls, ceiling, seats, etc. No posters, no slogans, no liberation flags, etc.

For the purpose of this piece, a three-sided seating arrangement should be best, with the last row in each section close enough for a tall actor to reach over and touch the occupant.

The place should not hold more than ninety people.

For this play, the audience must be at least two-thirds black. If more than a third of the audience that shows up is white, they should be turned away to maintain the proper ratio.

Psychic music, incense, colored lights.

At a small table, a tall BLACK MAN *methodically applies colored face paint. The stripes and circles and dots make brilliant contrast to his dark skin.*

Upon completion of this ritual, the BLACK MAN *carefully wipes his hands upon a towel, then places soft, black leather gloves upon his hands. He then picks up a large hand gun and deliberately goes to each white person in the audience and shoots him in the face.*

If there is need, he should unhurriedly reload as many times as necessary and complete his assignment.

Blackness.

Ritual drama dominated the stages and periodicals of Black theater in the late 1960s, attracting the likes of Amiri Baraka, Joseph Walker, Marvin X, Paul Carter Harrison, and Adrienne Kennedy. Generally such pieces blend a boldly drawn dramatic structure; a range of presentational techniques (chanting, choral movement, song); multimedia; and, especially, the deeply affecting invocation of the texts, movements, cadences, and intonations of Afrocentric spiritual traditions. This ritual was a collaborative creation with the other members of the New Lafayette Theatre Company and demonstrates Bullins's efforts to have done with, in his words, a "ragged" Western dramatic form that failed to "serve our purposes." Though it doesn't give its reader a sense of the music, design, and choreography that were an integral part of the ritual, it nevertheless provides a sense of the dramatic, poetic, and spiritual challenge that Bullins and his compatriots at the New Lafayette launched against white supremacy. The play was first produced by the New Lafayette Theatre, New York, in 1970 and first published, in pamphlet form, by New Lafayette Theatre Publications in 1970.

To raise the dead and foretell the future

(1970)

SPIRIT CLEANSING

Spirits of our people come
Take the evil from our hearts
Take the evil from our hearts
Spirits of our people come
Burn the evil from our souls
Burn the evil from our souls
Enter into our inner secret places
and cleanse us
Cleanse us
Oh cleanse us

Spirits of our people
Open our eyes to wisdom

Open our hearts to truth
Open our minds to knowledge
Open spirits to receive us

Spirits cut through the shell (OM)[1]
our ignorance
Cut through the skin of
not knowing ourselves
& release
& release
& release
us
to join our souls

THE WELCOMING

Welcome to the place of the dead
Welcome to the place where death is found
Come
Come enter
You are welcome

We are going
We are going to another place than here
We are going to the place of death

hold on to . . . hold on to each other . . . hold on to
us . . . we are going we are going . . . we are going . . .
don't fight against the journey give up and journey with us
come and release yourself up to the journey
THE JOURNEY OF LIFE IS THE LONGEST the journey to death
Is only part of the supreme journey come come come . . .
we are going we are going

PROCESSIONAL

Our bones	Our skin
bleached	black
white	strained

---

1. OM: A Sanskrit-derived word, described in one dictionary as a "word of solemn
affirmation and respectful assent," considered by Buddhists to be the sum total of all sound.

in the
suns of this waste land

Clack clack
our bones
clap

Our flesh
red
but the
tight press
of history
drains
blood
from our
eyes
drip drip the blood drops

over our
black shapes

Our
bones white
our
flesh tight
our skin night
black

we come
from
the wilderness

tramp tramp
stamp stamp
vamp vamp
clip clop
hip hop
oyee
oyee
oyee
oyee

THE WE SUTRA

We are the Black and deprived
We are the Black and Ones who have survived
We are the Survived
We have made the long journey
the middle crossing
We have lived
We have lived
and now we rise
We rise
We rise
to life
to life
We move toward
We move
move
Our bodies
Our spirits

Our souls
Our energies
Our loves
for one another
Black and One
we rise and
move
move Black people
rise Black nation
we move into life
we move into spirit
we push
we push
we push ahead
we go
for we have come from so
far
so far
far far far we have traveled
and far we have to go
into the future
that we only know is
awaiting us
we have come from
so far

Africa
Africa
our home
Africa
we come from
the belly and breast
of we who were
stolen
we who were wiped from
the slavers' decks
and dumped here
we who survived
we who conquered dead things
for a while
for a while

we who are slaves
we who will
rise
and make the nation
we who are homeless
and once lost
spirits in this wilderness
and live the life of the dead not knowing peace or a home
We are dead and must rise ourselves
must rise as One
as One
as one people
the Black nation
We are the African nation
of the West
We are the African nation
of the West
We are the African nation
in this dead place
we are the lost found colony[2] of Black men in this
Western tomb
we are the lost found colony of Black men in this
Western grave

We rise from the grave
We rise from the grave
We rise to the farthest extensions of our future possibilities
We rise to the farthest extensions of our future possibilities
We rise to the supreme Black presence in the universe
We rise to the supreme Black presence in the universe
We rise as One
We rise as One
We rise as one Black force
We rise as one Black mind
We rise as one Black intelligence
We rise as one Black spirit
We rise as one single Black soul
We rise as a smashing Black fist

---

2. "Lost found colony": An allusion to Elijah Muhammad's Nation of Islam, also known as the "Lost-Found Nation of Islam."

as a smashing Black energy
as a screaming strength of Black will
aaaaaaaaaaaaaaaaaiiiiiiiiiiiiiiiiiieeeeeeeeeeeeeeeeeeeee
aaaaaaaaaaaaaaaaaiiiiiiiiiiiiiiiiiieeeeeeeeeeeeeeeeeeeee
aaaaaaaaaaaaaaaaaiiiiiiiiiiiiiiiiiiieeeeeeeeeeeeeeeeeeeee
aaaaaaaaaaaaaaaaaiiiiiiiiiiiiiiiiiiiieeeeeeeeeeeeeeeeeeeee
rise Black bodies
from the dead
rise Black minds
from the dead of negro thought
rise Black souls
from the bed of white culture
rise Black spirits
from the crypt of christianity
rise dead Black men
rise dead Black men
rise dead Black men

rise dead Black men
rise and take the journey
rise and take the ultimate journey
rise and enter the future
rise and take on the journey
of life
rise and take on the journey
of life
of life
of life
We will inspire the dead
to rise
We will inspire the dead
to rise
We will inspire the lost
to sing
We will inspire the lost
to sing
We will inspire the blind
to see
We will inspire the blind
to see into the
Black future

We will inspire the crippled
to dance
We will inspire the crippled
to dance
We will inspire the spiritually
crippled to dance to the Black future
We will inspire the spiritually
crippled to dance into life
as One

as One
as One
we are one and know this
we are one and know this
we are one and know this
we know that our future is ahead of us
we know that our future is at the end of the journey
we know that our future lies in our nation
we know that our future lies in our nation
from slavery to nationhood
from slavery to nationhood
from the enslaved to rulers
of our own
from the enslaved to rulers
of our own
in our secret inner hearts
we promise to rise
in our secret inner hearts
we swear to be born again
in our hidden knowledge
we find the truth
in our occult wisdom
we bear witness to prophecy
we see into the future
we stare into the history
we move as one toward
what will be
we move as one
as one

as one
we know it is no use to wish about freedom

we know it is no use to wish about freedom
we know it is futile to pray
for freedom
we know that we can only gain freedom
through creating the future
by waking our dead selves
by waking our dead brothers and sisters
by raising our negro ghost mama
by breathing blackness into our dead negro daddy
by creating the nation we rise
by creating the nation we rise
we who were in the pit of death
we who were in the belly of the lost
we who have cried and were not
heard
we who fought against unseen enemies
we who were righteous and died for being
we who were saved but fell away into limbo
we who are Black and here
we who are Black and here
we who are Black and will live
rise from the dead and claim our own
with our brothers
raise up oh holy beaten down Black
people

raise up and live
as masters of the future
we who left the gold shore without any gold
we who were the black gold of Africa and the beast nations
we who were chained one to another
locked as unhuman things together for the long passage
who were dealt with as vermin as pigs as cattle never to gain their
freedom because they were black because they were unhuman
and black from Africa
   We who left the big place left the place of gold and traveled out
against our will against our knowledge of where we were traveling over
the big water to a cold place of death and savagery of white things and
work of work of work without pay or praise into the generations here
now of toil of hunger of beatings of lynchings of begging of whipping of
rape of defilement of slavery of slavery we who were killed and tortured

who were branded and beaten we who fell as a drunkard on the Boston
common in the blood shed for him we who walked from one end of the
land to the other preaching against slavery against inhumanity against the
most foul system devised in the universe
we know and come together
we know and collect ourselves together
together against he who would poison your babies
who would force on you the brine and staleness and emptiness
of living but not living of total emptiness of being a people
but not having a land a home a nation a country
who would kill your mind and image
together against this monster we collect together
this thing who would feed you the narcotic poison of
his way his dream his lie

we come together against his mind killing lies that
sap our will to fight and rise from the grave of ignorance
of our collective being
    we collect ourselves for the battle against the enemy we know the
enemy who has ravished our women bore off our children snatched away
our manhood cut off our choices damaged our wills befouled our bread
blinded us to our land and birthright destroyed our power crushed our
voices our voices our sounds our scream our screams our war song
eeeeeeeeeeeeeeeeeeeeuuuuuuuuuuuuuuuuuuuhhhhhhhhhhhh
eeeeeeeeeeeeeeeeeeeeuuuuuuuuuuuuuuuuuuuhhhhhhhhhhhh
eeeeeeeeeeeeeeeeeeeeuuuuuuuuuuuuuuuuuuuuhhhhhhhhhhhhhh
IT IS TIME FOR THE COMING TOGETHER
IT IS TIME FOR THE COMING TOGETHER
TOGETHER
together
together
we shall collect together in song and give the small
offering of your soul just a small donation of your soul

CURSES ON THE ENEMIES OF OUR PEOPLE

I.

Enemies of our people
You will live a life of soulessness
You still die in living death

You will wander in eternity without eyes
You will wander in eternity without souls
You will be in time without form
Your spirits will be as vacant as your
souls are

II.

Enemies of our people
go back to death
do not come near us
go back to death
do not come among us
do not come among us
do not attempt to enchant us
with your beastly white things
do not attempt to enchant us
with your blue devil eyes
do not come near us
for we are too strong
we are too strong
we are too strong
For we are too strong for you
we are too strong for evil
we are too strong to allow your evil
near us
near us
Oh, Yes, near us

III.

Enemies of our people
we are strong
dare not attack us
dare not attack us
we are mighty
we are mighty
retreat and escape to the white places
retreat and escape to white places
for we will fight
we will fight and destroy you
we will fight and destroy your name
and bury it in the farthest regions

of space where it will be
whispered or imagined
no more

CALL ON THE DEATH SPIRIT FOR THE PEOPLE[3]

AID US DEATH AND CAPTURE OUR ENEMIES
AID US SPIRIT OF DEATH
SEDUCE THE BEAST TO HIS GRAVE
AID US DEATH

CONQUER THE DEMONS THAT
DESTROY OUR PEOPLE
THAT DESTROY US

AID US DEATH
FOR WE HAVE GIVEN YOU
OUR PAST

---

3. Note in program: "Do not conjure this spirit unless you feel pure and righteous, for it is told that when this deity is summoned it never returns from where it comes from without a soul, and if the caller is not righteous in the way of his people, then his dearest loved one will be taken back to the land of the dead to return never again."

The Box Office

A Scenario for Short Film,
as Related by Robert Macbeth

(1969)

In the hot September noon, the old black man stumbles with shuffling steps to the box office of the moviehouse. Spittle glistens dewy in his grey, stubbled beard. He has a paper bag in one pocket of his great, large-pocketed coat. A bottle, surely red wine, pulls at the far side of him, making him lean or seem that a leg is shorter on that side as he finds his way to where he's going. Black children play, not seriously, for they play on a special sidewalk, today watching two men and two young women work at the front of the moviehouse. A tall, brown, bearded man has a camera strung from his neck. The children know that he will take their pictures, if they are careful not to move too far away, or seem that they would resent his intrusion into their mock play.

The old man rocks in front of the box office.

A young man is upon a ladder. He has a beard, too. He is browner than the taller man and his hairline prematurely recedes. He carefully arranges large black letters upon the marquee.

The children are now a crowd. They talk as bystanders, apart from the scene.

Traffic goes by both ways on the wide street. The girls hold the ladder and pose, as if they are being natural, waiting for the man with the camera to snap their pictures when they look candid enough.

Originally published in *Black Theatre* 3 (1969).

Into his pockets the old man puts his hands, his fingers fumbling over the hard quarter, the begged-for dime, and the other last coins of his day.

People pass, old but mostly young; all pass by, barely slowing, but some of the men smile at the girls.

The tall man has moved back. He aims his camera at the ladder, then the marquee, and the back of the head of the younger man on the ladder.

A jet flies over. Its jet stream is soon left behind, pointing toward California.

Two uniformed policemen walk by—a Black, a white. They try to look casual, but see everybody, everything.

The sun is hot. The girls have on Afro-outfits and the men wear dashikis. They all wear sunglasses except the tall man who snaps the old drunk's picture. His dark shades jut from a pocket.

When no one takes his change, the old man looks up and stares into the vacant box office.

The young man climbs down the ladder. With taunts, the children approach the old man.

The weary man backs away. He stares at the empty box office again, then at the children. Then he is lost, his eyes on the ground. His picture is taken once more.

A roll of paper is under the arm of the younger man. One of the girls mixes watery paste as the other girl encourages her.

The old man turns and walks back up the street. The game is over; the sun's too hot. The two men talk as one unrolls a large picture of a puffy-faced young man.

The ends of the giant photo are held by the girls, and the men measure and paste black paper over the box office front and sides.

In the distance, the old man has merged into the thickening crowd. Some people stop to watch the group as the girls stand and catch their breath and stretch their young bodies.

The girls look at each other and smile.

Unnoticed, the tall man takes their picture.

"No, plays."

"Oh?"

"Yeh, tell your mother to call up for tickets to the theater so she can bring you."

"There ain't no movie today."

"The movie's closed. They gonna open a theater here."

"I'm gonna come with my father."

"Do your stuff, baby. Gone, girl."[1]

---

1. Gone, girl: Go on, as in "Do your thing."

"Where you want this?"

"Let's put it right out front."

"Yeah, I was wonderin' what we were going to do with this funky-lookin' box office."

"Whew."

"I sho don't like this stoop labor, honey. I ain't no sharecropper."

In his New York Times *review of this collection of early short fiction, the respected Black Arts Movement critic and theorist Addison Gale Jr. described* The Hungered One: Early Writings *as "reading like an odyssey of one man's experiences of the world." Divided into two sections, the first dedicated to "the Absurd One," the second to "the Hungered One," it explores a variety of genres. The two stories included here exemplify Bullins's spare, off-kilter, palpably formed style; likewise, they illustrate the existential isolation and passionate commitment to absurd causes that made Bullins, in his own words, a "frustrated and evil cat" before turning to drama and theater. It was first published by William Morrow and Company, New York, in 1971.*

From The Hungered One: Early Writings

THE ENEMY

To Norm Moser[1]

I am an enemy of the State. I do not mine bridges nor take over the national airways or private airlines at gunpoint. I do not preach revolution against the Republic in its overt dialectical forms. I do not even care what political elements make up the State at the moment, unless these factions jeopardize my personal desires, caprices, or concerns. Nor do I care who holds the balance of power within the government. I simply do not care for the presence of the State; it is the supreme evil to my existence, for I am against all factions, groups, agencies, and alliances which make up the State, and I know, not so secretly, that they are against me. For I am their constant threat, for I am in essence against everything the State purports to be. I stand against the institutions of the whiteman.

One can easily find me. I am on the streets of the cities. I walk and wait on streets with names like Broadway, Market, Central, and Main. I stand

---

1. Norm Moser: The editor and publisher of Illuminations Press; Instructor at the University of California, Berkeley, Downtown Extension, San Francisco; poet and playwright.

huddled in stupor in the doorways of transient hotels, occasionally freeing myself from the shadows and pleading for pennies from pedestrians. I am found asleep in the early mornings, in the waiting rooms of bus stations, last night's newspapers my sheets, the black-booted policemen tapping upon the soles of my shoes with nightsticks, awakening me to arrest or sending me on my unknown way. I am seen peering for minutes at the billboards under the marquees of four-bit, all-night movie houses, my fingers in my last holeless pants pocket, rubbing my last two quarters together.[2] Sometimes, I look like a man, sometimes a boy, sometimes a woman, sometimes a girl. Sometimes, I am none of these.

And at times I can be discovered inside, inside green- and grey-painted jails, pacing off the days and years in my dirt-colored cell. I sleep fitfully and wake screaming with nose bleeding, trembling, in drunk-tanks, until hauled desperately out and straitjacketed by annoyed guards in tan and grey uniforms. I lie awake inside of one-dollar-a-night flophouses dreaming of old loves and clean smells. I sit up all night scratching bedbug bites and stalking juicy roaches in lonely rooms on skid row. I hear the bump bump de bump of the strip joints under my tenderloin window, the visions of the aging showgirls grinding and rolling up to my window like the din. From across the tracks, the whistle of no-longer-scheduled trains reach me, and the *din din* of the life buoy in the harbor and the bellow of ships shoving off to sea and the shrill work whistle at the plant that does not shriek for me. All this comes to where I sit, inside my deserted soul.

THE HUNGERED ONE

He suspected no unnaturalness in the flock. The pigeons were feeding upon salted nuts that some other passer-through had scattered down. He walked among the birds, tolerating the nearly tamed ones who grudgingly strutted from his path, hindering him on his tour.

His shoes crushed nuts, making his soles slip; he scraped them as he walked, startling the flock to leap briefly from the ground. It was during their resettling that he saw the strange one; it had remained aground, determined, pecking with its vicious beak about its companions' flitting feet.

It was larger than the other birds, weighing as much as a kept duck, and was a pale blue shade. No feathers clothed it; its tinted skin looked scaly, thirsty, and hot. More important to the young man were the bird's four legs, which sprouted from its muscular, squat body, grey and coarse.

---

2. Four-bit: fifty-cent.

Black talons shielded its toes, and splintered dewclaws dangled from the backs of each leg.

The man gaped at the blue creature. The flock remained aloof, leaving it isolated, spinning counterclockwise like a dog, in an island of goobers, awkward, unable to lower its short neck completely to the ground. Its hooked beak came within a hair of the nuts, causing its labors to be of little profit, but, fortunately, the bird discovered occasional kernels lying upon small protuberances that jutted from the pocked, uneven ground. Then it would snap them up with clicking sounds.

Most of the flock kept clear of this vortex of frenzy; for, the unfeathered one tore after its meal, a hundred pecks to their one, although receiving only a hundredth of their portion, and so furious were its random actions that, at times, in the fury of filling its craw, it snapped up careless birds which had gotten too near to it, and it devoured them wholly.

The young man stood until twilight, observing the movements of the creature. No other human passed that way; night was an awaited arrival. Many of the feeders took to wing, to soar in coveys, coated by the crimson rays of sun. One by one, the birds rose to race in scores about the treetops, until singly landing exhausted in their nests to chirp, fretful, into sleep.

As night sulked down the green paths, there was still enough light for the young man to fully distinguish the bird, which seemed to feed more rapinely upon its feast. The creature appeared to seize even fewer tidbits, almost none now, for its clicking beak erred when a morsel came within reach, and it would bite into the crumb instead of gobbling, resulting in the pieces falling from the bird's beak as it adjusted its hold.

The young man became impatient and approached the nut-gatherer. He knelt down and scooped up a handful of the nuts and offered them to the distressed one. The naked thing fixed the interloper in its stare. Its eyes were round and yellow, more suited for a snake's than a bird's. The yellow orbs scrutinized the bits lying in his extended hand, now easily within reach, and then the bird flicked out its stubby neck; its cruel beak snatched at nourishment. It tore off the outer joint of the index finger from the young man's hand.

"Yeee . . ." filled the small glade. The victim sprang away and flapped his hand at the end of his sleeve; then he placed the stump in his mouth and sucked at the spurting blood before taking out his handkerchief and wrapping his finger in a bandage.

The bird had resumed feeding. Light flared on; the swift pecker was revealed standing in shadows, whirling in its continuous circle.

After he had reduced the bleeding, the young man again returned to the creature. He crouched over it, waiting for it to skip away, but the thing stopped its spins and stared up at him. The gas lights glistened in the reflection of its eyes, and a luminous halo surrounded each iris when the man looked closer. He reached down and took the bird in his hands. With maimed finger extended, he gripped the thing's drumsticks, his thumbs and forefingers encircling the forelegs, his remaining fingers helping to brace the bird's hind legs and tail.

"I'm taking you home with me, strange fellow."

He began walking toward an exit; the creature roosted, tranquil, upon his knuckles; they reached the gate in minutes.

Night was dabbed with jasmine; it was a black interlude when crickets tuned their bows and mockingbirds pursued low melodies. The stars hung like trinkets against night's sordid veil.

A cab was waiting at the corner; its driver drew on his cigarette, shooing away the fireflies which sought to mate with the fiery glow.

"Can you take me home?" the young man said.

"That's my job, son."

"It's over on Dixon Street."

"Okay." The driver pushed open the door; the passenger light uncovered the weird cargo. "Christ! What's that?"

"I don't know . . . found it in the park."

"Well . . . just look at it . . . those eyes . . . Hey, what happened to your hand?"

"My friend bit part of my finger off."

"Hey . . . I don't know if I can take you. I don't carry dangerous animals."

"It's okay. He's quiet now, and I've got him back here with me. He'll never bother you."

"Well . . . if you say so. But I should take you to a doc first. Animal bites are dangerous."

"Later. I want to get my little friend home safely."

The cab started. The silent bird turned its broad head toward the park which fell away through the rear window. It then fastened its eyes upon its captor and beat its false wings three swift times.

"How did you find him, buddy?" the cabbie said.

"Just walked up on him. I couldn't believe my eyes at first. God, I'm really lucky."

"You sure are . . . that thing will bring you a nice hunk of dough."

"Oh, I ain't gonna sell him."

"No? Then what's the good of it . . . what do you want a thing like that for?"

"I don't know. I just want to get him home right now and feed him. He looked so starved out there in the park"

The bird didn't change its gaze but lunged for the young man's mouth; its beak fell short of the tongue but dug a furrow down the chin and along the man's breastbone.

"Oww . . . dammit, he's started up again."

"Well . . . let him go, fellah, he's not worth it."

The blue creature was now jerking its legs, causing its restrainer to rearrange his hands. The wound bled freshly. The driver braked to a halt and bolted from his door, reaching back and pulling open the rear.

"Quick, throw him the hell out. It ain't right to keep a thing like that."

"Please help me; I've got him."

"No, no, I won't touch that thing. Look how he's trying to reach down after your blood."

The creature was pecking, frustrated by its stump of a neck, at the young man's hands; it was unable to reach the wound but pecked the bandage several times, shredding it.

"Stop," the young man screamed, "I'll feed you when we get home. I'll feed you."

"It's a devil," the driver said.

The heavy bird wrestled one foreleg from the clutching hands and fastened its claws upon the young man's wrist. The claws gripped like tongs and dug in, immediately bringing blood, until the man's whole arm was slippery red. The creature swarmed over the man's fists, ripping spots from his palms which he now used to shove the bird from the door.

"It's horrible," the driver moaned. "Get rid of it."

"Help me," the young man cried.

With a lunge, the man forced the thing from him and out the cab's door. The terrible beast landed upon its back with its four legs kicking in the air. The driver swiped at it, hoping to stomp its head, but the featherless thing regained its legs and rushed its new assailant. The driver was routed, filling the blackness with quakes and babbles.

The berserk thing scurried back to the cab and leaped through the doorway; the young man was now upon his knees with hands protecting his eyes, showering tears down his shirt front to converge with the rivulets of red. As the bird extended its neck to examine its prey, the man shot out his mangled hands and encircled the thing's throat and beat its head against the car's footrest. The creature kicked out with its many claws, attempting to disembowel its foe, but before the man fainted, he split the monster's head, exposing its brains. Finally, the blue thing wriggled out of the clamped fists, displaying a limp wing and a partial view of its skull. It didn't bleed; its eyes, still yellow and alert, stared at its host. Then it made one more move toward the unconscious human, to tear a strip from his thigh and turn, to hobble from the vehicle. It scrambled along the street, in the direction of the sleeping flock, looking like some huge rodent or totally diseased hen with a large worm in its beak. It was an earth-bound thing which would never leap into the sky to circle treetops, camouflaging its strange complexion against the backdrop of the heavens.

When the ambulance arrives, the young man has been taken by shock.

"I wonder what happened to the poor bastard?" a bystander questions.

"Who knows, probably a teenaged gang," she is answered.

Inside the ambulance, the plasma is being rigged and sedatives rush the young man into nightmares. The attendant asks him, "What happened, mister? What happened?"

"He was so hungered," the hurt man says. "I only wanted to take him home . . . to feed him . . . to feed him well."

Among his most controversial works, The Reluctant Rapist *was one of the exhibits used against Bullins by Erika Munk in her 1976* Village Voice *pronouncement of his banishment from the A-list of Manhattan's alternative theater scene. His first and only novel, it was written over the course of the 1960s, originating both in Bullins's life experiences and, as he put it, in "the image of a Black outcast, outlaw of society moving through the social/cultural and political climate of the day." Inspired by the works of Jack Kerouac, Henry Miller, Eldridge Cleaver, and the great blues singers, it describes the life of Steve Benson, a regular in Bullins's work, as he passes from youth to manhood in a dog-eat-dog world of economic and sexual exploitation. The selection here includes the novel's epigraph poem and two passages from the middle of the text. These passages include the material quoted by Munk in her article but provide context for it. In particular, the reader should note the vampiric image that immediately precedes the account of his rape of Delores; the juxtaposition of the initial introduction of predatory Reverend Parsons to the story of the narrator's political development; and the tangle of sex, politics, and power among the young African-American students with whom he associates in Los Angeles. A portion of this section has not been included, introducing those students and their community, as indicated by bracketed asterisks [***]. The novel was first published by Harper and Row, New York, in 1973.*

From The Reluctant Rapist

(1973)

STREET JONES

I got a street jones
baby
run 'til the wheels
roll off

I got a steet fever
lil' mamma

turnin' corners
cause I'm
fly

My habit's runnin'
honey
so you know
not to have
an attitude

I'm a corner boy
sister
so you know
where I'm
comin' from

I'm a street nigger
girl
so any
tears for
me don't
lose too
soon

It's a cold shot
sweetmeat
but I've
known your
mamma
a long time
before I've
known
you.

The bus pulled in almost at dawn. It had been a long trip for the man, a trip extending across the country, meandering back through his past and criss-crossing a life style that he had dropped through disuse and age. Where he started out he knew had been once called home, a place he had begun from many times before, but this time it no longer seemed as home, a place of warmth and security, a memory to be forgotten, to be placed outside of his mind, for he knew he would never return there.

This place, the place the bus had come to, was different and he had just landed with fifty cents in his pocket.

A bus ride across country is a horrible experience, he thought. Slow. Torturous. Grinding. Cruel.

He had begun at New York, then headed south along the coast, visiting old friends and relatives and drifting from one place to another. And when he had gotten near the Deep South, he had turned back northward and continued as far as Boston, where he laid over and became acquainted with the city briefly. But growing tired of the aimlessness of not settling in the East, where so many of his starts had become dead ends, he decided upon the West and headed first back to New York and then outward across the middle country he had never seen before.

His money had been short. Hardly more than enough for his bus ticket and a week or two of living money after he landed, but he was strong and knew that he would survive under almost any conditions, for he had survived up to that moment under the duress of living in an urban desert and of being a loner and a traveler after whatever he sought.

The memory of the past, of his wasted years from where he came, from his previous trips searching for that something he sensed but hadn't found, had left him open to accept that there might not be anything to discover on this shore, like the bleakness, the lost and hurt of the shore he had just left, or the shores he had touched previously in Europe, in Africa, in the West Indies, and in South America. Shores that promised life—life in terms of adventure and hope, life in terms of promises fulfilled and dreams realized. Though he never found the wealth of the land. Not in its reserves of minerals or produce, not in its people and cities. Not in the bodies of its women.

And so he stepped now upon this new shore, a last shore for him for many years, and he headed toward light. The bus station was near empty this time of the day, and he kept on through, only stopping to check his one heavy suitcase and small travel bag, for bus stations are the same, he knew, so it was for him to scout the city and find newer things before he returned for his belongings.

He scouted along Main Street, perceiving the area he was in, an area not too unlike the Boweries across the land in most metropolitan districts. A sign flashed COME TO JESUS, and he knew where he would eat that morning. The men were lined up waiting to enter, and he took his place in the line, silently, with hardly anyone noticing him. A drifter is a drifter, black or white, and even if he wasn't soaked with cheap wine, anybody could see that he was down and out.

The door up ahead of the men cracked, and the line stumbled forward, then halted, and then the men waited again. A pint of sherry was passed. He waved it by. Someone went past him; he did not see who, for his eyes were upon his shoes, and he was handed a grimy card. He looked at it in light of the coming day. "If you want work come to . . ."

The card gave an address and directions. He pocketed it before the line moved again and he entered the cool dimness inside to drink his watery coffee and mouth glue-like oatmeal.

Later, he passed down the street, now filling with bodies bustling to work or to hustles which required the light of day. He belched. Coffee sometimes did that to him when it was cheaply made. A sign read DONORS WANTED. He turned inside.

I felt bad about taking it the first time. Though it was nice, so much better than I had imagined. The firmness of her box surprised me. She was so drunk she couldn't handle the strength of my attack, so I had my way with her like I wanted.

I had been away several years. To the service, to prison, to sea again, and back to the home town. She had been on wine, I knew, even before I left. Once, I visited her after we had gotten out of school together. I was back from some trip of a year or two and ran into her on the avenue. She invited me to her place and I went. She was looking much older, worn. In school, somewhere among my dreams, she had been my heart's desire, Delores. Black, fine, with pearly pearly white teeth and a shape that burst my heart almost since she wouldn't give me any but told me many times that she loved me.

And I went to her dirty apartment, drank some wine, and laughed with her. She loaned me some money; her welfare check was cashed before picking up the wine. We listened to her record player and whispered of the old times until her kid woke up and some of her drinking buddies came by, so I split.

Passing through home base a couple of years later, I met her again, in some bar. She was still drinking wine; two of her once pearly teeth were missing from the front lower half of her mouth.

"Some motherfucker beat my ass," she said, as I ordered her a double. "You still my play boyfriend, Chuckie?" she asked.

"Always," I said.

She kissed me on the cheek and struggled to the ladies' room. "I got two kids now," she said when she returned. "Cute little motherfuckers. . . . Both got different daddies and the welfare people wants me to turn them in."

"That's too bad," I said.

"I ain't even got no man now," she said and drained her glass.

Two more drinks and she was almost too drunk to walk. The bartender winked at me, and I paid the bill, led her out to my car, and drove to a dark side street I knew of, took off her black panties, and used her until dawn.

The only thing she said was when I first entered her: "You're a sonnabitch."

She stumbled up her front stoop later, me watching that she got into the house okay, and she didn't look back, only headed for home, while my eyes misted up, thinking of my beautiful, lovely, black black Delores of the flashy smile from the time that I didn't believe in from then on.

And the last time I met her I had returned to one of my many schools under the G.I. Bill and had been there for a year or so.[1] I ran into her on South Street.

She didn't recognize me at first. By the second drink, she had put my face together. So she smiled because she knew we were friends.

I took her to my apartment, gave her a beer, and undressed her. She resisted a little but, just before my second orgasm, she kissed my face and asked me why hadn't I stayed nearby her, before, when we were innocents and had been play man and woman?

She was snoring in my bedroom when I left her and got a fresh beer, and I was looking at a monster movie on the late late show by the time my roommate came in.

He had been to the library, he said, studying for an exam in sociology or something like that which I didn't understand.

"Who's in your bed?" he asked.

"Something I found," I said.

"Sharing?" he asked.

"If you take my sheets with yours tomorrow when you go to the laundromat."

He put his books in his room, went in the bathroom to get some rubbers, and came out and went to the icebox.

"Ready for a fresh one?" he asked.

"Yeah."

He handed me my beer on his way into my room and shut the door. Sweet sweet Delores cried out once: "Please, no!"

Then all behind the door was silent.

I popped the top on my brew and watched Dracula fly through a window.

---

1. G.I. Bill: The "Servicemen's Readjustment Act of 1944," better known as the "G.I. Bill of Rights," has provided billions of dollars to U.S. veterans for vocational training and higher education.

Forty-five minutes later he walked out with his blood money. Four brand-new, bank-fresh one-dollar bills were tucked safely inside his slim wallet.

He didn't care that prices out here were the lowest in the country for selling blood. A bit lower. But not so he would mind. He had sold his blood regularly in other cities. And used the money to pay his rent or buy meals or even to go to the movies.

He knew his blood was still good, good for something. And he smiled knowing that he was worth something.

It was mid-afternoon before he reached the other end of town and found the address that was on the card. He looked across the lawn to the house, tucked behind hedges with a long, low roof sloping over the porch. The front doorbell rang silently within the depths of the sprawling house. He waited, practicing a trick he had learned as a door-to-door salesman: standing well away from the door with his body half-turned toward the street, looking absent-mindedly sideways so his full face wouldn't be seen. The door cracked and a voice said, "What can I do for you?"

He turned and handed the old black woman the card.

"The reverend ain't in. Come back tonight."

"I thought you wanted me to work," he said.

"Come back late tonight," the woman said behind the screen door. "He'll be in then."

The man moved away.

"And come 'round the back next time, ya here?"

The door slammed.

The first woman I really raped was white. I mean really raped. Of course, I had tried with most of my play girls during my growing up time, but they had too much tomboy in them or their brothers would exact awful punishment from me, so these token attempts didn't pan out until I was older and wilier. But the summer night I first really scored was like many other summer nights back then on the corner. We were boozing port wine this time. Some of my partners: Bam'alam, Coozie, Foots, and Nate. Most of the Snakes—that's who we were, the Sepia Serpents, Snakes for short—were off somewhere and we were doing what we did every summer night. Goin' down with what change we had or could hustle and gittin' down with a jug. Somewhere along the line, after a couple of jugs had been wasted, Lump Lump from down on Thompson came up on the corner. Now Lump Lump is okay, ya know, but bein' that he from down the way and not from up the way, we cool on his case.

"Lump Lump . . . you crazy mahthafucker . . . ," Coozie said.

"What's happenin', nigger?"

Coozie's the actor among us. A sucker never knows where he's comin' from until ole Cooz moves on him.

Lump Lump, being forever a supercooly himself, said, "Dig, niggers, if you want to git you some white pussy, just follow me."

"No shit!" Bam said.

"Really," my man Lump replied.

And, juiced as we was, we didn't ask too many more questions but followed ole Lump, good though jive nigger that he was.

Just a block away, down in an abandoned basement, just like Lump had said, was this old drunken white woman. It was dark down there, since there wasn't nothin' but candles, but she was white and drunk and had her dress above her hips and no drawers showin', seein' that Cisco from over on Camac was humpin' for all his skinny black ass was worth. There were other guys down there, but I didn't notice them too tough, just waited my turn at the meat and then worked out.

"Uuuhhhggg . . ." I moaned. And somebody was tapping me on the shoulder saying it was their chance. While I had her, she kept muttering and saying, "God, won't it ever stop." And I rolled off and got myself together and split.

Half an hour later, I was sittin' up in the Heat Wave Cafe when Jelly-man, the number man, passed through and stopped.[2]

"I heard about you dumb young niggers," he said to me.

"Who, me?" I said.

"Stop tryin' to be so goddamn smart, little nigger! Look at the mud on your shoes and the shit on the front of your pants. If I was a cop, I could get you thirty to life, little wise pussy-hungry nigger."

"Thanks, Jellyman . . . . If there's anything I can . . ."

"Shut up! . . . and get your ass out of here," he said.

It was near midnight when he went through the gate and followed the cement path to the back of the rambling house. A dim light showed the back screen door. The man was careful not to stray off the path and step onto the well-clipped grass, and he placed his feet gently so as not to awaken any sleeping dogs, for he thought that such a wealthy-looking establishment must be provided with some kind of security measures. Behind the house, the land opened out into a large yard; the moon did not outline its full depth or dimensions, but the man knew by various shapes

2. Number man: The "numbers" was a lottery-style game, illegal though popular. The "runner" took customer picks, ran those picks back to headquarters for processing, and delivered to winners. Replaced by state-run lotteries starting in the late 1960s.

and shadows that there were garage and shed-like buildings on the property as well as the house he now stood at the back door of. A light shone secretly from within one of the low structures off the yard.

He stepped up to the back door and knocked softly. "A sucker's knock," he muttered to himself. But there was sound somewhere inside the house, then a light went on and a large shape was at the door.

"Yes," a male voice said.

"I got a card . . ." the man began.

"Yes, you're the one. Wait . . . I'll be right back with you."

The figure disappeared for a moment, and it came back holding a flashlight.

"Follow me," it said.

Farther back in yard, behind foliage, was the source of the light, a small barn-like building where inside burned a kerosene lamp showing several beds with occupants reading or playing checkers.

"Good evening, Reverend," a white-haired man said.

"Evening, Ted," the man's guide said. "Now I told you about that light burning all night. You want to fall asleep and catch the place on fire and burn you all up. What would the state say about that, now? Come now, turn it out and be good fellas and go to sleep now."

Before he left, he asked the white-haired man, "How's Jeff doin'?"

"Fine, Reverend. He's 'sleep."

"And Annie?"

"Just fine, Reverend."

The light went off and the pudgy man was gone and the new man lay down on the unmade couch, his nostrils stinging from the old urine smell, the disinfectant, and the scent of age and death as he closed his eyes to fall asleep.

"Hey, mister," he heard from somewhere in the room. "Hey, you," a female voice said. "You got any smokes?"

"Nawh," the stranger said. "They cost more than I could afford."

Then all was black and silent and he did not know anything more until the sun rose.

I guess the first Black Nationalist I knew was my mother. Not that she was a real doctrinaire nationalist like a Garveyite or a follower of Elijah Muhammad, but she believed in art and culture in a general sort of colored way and believed that colored folks, as she would say, could be artistic too.[3]

---

3. Garveyite: Marcus Mosiah Garvey Jr. (1887–1940), one of the most influential Black Nationalists, founder of the Universal Negro Improvement Association and the Black Star Line, a fleet of ships intended for African repatriation. Elijah Muhammad (1897–1975): Founder of the Nation of Islam, a key Black Nationalist organization.

She must have read W.E.B. DuBois, though I've never asked her.[4] But she was a great reader and once a chorus girl and childhood friend to Marian Anderson, but in later years disliked Marian for being so dicty and hiring white servants and such.[5] But my mother took me to the church and community center cultural events and programs, and there I saw black people singing and playing instruments and reading poetry that put me to sleep. And she would somehow put things in a colored-folks context no matter if they were subjects like the Second World War, Joe Louis, school integration, Jackie Robinson, or FDR.[6] But more important, I guess, she stressed that I become an accomplished reader, which I am still working at in my lackadaisical style.

He didn't sleep soundly. All night, he sensed movement inside the small building and several times mutters nearly woke him from his light sleep, but his breathing relaxed and his brain did not call him through the threshold of slumber, but his senses found the sounds seeming to come from one of the beds against the far wall.

At dawn, someone entered the building and a rooster crowed somewhere out in the dimness. He opened his eyes and saw a cobwebbed ceiling and the dim illumination showed that no one moved inside the room but him. He pulled on his shoes and wiped sleep from his eyes. Soon, at the back door of the house, he knocked and the old woman appeared.

"Come in," she said. "The reverend is out this morning, but he left your instructions."

She showed him a small toilet off the back porch where he washed and relieved himself. Upon entering the kitchen, he was shown a bowl of oatmeal and poured a cup of coffee. It was the best coffee that he had drunk in months, he thought. After breakfast, he was given his duties. To mop the downstairs of the large house, which he found to be a home for old black people, then to clean the yard and clip the hedge or mow the lawn or do whatever the taciturn old woman demanded.

By early afternoon, he was through with his duties.

---

4. W.E.B. DuBois (1868–1963): Essayist, novelist, journalist, playwright, founder of the Niagara Movement, critic, scholar, and activist.

5. Marian Anderson (1897–1993): African-American concert singer whose debut at the Metropolitan Opera in 1955 marked the first time an African American had sung on that stage. Dicty (also "dichty"): Snobbish.

6. Joe Louis (1914–81): The "Brown Bomber" is considered by many to be the best heavyweight in boxing history. Jackie Robinson (1919–72): African-American baseball player who played in the Major League in 1947, breaking a forty-year-old color line. FDR: Franklin Delano Roosevelt (1882–1945), U.S. president from 1933 to 1945 and the driving force behind the New Deal, which resulted in, among other things, the Social Security Act of 1935.

"Is there anything else?" he asked the woman.

"Nawh, not till the reverend comes and tells you somethin'. You ain't supposed to get no lunch but dinner will be ready this evenin'."

He went downtown and got his bags. It wasn't hard to figure out the bus routes. There were so few of them on this end of town that he walked to the larger uptown-downtown streets and waited, then made connections or walked across.

When he returned with his bags, the old woman wasn't in sight. He placed his bags inside the back porch, to the side of the door, and not knowing whether to go back to the little house where he had slept, but knowing it wasn't a wholesome place in smell and appearance, he walked about the neighborhood.

This part of the city was well taken care of by its almost completely black residents. The lawns were clipped uniformly. And sprinklers spewed water in rainbow swirls about the feet of the palms. Not many people were seen, only the stark emptiness of their curtained windows, except for an occasional child or teenager who rode a lonely bike or bounced a ball. The man later learned that the residents of this black island of affluence came in from their jobs at evening and entered their homes and remained in front of their televisions until past midnight and then went to bed, to appear just past dawn driving away to their employment, unless they had already left sometime in the night to other jobs. On the weekends, these workers were seen in comparatively large numbers washing their late-model cars or burning meat over outdoor grills. They drank whiskey and some beer, name brands certainly, and strove to enjoy their good lives desperately, so desperately that the soft hysteria lurking behind their eyes could only be shielded by their sunglasses.

The sun burned down, uncompromising, and the wide streets threw back shimmers of heat in their emptiness. The man walked, coming finally out to larger boulevards and avenues where the machines of commerce belched and rolled, intimidating the varied smaller autos to keep out of their way. A sign across a road showed TACOS. He had never had one. The words looked unfamiliar, but he recalled the word from the back of his mind, though he had never tasted or experienced this thing, a taco.

There was a brown-skinned Mexican-looking girl working alone in the small stand. "Whatta ya have?" she asked.

"A take-co, please."

"You want a *taco?*"

"Yeah, a taco."

She turned, did some swift exercises, and turned back soon with what he ordered. Shoving it on the counter, she asked, "Where you from?"

"The East."

"Oh . . . Like it here?"

"Don't know yet," he said.

"Want anything to drink?"

"Yeah, give me a Coke."

He ate his taco, drank his Coke, and watched the traffic go by. The girl had the radio turned to a rock-'n'-roll station and she occasionally popped her fingers and bobbed her head.

"How did you know I wasn't from around here?" he asked her.

She smiled and shrugged her shoulders. After a while he left.

Before he had disappeared down the street, the girl said to the beat of the blues, "Because you're so dumb, brother."

I knew about politics from an early age. I didn't know what politics was, but I knew about politics. Like when my cousins and I picked up on the slogan "Fooey on Dewey" and were laughed at and joked with by our family members who were older than us.[7] They agreed with our childish jingle about sentiments they did not express. Roosevelt was my mother's and aunt's savior. And I knew about the campaign workers who came through whatever neighborhood we lived in then, workers from all the parties, and how, when the communists came, my mother wouldn't open the door because she did piecework in a government plant, but my stepfather, who read a lot and had been in the war, would go out and talk with the sincere-looking men and women in extended conversational raps to the distress of our neighbors, newly from the South, though my mother took secret pride in my stepfather's daring. And I saw how the local ward politicians got out the vote on election days, which were school holidays as well, and the liquor stores were closed. Later, when I was older and in the white-lightning whiskey business, election days became some of my most profitable business days. But when I was a child, I saw the committeemen come with one-, two-, and five-dollar bills in their tight fists to get out the vote. And for some of my neighbors, only a swig of a bottle of "good stuff" was enough to get them to walk up the block to someone's house, converted for this great occasion into a democratic institution, a polling place, and pull whatever lever they had been guided to. But neither my mother nor my stepfather bothered to vote. They were of the new breed, I guess. So they never voted for anything I know of, anyway, but worked hard each day for the things they wanted and left voting to the innocents and idealists. Peo-

---

7. Fooey on Dewey: Republican Thomas E. Dewey ran against Harry S. Truman for the U.S. presidency in 1948, losing narrowly.

ple would ask them why they didn't do more about the conditions of the nation and get out there and pull that lever, but they only looked away, or my stepfather would go into strange stories of what he saw when he went off to fight for his country. They never voted; *never* did, not in that period of their lives, at least. Not for the party of Lincoln.[8] Or for FDR, who they said had led the country out of depression over the bodies of millions through creation of the war.[9] They read too much, you see. And would not even cast their lots with the silly socialists or the crazy communists who they said promised to save the world for we workers, black that we were, yet not understanding the world we blacks lived in. But I never could understand how these beliefs, this huge faith, politics, that pressed men into its service on a do-or-die basis, had anything to do with me. For I learned early that I was black. And being black, I was outside of systems made by white men for the place and people I lived among, wherever that was. Things are supposed to be changing, I hear. But I would be very surprised if the Second Coming overtook me in this life and country.[10] At least I'll never be caught attempting to vote it in on a machine ticket.[11]

He knew she had seen him watching her. Or he wished she had. By the extra swing she put in her hips. By her back-of-the-hand nose-wipe and frowning at the boogie that tickled the back of her nose. By the extra popping of her gum as she crossed the street and came up on the curb behind him.

He liked dark girls, but she was light, almost albino, and was a superbad street mama.

"Hey, girl, how's your baby?" she said.

He saw her join a dark girl in pink leotards covered by bright hot pants. They walked almost abreast of him, smiling, rolling their big young behinds, and popping their gum.

"Butchie's fine, honey," the girl said. "How's yours?"

"He's so bad. My mother took him out to the park. I'm sure glad she did. Mom and me smoked some boss reefer, girl.[12] And I got so high I couldn't deal with the little bastard. Then Mom took the little mahthafukker to the park, girl."

---

8. Party of Lincoln: The Republican Party, which Abraham Lincoln helped grow into a strong national organization.

9. The war: World War II (1939–45).

10. Second Coming: In Christian theology, the reappearance of the Messiah and the advent of the Last Judgment.

11. Machine ticket: A slate of candidates promoted by a group (the "machine") that controls the activities of a political party.

12. Boss reefer: Good marijuana.

The girls went into a candy store on their block and the man kept walking. He knew he would see her the next time he walked on that side of the street.

Bennie and I had this real estate company. Seems funny now, but we really had these broken-down buildings. We met in the post office. Both of us were working killing hours, sometimes twelve, sixteen hours a night, and going to school too under the G.I. Bill, and we both had hustles on the side. Bennie cut a tonk game over on the west side of town and I sold some white lightning—you know, cooked corn whiskey—at a low-lights joint up around my neighborhood.[13] I had a big family by then, so I had to keep my behind in gear, and Bennie was just greedy.

We began talking money, future, business, etc., while tossing mail. And, after a few months, we had our company, Ben & Benson, Inc. I was going to business school so could keep some light books, and Bennie was from one of those big southern colored families and grew up around undertaker/grocery/dentist/schoolteacher/doctor/business and allied activities, so could wheel and deal with a country flourish. We saved our money, put in more killing hours at our various jobs and schemes, and, in several more months, we had our first deposit.

After looking around a bit, we found a run-down tenement that we could pay down on. We found a flashy/slick Jewish real estate family—a father, wife, and platinum daughter—who would have sold us a cemetery if we had enough to make the first payment. And the properties we invested in weren't too far from graveyard city, at that. The bank didn't like our being so young, with me just turning twenty-one but able then to sign contracts, but money talks, and, with our shyster real estate agents, we walked with the deeds.

In eighteen months, we had two more buildings and were foolishly pushing for more. I guess we thought that quantity could make up for absence of any redeeming values. It's hard to think of it now for me; it's so painful. We had to borrow to make the notes and the fuel bills were always behind. The properties were in such bad shape. Talk about slumlords—we made ourselves actually slum slaves to those death traps, chasing the dynamic dollar, caricaturing the American dream.

I got my cousin Elvin to do some painting, plumbing, and plastering, but we could hardly even afford his minimal expenses. For every spare penny had to go into the buildings.

My family suffered for my ambition. My wife was always going home

---

13. Tonk game: A card game that combines elements of gin rummy and blackjack.

to her mother. As soon as I went and got her and brought her back to our house, I would have to be off to work or school or to see about the business, and by then most of my income was going to the business, not my home. And the only thing my ole lady could see and understand of my hyperactivity was that we were living worse and not hiding our personal misery.

Whenever I would go to my mother-in-law's place to collect my wife and children, my wife's mother would say, "Are you crazy, man? You're too far into this thing. Look at your family. They can't take this kind of stuff. Get out. It's not paying. Get out!"

But how could I explain to her that I had sunk all my savings into those ghetto holes, all the money I had saved in the service and going to sea, from days on end and sleepless nights of poker, from smuggling contraband in the ports my ships touched in Europe, Africa, the West Indies, and South America? How could I describe to her all the hours of mind-deadening labor I had done on all jobs I had worked the past three years to achieve the success of being a man of property?

How could I tell *anyone* that I had nearly killed to get some of the money and these blemishes on my soul could only be moved through work and study and, finally, when I could afford to, sometime in the future, through service to the people. But even then, there was more I could not admit to myself, as my dreams dissolved like wet plaster, than to anyone else, and who could understand a word I spoke or any single feeling that I had?

When my wife would appear from the interior of the protective confines of my in-laws' household, we would quarrel briefly, then I would help her pack for the last time, of course, to return to our home.

But then I almost immediately had to leave her after our welcome-home lovemaking and storm out to conquer the world.

My partner Bennie was a vulgar, ruthless, and stingy small-town talent, and gradually I grew not to trust or like him. And he had the traditional southern dislike for northern street niggers. Not that either of us had much to worry about in terms of each other ripping the other off. The real estate agents and the bank had done such a good job there wasn't anything in the pot left to cop; we could only turn out our pockets and keep shelling out to forestall foreclosure. A real estate agency handled rent collections except for an exception or two which I'll get to in a minute.

And I began to change visibly. I didn't go to my old haunts. I dressed conservatively, at least to my way of thinking then. Sports jackets. Slacks. Lavender shirts with orchid-colored ties. Stingy-brimmed Dobbs "sky pieces."[14] Something called the Bold Look was in then. I even took to

---

14. Stingy-brimmed Dobbs "sky pieces": Fedora-style hats with their narrow brims.

carrying a briefcase, for I was studying for my real estate salesman's license.

And I tried to change my speech. Began using the big words that I heard in school and encountered in reading, and, more often than not, I mispronounced them. Even when I would stop into a bar on the avenue and meet some of the old dudes from down the way, I would throw my new vocabulary on them. Hardly anyone said anything to me, though eyebrows were raised; mostly, I guess, they remembered that just a couple of years before that I would knock most monkeys out for batting their eyes at me, but my new credit-bought clothes didn't hide my heart. Oh, I would come on like, "Good afternoon, gentlemen. Would you care to partake of spirits and endeavor to render a discourse concerning the exceptional circumstances of our existential beings existing *a priori* to this philosophical incident?" Wow, talk about going corny. I could hardly stand myself most of the time. But I was out to make it in the big world, and I knew there was some kind of game to be learned and played. And I had to learn it. So I was getting my education, all right, though my style was turning off my old crowd and had me moving into some life patterns that developed out of my oversized head, rather than those I found in my surroundings and experience.

I even acquired a subscription to the *Wall Street Journal* and read it on the subway to work at the post office. When Bennie and I could get places next to each other to throw mail, we would discuss stock prices, although neither of us owned any shares, and our next projected real estate acquisitions, even while part of our pay and hustling money was drained off to meet our mortgages and fuel expenses.

I would have voted Republican, if I'd had the chance or taken the time to register. They were the party of the rich, right? I shudder now at my mental condition then, but for almost three years I was cut off on a success-American-style trip, and that's more than enough to damage any black's brain.

But things weren't too successful for me at my household.

He came in just past dusk. Dimly, a light shone from the house, and, following the path to the back, he knocked at the door and saw a shadow. The middle-aged pudgy brown man that he met the night before came to the door. He switched a light on.

"Hello there, young fellow," the man said.

"Yeah . . . I was here . . ."

"Yes, you're the young man who is helping us out. Come in," he said, holding open the door. "Have you had dinner?"

"Nawh, sir."

"Well, just come in then. The cook must have left something."

The older man fixed him cold cuts and chatted. The stranger hungrily scarfed his food while the older man told him that his name was Parsons, Reverend Parsons, and that he owned the house and kept it to help the sick and aged. "The state and social security pays the bills, of course." Somewhere in the house a television broadcast the news.

"Have you any family, son?" Reverend Parsons asked.

"Some, but they all back east."

"Then why are you all the way out here, young fellow?"

"I heard that schools are less expensive out here."

The reverend agreed with that, then he poured the young man some lemonade and patted his shoulder. "Well, I'm glad that you like it here, son. You do like it here, don't you?"

"Oh, yes. Yes, I do."

"I sent out the word some time ago among the local missionaries to send me any young colored men who came through their houses. Of course, they must appear to be only a victim of hard times or lost and strayed from the path of salvation. No drug addicts. No imbibers of the devil's grape. No, my son, only poor, homeless colored boys. Oh, how I do like young boys." The reverend smacked his lips at this last statement and tied an apron about himself. The young man ate silently, watching Reverend Parsons busying himself about the kitchen. After the food was gone, the reverend took the plate and set it in the sink.

"Your bags are in the broom closet," the reverend said. "Get them and I can take you over to the little house and introduce you."

He got his bags and followed the soft-bodied, heavy-set man out of the back door. They walked to the place where the man had slept the night before, and the older entered without knocking. In the light of more kerosene lamps, the younger man saw that there were four people in the room, sitting in beds: the dark, white-haired man named Ted that he had seen the night before, a nearly bald, equally dark older man, and a skinny old man in long johns. The other person in the room was a plain-looking, work-worn black woman of undeterminable age.

Everyone greeted the reverend with a degree of deference, though the woman only looked absent-mindedly at him, as if she had forgotten his name and face.

"This young fellow will be staying with us for a while," said Reverend Parsons. "Please make him comfortable and put him at ease, won't you?" Then he cautioned them not to burn themselves to death and not to drink too much of their cheap wine and not to ruin their eyes playing that devil's game, cards.

"If our eyes ain't bad yet, Reverend, we goin'a see till you bury us," the old man named Jeff said.

They laughed at that.

"Annie," the reverend said to the woman. "Why don't you come with me? I got something for you to do. Good night, everybody. God bless you."

And he was gone, the woman following him through the door.

The skinny old man in long johns began wheezing, then spoke. "Ole rev . . . ole rev gonna keep gettin' his self a little bit of Annie till there ain't none left for you, Ted."

"Huhn . . . Ted couldn't get a hard-on if his ass depended on it," Jeff said. "All he could do is suck on ole Annie like a hound dawg suck on a bone . . . if'in Annie would heist up her leg fo him wit' her ignorant self."

In mock anger, Ted said, "At least I ken git outta bed an' go ta tha bathroom."

"Sheet. . . then why you bed so funky?" answered the old man in the soiled long johns.

"Sheet . . . you niggers better stop talkin' about Annie like ya do," said Jeff. "And you better stop treatin' her like ah dawg or she won't go to the store fo you on check day 'n' git ya wine."

"Sheet . . . ole pappy Clark there would walk to the store for wine on his hands if he had ta," Ted said.

The three men kidded like that for a while, slapping their cards down on the table pulled between their beds, puffing at their pipes and Bull Durham, not bothering to notice the new man, until they began snuffing out their oil lamps one by one.

"Night . . . sleep tight," one of them said to the younger man. "Don't let the bedbugs bite."

The man slept better that night, but he could distinguish the snores and breathing of the three old men he shared his quarters with, and he wondered why he hadn't noticed their pronounced sounds the night before. Later, toward dawn, his sleeping mind told him that he heard someone enter the little house and pass his sleeping place, muttering in his mother's voice, "Lord, forgive me . . . . Lord, forgive me . . . . Lord God, have mercy and forgive me."

I have wondered why some women I have raped have forever since believed that I disliked them. I never could understand this misunderstanding on their parts. How could they believe that? On the contrary, rarely is the case that I dislike a source of pleasure. And I would not knowingly take a woman's body that I did not desire, unless I was drunk, or terribly horny, or depressed, or it was very dark, or someone offered her to me and out of comradeship I couldn't refuse the generosity . . . or some other good reason along these lines. But, for the most part, I find the objects of my assaults very desirable. And some of my conquests understand this and treat my predatory acts as the compliments they are, once having recovered their composure after having been taken advantage of against their will, if it really was against their will. And some women I have raped have remained loyal lovemates to me for years, yes, years. For several, for more than half a dozen years. You see, after the initial taking was done, they came to me, some after a few moments, some after several days, even years, and we started something long-lasting and permanent in a transitory sort of way; we became passionate and long-ranging, long-distance lovers. Now, I'm a traveling man. I pass through a lot of places and I can usually be found some part of the year in one or two special places, so when I pass through one of my women's cities or they swing through mine, the word is passed and somehow we make it together to refresh and complete our lasting union. For they know that it is *they* I desire above all else, and most real women at least in some part of their lives wish to be wanted by a man more than anything else. And I humbly become a servant to this need. So our lovemaking lasts over decades, it crosses state and national boundaries, it surpasses the vows made to husbands and friends and families. For they know that at least I'll take them and appreciate them and do my best for their total satisfaction.

It seems strange to me that I become lumped with some type of freak or sex deviant who gets a charge out of hurting women because I take them sometimes against their will. But I use only the necessary degree of force to accomplish the act, none at all when none is needed. For when you embark upon an act as total as rape, there is seldom a chance nor is it wise to turn back. I have engaged in fierce knuckle-bruising, biting, hair-tearing, and throat-throttling battles with women to take possession of them and midway through my love-making they have become some of my most responsive and ardent bed partners. These are the types of women who will follow a man from state to state, from country to country, and live with him under any circumstances that he demands. For they belong to their ravishers wholly, for they have been stripped of everything but their pride, and as long as the man will love them and desire to touch their minds, bodies, and souls, they retain all that a man can allow one of his women, her pride. She is desired above all else, even life, and the proof of his faith in her is that he leaves his life in her keeping after he walks out the door. For to commit rape is to commit oneself to one's own death, if the woman so wills it, and if one allows her to live with this power to speak of it to the authorities, the official state protectors of female chastity and honor. So you live for that moment of life with her and gamble with death for her, and she understands the stakes and knows that she is your woman like no others can be, for out of her has been born another existence, more fragile than an infant's, that she alone can guarantee—*yours*. Truly, I am reluctant to rape any woman I could not love, if I willed myself to, and in whose hands I could not sense my life was safe, within limits, of course, though frankly, I would rape a snake if the opportunity presented its slinky self. After all, it's all relative to where one is, who one is with, and what condition one is in.

So, she is taken, for it is not for her to decide how her man is to use her. She is cherished as a separate and distinct part of a union, a union that binds man's universe together—man and woman. And there is no sexual pretense for her after her underclothes have been ripped away, her private parts exposed, and the man enters her forcefully as if he were storming a divine citadel to take possession of a holy treasure that he alone knows the real value of.

After I take a woman's body and she has lost all fear that she'll be abused by me, then we can look into each other's eyes and discover everything, ourselves. For we are together then. Physically, in the *real* world, we are together: the lowest common denominator of our collective existence—man and woman—and this is all we ever truly wanted to be, if we will allow ourselves to release ourselves to this realization. For then body awareness falls away and we have our minds, our spirits, our sense of ourselves together as a unit, even while the individual parts may break and go separate ways until some accident of time in the future fuses us again. Our body falls away and we enter the psyche, for I do not desire dumb women, really dumb women, except as a release, and cannot tolerate a woman I cannot communicate with outside the physical plane, because some of my most profound learning has been in the company of women who are the moon to the sun of my manhood.

Reverend Parsons came for him after lunch. The younger man was doing yard work, trying to complete his duties satisfactorily and get some time to himself.

"Son . . . how're doin?" The reverend asked him.

"Fine, sir," he answered, raking some palm fronds into a large burlap bag.

"Have you seen the entire grounds yet, young man?"

Still working, the yard worker shook his head, swept some foliage into the bag, and said, "No, sir."

"Then come with me," the middle-aged man said. "I have something to show you."

The young man followed his employer away from the big house, past his small building, hidden by a clump of bushes, out of which came sounds of the old and invalid state-supported people he shared the premises with, and then behind a windbreak of trees to the very rear of the large lot. They followed a path that led through the trees to a sunny clearing. Here stood a small, single-story cottage, well painted and kept, with a goldfish pool in front of it and a small wooden bridge that had to be crossed before one could enter the little house. A birdbath stood to one side, in the space of land fronting the house and bridge, and on the other side of the path a sundial told the time of day to anyone who could calculate by the ancient ornament.

"After you, young man," the reverend said, indicating the bridge.

The young man crossed it, stepping off upon the porch, and turned and waited for his chubby companion.

"Here we are," said the reverend, after he had crossed over the bridge and turned his key in the lock of the cottage's front door.

When they entered, the older man touched a light switch and low-keyed, tinted lights revealed the curtained room. It was done in velvety maroon and black—walls, ceiling, carpets, furniture, and drapes.

"This is my study," the reverend said, smiling and waiting until the younger man's eyes drank in all of the splendor.

"You live well," the young man said.

"When I can," replied Reverend Parsons.

He moved to a black shellacked cabinet with fittings of white metal. From it he took a bottle and two glasses.

"I don't normally take spirits, but this is a special occasion."

"It is?" said the young man.

"Yes," Reverend Parsons said. "We're celebrating your joining our household."

"Well, Reverend." The young man sighed. "I want to talk to you about that . . . I'm only goin'a be here until I can get myself together. I didn't have any money when I got off the bus, so I was ready to take almost anything to keep eating and get a place to stay. I . . ."

"I understand. I understand, young man."

"See . . . I came out here . . ."

"Why don't we have our little drink first before you tell me *everything*," the reverend said, smiling.

He handed the younger man one of the glasses, now filled with an amber liquid.

"No, thanks, sir. I have work to do. The cook told me that I was to finish the yard this afternoon."

"You mean Mrs. Parsons?"

"Oh, I'm sorry, Reverend Parsons," the young man stammered. "I didn't know she was your wife."

"Yes . . . yes . . . we don't talk much anymore . . . but we are married." He showed the young man the couch. "Come, why don't we sit down? No use standing in the middle of the floor like two idiots, is it?"

The younger man sat while the older turned on a stereo. Old-time negro spirituals played.

After the reverend was seated at the other end of the couch from his guest, he said, "Why don't you try your drink? It's cognac . . . good stuff." He drank his neat and poured himself another full glass. "Don't you find religious music restful?" he asked.

The young man nodded his head and sipped his drink. The cognac was good stuff. He turned his head and looked at the room's paintings and tried to make out the book titles in the case across the room from his seat, and, while his head was turned, the reverend slid across the couch and tried to unfasten the young man's buttons on his trousers front. He stood up immediately, telling the older man, "Hey, mahthafukker! I don't play that kinda shit!"

After my marriage finally broke apart, I mean final, without recourse to reprieve or patchwork, my mind began fast disintegrating. And I hadn't expected that. I thought I was more stable than that, more together. But I found myself drinking progressively more and barflying again. I pawned all my suits, quit the post office, which was the best thing that I did that year, dropped out of school, and moved out of my mother's flat after a brutal, screaming tirade against her and all she had done for me, even bringing me into the world, to an apartment in one of my own buildings. The center had fallen out of that part of my life. And that's when I started daring trouble to come to me, myself.

From somewhere, her mother certainly, my wife had heard that she would receive more money from the welfare than I could give her. My wife already had a boyfriend, someone who had been keeping her occupied the weeks and months that I was in the service, at sea, or in jail. I could deal with that; I had lots of other women, didn't I? But she was my wife, I thought. And though I suspected who her nigger was, I still was on the move to "make it" land, and I couldn't stop long enough to get hung up in trivialities and waste time. I was so cool, I was stupid. So one day, my ole lady had her new man move her and my kids out of our place, my mother watching mutely with tears in her eyes, while my children, who my mother had raised, gaily told her, "Good-bye, Granny. We're going bye-bye."

My wife moved from my mother's place to her mother's run-down joint over in the ghetto part of town we had moved away from. But my mother-in-law knew she could fix her place up better with a share of the welfare money that was coming.

I called over there and my father-in-law told me to stay away if I "knew what was good" for me. Now he knew my nature, my temperament, so if I forced my way past that point, there would be bloodshed.

I was at work when my wife made her move, but I knew it was coming, so I didn't fight city hall. She had three more kids by me before I left that town for good, there's no need asking me how I know my children, but I would never consider taking her back after she had her boyfriend come to my mother's place when I was away at work and move her. Some things you can't allow a woman to get away with.

I drank more and became involved with a girl in the building that I moved to and several more in the neighborhood and I began doing a light pimp thing with them, having them use my place above the bar in the basement that I used for an after-hours joint. But I stayed drunk or high on pills so much I didn't know what was happening for days. But they were good, mainly clean girls out to make some money to take care of themselves and their kids, and just breaking into the life, so they treated me good because my head was too messed up to be putting them in a heavy hustle game, and I ran a straight house that paid off the cops and kept violence outside. With me being in poor condition, the house limped along the best way it could, only because I had a good woman taking care of things. The girls took care of me and the house and kept me out of trouble the best way they knew how. That evil, self-destructive thing of mine was feeding inside of me, operating off of liquor and my pill diet, and I took to carrying a pistol, which I pulled a couple of times to cool out the weekend crowd, and word went around that a contract was out for me to move me out of my lucrative spot. But I was meeting the mortgage on the joint by then and I wasn't ready to share that. But more scary, I was relieving white cab drivers and johns of their wallets when I got drunk and mean and would wander the neighborhood, daring death to do his best.

Bennie kept his distance from me, not knowing this side of me, and not wanting to get pulled into any beefs. He finally split town to settle his family's estate; his father was already dead, then his mother died, and he and his brothers and sisters began fighting over the spoils. While he was down in Florida, where he came from, he met and married a girl, a mortician's daughter, and sent me her picture. She was so light I put the picture on the mantelpiece and the girls in the house would rank me by saying that I had gone and gotten me a white "hoe."[15]

Sometimes my wife would come by when she got drunk. She was drinking heavily too, something she had never done before, and she would search me out, ask me to return to her for the sake of the children, then get furious when I said no after we had made love like we had done when we were teenagers and ridicule me by telling me that I didn't do it to her as good as her new men. I didn't mind too much. Somewhere inside, I was numb and dying. And the stuff she was drinking made her breath and skin smell so bad that I could hardly bring myself to have anything to do with her, even for old time's sake. And she had some kind of female trouble by then and most of the time I couldn't do anything with her because of the odor and slime.

One morning I woke up, hearing the rats scuttling through the walls, after being drunk for I don't know how many days. The house was empty. None of the girls' voices could I hear. Nor was a black music soul station on. And a fresh smell of coffee wasn't in the house. I checked the mailbox. A letter with a bus ticket was in the mail from an old friend, Jack Bowen. The letter said he had heard from my mother that I wasn't doing too well since my marriage had broken up and if I could come down and sit on the farm for a while and relax.

I shook my head and laughed, not believing that things like that happened. I checked my pockets and found a couple of hundred dollars in my wallet. My main woman was taking care of things just like she always did.

I went back inside the house, cleaned up, changed into a fresh shirt and pants, left half of the money in my woman's drawer with the pistol, wrote her a note, put my key on top of it and walked out the door.

I've never been back and that was several lifetimes ago.

What unsettles me most with women is when they are aggressive. I never learned how to really handle that. After I make the first advance, sure, they can go for broke. But I want to make the first heavy hit. I'm not hung up, really. Some of my most lasting relationships with women were those who wanted to get into the sex act as much as me or faster and didn't have any qualms about it. 'Cause if I don't make a broad on the first time go-round . . . well, there might not be any more go-rounds, unless I can get a chance to take some.

But there is a kind of woman I could never handle. Like I was walking up a street somewhere one day, and this hoe was standin' on the corner.

---

15. Rank: Insult.

I've seen hoes before. I've even had one or two throwin' me some chump change. I'm not exactly dumb, ya know. And when I got abreast of her, this funky whore said, "Lookin' for goodies, sport?"

I turned and replied, "I got six bitches that look so good that you can't even stand in their shadows, mamma!" You see, I was insulted that this woman would mistake me for a chump. And she said, "You may have six, papa, but mah thing's better!"

Our eyes really met for the first time, then I pulled away, not breaking my stride, and kept on round the corner.

You know, next day I went back and looked for her. She was gone, of course, and I've never found her. But I think of her sometimes and smile to myself and know that she'd make some man a mean bottom woman.

He had left Reverend Parsons standing in the middle of the gilded room called the "study." He hadn't hit the older man; no, he had more sense than that. Being a stranger in town with no money or contacts made him ripe for any accusation brought against him, he knew. He just walked out the door, slamming it, crossed the small bridge, and walked up the path toward his cottage.

It wasn't that he was entirely naïve; he had suspected that Parsons was a faggot, but he had to put on this show of injured indignation, he told himself, if he was going to stay there and keep the old man at a distance while he looked for a way out of the situation.

The old people were sunning themselves outside their houses when he approached. Annie was shelling peas on the front step, humming one of the old-time spirituals that he had heard in the reverend's study.

He passed them and entered the door. Ted was inside, feebly relieving himself in a bucket.

"How ya doing', young fella?" he said.

"Okay, I guess."

"I see you're upset . . . so the rev's explained your job to you."

"What do you mean?" The young man tried to act angry.

"Ahhh . . . don't get riled up now, young fella. I'm from Nevada. And I don't talk city talk so good, ya understand? Bet you didn't know there was colored folks in Nevada, did ya? Nawh, I bet ya didn't. Well, mah family was there ever since the Injun wars back after the Reconstruction . . . ."[16]

---

16. Injun wars back after the Reconstruction: Successive wars were fought against various indigenous American tribes following the American Civil War during Reconstruction, which dates from the creation of the Freedman's Bureau and the passage of the Thirteenth Amendment (1865) to the conclusion of the Federal military occupation and the start of southern "home rule" (1877–79).

"Yeah . . . yeah . . . I heard about it," the young man said impatiently.

"But there's other things you ain't heard about, junior. So listen to an older man for a while. Now I can't pee so good, I know. But I know what I know from all these years that God allowed me to live on his land . . . . It was in the war, the First World War, where I caught the claps . . . bad, real bad.[17] They didn't have no miracle drugs and things like that, not even over there in France then, so I ain't been able to piss so well these later years, but I seen the years go by."

"Look, old man . . . I don't feel so good."

"Why? Because the ole rev wanted to suck your thing for you?"

The old man was sitting back on his bed again; he reached under his mattress and pulled out a pint of sherry. "Do you bother any with this stuff?" he asked.

The younger man shook his head solemnly.

"Then get a glass over there outta that box."

When his glass was gotten, the old man filled it up.

"Now, let's talk some, young man . . . Now, why and how did you get yourself in this predicament?"

"I wanted to go to school and I heard they were cheaper out here in the West."

"Well, that's the best reason that I found yet amongst you young shavers passing through here. Yeah, lots of youngsters come to California for one reason or another. Yeah, lots comes through here. The rev has his eyes out for young stuff like you. Now don't go blamin' him too much. He's a pretty nice guy, in his own way. Lots of the people who run these kinds of places are lower than dawgs, nothing but scurvy critters. But ole rev feeds ya well and don't cheat you out of what's due you from the government or what your kids sends ya. C'mon, drink up . . . . Yeah, the rev's okay . . . . What's yours you get."

"But he tried to put his hand on me."

"Well, to him, you're like a sweet little girl . . . . Now, don't get upset. The rev's just funny like that. When his wife and him got married, they were in the service of the Lord, ya know, some kind of missionaries, and they promised that they would never have anything to do with each other in a sexual way at their wedding. The rev told me all this hisself, of course. Sure seems funny to me, but they been together for over thirty years now and he tells me he's never even seen up under his wife's skirt."

"That's weird," the young man said.

"Maybe so, but it's the truth . . . . But the rev couldn't hold to his vows.

---

17. Claps: Gonorrhea, the cure for which wasn't discovered until 1943.

He's got a couple of grown children who come to visit him every several years. His wife doesn't seem to mind. She just goes off to pray for his soul and leaves him alone with his kids he had out of wedlock. And now that he likes young boys and fools around with Annie some, she just acts like it's not happenin'."

"I don't know what to say," the young man said.

"Well, don't say nothin'," the old man said. "Just drink up. . . . But if you want to find out about school, you'd better get over to the high school over there on Vermont Avenue."

"But I'm too old to go to high school."

"Adult high school . . . evening school . . . Where you been all your life, son?"

"Oh, I thought . . ."

"Don't think so much. That's the trouble with you young fellas, you think nobody's got any sense but you. Now, they got counselors over to that there school that can tell you how to get a Ph.D., if ya wants one."

"Thanks," said the young fellow. Before he left, he asked, "Hey, Mr. Ted, what did you do when you were in Nevada?"

The old man took a swig of sherry and frowned. "Let's see now . . . I worked my daddy's spread some . . . an' I prospected for gold and silver, worked in the rodeo . . . was in the cavalry for a spell . . . and was a deputy marshal . . ."

"A marshal!"

"Yeah . . . where ya think mah pension comes from? Ya youngsters think all we niggers did was pick cotton in the ole days, huh? There's a lot you should find out about colored people, son . . . and a lot you better find out about yourself."

The school was found easily by the directions Mr. Ted gave him. After a wait of half an hour, he saw a counselor who discussed with him his plans for the future. He found that he only had to remain in that school for one semester before he could receive a California high school diploma, if he passed a G.E.D. test, due to his service background, his business and college prep schools, and could then enter college.[18]

"The registration fee here is fifty cents and the board of education textbooks are free of charge," said the counselor. It was some of the best news that he had gotten for some time.

It was dark when he returned to the big house. A light was on the

---

18. G.E.D. test: The General Education Development Test documents the attainment of high-school-level skills for those lacking a high-school degree.

porch and when he started to enter the gate to the back of the house, a woman's voice called him.

"Son . . . oh, you there, son!"

It was Mrs. Parsons. It was the first time she had spoken to him like that. He stopped and looked up at her.

"Yes, ma'm," he said.

"Son, the reverend told me to tell you that his cousin is coming tonight from down home. The reverend said he just got the wire today and is expectin' him anytime now. So we'll have your room."

"I see," the young man said. "Well, as soon as I get my things, I'll be gone."

"Your bags are here, son. The reverend didn't want to bother you none, so they're here on the porch."

He walked up on the porch and found his bags. Lifting them, he said, "Good night, Mrs. Parsons."

"Good-bye, son. My prayers go with you. Bless you."

He thanked her for the hospitality of the house and disappeared into the night.

Now allow me to restate my refrain. And don't misperceive me. My relations with women aren't only that of an exploiter of their flesh and a crusher of their spirits. I'm actually a lover. And I love to love and be all things that a man can be in a love involvement with a woman. But in the same breath, I'll tell anyone that I want what I want and that's the name of the game. And when the game deals with female meat, I'm out to score, baby. Make no mistake about it. I wouldn't lie to you. I love being in love and having a lovely lady to release myself in and fondle and fantasize about and free her from ever feeling that she is not the most important thing in the world to me, at least while I am getting into her and getting around her and just being her man. For I am very reluctant to rape any woman I don't relate to.

*　*　*

Marco Polo Henderson and I lived on a palm-lined street beside the Hollywood Freeway. Our two-bedroom apartment was upstairs over the mostly absent landlord's flat. The landlord found it necessary to be missing from his buxom wife and two kids the majority of the time because he worked full time as a sports car mechanic and kept a girl in a Western Avenue apartment who was possessive as well as being young, slim, and without children. His extended stays taught his wife how to collect our rent, clean and decorate our bachelor quarters, and determine what other needs of her tenants she could attend to, all without aid from her husband.

Marco Polo and I attended the same school. At the same time, our ambitions didn't seem too dissimilar. We made almost perfect roommates: We didn't like the same type girls, our friends loathed one another and would hardly have anything to do with us separately when one or the other was about, and we did almost nothing together except gamble and meet each afternoon after classes at the chess tables.

It was in the school patio at the table where our chess group met. A canopy covered the tables and benches, shielding us from the sun. The regulars and drift-ins were there every day, and we played for low stakes. I played with the class "D" players for fifty cents, being I'm about a "C–" player, and Marc played for better stakes of a buck or two, for he was one of the near best.

I was the only one who beat him regularly. Afternoons, to get things going, I would generally play a game with Marc, and if a new face showed among the kibitzers and asked for winners, Marc lost a close game to me. Nine out of ten of the new players beat me easily the first game, though being determined, I played my opponents a better game the next time, and then one last with the same results, except that I had just about pulled it out of the fire in the end game.

Having destroyed me and pocketed my two bucks, the winner would nearly always ask Marc, if he hadn't been tagged yet, "Hey, buddy, how about a game?"

That's how we made our bus fare and cigarette money.

One afternoon, one of the new players threatened to turn our gambling in to the dean of gambling or whatever dean takes care of that sort of thing. After Marc returned his ten bucks and the sucker had left, someone had gotten the idea of forming our loose group into a campus club. It was to be for our greater benefit, or so they said, by being sanctioned under the school charter. Among other compliances, we found that we had to collect dues before we were allowed on campus. We had been meeting together for months for profit and comradeship; then we tell a dean that we want to get into the yearbook and maybe represent the school in intercollegiate matches, and we find that we're illegal. So we had to collect dues, find a name, which finally was the Chess Club, get an adviser, and elect officers.

I was the first president of the Chess Club to attend our college's Associated Men's Smoker.

After the dinner of burnt beef and before the entertainment, which was to be several cheerleaders wearing hula skirts over shorts doing the twist in turtleneck sweaters with school letters pasted on and two myopic linemen from the football team in a wet pillow fight with we elected officials on the sidelines with cream pies to assist our favorites, some dean of something made a speech about fellowship, excellence, and manliness and announced, "Gentlemen, I give you your new student body president, Mr. Ricardo S. Evans."

Applause and cheers deafened me, with me even joining in, as it seemed the right thing to do, and, after the crowd quieted, Rick stepped to the podium wearing a dark suit and white bow tie. He nodded to some he knew in the audience and took a white sheet of paper from his inside suit pocket. His plastic-rimmed glasses shone under the spot and he stuck out his chest, a gesture that I would come to know well.

"Good evening, gentlemen," he started, and glancing over to the waiting cheerleaders, he added, "and ladies . . . ha ha ha. My topic tonight is . . ."

He had begun, and just as he began, there were titters in the audience. He paused and smiled a moment and then continued, and there was more and louder laughing. I wondered if there was a supreme joke or some game being played. What were they laughing at? I thought, and by *they* I meant the white boys. What was so hilarious? Rick and I were the only negroes there, so why were they laughing when he stood before them? I became furious. Rick began again and the snickers started; the dean stirred and a partial hush fell, and Rick continued once more; the giggles were with him throughout his speech. I didn't even hear what he had to say.

They are laughing at *him*, I thought; those little white bastards are laughing at a colored boy who stands before them as a man. Someone who represented them. I wanted to shout and grab the nearest white throat. I could even have throttled the dean. And I wanted Rick to get down. I wanted him to just leave their white faces laughing and let them get on with their costumed, untouchable pompom girls and have their muscle-and-cream-pie orgy without their pure and boyish innocence being damaged. I wanted to scream. I wanted him to help me kill them. I wanted him to come out into the audience and begin swinging, not wet pillows, but knives, fists, and feet. Kill them first, I thought, but don't let them chuckle at your manhood and giggle at your natural ability; don't let them think you a joke for competing with them and being something and doing what few others could. I thought: *Kill them! Kill them! Let's kill them, Rick, brother! Two blackmen are more than a match for a hundred soft-minded, weak-faced college whites.* But I only thought and remained silent, and we didn't act out my dream, not that night.

As the only other black in the large room, one who would have raved and ranted and threatened and cursed and drawn blood in the hallowed halls of the academy, I suddenly felt contempt for Rick when he smiled and went on with his speech. And I felt contempt for myself for sitting there among them and with my steak knife stabbing each and all in his white smugness that night of the cheerless cheerleaders and orgiastic athletes. I felt hate, the hate that had propelled me to see only ahead to a new future, not believing in the past or present filled with ignorance, violence, cruelty, and ridicule. I was so filled those moments that I never heard Rick nor suspected until months later that they were laughing at him because he was speaking to them in a very proper British accent, one with a refined southern drawl.

"Can I ask you a favor, Steve?" Len asked me when he came in from the back room.

"Sure."

"Will you stay tonight?" He looked concerned. "Lou is a bit distraught tonight, and when she gets like this, I think it's best to have people around she likes. I can never tell what she might do, and when she gets this way anything can happen."

I agreed to stay.

After Len left to speak with Rick, I told Jay that I would not be riding back with him.

"Well, what a pleasant surprise, Benson," he said. "My word, but I'm fortunate tonight. I was planning to take Evelyn home."

He fell into very precise speech when out with girls, and his show for the tall girl was complete. One would hardly believe he was from Alabama.

"Yes, the best thing you could do is learn about your homeland," the slim boy told the plump girl. He sagged on the couch, a beer can in his hand.

"Yes, I've been wanting to begin learning about Africa, but . . ."

A pudgy boy who had stayed close to Rick now stood alone; the crowd had moved away from him following Rick's jittery path. The boy did a private dance of his own making and pulled a pocket knife from his sleeve with a flourish, opened the shining blade with a snap of the button, and whirled and tossed the blade as he danced. He seemed the youngest in the room. Whenever a girl got near, he called out to her and said several phrases before she moved away in the crowd. I hadn't seen him drinking.

"Yes, I'd say that the repressed Oedipal urges in whites cause them to act with hostility toward we blacks.[19] If you'll notice, the most blatant homosexuals are nearly always white," someone told a large-eyed girl.

---

19. Oedipal urges: Sigmund Freud (1856–1939) theorized that males unconsciously desire to seduce their mothers and murder their fathers.

"Really!" she answered.

"Yes, the keeping of slaves has a definite correlation with masochistic and sadistic tendencies, plus many of the other more severe psychotic traumas . . ."

"Really!"

The crowd had thinned. Slower records played in the back. My head was light from the drinks.

"Will you dance with me?" Lou asked.

Inside, there were three other couples; Len and the small girl with pointy breasts made one pair. Lou danced as she looked: coarse and brisk with unexpected moments of grace and charm. It was my first time on the floor that night and, with beers and not having to compete with the serious dancers, I enjoyed holding Lou in my arms. Len and the other girl stayed to their corner until the record stopped, then he led her over.

"Hello, Steve. I want you to meet Tanya," he said with a slight bow. "Tanya Jefferson, this is Steve Benson."

We changed partners and the next record was another slow one and the small girl felt very close to me.

"Enjoying yourself?" I asked

"Why, yes. Len is so enjoyable."

She had been in Los Angeles since she was a baby; her family came from Ohio. Her hair was cut short and she smiled a lot. I thought that she must be some sort of Black Nationalist because of her haircut, but she didn't act the part, and I didn't think I should inquire.

Len and Lou argued quietly, with Len shaking his head and widening his mouth to emphasize words as he did when he wished to speak clearly. Lou glared at him, not allowing him to hold her too close. But the evening was becoming right for me.

"Eeee . . . *Oh, gawd!*" came from the front room. We looked around at each other, and then Len raced out the door to the front, followed by Lou.

The large-eyed girl stood in the middle of the front room, holding her dress out away from her body. The red sheath had a wide stain down the front.

"He poured beer on me," she said, pointing to the pudgy boy, who stood and grinned against the wall.

Len peered into the girl's face and turned to the boy.

"Brother," he began, and Rick stepped between them.

"There must be some confusion as to the circumstances in what happened here, Lenard," Rick said.

"Why the hell he throw that on her for?" Lou shouted.

"But, sister, you weren't here," Rick began.

"When I wouldn't dance with him and told him he acted like a fool, he told me I had to drink his beer or wear it, and then he threw it on me when I wouldn't drink," she said while crying.

Rick spoke softly to Len in a corner; some of the crowd muttered. A few went for their coats.

"Take care of yourself, Benson," Jay said, patting me on the back. "Sure you don't need a ride?"

He and the tall girl, Evelyn, left.

"I just want to know why he did it," Lou said. Len tried pushing her across the room; she resisted. "Just get him out of here, the little punk," she yelled from behind Len.

"Sister, why don't you refrain from making inaccurate statements?" Rick asked.

"Go to hell, Rick," she said. "Go to hell!"

The boy started talking to the offended girl in a low voice. He had a round moon face, and a glistening coating of scented pomade clung to his hair in pasty patches. I had seen boys like him before, ones who had not been outside their farm communities or small towns until they were in their late teens or older. They were like immigrants from strange lands, carrying secret knowledge that they could not communicate, but were the first ones to pick up the poorer habits of the new culture, faster than they could blend them into their old personalities. Usually, the worst aspects of the new showed through in displays of brash behavior, and they sometimes formed rebellious, overbearing natures to cover their inexperience.

Lou talked loudly in the kitchen. "Why do you invite a mahthafukker like that for?"

"Now, Lou Ellen," Len said.

"But, sister . . ." Rick pleaded.

She charged from between them straight to the fat boy. He smiled and waited for her rebuke until her gob of spit splattered against his forehead. I inched forward, hoping the boy wouldn't produce his knife again, but Lou had already spun and stalked into the bathroom, seeing the boy's stare of horror when her spit stuck upon his face. She jerked the bathroom door so violently it shook the house.

The fat boy wiped his face with a large pink handkerchief. Many of the crowd seemed ashamed for him and turned away; more got their coats and said good night.

"My people, my people," the dark man with the skull-like face said.

With the stain drying on her dress, the girl spoke to the pudgy boy. They seemed both to console each other about their separate calamities.

"Lou, open the door," Len said.

"Sister, sister, please." Rick stood with Len and pounded and called out.

"Will she be okay?" the skull-faced one asked.

"I don't know, Jacob," Len answered.

The knocking kept up another five minutes, and I got a fresh beer for myself and took Tanya a paper cup of wine in the back room.

"I guess the party's over," she said.

The slim youth and the girl he had been talking with the last part of the evening entered and began kissing. Tanya and I stopped our conversation and went back into the front, but we stayed out of the way of Len, Rick, and Jacob, who were deciding if they could take off the bathroom door from their side without splintering the frame. Tanya and I went into the kitchen.

"Do you live far?" I asked.

"No, not too far."

I told her that I had promised to stay overnight, but I could see her home and return. She let me know that Rick was seeing her home.

"Steve," Len said. "Will you please come with me? I want you to help me get Lou out of the bathroom."

I couldn't tell him that I didn't want to get involved.

We went out the kitchen door, which faced the front of the building, and walked past the rows of apartment doors to the end of the court and then turned in back of the units. It was a tight squeeze sliding through the narrow weed-filled space between fence and building.

When we came opposite the rear of his apartment, we peered through a small window.

Lou sat in the bathtub with her arms folded and stared at her ballerina shoes. Her sharp face was poised like a dagger waiting for a sound or a signal, and I wondered what cutting words and tearing of emotions her thin mouth would bring.

"She's all right," Len answered. "She's cut her wrists and taken overdoses of pills several times."

Back in the apartment, Len called through the door to her. Jacob was sitting on the couch next to the slim boy, and the fat one who had started the trouble and the girl were gone. About ten people remained. The record machine played once more in the back though the beer tub was empty. Someone had opened a gallon jug of red wine.

"Lou, I know it's cold in there," Len said. "Let me give you a blanket. I have a blanket for you, Lou Ellen," he pleaded. "You don't have to come out, but please don't stay in there all night and be cold. Let me give you this blanket to keep you warm."

"Brother Len," Jacob said, "that's not the way a sister should act. It shows a definite erosion of authority in the home situation and in the cultural values of her peer group."

"Sister, she's something else," Rick said, falling into a disdaining dialect. "Brother here is callin' to her, worryin' 'bout her comfort, and she's playin' suicide . . . my my my . . . Lenard, you should instruct the sister in the proper ways of conduct that a sister should observe in your presence and in the presence of your guests."

Len stood red-faced, his hair sprouting atop his head. There was a noise on the far side of the door.

"Lou, if you just open up a little bit, I'll give you this blanket so you can keep warm."

"That's right, Lenard, appeal to her reason," Jacob said. "Appeal to her reason. She seems like a reasonable girl." Jacob acted tired of the part he played in the activity, so he walked backwards to the couch and nearly sat in the laps of the couple there.

The couple squirmed out of his way and resumed hugging and kissing, but Jacob didn't seem to notice. They leaned farther back, almost lying down, even across Jacob's legs.

The door cracked and a thin brown hand extended. And then Len had the wrist, pulling Lou from the bathroom.

"You dirty mahthafukker!" she screamed when he had her out into the room.

"Now, sister, that isn't the way one should . . ." Rick began.

"Keep out of this, Rick; if you hadn't brought your damned punk cousin in here from the country, he wouldn't have fucked up my party."

"Sister's right," Jacob said. "The fault should be shared by more than one."

"Where is that fat bastard?" Lou wanted to know.

"He's gone home with Ceola," someone said.

"Why would she go home with him after he poured beer on her?" she demanded.

"Now, sister . . . the ways of man and woman are . . ." Jacob began.

"Yeah, what goes on behind locked doors ain't . . ." somebody interrupted.

Jacob was in the circle surrounding Lou; the couple on the couch mumbled at being disturbed by the others. Len held Lou's arms and Rick made a speech.

"Now when a man and a woman become . . ."

What's happening? I wondered. And then I knew.

I was back again at the night of the smoker. But there was a difference. Really many differences, but I didn't know most of them then. Rick was speechmaking, but there was no laughter. He made similar high-sounding noises as before in the nearly exact voice. In his most precise, clipped, very British accent, he arbitrated the issues of the day, handed down the laws, paved the way for peace. But how different the attitude of this group from the others at that lost night of cloaked sex and unaware, pantomimed homosexuality.

I looked about. The couple on the couch had stopped fumbling with each other and sat still, listening to Rick's words. Tanya was at his elbow now, her little brown face expressing joy and respect. Lou was quiet, standing counseled, and Len held her gently with a bored expression. The group was quiet, attentive to Rick; the music had been stopped in the back and everyone was in the living room listening to his many words about man and woman and the conduct of each to each, especially and entirely if they were black. He was speaking to them in a weird tongue, one more guise he used that night, and they listened and revered. His trace of earlier speech remained strong enough for him to be known; he was still one of them, he was merely a black boy from the country speaking to other blacks, but he spoke the language of power. How differently this group reacted to his style than those at the smoker. All those white faces had grinned, and their breath had snuffled in strained wheezing, and this black group were blank, their masks were exposed and torn away, the look of awe was open in their eyes.

What mask did Rick use to entrance these people? Not the unsuccessful ones he had worn earlier that night. The face of the jester and sport can hypnotize few. But now he was speaking in the same voice, with the same mannerisms, but was it all exactly the same?

No. Not just the same. A hint of mirth at a certain moment when a turn of dialect was made, making a common phrase an absurd pun. A twinkle in his eyes accompanied by a slur to remind all there that night of their low, or rather real, beginnings, a shuffling of feet to mock a half-remembered character, a foolish scratching of the scalp, a "yawhl" exclaimed, zooming in like an idiot's scream and followed by a hesitant triple chuckle of emphasis. No, it wasn't exactly the same as before. But it was a speech, nonetheless, and I would never forget it, though I didn't hear the words the same as that first night. It wasn't the same, but the voice spoke the same, the Queen's English as she had never heard it.

What guise was this? The magician of mood, what part did he play to bring life in that room to a standstill? This was all so new to me. What was it all about; what were Rick and Len and Lou and Jacob and these Black Nationalists and intellectuals about? Just what was *their* game? No one else there seemed surprised or estranged. They all accepted as ordinary this spare, obviously southern negro speaking to them in an imperfect approximation of an Oxford accent. That moment, I believe, was when I became determined to find more about what had happened during that night . . . and since that night, as well as many others, my life has never been the same.

After the speech, Len released Lou, and she spun, calling him a foul name and scratching a narrow streak down his cheek. He grabbed her throat and wrestled her to the floor with a strangling hold.

"Now, Len, Len . . ." Jacob pleaded, having hurried from his seat.

"Lenard . . . *brother!* You should know better." Rick hovered over them, trying to pull Len off without using force.

I could see that Len wasn't pressing hard, only attempting a convincing scene. Finally, he relaxed and Lou sprang up, snatching the dropped blanket, and, with mutters and sobs, she raced back into the bathroom and slammed the door. No one tried to get her to return.

"Well, the party's over, brother, so you'll have to go," Rick told me as he had most of the others he had ushered out.

"I'm staying tonight," I said.

"But you have to go when the man wants you out of his house, brother! What sort of statement is that to make?"

"Well, I'm a friend of theirs and they invited me to stay," I said.

He shrugged and pushed out his chest and looked furious when I wouldn't follow his orders.

"Good night," Tanya had said.

I waved at her and caught a flashing glimpse of her brown legs and narrow ankles turning a corner.

Soon, most were gone except for Len, who locked himself in the back room, the slim youth, long abandoned by the plump girl, who snored upon the couch, and I, remaining out front. Even Rick had left with pretty Tanya and the rest were gone, whispering what an awful party it had been. The light under the bathroom door snapped off, and I could hear the record player drone softly through the back door.

I snuck out into the darkness of the court to relieve myself of the fullness of the beer, the Southern California sky a starry and smogless expanse above. I drew in a whiff of night air, but only filled my chest with the odors of tenements, poverty, and the sickness of loneliness. No use thinking that Lou would open the door to me, I thought, any faster than she would to her lover.

ESSAYS
&
LETTERS

The Polished Protest

Aesthetics and the Black Writer

(1963)

... With stand-up sex and white hatred going for him, he (James Baldwin) had about as much chance of escaping the embrace of the bestseller list as William Burroughs has of copping the Orville Prescott Uplift Award.[1] As Herbert Gold has pointed out, the sharper publishers, having sniffed the market for rubbing the white man's nose in it, are busy setting up Negro Departments. It figures. (In recent days, I have received several specimens of The New Negro Novel; they happen to be pretty bad, but again that is not the point. They might just as well have been good. What signifies is that even Negro bohemia is on its way out ...)
                    —Harvey Swados, *Contact Magazine*, April 1963[2]

A philosophical conflict exists among Negroes, though much of their animosity and energies could take more appropriate direction. The visible split between the militant, passive-resistant groups and the numerous Black Nationalism coherers discloses but two radical positions (radical in relationship to where one is standing). Though other extremely tangential viewpoints exist in Negro communities, they are mostly stagnant for not having freely circulated.

First published in *Contact Magazine*, July 1963.

1. William Burroughs (1914–97): Intransigently experimental writer often associated with the Beat movement and notorious for his depictions of sex, drug use, and violence.

2. Harvey Swados (1920–72): Socialist, activist, factory worker, literary critic, and author of *Out Went the Candle* (1955) and *Standing Fast* (1970).

Contrasting views are not even being shown in contemporary Negro writing, although it has been proclaimed by some optimists (for example, J. W. Schulte Nordholt, *The People Who Walk in Darkness*, 1960) as having taken an historical pivot away from the stereotypes of the recent past. What gives this pertinence is its occurrence coincident with the increased activity in the Civil Rights movement. Negro militancy, of course, makes Negro subjects topical, and publishers can capitalize upon these phenomena.

The newer Negro writing generally is no longer *only* hard-scolding, embittered denouncements of whites, the South, the aloof North, and the overall tragedy of being a black man in America. Nor are there many of those tiring multitudes left in print, today, who achieve minor recognition in exploiting the plausible by claiming conclusive answers for the Negro problem in the same standard generalities and clichés. This work is not experimental, but is intentional; much of it is distinct from the main body of Negro letters, not so curiously, by its sophisticated treatment of unstereotypic Negro characters and situations. But recent events seem to forebode this movement of mature development and continual momentum. The publishers, who once encouraged the emergence of this more universal form of expression (when the market was right), now stifle it when it should, at last, be ready to move onward and state essential implications concerning the Negro, or better, to rise into creatively imaginative literature, unencumbered by the emotional motivations of resentment and vindication.

The stale, oft-chewed phrases and arguments of thirty or more years ago are currently being restated for a newly curious *white* readership. The bitter, black protest of yesteryear is now a modern, more polished protest in professional, stylized prose, directed to already sympathetic whites. Today's polished protest is cathartic and, occasionally, admirably written. With the typical image of the zealous, recriminating black writer long established, this form has a "made," awaiting, masochistic market. Since it is written by Negroes for primarily white audiences, it is all at once engaging, flagellant, and highly saleable. It is "hip" today for a black writer to take "Charles" to task and, under these conditions, it is doubtful whether a writer of Negro ancestry can remain aesthetically detached, even if he wishes, and not fall victim to those publishers who induce him to accept their accommodations in the newly popularized ghetto of the "New Negro" writer.[3]

---

3. Charles: As in "Charlie" or "Mister Charlie," a generic name for white men who exploit and oppress blacks.

Paralleling this movement is the violent nature of Negro demands in other areas. Though the Negro is at odds concerning methods and philosophies of action to achieve total success, his aggregate groups, separately, cry, "Freedom Now!" It is paradoxical that, at the moment the Negro is ready to make his most active and violent protest, he finds himself practically mute and he is unable to rally his fellows through written communication.

The present phase of Negro literature takes its identity from James Baldwin (*Go Tell it on the Mountain*, 1953). Baldwin seemingly revolutionized the field by vigorously attacking the standard black protest novel and achieved some amount of success in his attempt. Few Negro writers before him had escaped from the stereotyped trap in which Negro writing was enclosed. Baldwin consciously presented believable, multi-dimensional black characters doing the routine but difficult job of living their anguish-filled lives in their ghettos. And though there was cause for celebration in this breakthrough, the sinister implication now arises, as Baldwin's newer fiction and caustic essays are being read (though Baldwin himself feels artistically sincere in what he is now writing), that an insidious commonness has replaced the traditional types of Negro writing, and this new "slick" version is being imbued with gimmicks and cuteness. If there is any merit in this supposition, then there is one overriding reason for its validity; and if it is totally hollow, then the same reason applies to why Negro writing appears so limited and shallow that it can be wholly condemned by a few prejudiced generalities.

It is the publishers—both black and white—who will not take a financial chance on topics which may, they fear, alienate a large segment of their market and so exploit controversial themes. The publishing business seems pervaded with sensation-minded journalistic types. It is now smart for these businessmen to capitalize on the "black" market and grab a fast buck. It is now more "modern" for Negro authors to analyze the hate which exists between the races, comment upon the unsavory aspects of random (and certainly taboo) miscegenation, expose the circumstances of misunderstood homosexual love, and, incidentally, examine the inequalities which confront black Americans. Negro authors urging Negroes to act collectively in their own behalf outside of the limits established by organizations dominated by liberal whites, for instance, are seen scarcely (if ever) in white and black national publications. Nor is there much evidence of attempts at objectivity in fiction by Negroes since Baldwin's early novels and Lorraine Hansberry's play (*A Raisin in the Sun*, 1959). The inability to realize aesthetic distance has been one of the Negro writer's severest handicaps, and it is sad if the transition to active social critic and essayist has caused Baldwin's latest novel (*Another Country*, 1962) to suggest the bogus and contrived.[4]

If the black writer is published, today, it is usually the interested and partisan whites who sustain him. If he offends these "liberal" whites, he is branded as too radical, while being condemned by his own race as being "unready." Publishers see no profits in antagonizing and alienating readers. Consequently, the serious Negro writer is not in the vanguard of Negro thought (even if he wants to be)—not in the published and widely circulated vanguard, in any case. And Negroes have been burning for a new identity in their letters for many years; perhaps, unknowingly, this desired image is a more secular and universal identity. Negroes, most of all, splinter in thinking of their national worth, role, and identity, but only the activities of a passive minority are getting belated recognition by the mass media. It is bitterly ironical that, in the area of ideas concerning himself, the heaviest weight upon the black man's shoulders is his white liberal friend who sits astride his mind and cautions him to listen exclusively to those who have the Negro's welfare at heart. No new forms of Negro intellectual activity are being widely circulated today; it is even suspect how much innovative thought is being discussed in "Negro Bohemia" (granted that this exotic locale is not bordered by the naive imaginations of romantic whites and "New Negroes").

Currently, there are as many or even more dark individuals concerning themselves with "their" problem, but those claiming to be the "New Negro" or the "New Breed" remain as self-deluded as their cotton-patch brethren, and as irrational as their black-nationalistic kin who race into the arena of ideas in a chariot of emotional slogans and incredible panaceas. There can be no new forms of widely broadcast Negro ideas in America until the Negro himself realizes that he must break out of the blackest ghetto of all, the stereotyped "Negro" mind. The black writer must realize this above all else. With such fragmented and isolated areas in the whole of *Negritude*, it is unfortunate that the black writer is not creatively weaving these shreds into a comprehensible cloak which can be worn or identified by all black people, instead of dressing the empty statements of yesterday in loud and flashy outfits manufactured in commercial, mass-produced lots.[5]

---

4. *Another Country*: Generally regarded as both a formal and thematic departure for Baldwin, the novel graphically portrays the bisexual, interracial relations of a group of friends attempting to find meaning and identity after the suicide of Rufus Scott, a black jazz musician.

5. Negritude: Originating in the 1930s among Francophone blacks, this literary and ideological movement asserted a common cultural and historical identity across the African diaspora.

The Negro publishers—like the black middle-class they toady to—are smug, narrow, and stupid. The black figure who should hold the commanding position in the field has no place in it at all. True, Negroes as a group are notoriously unread, but it is not entirely because of the dreadful schooling and low cultural levels in black communities. Where can a reading Negro find significant ideas about himself (or even worthwhile entertainment)? Can he find them in the prosperous, nationally circulated, black-faced facsimiles of *Look*, *True Confessions*, and *The Reader's Digest?* The few Negro presses and publishers are concerned with crowing about the mediocre achievements of the few blacks who have won marginal success in the white world, and this is of too small importance for the black writer to consider.

So, in the end, it is the publishers who ignore and suppress more rounded forms of Negro writing. The black writer with an artistic bent is left lingering on the fringes of the literary community. The white publishers shun him and cultivate those black writers whose forte is to "make" the ready white market, which pleasurably squirms in the wrath of each new example of black indignation. And the black publishers wait for the whites to bring a Wright into vogue before claiming him in saccharine obituaries, or a Baldwin (who finally, perhaps, has had to compromise his art and artistic ideals to get his "message" fully across and gain currency).[6] The Negro publishers are the "Uncle Toms" of the literary world. They wait like curs to nibble the scraps thrown them by the sponsor of the "accepted" black writer, but fight to bury another that smacks of quality beneath the garbage of materialism and pseudo-hipness. These same publishers will print nearly anything which they feel will bring an enormous profit without the risk of legal action, unfavorable public opinion, and too many disgruntled comments from other segments of the business community. Knowing this, the serious writer (whatever his color) should first seek *honesty* with himself concerning his work; he must honestly consider what he wishes to make of his writing—art or facile craftsmanship for money, recognition, glamour, or proselytizing for a cause.

---

6. Wright: Richard Wright (1908–60), whose novel *Native Son* (1940) set the terms for black radical writing for two decades.

The So-Called Western Avant-Garde Drama

(1967)

It would seem that in America there is no way to break away from the historical (in the Western sense) definitions of drama, though never-ending revolutions occur in theater which are usually inappropriately named "avant-garde." These "avant-garde" movements are not attempts, in most cases, to break or separate from Western theater's history, conventions, and traditions, but are efforts to extend Western dramatic art, to perpetuate and adapt the white man's theater, to extend Western reality, and finally to *rescue* his culture and have it benefit *his* needs.

Avant-garde theater is difficult to recognize, for it may not be truly indicative of the future and may have little other effect upon the current drama other than to be pretentious. Its characteristics may only be bizarre, e.g., penis worship, masturbation, incestuous narcissism, and ego projection. And often, avant-garde mannerisms are a collection of rediscovered conventions of a forgotten era, newly foisted upon the new generation to become clichés in themselves.

Most conventions fall into a series or set of mannerisms. After a time, men (usually of the coming generation) rebel against these arbitrary rules; they break "tradition," rail against dogma, and smash the molds established by custom and time as well as complacence. These are the avant-garde. But, nevertheless, they work within a tradition which is particular to the West.

So are they avant-garde? Are they not actually only so-called avant-

First published in *Liberator*, December 1967; reprinted in *Black Expression*, edited by Addison Gayle Jr. (New York: Weybright and Talley, 1969).

garde? Is what they are doing really new? Is there anything under the sun that is new, especially in the theater, in the Western tradition of that institution?

Currently, the so-called avant-garde theater, as opposed to contemporary commercial, academic, and "experimental" theater, is identified chiefly with France and the absurdist school of writing (defined not by the playwrights, but by critics) or with Piscator and Brecht and the Epic theater, or with actor/director movements, e.g., the Polish Lab, the Living Theatre, Peter Brook's Experiments at the Royal Shakespearian Theatre Club, or the Berliner Ensemble. (I shall not even enter into a parallel argument concerning Black Drama and Western Theater, for the separation is so innovative and startling that they cannot be spoken of in the same vocabulary, much less classifications. This statement should be approached as a jumping-off place to various discussions which will lead to that unique entity known as Black Drama.)

But is any of the above really new? For instance, the paragon of *their* movement and history, *Waiting for Godot* by Samuel Beckett, has a linear story action, a timelessness, universal characters, and a plot with continual expansion of meaning. (This is the white man's language, which I use in connection with his culture; in speaking of Black culture, we Black artists are continually developing a vocabulary and dialogue.) Many of the other plays in this tradition have similar effects and are equally as identifiable. These effects are all found in previous dramatic literature, conventional or archaic, in our period, but equally vanguard in theirs. But to cut through the academic and critical verbiage, it is the white man's vision of reality that is most identifiable in his drama, and Black dramatists are not heir to that type of madness.

The trick or innovation that the present-day absurdists seem to have come upon, out of their conscious or unconscious wills and motivations, is the ability to express *disbelief.* They disbelieve in themselves, in their sources, in their creation, in their present moment in time. The conventional drama aims at telling a story. The absurdists feel little or no story is necessary. The tradition of theater has been to deal in character. *Krape's Last Tape* by Eugene Ionesco[1] has a tape recorder as one of the principal characters, not giving it anthropomorphic characteristics like Mr. Ed, the talking horse, but leaving it in the realm of being an object. Objects remain the phenomenological items they are, and humans become dehumanized in this drama. Quite a step away from traditional humanistic thought, but not too far removed from Medusa (of Greek legend) turning men to stone or of Lot's wife who couldn't allow her damned city to burn without a

---

1. *Krape's Last Tape* by Eugene Ionesco: Should be *Krapp's Last Tape* by Samuel Beckett.

backward glance. (The portrayal of the great white Bitch figure in Western literature and philosophy has some interesting associative material for contemporary Black writers.)

The new technological culture (ology) seems to be the one factor or aggregation of factors which might change Western theater drastically. (Western theater: a theater which shies away from social, political, psychological, or *any* disturbing [revolutionary]² reforms, just as the reactionary society which it reflects does) and may throw this backward institution into the twentieth century. If the media is the message, we Black artists have been far ahead of anything the white man has conceived.)³

For the white man, there are no new stories or plots or characters; and somehow, by the time they filter down to present-day theater, there are *no* really new ideas in his culture. His sense of reality cannot extend far enough to encompass what is not merely himself or to perceive what is really happening, i.e., *Black*.

So, the electric light hasn't really changed *Hamlet*. The arena stage was known when the threshing floor existed and the hero-warriors danced the lion and spear dance. All are there and remain, and not just as some footnoted reference in anthropological data. The use of mechanical sounds and film devices were used before Piscator and Brecht.

There may be nothing which can really be properly regarded as avant-garde in Western theater. (Surely, Black Drama doesn't wish to exploit this pretentious, effete, white, bourgeois term.) And this pale label (avant-garde) must not be confused with "experimental." "Experimental" is generally the refuge of the inept. Experiments, and especially in theater, must be designed to go somewhere, to have a positive direction and goal, even if that place is predetermined to be "nowhere," e.g., (and only in rare cases) a *happening*.

An experiment can only be a handmaiden to the so-called avant-garde and quite in keeping with the times; for as stated above, there may be no such thing as avant-garde in white America.

To paraphrase Brother LeRoi Jones: It is a post-American form of Black theater we Black Artists should be seeking. It is Black Art that is like a dagger pointed at the vitals of America, and through the rips "we" (US) can enter the new epoch.⁴

---

2. Brackets in original.

3. Media is the message: A phrase coined by Marshall McLuhan (1911–80), a best-selling media theorist who legitimized academic mass-media studies.

4. US: The name of the Black Nationalist organization founded by Maulana Ron Karenga (1941–) in 1965.

A Short Statement on Street Theater

Street Theater is the name given to the play or dramatic piece (i.e., skit, morality or political farce or black "commercial" that subliminally broadcasts blackness) written expressly to be presented upon the urban streets or adapted to that purpose.

When one envisions contemporary America, one is compelled to think of faces moving, faces facing upwards, faces in crowds, faces in dynamic mobs—expanses of faces in the streets.

Faces in the streets and in the cities: Broadway, Main Street, Market Street, Broad Street, Grand Avenue, the thoroughfares of New York, Detroit, Providence, Chicago, San Francisco, Philadelphia, Atlanta, L.A.—BLACK FACES.

STREET PLAYS (BLACK REVOLUTIONARY AGIT-PROP)

1. Purpose: Communicating to masses of Black people. Contact with Black crowds. Communication with diverse classes of people, the Black working class, or with special groups (e.g., winos, pool hall brothers, prostitutes, pimps, hypes,[1] etc.) who would not ordinarily come or be drawn into the theater.
2. Method: First, draw a crowd. This can be done by use of drums, musicians, recording equipment, girls dancing, or by use of a barker or rallying cry which is familiar and revolutionary and nationalistic in connection (Burn, Baby, Burn).[2] Or the crowd can be gotten spontaneously

First published in *The Drama Review* (*TDR*) 12 (summer 1968).
1. Hypes: An addict hustling for drugs.
2. Burn Baby Burn: A phrase coined by H. Rap Brown (1943–), now Jamil Abdullah Al-Amin, in 1967 while he was serving as national director of the Student Nonviolent Coordinating Committee. It is also the title of a poem by Marvin X.

where masses of people are already assembled—the play done within the mob (Mob Action—Mob Act): Immediacy—or done with a minimum of fanfare, in the street, upon a platform or a flatbed truck. The truck can carry the equipment and be used as an object of interest if decorated attractively. Also, girls can ride atop the truck and aid in crowd-gathering (fishin'). Monitors can circulate throughout the crowd, distributing printed information, doing person-to-person verbal communicating and acting as guards for the performers and crew (The Black Guard).

3. Types of plays: Short, sharp, incisive plays are best. Contemporary themes, satirical pieces on current counter-revolutionary figures or enemies of the people, humorous themes, also children's plays with revolutionary lessons are good street play material. Also, startling, unique material, something that gives the masses identifying images, symbols, and challenging situations. Each individual in the crowd should have his sense of reality confronted, his consciousness assaulted.

Black Theater, Bourgeois Critics

(1972)

In the mid-sixties, when most of the now working Black artists entered what soon became known as the Black Theater Movement, there was an open contempt from the Negro middle class, or Black bourgeois class, for this artistic and psychic thrust of Black intellectual self-determination growing out of the Black Power impulse of the day.

The young Black artists that formed LeRoi Jones's (Imamu Baraka) Black Arts Repertory Theater/School in Harlem, Marvin X and Ed Bullins's Black Arts/West in San Francisco, Woodie King's Concept-East Theater in Detroit, John O'Neal and Gilbert Moses's Free Southern Theater in New Orleans, Robert Macbeth's New Lafayette Theatre of Harlem, Black House, The Negro Ensemble Company, the National Black Theater, the Afro-American Studio, and, presently, the more than sixty functioning Black community theaters throughout America were mainly from the Black urban ghettos of America, a class that the Black bourgeoisie has traditionally hated for being less than "civilized," or not imitative of European culture and values, and, hence, a conscious threat against the status quo values of Black middle-America.

When the Black artists from the ghettos of Harlem to Watts began challenging, then changing, the aesthetic assumptions of America through art and theater, the Black bourgeois intellectual became one of the major active enemies to this Black People's Theater movement.

The commonality of aesthetic stance among the artists of this period was in the impulse to migrate away from European references in their concep-

First published in the *New York Times*, August 27, 1972. Copyright © 1972 by The New York Times Co. Reprinted with permission

tualizations, in the practice of their arts, and in their very lives. For Blacks seeking advanced degrees in English Victorian literature, for Afro-Americans militantly struggling for integration armed with little else than 19th-century European ideas, for Negroes waging pyrrhic battles upon the marriage beds of Euro-America, for all those niggers who in their heart of hearts believe that Black Men cannot create original works and discover a contemporary aesthetic founded in a Black Ethos, the attempts to establish a working Black Arts community verged upon irrationality and were extremely threatening.

This dichotomy between the Black artists and the reactionary Black pseudo-intellectual elements that exploit the community is most evident today in the "Destroy Black Theater" propaganda of the so-called Black critics who have access to national publications. These untalented few attempt to hold forth as the arbiters of the values that they want infused within the Black theater artist's work.

These parasites, sucking a living off the energies and talents of Black playwrights, actors, directors, designers, musicians, and technicians, feel so above their prey, the artists, that they are very seldom seen in their company, feeling threatened by the strong, positive presences of the artists—surely, but smugly, thinking that they cannot learn anything by the association.

Nor are these so-called Black critics found in the Black community, except when they are on assignment for their publications. Picture the group, if one can: almost without exception they wear glasses and are never out of their uniform of suit and tie, resembling unsuccessful colored insurance men; as they stand around the lobbies of Black theaters before curtain, among clusters of grassroots Black people which cause them nervous perspiration, they grin insincerely like morticians' apprentices and talk out of the sides of their mouths to each other.

When they leave to write of how far the Black production was from their preconceived models, this cadre of mediocrity returns to little pockets of integrated Black bourgeoisie/dom and carries on what passes for intellectual conversation with other Black pseudo-intelligences and their white cronies.

One such critic type, [P.B.], associate editor of *Ebony* magazine, in the Sunday, August 13, issue of *The New York Times*, reviewed the work of J.E. Gaines (a.k.a. Sonny Jim), "Sometimes a Hard Head Makes a Soft Behind," which is presently running at the New Lafayette Theatre, Seventh Avenue and 137th Street. [Mr. B.] apparently did not like the play, what the playwright did and did not have to say, the performances, the direction, and he ridiculed the almost entirely Black audience's wearing apparel.

[Mr. B.] also questioned the presence of teenagers in the audience and was contemptuous of the audience's positive responses to the play, and he ended by pulling out some moralist clichés while telling the reader what the author should have written instead of recognizing that his middle-class consciousness had been mugged by a work of art that came from the hard core of the dispossessed Black ghetto of Harlem. He was literally disoriented and alienated by a true depiction of current Black street/life.

This lack of recognition by many Blacks and most whites of certain aspects of the Black aesthetic and ethos has caused a great antagonism by them against contemporary Black Art that falls outside of the Euro-American reality.

The newer phase of Black writing is in the dialectic period of evolution. Black artists are discussing ideas, discoursing about the problems and concerns of their Black audience, readers, and peers, among a body of evolved Black Consciousness, hence, it is a Dialectic of Black Contemporary Literature/Art/Theater that this generation's artists are engaged in.

The Dialectic of Black Art has a give-and-take quality among its practitioners, with certain cultural contexts and recognitions assumed.

Currently, there are two main branches to the mainstream of new Black creativity: the dialectic of change (once called "protest writing," then called "Black revolutionary writing" when it turned a decade ago away from a white audience to a Black) and the dialectic of experience. Sometimes the branches merge, but variety in the overall work is generally the rule. And there is little conflict among the artists working within the forms.

The dialectic of change has a distinguished history founded in the slave narrative/abolitionist/protest phases of Black literature. The dialectic of experience has roots that antecede the arrival of Black slaves on this continent and is traceable to oral literatures of Africa and cultures of temperate zone non-European peoples. Both are strong strains in Black Art and play vital functions in the Black Ethos in Black American writing.

It is dreary when a self-righteous censor such as [P.B.] would recognize the need for change in Black/white American lives but shun the recognition of the experience, an experience so barren and oppressive that "Sometimes a Hard Head Makes a Soft Behind" does not have to explain the obvious to its Harlem audience—the retreat into the Mosque by the sister in the play, the retreat by other characters into liquor, drugs, and sex. [Mr. B.] apparently lives by utopian ideals suggesting final solutions in marriage, family, and middle-class nation building.

"One who does not know his history is bound to repeat it," surely, but one who denies the experience of ninety per cent of his brothern [sic] is making a grave error. The self-deceit of so-called "Black critics," "intellectuals," and "moralizers" should be beyond the "talented-tenth" elitism that should have gone the way of the "blackbottom" and other cultural memorabilia.[1] Perhaps this type of prejudice against the Black people's artists and their creative institutions exists in the *Ebony* minds of some few journalists with pretensions to artistic and literary judgments, but it won't change the degree of truth in the community artists' Black visions.

---

1. Talented-tenth: A term coined by W. E. B. DuBois (1868–1963) in 1903, in reference to the "exceptional men," the 10 percent of African Americans who "have led and elevated the mass" and "may guide the mass away from the contamination and death of the worst, in their own and other races."

Black Theater:
The 70s—Evolutionary Changes

(1973)

During the recently left behind 60s, some young Black people in these white, bleak lands imagined the metaphor of the times to be revolution. All were inheritors of a radical Black political and social activist past in America that most were ignorant of, being that they were Black and victims of their oppressors' school system and lack of system for them, members of an alien culture. America's educational institutions are predicated upon keeping Black men ignorant of themselves and the other non-white four-fifths of the world. Actually, it is many times a misfortune that Blacks go through these white cultural propaganda mills, places that produce schizoid misfits, properly called "Black intellectuals." (Black from their Afros to dark behinds, but at their psychic centers a mortal conflict rages between the Hellenistic Ideal and their *soul*.) Programming for the Black man, the white man's schools are slick job-training centers for induction into the military machine for negroes to become twentieth-century global mercenaries.

A segment of this ill-informed Black youth movement, spurred on by the mass media that fed upon the urban ghetto upheavals of the times, identified themselves with some species of Black Revolutionary Nationalism. A handful of these "revolutionaries" evolved into what can best be described as *Black artists*, using the tired and wasted Western theater form as a medium to effect the most profound changes in Black people here in America, that process termed "altering consciousness," at the same time

---

First published as the introduction to *The Theme Is Blackness: The Corner and Other Plays* (New York: Morrow, 1973).

revitalizing the form aesthetically and literally by attacking the intellectual and ideological premises of Western civilization. Their models for future Black conceptualization came through the evolutionary struggle of *creative practice*, and brought about a confrontation with reality that developed into what is now known as *Black theater*.

The Black Revolutionary Nationalist's ideological antecedents reach back to early negro American history, representing the essential conflict among Black thinkers in America—nationalism vs. assimilation. The teachings of the older, traditional nationalist philosophers, fused with contemporary Third World revolutionary thought, became rockbed references of the civil rights and Black Power generation seeking social change through social action, though for the most part remaining unknown in philosophical perspective and not historically understood by the Black youth movement. Some of these intellectual forebears are Booker T. Washington, Marcus Garvey (who initially came to America to study and learn from Booker T.), W. E. B. DuBois, Richard Wright, Elijah Muhammad, Kwame Nkrumah, Sékou Touré, Frantz Fanon, Chairman Mao; then came Malcolm X, and nothing has been the same since in the Black urban ghetto.

Infused within the Black nationalistic ardor of the young activists were the confused tenets of dated negro radical activism of early twentieth-century America, which has been always Black Nationalism's most hostile adversary within the Black community. Those influenced by the militant integrationist syndrome—the once far left of the negro C.P. membership, the colored trade unionism, protest as practiced historically by the NAACP, the Urban League, CORE, SNCC, and culminating in the reactive rhetoric and revolutionary suicides of Black Panther violent integration (spelled *communalism*)—have traditionally psychologically abhorred and physically hindered most things to do with genuine Black nationhood and self-determination.[1]

Add to this political misbegotten identity—one having an *emotional* relationship to Blackness but bearing a modern legacy of a surviving leadership which worships the Hellenistic Ideal, whether through G.M., Jane Fonda or Marx—the culturally pervading influence in the ghetto of the Black religionists and Africanists, best examples being the Nation of Islam and the Yoruba Tribe of Harlem, and the image of a definite breed of political ghetto cat becomes clearer.[2]

---

1. C.P.: Communist Party. NAACP: National Association for the Advancement of Colored People. CORE: Congress of Racial Equality. SNCC: Student Nonviolent Coordinating Committee.

2. G.M.: General Motors, one of the biggest corporations in the world. Jane Fonda (1937–): U.S. actor and antiwar activist (in)famous for her 1971 visit to North Vietnam.

The remainder of the Liberation Movement people affected by politics, philosophy, Black cultural forms, and American repression are the Black artists/intellectual activists, the young street niggers, and, largest in numbers and the well of Blackness, the Black people people.

All of these elements met, fused, fought, and survived in some recognizable form in the strife of the 60s. For poems of actual social and political practice, in hybrid Afro-American style, were being torn from the dark, blood-drenched Dixie nights and the flame-sooted Watts and display-case rip-offs of Newarks across this spiritual wasteland, America, and published in obituary columns.[3] And Brothers Malcolm X and Martin Luther King, Jr., held in check the madness and their own murders, for a moment, through threats of retaliatory self-defense and radical nonviolence, in their turns, though Nixon, in the end, clambered across the mounds of made-in-America corpses to take the seat from where he now pushes buttons marked "Indochina," while ushering impatient, though conservative, Black politicos to the back of "benign neglect."

In the 60s, Black leadership transmitted visions of nationhood. Concrete images, asphalt smooth and stainless as steel, projected the freedom land, coating negro visions as never before, shuttering the sissy myths of the degenerate end-product of Western civilization. And colored people knew they were black, unique, separate, and had a future. For paeans of Blackness were videoed throughout Black America, between the staccato snipe of the assassin's slug, and the Black folk believed, as they are told to do, in the social, political, and cultural profundity of that most dramatic of eras. For they then had martyrs as immaculate as Jesus.

But not all the drama then was in the TV slap of a pigstick upside some sister's head in front of an Alabama courthouse, or the *Life* magazine punch of shotgun pellets deflating the heart of a Black thirteen-year-old for the crime of highsidin' among the flames of Burn Baby Burn U.S.A.[4]

No, when the shit went down under the palms on 103rd & Central, there were those of us standing upon a small stage, some miles north of

---

Yoruba tribe of Harlem: In the early 1960s, Baba Oserjiman Adefumi founded the Harlem Yoruba Temple, which, like the nearby Olatunji Center, devoted itself to the exploration of the Yoruba culture of southwestern Nigeria and profoundly impacted the Black Arts Movement.

3. Flame-sooted Watts and display-case rip-offs of Newarks: In August 1965, a routine traffic stop in South Central Los Angeles sparked a riot that lasted for six days, resulting in massive property damage, thousands of arrests, and thirty-four deaths. A similar event led to three days of violence in Newark, New Jersey, during the summer of 1967.

4. Burn Baby Burn: Coined by H. Rap Brown (1943–), now Jamil Abdullah Al-Amin, in 1967 while national director of The Student Nonviolent Coordinating Committee. Also the title of a poem by Marvin X.

Chief Parker, looking up into bewildered, mostly white faces, explaining why *Clara's Ole Man* might give them some insight as to why the City of Angels was burning that night.[5] And they pleaded ignorance of not understanding the play or why Black people were ready to destroy everything that they cherished, and left soon to invest in guard dogs, .30–06s, and security gates, being the good Americans that they were. (Though the night wasn't entirely wasted: There was enough dough in the box office that night to send bail money to a cousin caught on South Broadway [Watts] with a couch on his back, and to call around about a friend who got busted for burning down a bank, but is now a pre-med student at U.C.L.A.)

Those were dramatic times that we Black theater creators set about dramatizing. Black theater then was to be a revolutionary instrument of change. Not only did we have in hand manifestos of Black artistic, aesthetic, and cultural revolution, but a body of plays from the visions of the newer Black playwrights: Imamu Baraka (LeRoi Jones), Marvin X, Ben Caldwell, Ron Milner, Jimmie Garrett, Sonia Sanchez, and others who have since made some impact upon Black radical aesthetics and innovations to the Black theatrical form. But more important, in those times of action and activists, when the needs were said to be *relevancy* in everything, there were emerging theater groups, all a product of their collective place in history, and carrying some germs of Black consciousness, and bent on effecting revolutionary change. Black Arts [Repertory Theatre/School] (Harlem), Concept East, Black Arts/West, The Black House, Spirit House, The Free Southern Theater, and The New Lafayette Theatre had little to do with or use for predetermined theory or intellectual posturing. Then, as now, the needs of our generation were couched in terms which demanded definite action. Those of us then not playing revolutionary cowboys and pigs out in the really wild, wild West were touring through Lynchland, Mississippi (as were Roscoe Orman, Gary Bolling, and Gilbert Moses, now of the New Lafayette and the Negro Ensemble Company, respectively), or sweating out long, hot summers in store-front theaters in uptight places with names like New Orleans, Detroit, Chicago, Newark, and Harlem. As the saying goes, we Black theater creators, those of us working with and for *the people*, "paid our dues" through revolutionary struggle, by *creative practice*.

---

5. 103rd and Central: a street corner near the epicenter of the Watts uprising. Chief Parker: William H. Parker (1905–66). Appointed chief of the Los Angeles Police Department in 1950, he oversaw what many see as the militarization of police tactics, which led indirectly to the Watts uprising.

In the course of that brief period, the still functioning old men of the Black-theater movement—Imamu Baraka, Marvin X, Robert Macbeth, and myself—have had collectively and singularly half a dozen theaters shot out from under us (with genuine U.S.-made pistols pointed)—no stage joke here—or lost through ghetto fire. We have already seen the fire next time, dig? So, if some of the groups seem unduly close-knit and "parochial" today, there are historical reasons of survival that we have evolved special methods of work and life through social and artistic creative practice.

And my mentioning particular people and groups is not done to play down the efforts of numerous other important theater workers and institutions that presently work from under the Black umbrella because it's currently faddish, but in truth, most of the newer are derivative of their predecessors or plainly unseasoned, and when some continue to insist upon being designated as *Negro*, in this time of Black consciousness, and on public record as being non- or against nationalism, but can only emotionally relate to America and Europe through some abstract romanticism of a return to a Greco-Roman master-slave ideal—well, one can merely abide by their freakish desires and wish these brothers well in their existential dilemma.

I have said all this to give the reader some clues as to where I might be coming from, so that my references—alien, true—might be somewhat identified and not completely confuse, for I am concerned with clarifying some images from my hard-earned Black theater consciousness within this discussion. For I feel that I have some things to communicate.

The reason that critics—Black/white/American—cannot decipher many of the symbols of Black theater is because the artists are consciously migrating to non-Western references. Even while theater, as it is done in America, has models of form and aesthetics found in pre-industrial and technological societies, those beginnings are traced from Greece. Black theater creators, those who have done some *homework*, realize that Greece and the West were civilized by Africans, a superior mingling of cultures from the motherland of humanity, sub-Sahara *Africa*, and that the contemporary Black aesthetics requires that these prototypic sources be exploited, conveyed, and translated to *the people* through Black stylistic, symbolic, and literal image/renditions. Thus, an innovative strain of Black Art is continually revitalized.

So, the critic, like the Black Western-worshipping intellectual and street-corner revolutionary, comes to Black theater ignorant of the profound heritage that some artists are tapping. These "thinkers," their minds forever damaged by white racism, would believe that contemporary Black revolutionary theater could provide a matrix for their projected delusions;

by weird example, Venus de Milo and Othello copulating in a freaked/out Howard Johnson motel while shrieking passages from Chairman Mao upon orgasm.[6] What a useless bunch in a people's theater, alienated from the people who are using their instinctive folk/sense to rediscover all that they ever knew from the beginnings of mankind! The most perceptive of this breed that brings its smug mind to Black theater may merely distinguish the exterior edges of a deep dream, while blinded to the interior sense of this altered reality. But there is growth among certain Black and, surprisingly, white critics, which shows that some wish to evolve also with the theater of the immediate future. Though there is a trivial tragedy on the black/side: Two Black critics, more accomplished and conceptually endowed than others, are ambivalent concerning whether they will regard Black dramatic criticism seriously and not degenerate into professional press agentry.

Some of the obvious elements that make up the alphabet of the secret language used in Black theater are, naturally, rhythm (black, blues, African); the racial consciousness and subconsciousness of Third World peoples; Black Cultural Nationalism, Black Revolutionary Nationalism, and traditional Black people's familial nationalism; dance, as in Black life style and patterns; Black religion in its numerous forms (gospel, negro spiritualism, to African spirit, sun, moon, stars, and ancestor worship); Black astrology, numerology, and symbolism; Black mysticism, magic, and myth-science; also, history, fable, and legend, vodoun ritual-ceremony, Afro-American nigger street styles; and, of course, Black music.

Robert Macbeth, director of The New Lafayette Theatre, needs to be quoted here: "The music, the literature, the architecture and design art, and the art of human movement and singing. When these arts are performed together, in concert, it is called theatre."

When Robert Macbeth and I began talking in the summer of '67 of how to build a Black theater ensemble company, we committed ourselves to moving away from European references for our art and lives.

Macbeth had read one of my plays in manuscript, sought out my whereabouts, and called me in Oakland, California. I agreed to come east and work with the new theater, The New Lafayette, that he was just starting on a shoe string and hard-borrowed cash earned by *Black people*.

At that time I was preparing to leave the country. Immediately prior to

---

6. Chairman Mao: Mao Zedong (1893–1976), leader of the Chinese communist revolution. *Quotations from Chairman Mao* was both popular and influential among Black Nationalists.

Macbeth's call, I had been working with Eldridge Cleaver, Marvin X, Imamu Baraka (LeRoi Jones), Sonia Sanchez, and numerous other Bay Area revolutionary nationalists in a project we called "Black House," a Black cultural-political institution. The political factions fell out with the cultural and artistic members over coalition with white radicals. The Black artists told Cleaver that Black Art and white people do not go together; Cleaver said that Culture is a Gun. He brought in a goon squad to enforce party discipline; in fact, brother was fighting brother. (But in looking back, one can check out the paranoid romanticism, after reading Bakunin's *Revolutionary Catechism*, published in pamphlet form by The Party, under Cleaver's editorship.)[7]

The Black House fell; the Black Revolutionary Artists were the single body able to maintain a community institution of that standard, dedicated to positive community education and cultural-political organization.

So, there I was with a dozen finished plays, or more, having a recent history of four theater groups that my plays had built swept away in the Black revolutionary emotionalism and resulting fratricide of the 60s, a fresh score on my rap sheet, and a lot of bitterness.

Some of the Black Arts approaches and techniques that Marvin X and I had developed in revolutionary theater and literature workshops on the Coast were brought with me to Harlem when Macbeth sent me a ticket. With Macbeth, a creative genius, providing a strongly structured working situation, building a Black artistic complex from the bottom, teaching the company members and myself from his considerable theater lore, while exercising a creative will to organize thirty talented minds for a collective effort of the highest attainment, the New Lafayette Theatre has evolved to this point in history.

History may define Black theater's social function, but being near the center, I can only believe, like others, that Black theater's social function is immensely important. Being a past organizer of Black street theater, agit-prop drama, guerrilla theater, and revolutionary Black theater groups, I realize that we artists did what we could do best at the time. The activity was part of the *creative practice* of the social and cultural milieu, and conditions must be right for every type of action. It must be right especially for revolution.

Bobby Seale, long interested in the social function of art and media,

---

7. Bakunin's *Revolutionary Catechism:* Originally published in 1866, Mikhail Bakunin's (1817–76) text, now attributed to Sergei Nechayev (1847–82), concerns the immediate problems of the international anarchist revolution.

was an actor in one of the early Black revolutionary theater groups, before he "went for the pig."[8] (Yes, Bobby played the militant roles.) From working with Bobby as an artist, I am unable to believe that he could, psychologically, murder another Black man. I knew him as a natively gifted actor, badly in need of direction, but never a killer, unless defending his family and community. Some crummy politician talked Bobby Seale into jail, plus his own artlessness, and for the lack of values of some revolutionary political hustlers his last role, like Brother Rap's, might be militant martyr.[9]

The conditions must be created for sweeping social and cultural change. It is the Black artist's creative duty to plant, nurture, and spread the seeds of change. It is a deadly serious way of life to make some small contribution in this area of human endeavor which has an extremely high mortality rate. And there is little chance to contribute to this activity—altering human consciousness—when dead through revolutionary, reactionary, or ritual suicide, except that the work survives and is propagated. In Black theater, this continuity is achieved through *creative struggle:* ruthless dedication in creation of collective forms that will survive any single individual's life.

Working from these premises, then, Black theater becomes a citadel of evolving consciousness. True, this phrase has a noble ring, but that is what certain Black theater creators are about, *to inspire creation of the nation;* the playwrights not excepted.

(To make an open secret more public: In the area of playwriting, Ed Bullins, at this moment in time, is almost without peer in America—black, white, or imported. I admit this, not merely from vanity, but because there is practically no one in America but myself who would dare.)

The 20th Century Cycle is the title given to a group of plays about the lives of some Afro-Americans. When completed, there will be twenty plays in number, each of them individually intended to be fully realized works of art. There is already talk of this collective project surpassing greatness in its scope, though the work is not that astonishing relative to Bullins's abilities. He has now written more than thirty plays; being a comparatively

---

8. Bullins's note: "'Went *or* go for the pig' is a Black street-language term out of Philly (50s), meaning 'to be *chumped off.*' Neither term included in *Dictionary of Afro-American Slang,* compiled by Clarence Major (International Publishers, New York, 1970)." The "Black revolutionary theater group" was Black Arts/West, where Seale played, among other roles, Paul in *How Do You Do* and the troubled intellectual in Marvin X's *Flowers for the Trashman.*

9. In 1970–71, Seale and eight others (the so-called New Haven Nine) were tried for the torture and murder of a fellow Black Panther suspected of being a police informant. Seale would be acquitted by a hung jury. H. Rap Brown was in hiding during 1970, eluding charges of inciting a 1967 riot in Cambridge, Maryland.

young artist, there is little reason to believe that he won't easily surpass his early work, in depth of vision and in pure quantity.[10]

Many of Bullins' plays were written for the New Lafayette Theatre because he has worked as a writer to build one of the finest Black community institutions of its kind in the world. Not only has the theater inspired and sustained him as an artist, but, with the association of a practicing body of Black artists, there has been an untold influence upon his work. His work and the New Lafayette's cannot be exactly separated or identified. There is no other place, to his knowledge, where a collective entity of Black artistic knowledge, talent, craft, experience, and commitment exists. In many ways, the New Lafayette Theatre is the true Black theater.)

The manner that the New Lafayette approaches productions is completely different from those of commercial theater. Commercial Black/white theater would find it physically impossible to achieve what a precision trained ensemble group like the New Lafayette can, though I discover at times a need to see some of my work done elsewhere, and there are many dynamite plays of other Black playwrights the theater is now presenting.

Black theater is part of all theater, whether this fact is liked by Black theater creators or denied by ignorant Americans. Black theater's evolution to a visible force in the arts and the cultural life of Black America has changed theater very profoundly, though this change is not yet immediately evident to the white theatergoer.

For one, in Black theater the audience is different. This audience contains all the elements that will create the revolutionary changes among Black people of the near future. This difference causes the audience to have separate needs, desires, and behavior. And two, for this audience, the material must be original and innovative. Because of these differences, the criteria of what encompasses theater is radically altered in America.

In speaking of some Black playwrights from where Black theater begins: Imamu Baraka has already received my full regard and respect; J. E. Gaines is the best playwright I know; watch Richard Wesley; Melvin Van Peebles is boss; Charles Gordone is separated from reality; Lonne Elder III can, perhaps, quietly disappear with grace; Lorraine Hansberry preceded contemporary Black theater, which isn't negative at all, merely fact; Ron Milner needs to write some more plays; Jimmy Garrett, likewise; Jennie Franklin is a queen; Sonia 15X, Martie Charles, and Adrienne Kennedy are

---

10. *The 20th Century Cycle:* For a discussion, see the headnote to *In the Wine Time* in this volume.

the revolution; and Douglas Turner Ward has my fondest hopes as an all-round theater man—from providing home bases for Black talents such as Gilbert Moses and Michael Schultz to providing Derek Walcott's inspiring *Dream on Monkey Mountain* with an excellent production, Brother Ward's *creative practice* is evolving in the Blackest sense.

A few other Black artists that interest me: I have spoken of Robert Macbeth—though accused of acting like the God of Black Theater, in truth, he is nothing but its Master, for all of its elements are under his control. There's no male actor working anywhere finer than Sonny Jim—his voice alone would rupture most white actors, if any dared to step upon the same stage with him.[11] And Whitman Mayo is almost unequaled in the variety of things he can do upon stage. There are others, but I shall leave them for the future, if I should have reason to introduce another book in this manner . . .

The future of Black theater will be in its evolution into a profound instrument of altering the slave mentality of Black Americans. In an evil, white world of ever-shifting values and reality, for the Black man there must be a sanctuary for re-creation of the Black spirit and African identity. In racist, madmen America, the Black theater has carved out this part of the future for itself. If all around us are losing their heads (spilled out by assassins on Harlem intersections, for some), it may be provident for the Black artist to attempt to hold onto his own, which is a conservative impulse, true, but radical in terms of heretical viewpoints. Political theorists of the Black Arts are confused and disappointing. They sloganeer that Art and Politics Should Be Identical—be serious! Today's politics are the politics of the pig: to murder all dissent and opposition. Black Art is to express what is best in us and for us Black people. Like the people, the people's art and artists have forever survived any opportunistic political expediency of some Fat Mouthin' leader. Black theater is not a Theater of the Lip, as is the style of Black/white hustling America, but a people's theater dedicated to the continuing survival of Black people. And the artists will continue to evolve with the people, swim within their mass, and emerge through creation after creation. For we know: "The dogs may bark, but the caravan passes on."

---

11. Sonny Jim: J. E. Gaines.

Should Black Actors Play Chekhov?

(1973)

It would be a pyrrhic gesture to summarily put down Anton Chekhov because he comes from a distant time and place and a race different from mine. This 19th-century Russian playwright's masterpiece, *The Cherry Orchard*, is being offered in an intriguing production of a near-Black cast at that totally American institution, the Public Theater.[1] Upon hearing of the production concept before attending a performance, I thought the idea abominable, but the man's work has survived revolutions, wars, and evolution, so one must remember that Chekhov was read and studied even before one matured enough to read and study himself.

Nor should the near-Black cast be rudely dismissed because of preconceived assumptions concerning Europeans, Black/white Art and correctness. For among the uneven company are several of the most gifted and important performers now working upon the stages of America—Black, white, or imported.

Frankly, before I attended a performance, I had my mind practically made up. I was ready for another weird and probably dismal evening in the theater. And as the play began with the Russian period music lilting in from the wings, I sank down into my seat and groaned to my companion that there would be four acts of this. And, strangely, that is what helps the evening to work so well—the length, the substance, and the enduring drive of a completed work of this strength.

First published in the *New York Times*, February 4, 1973. Copyright © 1973 by The New York Times Co. Reprinted with permission.

    1. Public Theater: In 1967, New York City's Astor Library Building was granted to the New York Shakespeare Festival and named the Public Theater. It was renamed the Joseph Papp Public Theater in 1992.

For the first act and a half, I fought grimly against falling asleep, or even yawning, but I was more than skeptical by now of wringing any enjoyment or relevancy from Chekhov. I was bored. My mind and temperament were yearning to exit when something was said by Gloria Foster to James Earl Jones that turned me around. Perhaps it was that line delivered with startling understatement, "You shouldn't go to plays, my friend, but look at yourself . . ." And from that moment, I was in the play but in a very interesting way.

I kept looking and listening and the reality turned on me. My mind continued cautioning me that this was turn-of-the-century Russia being played by Americans of that cultural/social/historical/ethnic minority known as Blacks. But somehow I was translating Post Reconstruction Southern American Plantation.

It was as if the American Reconstruction/Revolution had been successful to a point: The Blacks had gotten their forty acres, their mule, and more.[2] But the leaders of the movement, the Black Bourgeoisie, like Madame Ranevsky, were morally, materially, and spiritually bankrupt. In fact, the House Slaves had acquired the Big House. And they played the Masters with so much more flair, style, and soul than the absentee landlords who were out in the wings, no doubt, counting the receipts. It seemed so right, especially when one of the dark Yard or Field Slaves would mutter that things hadn't changed for them: They were "still with the master." And the old slave, Firs, died there too, in that cemetery of the mind.

The obvious parallels are there: Russian peasant/Southern slave, and the servant, serf, landowner, summer resident classes could easily have Dixie equivalents. And the slave-master/serf-owner metaphor can be readily drawn in that classic stereotype of imperialism, but there are numerous subtle and ironic elements operating within this production that make it special in its own way.

For one, there is the uniqueness of the color casting scheme used. The cast's shadings almost run the gamut found throughout Black America. From the fair, aristocratic ladies of the inner household to the rich, warm tones of James Earl Jones that suggest a peasant origin to the dark coloring of an "authentic" African who played a Field Nigger, now a slavish house servant, it was mainly effective.

The clever appearance of the Queen of Spades during the governess's

---

2. Forty acres, their mule, and more: Forty acres and a mule were promised to newly liberated African-American slaves by Union General William T. Sherman in a Special Field Order of 1865. Commonly associated with the land-for-slavery reparations movement.

card tricks, the dramatic devices and conventions of the times, i.e., pur-loined letters, hidden coins, and false mannerisms, blended together into the fabric of this strange production.

One image that continues to recur in my mind is that of the handsome, young Black man playing his violin for his social "betters" during the party scene. The music was Russian, but I kept waiting for the blues. And I knew, if the fantasy was complete, then this musician would soon put away his instrument and take his customary place outside at the hitching rack, wait-ing to be handed the reins of the guests' mules.

The Cherry Orchard is a cemetery of human failure and class arrogance. Even if the House Slaves were to take over the Big House but ape the deca-dence and dissolution of the Slavemasters, they would still not have their freedom. For if history is repetitive, then the truth is that before freedom, promised by each succeeding revolution, there is not integration among disparate factions, there is social disintegration.

There is little more that I can say than go see *The Cherry Orchard* with its near-Black cast. Miss Foster is a hypnotic performer—she'll gobble up your attention. And James Earl Jones is brash, almost niggerish in power, in portraying the once-serf Lopahin, but demonstrating a bridled strength. I can say little else, for one must see to believe.

From The New Lafayette Theatre Presents

(1974)

THE BLACK DRAMA OF NOW

Two of the positive characteristics of contemporary Black writing have been the attempt at honesty by the newer writers and the turning away from addressing Black writing to white audiences and readership.

In the past decade, the Black writer/artist/intellectual has been able to acquire an urban Black audience in the Black theater, for the independent and Hollywood-type Black film, and a wider range of Black readership for Black poetry, fiction, and drama.

In the early 1960s, with the advent of the new Black nationalism as espoused by Malcolm X and the Nation of Islam, the contemporary Black writer was influenced to migrate psychically away from strictly European values in his art and aesthetics. The Black people, in their struggle to survive in hostile white America, through revolutionary or reactionary means, again became worthy subject matter for the artists, especially when the examples of the Cuban Revolution, the African Liberation movement, the Civil Rights movement, the Black militant/revolutionary/student movement were spread by the media and influenced, perhaps even created, the Black arts movement of today.

INTRODUCTION

The Black masses were sought out in their ghettos and enthusiastically set upon by the new Black revolutionary artists through almost seemingly

First published in *The New Lafayette Theatre Presents*, edited by Ed Bullins (New York: Anchor, 1974).

spontaneous eruptions of Black street plays. An inevitable round of benefits appeared with revolutionary rhetoric and rap interlinked by Black revolutionary theater, music, dance, and art, to aid Black political prisoners that the social and political climate of the times generated. Black arts festivals proliferated, with numerous conferences and symposiums created to discuss criteria for evaluating Black arts, the role of the artists in the movement, and the creation of an alternate Black communications and media system throughout the Black communities of America. New Black magazines specialized in poetry, Black theater, Black scholarship, and Black community and Pan-African issues. The Black revolutionary theater did its thing upon the at-first makeshift stages of Harlem, San Francisco, Detroit, and New Orleans, while the new Black poets institutionalized the street rhetoric of the day, as Black arts centers and groups grew from Baltimore to Santa Barbara, having in common activities and arts efforts that incorporated African motif and Afro-American soul ethos, a commonality of words couched in Black ideological expression and using a Third World iconology.

The present phase of Black writing is in the dialectic period of evolution. Black artists are discussing ideas, discoursing about the problems and concerns of their Black audience, readers, and peers, among a body of evolved Black consciousness; hence, it is a dialectic of Black contemporary literature/art/theater in which this generation's artists are engaged.

In the recent past, preoccupation in addressing mainly social and political issues may have been Black literature's major flaw. Richard Wright, James Baldwin, and LeRoi Jones (now Imamu Baraka) have each in turn called for a Black literature that plumbed the human spirit for Black beings, but each has been mainly concerned by the social and political aspects of Black existence in America.

With present Black writers turned away from addressing an anticipated white readership and appealing the plight of Blackness in America to their masochistic delight, the literature has changed from a social-protest oriented form to one of a dialectical nature among Black people—*Black dialectics*—and this new thrust has two main branches—the *dialectic of change* and the *dialectic of experience*. The writers are attempting to answer questions concerning Black survival and future, one group through confronting the Black/white reality of America, the other by heightening the dreadful white reality of being a modern Black captive and victim.

These two major branches in the mainstream of the new Black creativity, the dialectic of change (once called "protest writing," surely, when confronting whites directly and angrily, then altered to what was called "Black revolutionary writing" when it shifted a decade ago through the pioneering work of Baraka away from a white audience to a Black) and the dialectic of experience (or being), sometimes merge, but *variety* and *power* in the overall work are the general rule. And there is little conflict among the artists within the forms.

The dialectic of change has a distinguished history founded in the slave narrative/abolitionist/protest phases of Black literature. The dialectic of experience has roots that antecede the arrival of Black slaves on this continent and is traceable to oral literatures of Africa and cultures of temperate-zone, non-European peoples. Both are strong strains in Black art and play vital functions in the Black ethos of Black American writing.

The six plays in this collection demonstrate the best dramatic writing of today coming out of the contemporary Black dialectic movement.

Richard Wesley's *Black Terror* is a play discussing the revolutionary ideas and situations of evolutionary change in the Black community among a cadre of revolutionaries. *And What If It Turned Up Heads*, by J. E. Gaines, perfectly represents the other side of this creative coin of Black dramatic writing. His character could almost be Richard Wright's symbolic "man who lived underground," but Jacob Jones is somehow more horribly real and grass-roots original.

The works of Goss, OyamO, Sanchez, and Bullins are fully realized works of the modern Black theater writers and are the best of the plays that are being done in the rising number of Black theaters throughout America and, sometimes, Off Broadway.[1]

---

1. In addition to the Wesley and Gaines plays named, the anthology includes Clay Goss's *On Being Hit*, OyamO's *His First Step*, Sonia Sanchez's *Uh, Uh; But How Do It Free Us?* and Bullins's *The Fabulous Miss Marie*.

An Open Letter to [D.W.]

(1976)

Dear Mr. [W.]:

I read your review of Neil Harris's new play *So Nice, They Named It Twice*, presently running at the Public Theater.

Frankly, I was dismayed and enraged by some of your comments. You write: "Very little of this [black lifestyle] rings true." I wonder if you are acquainted enough with black lifestyle to make such a presumptuous statement. You go on to say, "This [the play] doesn't appear to be a very convincing reflection of black life." Do you mean it doesn't appear to *you* to be a convincing reflection of black life? Well, *you* aren't qualified to say such a thing. You aren't black, nor do I believe that you can make that type of value judgment on a writer's work whose materials are the stuff of the existence he lives. You also say that you see "little purpose behind [the play]." Of course, *So Nice* is a depiction of black life in its gushing, throbbing realness. And your experience alienates you from that realness.

Neil Harris is a strong, vital, emerging stage talent of high caliber. He conceived his play to be an entertaining comedy on black life with serious subject matter. If you can't see that, then that only points up your cultural and racial myopia and elitist persuasion.

It comes down to this—are certain white newspaper critics qualified to review *all* black theater works? By qualified, I mean, are these critics knowledgeable and have empathy for the black aesthetic[1] to the degree

---

First published in the *The Soho Weekly News*, June 10, 1976.

   1. Black aesthetic: The philosophical system of the Black Arts Movement. See *The Black Aesthetic*, edited by Addison Gayle Jr. (Garden City, NY: Anchor, 1972).

that they can pass valid judgments on the work, or are the separate realities between the white cultural arbitrators (critics) and the black creative artists so disparate that the reality of the situation has caused an impossible gulf between the two camps? This critical crisis which exists in black theater today survives precisely because blacks do not have critical voices to speak for themselves in the nation's major media, and white critics apply standards which make them appear vindictive, ignorant, and reactionary toward new black work. These attitudes seem bent upon destruction of black creative potential.

Sincerely,
Ed Bullins

Black Theater

(1980)

When thinking of what to write about today's Black Theater, my first impulse is to be positive. To find and point out some encouraging signs and portents on the Black Theater landscape, to signal that a rainbow of hope has been sighted upon the Black theatrical horizon. But, alas, in my estimation, the once Garden of Eden of Black Creativity, Black Relevancy, Black Thought, the modern Black Theater, is now nothing but a pot-holed expanse, a desert of ineptness, dotted by a few oases of skill, craft, and art, but generally bleak, barren, and containing bitter elements, such as the amateur.

Where is the Black Theater which speaks to Blacks of Miami? I wanted to make something of this position. When I entered theater in 1965, I was told then that there was no such thing as Black Theater, which I refused to believe, so some of the Black artists of then and now went about the job of creating a Black Theater which would be indisputably recognized throughout the world, and even some distant segments of America, as being a product of us Black people, being our expression, our visions, our "thang." It was a theater which was meant to speak to Harlem, Watts, Oakland, and wherever Blacks found themselves oppressed in the small black corners of America.

But somehow, many of us modern Black creative pioneers must have succeeded too well. For now, almost everybody is doing something called "Black Theater." In fact, everything and anything with Blacks in it, from it, or of it is thrown in this grab-sack and tossed at the stage.[1] And at this

---

First published in *Other Stages*, July 10, 1980).

1. In it, from it, or of it: Recalls W. E. B. DuBois's axiomatic call for theater "about us," "by us," "for us," and "near us."

moment, the standards have become so appallingly mediocre that a veteran like myself nearly retches when viewing one out of three Black theater productions. Of course, there are some occasional good-to-brilliant works, done with high style and flair, but mostly Black Theater has become the refuge of the inept, the ill-prepared, the wrongly-conceived, and just plain embarrassing. There's a workshop theater saying: "Everybody should be allowed to fail." Well, maybe, but we don't have to make a cult of it, do we?

So, here we have Black Theater. Now, this instant, as you read this, the future looks dismal. Where's the money coming from? Where's the audience coming from? Blacks, especially in New York, will not support most of what's passing itself off as Black Theater—and why should they? I know their absence and apathy is blamed on ignorance or cultural backwardness, but they have been burned too often by "hot" crap and "hip" corn passing itself off as being the Second Coming of Malcolm X/Martin Luther King, Jr./Father Divine/Booker T. Washington and Diana Ross rolled into a "smash Black Hit!"—or so the commercials blare.[2]

Recently, I was muttering to myself about these grave philosophical matters at my desk at the New York Shakespeare Festival's Public Theater, when a friend of mine asked me if I had a hangover or something.[3] So I told him what was troubling me: Black Theater and its existential place in the modern moment.

He shrugged and told me that I was looking at things all wrong, that if I knew anything about theater like I pretended, that I would know that "Joseph Papp has made the single most impressive and important contribution to the emergence of Black Theater in America."[4]

Needless to say, I was astounded, confused, and put on the defensive. "How, how, how . . ." I attempted, but he went blithely on.

"As producer of the New York Shakespeare Festival, Joe Papp has presented 112 or more productions to date with Black, Hispanic, and Third World Artists."

"So!" I challenged.

He has presented these artists in a range of plays," continued my men-

2. Father Divine (1880?–1965): Regarded by his followers as a messiah, Fr. Major Jealous Divine founded the Universal Peace Mission Movement in 1914 in Sayville, New York, to help the downtrodden, especially African Americans. Diana Ross (1944–): African-American singer noted primarily for her work with the Motown group the Supremes, which scored an unparalleled twelve top-selling songs between 1965 and 1969.

3. New York Shakespeare Festival's Public Theater: The non-profit New York Shakespeare Festival was founded in 1954 to expose the public to theater, most notably with free performances in Central Park.

4. Joseph Papp (1921–91): American theatrical director and producer, founder the of New York Shakespeare Festival, and tireless promoter of off-Broadway theater.

tor. "From contemporary to the classic, from street theater to Shakespeare, ranging from *for colored girls who have considered suicide/when the rainbow is enuf*, *No Place To Be Somebody*, *The Taking of Miss Janie*, to Chekhov's *The Cherry Orchard*, Shakespeare's *Coriolanus*, the Greek classic *Electra*, and, oh yes, Brecht's *Mother Courage*."

"But what does that have to do with what I'm talking about?" I said. "Joe's a producer. He produces a lot of things, but to make such allegations? What about Douglas Turner Ward?[5] What about Woodie King?[6] What about a whole lot of people, including me?"

"Tut tut tut, my young friend," he continued. "What about all the writers, the impressive body of writers, that have emerged under Joseph Papp's patronage? There have been Ed Bullins, Alice Childress, Phillip Hayes Dean, Charles Gordone, Bill Gunn, Neil Harris, Adrienne Kennedy, Ron Milner, Miguel Piñero, Ntozake Shange, Derek Walcott, Richard Wesley, and Edgar White."

"Well, I see that I'm not going to get very far with you," I said, and started to go visit the water cooler.

"On the contrary, Ed," he said. "Be patient just a bit more. Do you know, with the ongoing support of Mr. Papp, these writers have created major theater works that have won a Pulitzer Prize (*No Place To Be Somebody*), New York Drama Critics Circle Awards (*Short Eyes* and *The Taking of Miss Janie*) and numerous Obie Awards."[7]

He was beginning to get to me, because I stopped protesting out of reflex and began to take notes.

"When one considers that each of these 112 or more productions employed an average of more than twenty writers, actors, stage managers, directors, technicians, and musicians, Joe Papp's influence and impact on Black Theater becomes quite apparent," he told me.

"I have to think about all this," I told him.

"Well, you do that, Ed," he said. "And please do get back to me. I just so love controversy.'"

"You have some strong arguments," I told him. "But I'd like to put things more in perspective . . . you know, concerning Black Theater."

"What perspective?" he demanded. "Don't be afraid to look at the facts and admit that there is a lot of truth in my thesis!"

---

5. Douglas Turner Ward (1930–): Actor, playwright, producer, and co-founder in 1967 of the Negro Ensemble Company, the first all-black theater company in the United States.

6. Woodie King (1937–): American director, essayist, producer, co-founder in 1960 of Detroit's Concept East Theatre, and founder in 1970 of the New Federal Theatre and the National Black Touring Circuit.

7. Obie Awards: Since 1956, granted by the *The Village Voice* to outstanding off-Broadway theater and theater artists.

"Who's afraid?" I asked.

"Remember," he went on. "Joe has never feared to put his money where his sentiments and convictions lay. He has made a valiant effort to present new American writers and, in the case of Miguel Piñero and you, Ed Bullins, gifted Black and Hispanic writers at Lincoln Center."[8]

He went on and on, and I went away to think. I thought of a new beginning for my Black Theater piece: "When asked to comment on the current Black Theater scene, I dove at it much like a drake approaching a lake. I felt that, if there was still motion in the Black Theater ocean, I should at least float.[9] (Quack! Quack!) . . ." Finally, I tore it up and decided to begin again.

---

8. Miguel Piñero's (1946–88) *Short Eyes* was staged at New York City's prestigious Lincoln Center for the Performing Arts in 1974 and Bullins's *The Duplex* and *The Fabulous Miss Marie* in 1971 and 1979.

9. Motion in the Black Theater ocean: Recalls the adage, "It ain't the size of the ship that makes the wave, it's the motion of the ocean."

Chronology

by Mike Sell and Gabriel A. Smith

1935   Born July 2 to Bertha Marie (Queen) Bullins in Philadelphia, Pennsylvania. Attends several, largely white elementary schools, summers in Maryland Eastern Shore farm country, and spends a year at a black middle school in Denton, MO.

1952–55   Drops out of Ben Franklin High School in Philadelphia, holds menial jobs and hangs out on the streets of North Philly for more than a year, and joins the navy, where he serves from 1952 to 1955. Wins a shipboard amateur lightweight boxing tournament and considers turning professional. He personally encounters racism for the first time when he is made a ship's steward despite the fact that his IQ score is in the upper percentile of recruits. He begins a program of self-education through reading. Shortly after his discharge, he is stabbed in the throat while protecting a cousin and her husband from a street attack and has a near-death experience. During his recovery, he realizes that there are better paths to success than physical toughness.

1958   Moves from Philadelphia to Los Angeles, earns a GED degree, and enrolls in Los Angeles City College, where he begins writing short stories and editing the campus literary journal, the *Citadel*. Begins rooming and associating with a cadre of young African-American students and civil rights activists, including Maulana Ron Karenga, founder of the radical organization US and creator of Kwanzaa.

1961	Begins writing in earnest, mainly fiction, essays, and poetry.
1963	Publishes "The Polished Protest: Aesthetics and the Black Writer" in the magazine *Contact*. Affected strongly by the assassination of John F Kennedy. His sympathy for the nonviolence of the Civil Rights movement begins to erode.
1964	Moves to the San Francisco Bay area and enrolls in a writing program at San Francisco State College. Holds various jobs in the theater and begins writing plays.
1965	Shocked into militancy by the assassination of Malcolm X. Becomes discouraged at not being produced, but sees Amiri Baraka's *Dutchman* and *The Slave* and experiences a creative surge. *Clara's Ole Man, How Do You Do?* and *Dialect Determinism, or, The Rally* open on the night of the Watts rebellion in Los Angeles (a triple bill at the Firehouse Repertory Theatre, San Francisco).
1966	Cofounds Black Arts/West in San Francisco with Marvin X (Mavin Jackmon), Carl Bossiere, and Duncan Barber, and stages plays with San Francisco State students, including Danny Glover and Bobby Seale. *The Theme Is Blackness* (San Francisco). *It Has No Choice* (San Francisco). *A Minor Scene* (San Francisco). *The Game of Adam and Eve* (with Shirley Tarbell, produced Los Angeles). *A Street Play* (San Francisco). "Theatre of Reality" (*Negro Digest*).
1966–67	Cofounds Black House with Marvin X and Eldridge Cleaver. Bobby Seale, Huey Newton, and the newly formed Black Panther Party are soon enlisted to provide security. Though later purged from Black House, with Marvin X, on orders from Cleaver for refusing to put white radicals in leadership positions, Bullins serves briefly as the Black Panthers' minister of culture. He coproduces benefit shows for the Panthers at Bill Graham's Fillmore Auditorium (San Francisco), the Fillmore East (New York City), and the Roundhouse Theatre (London). After teaming up with Baraka and Sonia Sanchez at Black House, initiates other theater activities in the Bay Area but grows dissatisfied and considers leaving the country.
1967	Invited by Robert Macbeth to New York City to write plays for the New Lafayette Theatre. Begins six-year association as playwright in residence, heads its playwriting workshop, and edits the house journal, *Black Theatre*. Receives an American Place Theatre grant. Writes *Black Commercial #2* (unproduced) and

"The So-called Western Avant-Garde Drama" (essay published in the *Liberator*).

1968   Becomes associate director of the New Lafayette Theatre. Spends the summer in London after original New Lafayette burns due to arson. Wins the first of four Rockefeller Foundation grants and the Vernon Rice Drama Desk Award for the American Place Theatre production of *Goin' a Buffalo*, *A Son Come Home*, and *The Electronic Nigger*. *In the Wine Time* (New Lafayette Theatre, New York) and *The Corner* (Boston). "the electronic nigger meets the gold dust twins: Clifford Mason Talks with Robert Macbeth and Ed Bullins" in *Black Theatre #1*. "The Eugene O'Neill Memorial Theater Foundation" in *Black Theatre #1*. Edits a special issue on Black theater for *TDR: The Drama Review* (vol. 40), which becomes the "Bible" of the Black Arts Movement.

1969   The New Lafayette Theatre begins producing theater rituals, and attendance begins to decline. Publishes *The Gentleman Caller* (New York and London), *We Righteous Bombers* (as Kingsley B. Bass Jr., New Lafayette Theatre, New York), *The American Flag Ritual: A Short Play or Film Scenario* (unproduced), and *Go Go: A Story of Dancing Girls* (with Bill Lathan, unproduced). Publishes *A Ritual to Bind Together and Strengthen Black People So That They Can Survive the Long Struggle Ahead* (collective composition of New Lafayette Theatre, New York), *Five Plays* (as editor, Bobbs Merrill), "Lafayette Theatre: Reaction to *Bombers*" (modified transcript of panel debate in *Black Theatre #4*), "What Lies Ahead for the Blackamericans?" (in *Black World*), and *New Plays from the Black Theater: An Anthology* (as editor, Bantam).

1970   New Lafayette playwriting workshop is shut down after members stage their plays, with Bullins's permission, on the workshop's budget. Divisions grow between the Lafayette's acting and management units and the workshop group. Bullins attempts to be neutral but finally sides with the parent company. Public clashes with Jules Irving of the Lincoln Center over a production of *The Duplex: A Black Love Fable in Four Movements*, directed by Gilbert Moses. Writes *The Pig Pen* (American Place Theatre, New York), *Street Sounds* (La Mama ETC, New York), *The Helper* (New York), *A Ritual to Raise the Dead and Foretell the Future* (collective composition of the New Lafayette Theatre,

New York), *The Man Who Dug Fish* (New York), *To Raise the Dead and Foretell the Future* (collective composition of the New Lafayette Theatre, New York), *It Bees Dat Way* (London), *The Devil Catchers* (New Lafayette Theatre, New York), *A Black Time for Black Folk* (collective composition of the New Lafayette Theatre, New York), *The Bottom* (commissioned by Joseph Papp, unproduced), and "Comments on Production of *In New England Winter*" (*New York Times*). Publishes *Four Dynamite Plays* (Morrow).

1971   Wins Obie Award for distinguished playwriting and Black Arts Alliance Award for *The Fabulous Miss Marie* (New Lafayette Theatre, New York) and *In New England Winter* (New Federal Theatre, New York). Receives first Guggenheim Fellowship for playwriting. Attends Pan-African Cultural Festival in Algeria. Writes *The Psychic Pretenders: A Black Magic Show* (New Lafayette Theatre, New York). Publishes *The Hungered One: Early Writings* (Morrow).

1972   Receives first of two National Endowment for the Arts playwriting grants. Coordinates playwriting workshop at the New York Shakespeare Festival. Writes *You Gonna Let Me Take You Out Tonight, Baby* (New York) and *Next Time . . .* (New York).

1973   New Lafayette Theatre dissolves. Playwright in residence, American Place Theatre. Receives grant from Creative Artists Public Service Program. Writes *House Party* (music by Pat Patrick, New York), *One-Minute Commercial* (unproduced), *The Play of the Play* (unproduced), *A Short Play for a Small Theater* (unproduced), and *State Office Bldg. Curse: A Scenario to Ultimate Action* (unproduced). Publishes *The Theme Is Blackness: The Corner and Other Plays*, which includes "Black Theatre: The 70's—Evolutionary Changes" (Morrow); *The Reluctant Rapist* (Harper); "Black Theatre Art—Structured Black Collaboration: A Discussion between Romare Bearden and Ed Bullins" (*News of the American Place Theatre*); a review of *A Hero Ain't Nothin' but a Sandwich* by Alice Childress" (*New York Times Book Review*), and "Should Black Actors Play Chekhov?" (*New York Times*).

1973–83 Serves as playwright in residence and production director at various theaters and as a playwriting instructor at various colleges and universities.

1974	Edits *The New Lafayette Theatre Presents: Plays with Aesthetic Comments by 6 Black Playwrights* (Doubleday).
1975	Wins Obie Award for distinguished playwriting and the New York Drama Critics Circle Award for *The Taking of Miss Janie* (New Federal Theatre, New York). Writes *A Teacup Full of Roses* (screenplay, unproduced). Publishes *Malcolm: '71, or Publishing Blackness* (in *Black Scholar*). "Dirty Story" (*Black World*), and "Open Letter to Joan Little: 'Stay Off Fast Track'" (*New York Amsterdam News*).
1976	A review by Erika Munk of *Jo Anne!!!* and *The Reluctant Rapist* in the *The Village Voice* marks the start of rancorous relations between Bullins and the alternative theater establishment. He begins writing musicals, starting with *Home Boy* (music by Aaron Bell, New York) and *Women I Have Known* (production concept by Robert Macbeth, music by Pat Patrick, American Place Theatre, New York). Writes *The Mystery of Phyllis Wheatley* (New Federal Theatre, New York), *I Am Lucy Terry: A Historical Fantasy for Young Americans* (American Place Theatre, New York), *Jo Anne!!!* (New York), *The Taking of Miss Janie* (screenplay, unproduced), and "An Open Letter to [D.W.]" (*Soho Weekly News*).
1977	Writes *Daddy* (New Federal Theatre, New York), *Sepia Star, or Chocolata Comes to the Cotton Club* (music and lyrics by Mildred Kayden, New York), *Storyville* (music and lyrics by Mildred Kayden, La Jolla, CA), *C'mon Back to Heavenly House* (Amherst, MA), and "No Nothin'" (*New York Times*).
1978	Son Edward Jr. dies. Writes *Michael* (Northeastern University, Boston), *Steve and Velma* (Northeastern University, Boston), *City Preacher* (teleplay, unproduced), and *You Can't Keep a Good Man Down* (unproduced).
1980	Writes *The Work Gets Done* (Boston), *You Gonna Let Me Take You Out Tonight, Baby?* (New York), "Black Theatre" (in *Other Stages*), "An Open Statement on the Review of *Leavings*" in response to Thulani Davis (*Village Voice*), and *Hunk* (unproduced).
1981	Returns to California. Writes *Satchmo: An American Musical Legend* (unproduced), "Celebrating La Mama's 20th" (in *The Villager*), and "On Baraka" (in *Other Stages*).
1982	Writes *Blacklist* (unproduced) and "Playwrights Workshop at the Public Theatre" (in *Other Stages*).

1984	Writes *City Preacher* (San Francisco) and *The Hungered One* (radio play, produced in Berkeley).
1984–88	Serves as a lecturer at Sonoma State University and the University of California, Berkeley.
1985	Writes *High John da Conquerer: The Musical* (Berkeley), *Dr. Geechee and the Blood Junkies: A Modern Horror Yarn* (San Francisco City College), *Dirty Pool* (unproduced), *Ethiopian Comedy* (unproduced), *Snickers* (unproduced), and *A Teacup Full of Roses* (unproduced).
1986	Writes *Dr. Geechee and the Blood Junkies* (screenplay, unproduced) and "Black Theatre Roundup" (*Black Theatre Newsletter*).
1987	Writes *A Sunday Afternoon* (with Marshall Borden, San Francisco) and *Sinning in Sun City* (with Selaelo Maredi, San Francisco).
1988	Founds the Edward Bullins Jr. Memorial Theatre in Oakland, California, then moves it to live-work space in Emeryville. The group produces more than a dozen plays, including work by Bullins, Amiri Baraka, and Ishmael Reed. Begins publication of the *Black Theatre Newsletter*, which features the work of Lorraine Hansberry and Ntozake Shange Directs *Bullins Does Bullins* (Oakland, CA).
1989	Loma Prieta earthquake damages the Bullins Memorial Theatre. With assistance from the government and the Black United Way, it reopens, but audiences dwindle. Bullins earns bachelor's degree from Antioch University, San Francisco, in liberal studies (English and playwriting). Writes *I Think It's Gonna Work Out Fine: A Rock and Roll Fable* (with Idris Ackamoor, Rhodessa Jones, and Brian Freeman, San Francisco).
1991	Writes *Salaam, Huey Newton, Salaam* (based on the writings of Marvin X, New York), which is included in *Best American Short Plays of 1990*; and *American Griot* (with Idris Ackamoor, New York).
1992	Writes *Raining Down Stars: Sepia Stories of the Dark Diaspora* (with Idris Ackamoor and Rhodessa Jones, San Francisco), *Judge Tom Strikes Back: A Seriously Vicious Satire* (unproduced), "Baseball Bill" (in *Ink Margins*), "Miss Minnie and Her New Hairdo" (fiction in *Discourse*), and "Two Days Shie . . ." (in the Contemporary Authors Autobiography Series).

1993	*New/Lost Plays by Ed Bullins*, edited by Ethel Pitts Walker (That New Publishing Company) is published. Writes *Emergency Report* (with Rhodessa Jones and Danny Duncan, San Francisco).
1994	Earns a master in fine arts in creative writing at San Francisco State University.
1995	Returns to East Coast. Appointed Professor of Theatre at Northeastern University in Boston. Writes *Boy x Man* (Greensboro, NC).
1996	Writes "Like It Was: Review of Jones' *The Dutchman* and *The Toilet*" (*Black Dialogue*).
1997	Honored as a "Living Legend" at the National Black Theatre Festival.
2005	Writes *Storyville* (music and lyrics by Mildred Kayden, Galveston Island, TX) and *Harlem Diva* (Bullins's Roxbury Crossroads Theatre, Boston).